Turkish Contract Law

İlhan Helvacı

Turkish Contract Law

Springer

İlhan Helvacı
Faculty of Law
Istanbul University
Istanbul, Turkey

ISBN 978-3-319-86768-7 ISBN 978-3-319-60061-1 (eBook)
DOI 10.1007/978-3-319-60061-1

Softcover reprint of the hardcover 1st edition 2017

Printed on acid-free paper

This Springer imprint is published by Springer Nature
The registered company is Springer International Publishing AG
The registered company address is: Gewerbestrasse 11, 6330 Cham, Switzerland

To Füsun . . .

Preface

In Turkish law, obligations may arise from legal transactions, in particular from contracts, and also from torts, cases of unjust enrichment, agency relationships without authorisation (*quasi-contractus*) and the law itself. However, since the most important source of obligations is contracts, this book focuses on contracts.

With the objective of providing an overview of the subject, the author analyses in particular the general provisions of the Turkish Code of Obligations (TCO arts. 1–48 and arts. 83–206) in five parts. The first part is concerned with the provisions pertaining to obligations arising from contracts (TCO arts. 1–48). In the second part, the provisions relating to the effect of obligations, especially performance and non-performance of obligations (TCO arts. 83–126) are analysed. The effect of obligations on third parties (TCO arts. 127–130) is also discussed in this part. The third part focuses on the extinguishment of obligations and limitation periods (TCO arts. 131–161). In the fourth part, joint and several debtors and creditors, conditions, earnest and forfeit money and penalty (TCO arts. 162–182) are explained. The last part concerns the assignment of claims, assumption of debt, transfer of contract and the joining of parties to an existing contract (TCO arts. 183–206).

It is evident that contract law is a broad subject. However, in this introductory book, the objective is to provide the reader with the main principles of Turkish contract law. That is why the author analyses particularly the general provisions of the Turkish Code of Obligations. Nevertheless, in order to provide a complete overview, certain provisions of the Turkish Code of Obligations relating to specific contracts, which are regulated in the second part of the Code, are also analysed. Moreover, in order to clarify certain subjects, provisions of the Turkish Civil Code, the Turkish Commercial Code and the Turkish Bankruptcy and Enforcement Law are also considered to the necessary extent.

Having regard to the objective of giving a complete and clear overview of Turkish contract law, the author seeks to avoid contentious arguments and to explain the subjects with the use of simple examples.

The author hopes that this book will be beneficial, especially for law students and practitioners who are not familiar with Turkish contract law.

The author wishes to express thanks to Istanbul University faculty members Catherine McKimm and Paul Sludds and to Peter Murphy, who helped in the discussion and refinement of the legal terminology in this book. Further thanks are due to M. Cansu Ünal, Samed Can Yılmazlar and Binesh Hass for their assistance with the book prior to publication.

Oxford, UK İlhan Helvacı
May 2017

Introduction

Contracts usually constitute an obligational relationship (*rapport d'obligation, Schuldverhältnis*) between the contracting parties and specifically give rise to obligations. The obligational relationship created by a contract is referred to as a contractual obligational relationship, and the obligations arising out of it are referred to as contractual obligations.

However, certain contracts do not give rise to an obligational relationship; they amend or terminate an existing obligational relationship between the parties. Indeed, a contract that is concluded in order to amend the place or time of performance of an existing obligation is an example of a contract of this nature. Moreover, certain contracts are concluded in order to transfer, to amend, to terminate or to restrict a right. These contracts are further examples of contracts that do not give rise to any obligations.

Furthermore, there are also certain contracts concerning family law, for example, contracts relating to engagement or marriage, or the law of inheritance such as testamentary agreements and inheritance partition agreements. The Turkish Civil Code No 4721 of 22.11.2001 governs these contracts.[1]

The contracts that give rise to an obligational relationship are governed by the new Turkish Code of Obligations No 6098 of 11 January 2011, which came into force on 1 July 2012.[2]

[1]Official Gazette 08.12.2001; No: 24607. The new Turkish Civil Code replaced the former Turkish Civil Code No 743 of 17 February 1926, which had come into force on 4 October 1926 (Official Gazette 04.04.1926; No: 339). The former Civil Code was heavily influenced by the Swiss Civil Code. The new Civil Code is also similar to the Swiss Civil Code, albeit to a lesser degree.

[2]Official Gazette 04.02.2011; No 27836. The new Turkish Code of Obligations replaced the former Turkish Code of Obligations No 818 of 22 April 1926, which had come into force on 4 October 1926 (Official Gazette 08.05.1926; No: 366). The former Code was heavily influenced by the Swiss Code of Obligations. The new Code is also similar to the Swiss Code of Obligations, albeit to a lesser degree.

The Turkish Code of Obligations arts. 1–48 regulate contracts that give rise to an obligational relationship. However, these and the other general provisions of the Turkish Code of Obligations may also be applied to contracts regarding family law or the law of inheritance. Indeed, according to TCC art. 5, the general provisions laid down in the Code of Obligations (and Civil Code) also apply to other legal relationships concerning private law, provided that their applications are appropriate to the nature of the legal relationship. In addition, pursuant to TCO art. 646, the Turkish Code of Obligations completes the Turkish Civil Code as it forms Part V of the Civil Code.

The Turkish Code of Obligations arts. 49–76 govern obligational relationships arising from tort, and arts. 77–82 govern obligational relationships arising out of unjust enrichment. As the subject matter of this book is contract law, these obligational relationships arising from tort and unjust enrichment are not analysed.

As mentioned above, contractual obligational relationships or, in short, contracts usually give rise to obligations. An obligation is a legal tie (*vinculum iuris*) between the debtor (obligor) and the creditor (obligee) by which the debtor is bound to perform or refrain from performing specified conduct. In this context, the creditor may be under an obligation to give (*e.g.*, to transfer ownership of a car), to do (*e.g.*, to build a house) or not to do (to refrain from doing) (*e.g.*, not to compete).

A contract may give rise to several obligations (duties). Some of them are primary in nature, whereas some of them are subsidiary in nature. For example, in a contract of sale, the primary obligation (main duty) of the seller is to transfer ownership of the subject matter of the contract to the buyer. However, the seller may be under certain subsidiary obligations (subsidiary duties) along with the primary obligation, such as packing the goods, giving necessary information or instructions for their proper use. The primary obligations are what define the contract.

As a general rule, the non- or improper performance of the primary obligation may give rise to secondary obligations such as compensation (damages).

A contractual obligational relationship or, in short, a contract may also be the source of formative rights (*droit formateur*, *Gestaltungsrecht*) such as the right to terminate a contract or the right to withdraw from a contract. Furthermore, a contract may lead to certain defences where there has been a non- or an improper performance on the part of one of the parties. For example, in a sale contract, if the subject matter of the contract is defective, then the buyer may raise the defect as a defence.

It should be noted that when persons engage with one another in order to make a contract, they are also under a duty to protect each other's assets and personal rights. The basis of these pre-contractual duties is the principle of good faith (TCC art. 2).

Contents

List of Abbreviations

art.	Article
BGB	German Civil Code
cf	*Confer*
DSA	Digital Signature Act
éd	Editeurs
eds.	Editors
e.g.	*exempli gratia*
etc.	et cetera
FCC	French Civil Code
ff.	*foliis*
fn	Footnote
i.e.	*id est*
LIA	Legal Interest and Default Interest Act
LRA	Land Registry Act
N	Number, Numéro, Nummer
No	Number
NPA	Notary Public Act
p	Page
par	Paragraph
RLR	Regulation of Land Registry
SCO	Swiss Code of Obligations
Sect.	Section
sent	Sentence
subcl	Subclause
subs	Subsection
TCBE	Turkish Code of Bankruptcy and Enforcement
TCC	Turkish Civil Code

TCO	Turkish Code of Obligations
TComC	Turkish Commercial Code
TCPA	Turkish Consumer Protection Act
TCPC	Turkish Civil Procedure Code
TL	Turkish Lira
TPC	Turkish Penal Code

Part I
Obligations Arising from Contracts

Chapter 1
Formation of the Contract

1.1 General[1]

A contract is a legally binding agreement (a legal transaction)[2] that is usually concluded between two parties. Therefore, it is generally referred to as a bilateral legal transaction. For instance, in a sale contract, there are two parties: a buyer and a seller. In a lease contract, there are also two parties: a lessor and a lessee. However, a contract may be concluded between more than two parties—*e.g.*, a partnership contract with multiple partners. Another example is an inheritance partition agreement made between more than two heirs. These kinds of contracts are referred to as multilateral legal transactions or, more precisely, as multilateral contracts.

The Turkish Code of Obligations regulates contracts as bilateral legal transactions. That is why the general provisions relating to contracts in the Turkish Code of Obligations are applicable to multilateral contracts only by analogy. As the Turkish Code of Obligations governs contracts as bilateral legal transactions, this book will also treat them as such.

The elements that are required for the formation of a contract are offer and acceptance. In addition, the parties must have the intention to establish a legal

---

[1]Antalya (2012), pp. 155–198; Aybay (2011), pp. 25–32; Becker (1941), art. 1–10; Berger (2012), pp. 207–221; Engel (1997), pp. 184–209; Eren (2015), pp. 227–263; Feyzioğlu (1976), pp. 59–101; Gauch et al. (2008), pp. 53–90; Honsell et al. (2003), art. 1–10; Kılıçoğlu (2013), pp. 52–75; Kocayusufpaşaoğlu (2014), pp. 165–213; Nomer (2015), pp. 36–48; Oser and Schönenberger (1929), Vorbemerkungen zum ersten Abschnitt (Art. 1–40), art. 1–10; Oğuzman and Öz (2015), pp. 49–79; Özsunay (1983), pp. 61–70; Reisoğlu (2014), pp. 62–70; Schwenzer (2009), pp. 182–210; Tekinay et al. (1993), pp. 81–99; Tercier (2004), pp. 112–129; Tercier et al. (2016), pp. 147–205; Thévenoz and Werro (2012), art. 1–10, and von Tuhr and Peter (1979), pp. 181–193.

[2]A juridical act, (*acte juridique, Rechtsgeschäft*).

İ. Helvacı, *Turkish Contract Law*, DOI 10.1007/978-3-319-60061-1_1

relationship.[3] This intention may be express or implied. An agreement cannot be binding as a contract if it was made without any intention to create legal relations.

The offer is the first declaration of will (intention)[4] in time,[5] whereas acceptance is the second. In order for a contract to be concluded, the offer and the acceptance must be mutual and consistent (TCO art. 1 par. 1). The offer and the acceptance may be express or implied (TCO art. 1 par. 2).

1.2 The Offer

An offer is a unilateral declaration of will (intention) expressed by the offeror. This declaration contains the offeror's proposal to enter into a contract with the offeree. An offer may be made by a person who intends to undertake an obligation, that is to say, who intends to become a debtor. Furthermore, an offer may also be made by a person who intends to be entitled to a right, in other words, who intends to become a creditor.[6] In certain contracts, both parties undertake an obligation. Such contracts are referred to as bilateral contracts (*e.g.*, a sale contract, a lease contract).[7] Any of the parties may also make an offer on the conclusion of these types of contracts.

An offer must be addressed to a prospective contracting party. In this sense, it may be addressed to determined or undetermined persons (*e.g.*, the general public).[8] For instance, when a seller S makes an offer to sell a chattel for a determined price to a prospective buyer B, this offer is addressed to a determined person. On the other hand, an example of an offer being addressed to undetermined persons is when a shopkeeper displays a chattel indicating its price in the shop window. Indeed, according to TCO art. 8 par. 2, displaying goods with an indication of their price is considered to be an offer, unless the contrary is understood readily and clearly.

By the offer, the offeror expresses his willingness to enter into a contract on a specific set of terms on the mere acceptance of the offeree. Consequently, the offer, as a rule, must contain the objectively and subjectively necessary elements of the contract so that the offeree can form the contract with his mere acceptance.[9] In order for an offer to be valid, there are no specific form requirements. However, in

[3]It is obvious that the parties must have the necessary capacity to act (*exercise des droits civils, Handlungsfähigkeit*) required to enter into a contract. For further explanations see Esener (2000), pp. 48–52; Ansay and Wallace (2002), pp. 84–87.

[4]*Déclaration de volonté, Willenserklärung.*

[5]Gauch et al. (2008), p. 69; Eren (2015), p. 244.

[6]von Tuhr and Peter (1979), §24, II, p. 182; Eren (2015), pp. 243–244; Feyzioğlu (1976), p. 69; Reisoğlu (2014), p. 64.

[7]Oğuzman and Öz (2015), p. 45; Eren (2015), p. 210; Reisoğlu (2014), p. 52; Thévenoz and Werro (2012), art. 1, N. 65; Tercier (2004), p. 59.

[8]Reisoğlu (2014), p. 65; Eren (2015), p. 244.

[9]For the objectively and subjectively essential elements of the contract, see Sect. 1.7.

certain cases, the contract to be concluded may require a specific form due to the law itself or due to the parties' agreement. In such cases, the offer must be made in compliance with this form requirement. Otherwise, the offer is invalid, and an invalid offer does not provide the offeree with the right to conclude the contract by accepting it. For example, a sale contract relating to real estate must be made before a land registry officer. Thus, if the owner of a field intends to sell it and erects a sign on the field indicating that it is to be sold and also indicates the price, then this is not deemed to be an offer.

As mentioned above, according to TCO art. 8 par. 2, displaying goods with an indication of their price, sending a price list, a tariff, etc. are considered to be offers unless the contrary is understood readily and clearly. However, merely sending unsolicited goods does not constitute an offer. In addition, the recipient does not have an obligation to keep or to return the goods (TCO art. 7).

1.3 Binding Effect of the Offer

The offeror is bound by the offer.[10] This means that the offeree's mere acceptance will result in the formation (conclusion) of the contract. In addition, the offeror, as a rule, is not entitled to revoke the offer and, thus, may not preclude the formation of the contract. The offeree (addressee) may reject the offer. Furthermore, he may make a counter-offer. In both cases, the binding effect of the original offer is terminated.

If the offeror dies or loses the capacity to act, which is necessary in order to enter into a contract, then the binding effect of the offer must be analysed according to two separate possibilities:[11] (1) if the person or the personal skills of the offeror are important for the offeree, then the offer is terminated. For example, an offer made by a well-known surgeon to a patient regarding vital surgery is terminated by the offeror's death or his subsequent incapacity to act; (2) in cases where the person or personal skills of the offeror are not important for the offeree, the binding effect of the offer nevertheless stands. For instance, if a seller makes an offer to sell a chattel to a buyer, then the death or subsequent incapacity of the seller does not affect the offer's binding effect. Consequently, where the offeror dies, the offer will bind his heirs. Similarly, if the offeror loses the capacity to act, the binding effect of the offer remains nevertheless. Another factor that may terminate the binding effect of an offer is the lapse of time, which is analysed in the paragraphs below.

---

[10] Eren (2015), p. 250; Oğuzman and Öz (2015), p. 57; Tekinay et al. (1993), p. 86; Feyzioğlu (1976), p. 71; Thévenoz and Werro (2012), art. 1, N. 84; Engel (1997), p. 194; Gauch et al. (2008), p. 73.

[11] von Tuhr and Peter (1979), § 24, III, p. 187; Reisoğlu (2014), pp. 67–68; Eren (2015), p. 260; Oğuzman and Öz (2015), p. 64.

1.3.1 Offer with Time Limit for Acceptance

If an offeror sets a time limit for acceptance, then the offeror will be bound by the offer until the fixed time expires. Where the addressee wants to accept the offer, his acceptance should reach the offeror before the set time expires (TCO art. 3).

1.3.2 Offer Without Time Limit for Acceptance

Where the offeror does not set a time limit for acceptance, it will be useful to consider two possibilities separately.

1.3.2.1 Among Persons Present

In cases where an offer is made without a time limit in the presence of the offeree, if the offeree wants to accept it, he must declare this forthwith. Otherwise, the offeror will no longer be bound (TCO art. 4 par. 1). It is worth noting that if the contracting parties communicate directly by telephone, electronically, etc., the offer is deemed to be made between persons present (TCO art. 4 par. 2). If, at the stage of the contract negotiations, both the contracting parties' agents are present or one party and the other party's agent are present, then the offer is nevertheless deemed to be made between persons present.

1.3.2.2 Among Persons Not Present

Where an offer is made without a time limit in the absence of an offeree, the offeror will remain bound for a reasonable time. That is to say, the offeror will be bound until such time as he might expect a reply, which is sent properly and in due time to reach him (TCO art. 5 par. 1).

A reasonable time is determined according to what a reasonable person would consider sufficient time to accept the offer.[12] It means that the offeree will need time for the offer to reach him, to think about the offer and to send the acceptance. Therefore, the expiration time varies according to the specific circumstances. For instance, the offeree in a contract for the sale of a car needs a longer period of time in comparison to the offeree in a simple book sale contract.

In certain cases, the offeror sends the offer properly but the offer is late in reaching the offeree. If the offeror does not know of this delay, then he may presume that the offer reached the offeree in due time (TCO art. 5 par. 2).

[12]Honsell et al. (2003), art. 5, N. 3; Gauch et al. (2008), p. 75; Eren (2015), p. 253; Reisoğlu (2014), p. 67; Tekinay et al. (1993), p. 89; Nomer (2015), pp. 46–47.

Moreover, although the offeree sends the acceptance in due course and time, it may reach the offeror after a reasonable period of time has expired. In this case, where the offeror does not want to be bound by the offer any longer, he must give notice immediately to the offeree of his intent not to be bound (TCO art. 5 par. 3). Otherwise, the contract will be formed.

1.4 Acceptance

Acceptance is a unilateral declaration of will (intention)[13] by the offeree and must be addressed to the offeror. For example, a seller S proposes to sell a chattel for a determined price to a prospective buyer B. Where this offer is accepted by B and this acceptance is addressed to S, the contract may be concluded. However, if the offer was accepted by a person other than the offeree (addressee), the contract may not be concluded. This is because, according to TCO art. 1 par. 1, the parties' declarations of will (intention) must be mutual. In addition, according to TCO art. 1 par. 1, acceptance must be in compliance with the offer. Otherwise, the contract will not be formed. For instance, despite the fact that a seller wants to sell a car for TL 10,000, a buyer may not wish to pay this amount and may propose to pay TL 8000 instead. In this case, the contract will also not be concluded.

There are no specific form requirements regarding the validity of an acceptance. However, if the contract to be concluded requires a form by virtue of law or of the parties' agreement, then the validity of the acceptance is subject to compliance with these form requirements. If the acceptance is non-compliant with the form requirements, then the contract is nevertheless concluded but is void.[14]

If the offeree dies or loses the capacity to act after sending the acceptance but before the acceptance reaches the offeror, this precludes the formation of the contract in cases where the offeree's person or his personal skills are important for the offeror.

Acceptance can be either express or implied (TCO art. 1 par. 2). When an offeree states his will clearly and explicitly to the offeror, the acceptance is deemed to be express. However, where the offeree does not state his will directly but demonstrates this will by any acts indicating assent, the acceptance is deemed to be implied. For instance, where a shopper selects an item in a supermarket and hands it to the cashier, such conduct demonstrates that he accepts the supermarket owner's offer at the price stated on the item. As mentioned above, TCO art. 8 par. 2 states that the display of goods with an indication of their price is, as a rule, considered to be an offer.

Even silence may constitute an implied acceptance. In certain cases, the offeror does not have to receive an express acceptance if the law, the special nature of the

[13] *Déclaration de volonté, Willenserklärung.*

[14] See Chap. 3.

transactions or the circumstances do not require it. In such a case, if the offeree does not reject the offer in a reasonable time, then the contract is considered to be concluded (TCO art. 6). For instance, TCO art. 503 does not require an express acceptance for the conclusion of an agency contract. Indeed, pursuant to said article, an agency contract is deemed to be concluded when an agent receives an offer with respect to the services he carries out in an official capacity or on a professional basis or he has publicly announced that he will accept offers relating to these services, unless the agent immediately rejects this offer.

1.5 Invitation to Offer (Invitation to Treat)[15]

Where the offeror, in his offer, declares that he reserves the right not to be bound by the offer or where such reservation arises from the nature or the circumstances of the transaction, there is only an invitation to make an offer (invitation to treat).[16] Therefore, mere acceptance of the invitation to offer by the addressee does not result in the formation of the contract. Accordingly, where the addressee intends to enter into a contract, he should make an offer.

The most common example of the difference between the offer and the invitation to offer is in ascending price auctions. For example, a seller wishes to sell certain goods by such an auction. If the seller declares that the subject matter of the auction is to be sold to the highest bidder, then the seller's declaration is deemed to be an offer and the highest bid is deemed to be an acceptance. However, if the seller does not intend to make a sale contract but merely wishes to collect certain proposals with regard to a probable sale contract and declares this intention, then this declaration is deemed to be an invitation to offer. Consequently, the participants' bids are deemed to be an offer (TCO art. 275 par. 1). These explanations are also applicable to reverse auctions (procurement auctions)—*i.e.*, a type of auction in which the price of the goods is decreased with each bid.[17]

Advertisements in newspapers, on TV or on the Internet[18] may not be considered to be an offer, even if they contain the price of the goods to be sold or the service to be rendered. On the contrary, such advertisements must be considered as an invitation to offer. Accordingly, the purchaser's conduct, such as clicking on an advertisement on the Internet, is deemed to be an offer. In such a case, the counterparty's acceptance may be express or implied. For example, accepting online

---

[15]*Invitatio ad offerendum.*

[16]Tercier (2004), p. 120; Gauch et al. (2008), p. 69; von Tuhr and Peter (1979), § 24, II, p. 183; Tekinay et al. (1993), pp. 84–85; Eren (2015), pp. 246–247; Reisoğlu (2014), p. 65; Tercier et al. (2016), p. 190; Kocayusufpaşaoğlu (2014), p. 182.

[17]For instance, a company intends to purchase certain goods or services and the price will be determined by the lowest bid. Thus, prospective sellers or providers underbid each other.

[18]For contracts that are concluded on the Internet see İnal (2005), Erten (2009).

payment by credit card is deemed to be an implied acceptance. However, in cases where a person is able to download a program online, the advertising of the program on the Internet is deemed to be an offer and the customer clicking on the advertisement is deemed to be an acceptance.[19]

Even though a vending machine displays goods and indicates their price, the conduct of the seller who operates the vending machine, in the view of the author, may only be deemed as an invitation to offer, rather than an offer. Consequently, when a customer puts the necessary money for the item that he wishes to buy in the machine's slot, then his act is deemed to be an offer and the machine's delivery of the goods is deemed to be an acceptance.[20]

Tenders are also considered to be an invitation to offer. Indeed, where a person invites others to submit tenders regarding a particular project, a sale contract or a lease contract, as a rule, this invitation is simply an invitation to offer. The offers are made by the persons who submit the tenders. If the person who invited them to submit tenders accepts one of them, then the contract is concluded.

1.6 Intention to Create a Contract

As a general principle, a person who makes or accepts an offer must have the intention to be legally bound. If a person makes a declaration of will[21] without having the intention to be legally bound, there is either a *reservatio mentalis* (mental reservation) or a declaration that is not serious.

In the case of *reservatio mentalis*, a person declares that he intends to make a contract but, in reality, he does not have such an intention. In this case, if the declaring party's real intention is hidden from the other party, then the contract is concluded according to the receiving party's understanding.[22] The declaring party is not entitled to assert that the contract is not concluded.[23] As an example, in a sale auction, a bidder does not intend to buy the goods to be sold. However, he participates in the auction and makes an offer by submitting the highest bid. The auctioneer, being unaware of the real intention of the bidder, accepts this offer. In this case, the contract is concluded and the bidder is not entitled to assert that his real intention was, for example, to increase the price of the goods but not to buy the goods.

In the case of a frivolous declaration, there is a declaration apparently made as a joke, on stage, or for teaching purposes. The declaring party's real intention is not to

[19]Oğuzman and Öz (2015), p. 54; Kocayusufpaşaoğlu (2014), p. 188

[20]See Kocayusufpaşaoğlu (2014), p. 181.

[21]*Déclaration de volonté*, *Willenserklärung*.

[22]Engel (1997), p. 223; Thévenoz and Werro (2012), art. 18, N. 76; Oğuzman and Öz (2015), pp. 90–91.

[23]See BGB §116.

create a contract. In this instance, as opposed to the above-mentioned case, the declaration of will has no legal effect. However, pursuant to the 'trust theory' (*théorie de la confiance, Vertrauenstheorie*), if the addressee does not know of and, as a reasonable person, should not know that this declaration is frivolous, then the contract is concluded according to his understanding.[24] In such a case, the declaring party (for example, the joking party) is entitled to rescind (avoid) the contract according to the provisions relating to mistake in the declaration of will (intention).[25]

1.7 Content of the Agreement

In order to form a contract, the parties must agree on all of the necessary elements of the contract. The necessary elements of a contract are divided into two categories: (1) objectively essential elements and (2) subjectively essential elements.

Objectively essential elements (*essentialia negotii*) constitute the minimum contents of a contract in order for it to be valid and legally binding. Such elements form the core of the contract by themselves (*per se*), and thus, they are indispensable (*conditio sine qua non*) for the conclusion of the contract. In other words, they must be determined in order to individualise the contract.[26] As a general rule, where the parties do not agree on the objectively necessary elements, the contract will not be concluded. For instance, in a sale contract, a description of the goods and the price are the objectively necessary elements. If the parties do not agree on these elements, the contract will not be concluded.[27] At this point, it should be kept in mind that in a sale contract, the price of the goods does not have to be determined. It is sufficient for this price to be determinable. Indeed, according to TCO art. 233, where the buyer has placed a definite order without indicating the price, the goods are deemed to have been sold at the average market price at the time and place of performance. Moreover, the objectively essential elements of the contract may be determinable. In other words, the parties may agree as to how these elements will be determined in the future.

Subjectively essential elements are subsidiary elements of the contract. They are not objectively indispensable for the formation of the contract, but they may be necessary for one or both of the parties in order to form the contract. In other words,

[24]See BGB §118.

[25]Oğuzman and Öz (2015), p. 91; Eren (2015), p. 348, See Sect. 11.1.2.

[26]von Tuhr and Peter (1979), § 20, VIII, 1, p. 155; Becker (1941), art. 2, N. 4; Gauch et al. (2008), p. 62; Tercier (2004), pp. 113–114; Reisoğlu (2014), p. 63; Eren (2015), p. 234; Oğuzman and Öz (2015), p. 72; Feyzioğlu (1976), pp. 65–66; Kocayusufpaşaoğlu (2014), pp. 174–175; Nomer (2015), p. 45; Tercier et al. (2016), p. 179.

[27]von Tuhr and Peter (1979), § 20, VIII, 1, p. 155; Becker (1941), art. 2, N. 5; Oğuzman and Öz (2015), p. 72.

they do not form the core of the contract by themselves (*per se*).[28] However, they are added to the core of the contract by virtue of the intentions of the parties or of one of the parties. For instance, a suspensive condition (condition precedent)[29] or a resolutive condition (condition subsequent)[30] may constitute a subjectively essential element for all contracting parties or for only one of them. If the parties do not agree on such a subsidiary element, then the contract will not come into existence.

Furthermore, there are also secondary elements of a contract, which neither form its core nor are a part of it. In other words, they are not objectively or subjectively indispensable for the formation of the contract. For instance, in a sale contract, the time of performance and the place of delivery of the goods are accepted as secondary elements. According to TCO art. 2 par. 1, if the parties have agreed on the essential elements of the contract, then the contract is deemed to be concluded, even if they have not negotiated the secondary elements at all.[31] It is also possible that the parties may negotiate the secondary elements before the formation of the contract and decide that they will be determined at a later time. In such a case, the contract is also deemed to be concluded.[32] Actually, TCO art. 2 par. 1 does not state this possibility; it only regulates situations where the parties have not negotiated the secondary elements at all. However, it is appropriate to accept that the scope of the provision may also apply to these situations.

Where the parties negotiate the secondary elements of the contract at the stage of contract negotiations but do not come to an agreement, the contract cannot be concluded. This is because a secondary element is deemed to have become a subjectively necessary element of the contract due to the wishes of one or both parties.[33]

1.8 Revocation of Offer and Revocation of Acceptance

If contract negotiations take place between persons present, then the offeror is not entitled to revoke his offer. This is because once the offer is made between persons present, it is known by the offeree.

If the contract negotiations take place between persons not present, the following rules are applied: (1) if the offeror intends to revoke the offer, he must make a revocation statement. This revocation statement should reach the offeree prior to the offer. In this case, the offer is deemed not to have been made (TCO art. 10 par.

[28]Tercier (2004), p. 114; Gauch et al. (2008), pp. 64–65; Eren (2015), pp. 235–237; Oğuzman and Öz (2015), p. 73; Kocayusufpaşaoğlu (2014), pp. 175–176; Nomer (2015), p. 45; Tercier et al. (2016), p. 179.

[29]See Sect. 29.2.

[30]See Sect. 29.3.

[31]Oğuzman and Öz (2015), p. 73.

[32]Oğuzman and Öz (2015), p. 73.

[33]Tekinay et al. (1993), pp. 75–76; Oğuzman and Öz (2015), p. 73.

1); (2) however, if the offeror's revocation statement reaches the offeree at the same time as or after the offer, then in order for the offeror to be able to revoke the offer, the offeree should have knowledge of the revocation statement before he has knowledge of the offer (TCO art. 10 par. 1). The above-mentioned rules are also applicable to the revocation of acceptance (TCO art. 10 par. 2).

1.9 Coming into Effect of the Contract

Where contract negotiations take place among persons present, the conclusion of the contract and its coming into effect occur at the same time.[34] In other words, the contract is concluded and comes into effect at the time the offeree declares acceptance.

If contract negotiations take place between persons who are not in each other's presence, then the conclusion of the contract and its coming into effect occur at different times. The contract is concluded when the acceptance reaches the offeror (*cf.* TCO art. 5 par. 1). However, the contract comes into effect when the acceptance is sent (TCO art. 11 par. 1).[35]

Where an express acceptance is not necessary, the contract is concluded when the reasonable time limit for the rejection of the offer expires or at the time the act that constitutes implied acceptance occurs.[36] In this case, the contract comes into effect at the time the offer reaches the offeree (TCO art. 11 par. 2).

1.10 Pre-contractual Duties

Persons commencing negotiations for a contract must act in accordance with the principles of good faith (TCC art. 2). During negotiations, each party must provide the other with any information that may affect their decisions regarding the conclusion of the contract.[37] In addition, they must avoid deceptive conduct. If one of the parties realises that the other is mistaken, he must warn the mistaken party. Moreover, the negotiating parties must take precautionary measures in order to protect the assets and personal rights of each other.[38] This duty to protect the other also arises from the principles of good faith. For instance, if the floors are wet in a restaurant, the owner must warn the customers of this fact. Another example is

[34]Thévenoz and Werro (2012), art. 10, N. 1; Engel (1997), p. 208; Eren (2015), p. 262; Oğuzman and Öz (2015), pp. 73–74; Feyzioğlu (1976), p. 94.

[35]von Tuhr and Peter (1979), § 24, VI, p. 191.

[36]Oğuzman and Öz (2015), p. 75.

[37]von Tuhr and Peter (1979), § 24, VIII, p. 192; Gauch et al. (2008), p. 202.

[38]Oğuzman and Öz (2015), pp. 77–78; Tekinay et al. (1993), p. 976.

that in a supermarket, the items on the shelves must be properly stacked so as to avoid harming customers.

If a negotiating party breaches these kinds of pre-contractual duties and is at fault (*culpa in contrahendo*, fault in contracting) and the other party suffers damage as a result, he must compensate the other party for that damage.[39]

References

Ansay T, Wallace D (eds) (2002) Introduction to Turkish law. Turan, Ankara

Antalya OG (2012) Borçlar hukuku genel hükümler, vol 1. Legal, İstanbul

Aybay A (2011) Borçlar hukuku dersleri genel bölüm. Filiz, İstanbul

Becker H (1941) Kommentar zum Schweizerischen Zivilgesetzbuch, Volume VI, Obligationenrecht, 1. Abteilung: Allgemeine Bestimmungen, Art. 1-183. Stämpfli, Bern

Berger B (2012) Allgemeines Schuldrecht. Stämpfli, Bern

Engel P (1997) Traité des obligations en droit Suisse. Stämpfli, Bern

Eren F (2015) Borçlar hukuku genel hükümler. Yetkin, Ankara

Erten A (2009) Türk ve Alman hukukunda mesafeli sözleşmeler. Banka ve ticaret hukuku araştırma enstitüsü, Ankara

Esener T (2000) Turkish business law, vol 1. Boğaziçi University Library, İstanbul

Feyzioğlu FN (1976) Borçlar hukuku genel hükümler, Volume 1. Fakülteler, İstanbul

Gauch P, Schluep WR, Schmid J (2008) Schweizerisches Obligationenrecht, Allgemeiner Teil, vol 1. Schulthess, Zürich

Honsell H, Vogt NP, Wiegand W (eds) (2003) Basler Kommentar zum Schweizerischen Privatrecht, Obligationenrecht 1: Art. 1-529 OR. Helbing Lichtenhahn, Basel

İnal E (2005) E-ticaret hukukunda gelişmeler ve internette sözleşmelerin kurulması. Vedat, İstanbul

Kılıçoğlu AM (2013) Borçlar hukuku genel hükümler. Turhan, İstanbul

Kocayusufpaşaoğlu N (2014) Borçlar hukuku genel bölüm, vol 1 (Kocayusufpaşaoğlu/Hatemi/Serozan/Arpacı). Filiz, İstanbul

Nomer HN (2015) Borçlar hukuku genel hükümler. Beta, İstanbul

Oğuzman K, Öz T (2015) Borçlar hukuku genel hükümler, vol 1. Vedat, İstanbul

Oser H, Schönenberger W (1929) Kommentar zum Schweizerischen Zivilgesetzbuch, Volume V: Das Obligationenrecht, Erster Halbband: Art. 1-183. Schulthess, Zürich

Özsunay E (1983) Borçlar hukuku, vol I. Filiz, İstanbul

Reisoğlu S (2014) Türk borçlar hukuku genel hükümler. Beta, İstanbul

Schwenzer I (2009) Schweizerisches Obligationenrecht, Allgemeiner Teil. Schulthess, Bern

Tekinay SS, Akman S, Burcuoğlu H, Altop A (1993) Tekinay borçlar hukuku genel hükümler. Filiz, İstanbul

Tercier P (2004) Le droit des obligations. Schulthess, Zurich

Tercier P, Pichonnaz P, Develioğlu HM (2016) Borçlar hukuku genel hükümler. On iki levha, İstanbul

Thévenoz L, Werro F (éd) (2012) Commentaire romand code des obligations 1: art. 1-529 CO. Helbing Lichtenhahn, Bâle

von Tuhr A, Peter H (1979) Allgemeiner Teil des Schweizerischen Obligationenrecht, Volume 1. Schulthess, Zürich

[39]See Sect. 22.6.

Chapter 2
Public Promise

2.1 General[1]

TCO art. 9 regulates public promises. At first sight, a public promise[2] might be thought of as an offer, since art. 9 is found between art. 1 and art. 11, being the provisions of the Code concerned with the formation of the contract. However, in spite of its place in the Code, a public promise is not an offer. It is a unilateral legal transaction,[3] according to which a public promisor incurs an obligation.[4]

2.2 Conditions

According to TCO art. 9 par. 1, a person who publicly promises a reward in exchange for the performance of an act is bound to provide this reward in accordance with the terms of his announcement. A public promisor may require the performance of any act as long as this act is not illegal or immoral. For instance, the

[1]Antalya (2012), pp. 114–120; Aybay (2011), p. 29; Becker (1941), art. 8; Berger (2012), p. 87; Engel (1997), pp. 209–211; Eren (2015), pp. 460–465; Feyzioğlu (1976), pp. 101–119; Gauch et al. (2008), pp. 224–226; Honsell et al. (2003), art. 8; Kılıçoğlu (2013), pp. 268–272; Kocayusufpaşaoğlu (2014) pp. 257–269; Nomer (2015), p. 48; Oser and Schönenberger (1929), art. 8; Oğuzman and Öz (2015), pp. 202–205; Özsunay (1983), pp. 127–131; Reisoğlu (2014), pp. 78–80; Schwenzer (2009), pp. 213–214; Tekinay et al. (1993), pp. 467–473; Tercier (2004), p. 44; Tercier et al. (2016), p. 54; Thévenoz and Werro (2012) art. 8, and von Tuhr and Peter (1979), p. 182 fn. 6, 324. See in particular İnan (1961).

[2]*Promesse publique*, *Auslobung*.

[3]A juridical act, (*acte juridique*, *Rechtsgeschäft*).

[4]von Tuhr and Peter (1979), § 24, II, p. 182 fn. 6, § 38, II, 6, p. 324; Becker (1941), art. 8, N. 5; Eren (2015), p. 460 *ff*; Oğuzman and Öz (2015), p. 203.

İ. Helvacı, *Turkish Contract Law*, DOI 10.1007/978-3-319-60061-1_2

object of the public promise can be the discovery of stolen property, the return of lost property or the apprehension of a thief.

A public promise should contain a reward such as a sum of money, a holiday or a travel ticket.[5] A public promise can be addressed to the public generally or to a class of persons, such as college students, or to the population of a small district.[6] A public promise may be made via television, radio, newspapers, the Internet or any other means of communication.[7] There are no restrictions on how the reward may be announced.

2.3 Consequences

When a person performs the act required by a public promisor, the latter is obliged to fulfil his obligation in accordance with the announcement.[8] For instance, if the public promisor offers a sum of money in return for finding a lost pet and someone finds the pet, the public promisor must pay the sum offered.

It should be noted that even if the performer does not know of the existence of the public promise at the time of his action, he may request the reward as long as he has fulfilled the conditions of the promise.[9]

2.4 Revocation

The public promisor can revoke the promise before the performance of the required act. For a valid revocation, the intention to revoke a promise does not have to be declared in the same manner as a public promise (*cf.* BGB § 658 subs. 1).[10] After the revocation, even if a person performs the expected act, he is not entitled to demand the reward.

However, where the public promisor revokes the promise before the performance of the act or precludes its performance, he must reimburse the expenses that are incurred by any person acting in good faith in order to meet the requirements of the public promise (TCO art. 9 par. 2 sent. 1). TCO art. 9 par. 2 sent. 2 sets a limit on the reimbursement of the expenditure. According to this provision, even if the

[5]Gauch et al. (2008), p. 225; Oğuzman and Öz (2015), p. 203.

[6]Gauch et al. (2008), p. 224; Oğuzman and Öz (2015), p. 203.

[7]Engel (1997), p. 210; Thévenoz and Werro (2012), art. 8, N. 3.

[8]Thévenoz and Werro (2012), art. 8, N. 8.

[9]Thévenoz and Werro (2012), art. 8, N. 8; Oğuzman and Öz (2015), p. 204.

[10]Becker (1941), art. 8, N. 11; Eren (2015), p. 465, Reisoğlu (2014), p. 80; Tekinay et al. (1993), p. 472; Kocayusufpaşaoğlu (2014) pp. 267–268, See on the contrary Engel (1997), p. 211; Thévenoz and Werro (2012), art. 8, N. 9; Oğuzman and Öz (2015), p. 204.

public promisor is obliged to reimburse the expenses of one or more persons incurred in good faith, this reimbursement cannot exceed the amount of the stated reward. Where the public promisor proves that it would have been impossible for the person demanding reimbursement of the expenses to satisfy the conditions of the public promise, then the public promisor can be released from his obligations (TCO art. 9 par. 3).

2.5 Prize Competition

TCO art. 9 does not regulate prize competitions,[11] though it may be applied to such practices by analogy.

References

Antalya OG (2012) Borçlar hukuku genel hükümler, vol 1. Legal, İstanbul

Aybay A (2011) Borçlar hukuku dersleri genel bölüm. Filiz, İstanbul

Becker H (1941) Kommentar zum Schweizerischen Zivilgesetzbuch, Volume VI, Obligationenrecht, 1. Abteilung: Allgemeine Bestimmungen, Art. 1-183. Stämpfli, Bern.

Berger B (2012) Allgemeines Schuldrecht. Stämpfli, Bern

Engel P (1997) Traité des obligations en droit Suisse. Stämpfli, Bern

Eren F (2015) Borçlar hukuku genel hükümler. Yetkin, Ankara

Feyzioğlu FN (1976) Borçlar hukuku genel hükümler, vol 1. Fakülteler, İstanbul

Gauch P, Schluep WR, Schmid J (2008) Schweizerisches Obligationenrecht, Allgemeiner Teil, vol 1. Schulthess, Zürich

Honsell H, Vogt NP, Wiegand W (eds) (2003) Basler Kommentar zum Schweizerischen Privatrecht, Obligationenrecht 1: Art. 1-529 OR. Helbing Lichtenhahn, Basel

İnan AN (1961) Türk hukukunda ilan suretiyle yapılan vaadler. Ankara universitesi hukuk fakültesi, Ankara

Kılıçoğlu AM (2013) Borçlar hukuku genel hükümler. Turhan, İstanbul

Kocayusufpaşaoğlu N (2014) Borçlar hukuku genel bölüm, vol 1 (Kocayusufpaşaoğlu/Hatemi/Serozan/Arpacı). Filiz, İstanbul

Nomer HN (2015) Borçlar hukuku genel hükümler. Beta, İstanbul

Oğuzman K, Öz T (2015) Borçlar hukuku genel hükümler, vol 1. Vedat, İstanbul

Oser H, Schönenberger W (1929) Kommentar zum Schweizerischen Zivilgesetzbuch, Volume V: Das Obligationenrecht, Erster Halbband: Art. 1-183. Schulthess, Zürich

Özsunay E (1983) Borçlar hukuku, vol I. Filiz, İstanbul

Reisoğlu S (2014) Türk borçlar hukuku genel hükümler. Beta, İstanbul

Schwenzer I (2009) Schweizerisches Obligationenrecht, Allgemeiner Teil. Schulthess, Bern

Tekinay SS, Akman S, Burcuoğlu H, Altop A (1993) Tekinay borçlar hukuku genel hükümler. Filiz, İstanbul

Tercier P (2004) Le droit des obligations. Schulthess, Zurich

Tercier P, Pichonnaz P, Develioğlu HM (2016) Borçlar hukuku genel hükümler. On iki levha, İstanbul

[11] *Preisausschreiben.*

Thévenoz L, Werro F (éd) (2012) Commentaire romand code des obligations 1: art. 1-529 CO. Helbing Lichtenhahn, Bâle
von Tuhr A, Peter H (1979) Allgemeiner Teil des Schweizerischen Obligationenrecht, vol 1. Schulthess, Zürich

Chapter 3
Form of the Contract

3.1 General[1]

The freedom of form is one of the main principles of the Turkish Code of Obligations. This principle has its basis in TCO art. 12 par. 1, according to which the validity of a contract does not require any specific form unless it is provided for by law. Consequently, the parties may enter into contracts that do not require a specific form depending on their own preferences as to form. In this context, subject to certain exceptions, a contract for the sale of movable property may be concluded in any form. A lease contract for movable or immovable property may also be made orally or in writing.

It is apparent that an orally concluded contract may give rise to disputes between the parties. When a dispute arises, if a defendant admits the claimant's assertion regarding the existence or the contents of the contract, then the claimant is relieved of the burden of proof to establish these facts. However, if the defendant denies the existence of the contract, the claimant must prove its existence. As a rule, if the value of the contract exceeds TL 2500 at the time of its conclusion, the claimant must prove the existence of the contract by specific evidence, which is not subject to the judge's discretion, such as a deed (TCPC art. 200). In other words, the claimant may not prove the contract's existence, say, solely by the testimony of witnesses. The claimant may only prove the existence of the contract by a deed, by the

[1] Antalya (2012), pp. 324–353; Aybay (2011), pp. 32–36, 61–62; Becker (1941), Vorbemerkungen zu art. 11–16 (Formen der Verträge), art. 11–16; Berger (2012), pp. 245–258; Engel (1997), pp. 246–266; Eren (2015), pp. 264–296; Feyzioğlu (1976), pp. 303–349; Gauch et al. (2008), pp. 91–119; Honsell et al. (2003), art. 11–16; Kılıçoğlu (2013), pp. 104–112, 122–171; Kocayusufpaşaoğlu (2014) pp. 270–330, 609–619; Nomer (2015), pp. 61, 99–120; Oser and Schönenberger (1929), art. 11–16; Oğuzman and Öz (2015), pp. 138–160, 176–177; Özsunay (1983), pp. 71–77; Reisoğlu (2014), pp. 80–97, 147; Schwenzer (2009), pp. 228–245, 18; Tekinay et al. (1993), pp. 99–136; Tercier (2004), pp. 130–136; Tercier et al. (2016), pp. 206–220; Thévenoz and Werro (2012) art. 11–16, and von Tuhr and Peter (1979), pp. 228–229, 233–247.

İ. Helvacı, *Turkish Contract Law*, DOI 10.1007/978-3-319-60061-1_3

defendant's admission (TCPC art. 188) or by the defendant's refusal to swear an oath (TCPC art. 229).

In brief, the Turkish Code of Obligations does not generally require a particular form for contracts. In contrast, the Turkish Civil Procedure Code sets certain strict rules for the proof of contracts in which the value exceeds TL 2500.[2] Due to these strict rules concerning proof, in practice, the contracting parties generally prefer certain specific forms, particularly the written form.

3.2 Form Requirements[3]

3.2.1 Sources of Form Requirements

3.2.1.1 By Law

As mentioned above, the Turkish Code of Obligations does not generally require a specific form for the validity of contracts (TCO art. 12 par. 1). Nevertheless, certain contracts do require a specific form. The reasons for this requirement are as follows:[4] (1) to invite the parties to consider the contract and (2) to provide certainty regarding the terms of the contract. Moreover, in certain cases, the legislature sets stricter form requirements (the official form) in order to give official registers a secure base.

3.2.1.2 By the Contracting Parties

Even though, according to the Turkish Code of Obligations, a contract is not subject to a specific form, the parties can agree on a specific form requirement. In this case, they will not be bound by the contract until such a form requirement is satisfied (TCO art. 17 par. 1).[5] For instance, a lease agreement relating to immovable property does not require a legal form, but the parties may agree that the contract will not be valid unless it is concluded before a notary. Under these circumstances, if the parties make the lease contract in a simple written form, it will not be valid.

If the parties agree on a written form, without providing any specifications, as a condition for the validity of the contract, the provisions governing the legal written form apply to this form requirement (TCO art. 17 par. 2).

---

[2]Eren (2015), p. 271; Oğuzman and Öz (2015), p. 138.

[3]For further explanations see Tuğ (1994), Kavak (2015).

[4]Tercier (2004), p. 131; Thévenoz and Werro (2012), art. 11; N. 4; Eren (2015), p. 265; Oğuzman and Öz (2015), pp. 139–140.

[5]Tercier (2004), p. 132; Oğuzman and Öz (2015), p. 139; Eren (2015), p. 269.

3.2.2 *Written Form*

3.2.2.1 Simple Written Form

According to the Turkish Code of Obligations, certain contracts must be in writing. For instance, the promise of a gift[6] concerning movable property must be executed in writing (TCO art. 288 par. 1).[7] Other examples may be a pre-emption contract (TCO art. 237 par. 3), an assignment of a claim (TCO art. 184 par. 1) and a life annuity contract (TCO art. 608). It should be added that a promise to conclude an assignment of a claim need not be in writing (TCO art. 184 par. 2).

3.2.2.2 Qualified Written Form

Occasionally, the legislature requires a qualified written form for certain transactions.[8] Article 538 is the only example of this rule in the Turkish Civil Code. According to this article, a handwritten will must be entirely in the testator's handwriting (including the year, the month and the day it was made) and must be signed by the testator.

In terms of the law of obligations, the sole example of a qualified written form is a suretyship contract. TCO art. 583 par. 1 states that a surety contract must be in writing and that the date and maximum amount of the surety's liability must be indicated in the surety's own handwriting. If the surety contract is joint and several, this fact must also be included on the surety bond in the surety's handwriting.

3.2.3 *Official Form*

According to the Turkish Code of Obligations, certain contracts require an official form. For instance, a sale contract relating to immovable property must be concluded as a public deed (TCO art. 237 par. 1). Contracts purporting to transfer the ownership of immovable property must be made before a land registry officer and authenticated by the officer (LRA art. 26).[9] The promise to make a gift of immovable property or of rights *in rem* requires a public deed (TCO art. 288 par. 2) and

---

[6]Although "donation" is widely used in European texts, the author has preferred the use of "gift" throughout this book as "donation" has a narrower and more specific meaning in English.

[7]However, even if the parties breach this rule, the promisor can deliver the goods stated in the contract to the donee. In this case, the contractual relationship between the parties will be treated as a gift "from hand to hand" as the delivery of the movable property by the donor to the donee constitutes a gift "from hand to hand" (TCO art. 289).

[8]Thévenoz and Werro (2012), art. 11, N. 19; Eren (2015), p. 283.

[9]Land Registry Act, No 2644 of 22 December 1934 (Official Gazette 29.12. 1934; No: 2892).

must also be made before a land registry officer and authenticated by him (LRA art. 26).

3.2.4 *Signature*

3.2.4.1 General

Where the contract requires a written form, the person who undertakes an obligation must sign the contract (TCO art. 14 par. 1). For instance, in a surety contract, the obliged party is the surety. The creditor undertakes no obligations. Consequently, in a surety contract, the surety's signature will be necessary, whereas the creditor's signature will not be required. However, in a real estate sale contract that is subject to an official written form, both parties incur an obligation, and thus, both parties' signatures are required. The signatures indicate that the parties accept all the terms of the contract, and therefore the signature must be at the end of the document.

Unless the contrary is stipulated by law, a signed letter or the original copy of a telegram that has been signed by the obliged party is deemed to be in writing. Moreover, recoverable texts that are sent by fax or similar means or by secure electronic signature are considered to be in writing, provided that they are confirmed (TCO art. 14 par. 2).

As a rule, a signature must be handwritten (TCO art. 15 par. 1 sent. 1). However, this rule has two exceptions, which are explained below. The first exception to this rule is a secure digital signature.[10] A secure digital signature will have the same legal force as a handwritten signature (TCO art. 15 par. 1 sent. 2). Nevertheless, DSA art. 5 par. 2[11] states that security contracts (*e.g.*, a surety, guarantee,[12] pledge,[13] etc.) and transactions that are subject to an official form (*e.g.*, the sale of immovable property, mortgages, etc.) or a specific procedure (*e.g.*, marriage) cannot be signed by digital signature. It should be added that negotiable instruments are subject to a similar rule as a handwritten signature is obligatory in such cases. The second exception to the aforementioned rule is a signature produced by seal. A seal is acceptable where its use is customary or in the case of the signing of securities that are issued in large numbers (TCO art. 15 par. 2).

---

[10]For further explanations see Keser Berber (2002).

[11]Digital Signature Act, No 5070 of 15.1.2004 (Official Gazette 23.01.2004; No: 25355).

[12]Performance bonds issued by banks can be signed by an electronic signature.

[13]The art. 4 par. 3 of the Act on Movable Pledge on Commercial Transactions, No 6750 of 20.10.2016 (Official Gazette 28.10.2016; No: 29871) in relation to digital signature is reserved.

3.2.4.2 Substitutes for a Signature

The legislature allows those who are unable to sign the contract (*e.g.*, disabled or illiterate persons) to substitute for their signatures a fingerprint, a handmade mark or a stamp, provided that these are duly certified (TCO art. 16 par. 1). In Turkish law, the authority that certifies these substitutes for a signature is the notary public (see NPA art. 60 subcl. 1).[14]

The provisions pertaining to negotiable instruments[15] are reserved (TCO art. 16 par. 2). Indeed, according to the Turkish Commercial Code, bills of exchange (art. 756), promissory notes (art. 778 par. 1 subcl. i) and cheques (art. 818 par. 1 subcl. r) must be signed by hand. This rule also applies to signatures on avals[16] and endorsements.[17]

3.2.4.3 Signature of Blind Persons

Blind persons may sign the contract by themselves or request the testimony of a witness while signing it (TCO art. 15 par. 3).[18]

3.3 Content of the Form

As explained above, in order to form a contract, the parties must agree on all necessary elements of the contract.[19] That is to say, the agreement must contain the necessary elements—specifically, objectively and subjectively essential elements. Therefore, if a contract is subject to a particular form, all necessary elements must be included in the form.

3.4 Amendment of the Contract[20]

After concluding the contract, the parties may wish to amend it. Where a contract does not require a legal written form, the parties may amend it either orally or in writing without any form requirement.

---

[14]Notary Public Act, No 1512 of 18.1.1972 (Official Gazette 5.02.1972; No: 14090).

[15]For further explanations see Ansay and Schneider (2002), p. 66 *ff.*

[16]For further explanations see Ansay and Schneider (2002), pp. 57–58, 73.

[17]For further explanations see Ansay and Schneider (2002), pp. 72–73.

[18]For further explanations see Helvacı (2007), pp. 1865–1876; Helvacı (2016), pp. 419–428, *cf.* SCO.art.14/par. 3, see Engel (1997), pp. 253–254; Thévenoz and Werro (2012), art. 14, N. 25–29.

[19]See Sect. 1.7.

[20]For further explanations see Öz (2016).

Where the contract requires a legal written form, every amendment must be in writing (TCO art. 13 par. 1 sent. 1). For instance, in a sale contract in which the subject matter is immovable property, which requires an official form, the parties determine, and clearly describe, the immovable property and the price in the contract. After this determination, if the parties wish to increase or decrease the price, this amendment must also be made in an official form.[21]

It should be noted that pursuant to TCO art. 583 par. 3, subsequent variations that increase a surety's liability will not be valid unless the form requirement for the surety is satisfied. However, in a surety contract, the parties can make an agreement that reduces the amount of the surety's liability without complying with any particular form.

As has been seen, the above-mentioned amendment relates to an essential element of the contract. As to the supplementary non-essential (collateral) amendments that do not conflict with the terms of the contract, the legislature adopts a different rule. Pursuant to TCO art. 13 par. 1 sent. 2, such amendments are not subject to any specific form.[22] That is to say, in a contract that is subject to a specific form by law, such as in a sale contract for immovable property, if the parties do not determine, for example, the due time for performance of the obligation in the contract and they determine it afterwards, such an amendment will qualify as a supplementary non-essential amendment. Consequently, such an amendment will not be subject to a particular form.

It should be kept in mind that according to TCO art. 132, even where the contract requires a particular form either by law or by the parties' agreement, the parties can partially or wholly discharge an obligation regardless of any specific form.[23]

3.5 Breach of the Form Requirement

Where the parties do not comply with the aforementioned form requirements, the contract will not be binding, *i.e.*, the contract will be invalid (TCO art. 12 par. 2 sent. 2).[24] Invalidity of this nature can be referred to as a nullity, and it arises by operation of law.[25] Consequently, it is not necessary to file a lawsuit in order to establish that the contract is void. However, if the validity of a contract is disputed,

[21]Oğuzman and Öz (2015), pp. 152–153, compare to von Tuhr and Peter (1979), § 30, VI, pp. 242–243.

[22]Thévenoz and Werro (2012), art. 12, N. 3; Oğuzman and Öz (2015), p. 153; Eren (2015), pp. 287–288.

[23]See Sect. 25.2.2.

[24]Becker (1941), art. 11, N. 8.

[25]von Tuhr and Peter (1979), § 30, III, p. 237 *ff.*; Eren (2015), p. 291; Tandoğan (1989), p. 242.

the party who asserts that it is invalid may file a declaratory lawsuit.[26] There is no limitation period for relying on the nullity of a contract. Furthermore, even if the parties do not assert the invalidity of the contract in a lawsuit, the judge must take this nullity into consideration *ex officio*.[27] Moreover, the ratification or good faith of the parties does not remedy this invalidity.[28]

As mentioned above, if the parties do not comply with the form requirement, the contract will be void. Nevertheless, this consequential nullity has two exceptions, which are explained in the paragraphs below.[29]

The first exception arises from TCC art. 2, which states that every person is bound to exercise his rights and fulfil his obligations according to the principles of good faith; the law does not protect the manifest abuse of rights. Indeed, in certain cases, the assertion of invalidity can be against the principles of good faith (*bona fides*). For instance, as mentioned above,[30] the sale of immovable property must be made before a land registry officer. However, it is possible for the parties to make the contract without respecting this requirement of form. Despite this non-compliance with the form requirement, both parties may perform their obligations according to the contract as if it were valid. After the fulfilment of their obligations, if one of the parties asserts that the contract is invalid due to non-compliance with the form requirements,[31] then this assertion will be against the principles of good faith and the judge must reject it.[32]

Moreover, in the above-mentioned example, despite the nullity of the contract due to the lack of form, if the buyer pays the sale price and the seller transfers possession of the immovable property to the buyer, the latter may demand that the immovable property be registered in the land register under his name. In such a case, if the seller alleges that the contract is void due to the lack of form, such a defence may be considered to be against the principles of good faith by the court and the court may grant the claimant's demand to register his ownership in the land register.[33]

The second exception is 'reinterpretation'. Actually, this is not regulated under the Turkish Code of Obligations. In contrast, the German Civil Code (BGB)

---

[26]According to the TCPC art. 106 in the case of a declaratory action, the claimant seeks a court declaration that a right or a legal relationship exists or does not exist. For further explanations see Kuru and Budak (2010).

[27]Thévenoz and Werro (2012), art. 11, N. 33; Engel (1997), p. 262.

[28]Oğuzman and Öz (2015), p. 175.

[29]For further explanations see Altaş (1998).

[30]See Sect. 3.2.3.

[31]See and compare BGB §311 b subs. 1.

[32]Tercier (2004), pp. 135–136; Thévenoz and Werro (2012), art. 11, N. 37; Oğuzman and Öz (2015), pp. 155–158; Eren (2015), p. 290.

[33]Tandoğan (1989), p. 242, See Decision to Unify the Jurisprudence of the Court of Cassation, 30.09.1988, File No: 1987/2, Decision No: 1988/2 (Official Gazette 21.12.1988; No: 20026).

In Turkish law, the decisions of the Court of Cassation are not binding with one exception; namely, decisions to unify the jurisprudence, resolving inconsistencies between its divisions.

regulates reinterpretation (*Umdeutung*) under § 140. Certain Swiss[34] and Turkish scholars[35] analyse this notion having regard to the approach of commentators on the German Civil Code under the concept of conversion (*conversion*).[36] Furthermore, the Turkish Court of Cassation has applied this principle in its decisions.

In the author's opinion, the concept of reinterpretation can be considered as follows: if the parties enter into a contract without respecting the compulsory form requirements, the contract will be void. However, if the form of the invalid contract satisfies the form requirements of another contract relating to the same subject matter and it can be assumed that the latter contract is covered by the presumed intention of the parties, then the invalid contract will have the same full effect as the presumed contract. For instance, parties make a land sale contract before a notary public, although such a contract must be executed before a land registry officer. Nevertheless, this invalid sale contract would be recognised as a pre-contract to a land sale contract if (1) it satisfies the form requirements of a pre-contract for the sale of land and (2) it can be shown that had the parties been aware of the invalidity of their sale contract, then they would have entered into a pre-contract for the land sale contract. The Turkish Court of Cassation consistently adopts this approach in its decisions.[37]

References

Altaş H (1998) Şekle aykırılığın olumsuz sonuçlarının düzeltilmesi. Yetkin, Ankara

Ansay T, Schneider EC (eds) (2002) Introduction to Turkish business law. Turan, Ankara

Antalya OG (2012) Borçlar hukuku genel hükümler, vol 1. Legal, İstanbul

Aybay A (2011) Borçlar hukuku dersleri genel bölüm. Filiz, İstanbul

Becker H (1941) Kommentar zum Schweizerischen Zivilgesetzbuch, vol VI, Obligationenrecht, 1. Abteilung: Allgemeine Bestimmungen, Art. 1-183, Stämpfli, Bern

Berger B (2012) Allgemeines Schuldrecht. Stämpfli, Bern

Engel P (1997) Traité des obligations en droit Suisse. Stämpfli, Bern

Eren F (2015) Borçlar hukuku genel hükümler. Yetkin, Ankara

Feyzioğlu FN (1976) Borçlar hukuku genel hükümler, vol 1. Fakülteler, İstanbul

Gauch P, Schluep WR, Schmid J (2008) Schweizerisches Obligationenrecht, Allgemeiner Teil, vol 1. Schulthess, Zürich

Helvacı İ (2007) "Özürlüler hakkında kanun"un borçlar kanunu, ticaret kanunu ve medeni kanun ve noterlik kanunu bakımından getirdiği değişiklikler üzerine (Türk borçlar kanunu ve Türk ticaret kanunu tasarıları hakkında bazı saptamalar). Prof. Dr. Hüseyin Ülgen'e Armağan, vol II. İstanbul, pp. 1865–1876

[34] Thévenoz and Werro (2012) art. 11, N. 44–46; Engel (1997), p. 265.

[35] Oğuzman and Öz (2015), p. 155; Eren (2015), pp. 295–296.

[36] For further explanations see Kaneti (1972).

[37] 13th Civil Division of Court of Cassation, 08.05.1985, File No: 1985/2723, Decision No: 1985/3153; 15th Civil Division of Court of Cassation, 13.05.1976, File No: 1976/811, Decision No: 1976/2152; General Assembly of Civil Division of Court of Cassation, 13.10.1976, File No: 1975/13-108, Decision No: 1976/2617 (Kazancı İçtihat Bilgi Bankası).

Helvacı İ (2016) Görme engelli kişilerin imzaları ve ispat yükü üzerine bazı düşünceler. İstanbul kültür üniversitesi hukuk fakültesi dergisi 15(2):419–428
Honsell H, Vogt NP, Wiegand W (eds) (2003) Basler Kommentar zum Schweizerischen Privatrecht, Obligationenrecht 1: Art. 1-529 OR. Helbing Lichtenhahn, Basel
Kaneti S (1972) Hukuki işlemlerin çevrilmesi (tahvili). İstanbul üniversitesi, İstanbul
Kavak Y (2015) Borçlar hukukunda yazılı şekil. Kayhan, İstanbul
Keser Berber L (2002) İnternet üzerinde yapılan işlemlerde elektronik para ve dijital imza. Yetkin, Ankara
Kılıçoğlu AM (2013) Borçlar hukuku genel hükümler. Turhan, İstanbul
Kocayusufpaşaoğlu N (2014) Borçlar hukuku genel bölüm, vol 1 (Kocayusufpaşaoğlu/Hatemi/Serozan/Arpacı). Filiz, İstanbul.
Kuru B, Budak AC (2010) Tespit davaları. On iki levha, İstanbul
Nomer HN (2015) Borçlar hukuku genel hükümler. Beta, İstanbul
Oğuzman K, Öz T (2015) Borçlar hukuku genel hükümler, vol 1. Vedat, İstanbul
Oser H, Schönenberger W (1929) Kommentar zum Schweizerischen Zivilgesetzbuch, vol V: Das Obligationenrecht, Erster Halbband: Art. 1-183. Schulthess, Zürich
Öz K (2016) Tadil sözleşmesi. Filiz, İstanbul
Özsunay E (1983) Borçlar hukuku, vol I. Filiz, İstanbul
Reisoğlu S (2014) Türk borçlar hukuku genel hükümler. Beta, İstanbul
Schwenzer I (2009) Schweizerisches Obligationenrecht, Allgemeiner Teil. Schulthess, Bern
Tandoğan H (1989) Borçlar hukuku, özel borç ilişkileri, vol I/1. Vedat, İstanbul
Tekinay SS, Akman S, Burcuoğlu H, Altop A (1993) Tekinay borçlar hukuku genel hükümler. Filiz, İstanbul
Tercier P (2004) Le droit des obligations. Schulthess, Zurich
Tercier P, Pichonnaz P, Develioğlu HM (2016) Borçlar hukuku genel hükümler. On iki levha, İstanbul
Thévenoz L, Werro F (éd) (2012) Commentaire romand code des obligations 1: art. 1-529 CO, Art. 8. Helbing Lichtenhahn, Bâle
Tuğ A (1994) Türk özel hukukunda şekil. Mimoza, Konya
von Tuhr A, Peter H (1979) Allgemeiner Teil des Schweizerischen Obligationenrecht, vol 1. Schulthess, Zürich

Chapter 4
Standard Terms

4.1 General[1]

During the formation of a contract, the parties generally negotiate the terms of the contract. However, in certain cases, one of the parties prepares the contract's terms in advance and, without negotiation, imposes them on the other party. Generally, banks, insurance companies, travel agencies and public institutions providing utility services use such terms prepared in advance, which are referred to as 'standard terms', 'general conditions'[2] or 'adhesion contracts'.

4.2 Definition and Interpretation

According to TCO art. 20 par. 1, standard terms are the provisions that are prepared in advance by the imposing party to use in several similar contracts.[3] The preparing party imposes these provisions on the other party without negotiating with him. It is irrelevant whether these provisions appear in the contract itself or in its annexures. Also, the form, the font or the typeface and the scope of these provisions are not relevant to their status as standard terms (TCO art. 20 par. 1 sent. 2).

---

[1] Antalya (2012), pp. 285–323; Aybay (2011), pp. 44–46; Berger (2012), pp. 309–321; Engel (1997), pp. 165–175; Eren (2015), pp. 214–223; Gauch et al. (2008), pp. 244–258; Honsell et al. (2003), art. 1; Kılıçoğlu (2013), pp. 112–122; Kocayusufpaşaoğlu (2014), pp. 225–257; Nomer (2015), pp. 72–76; Oğuzman and Öz (2015), pp. 160–169; Reisoğlu (2014), pp. 70–78; Schwenzer (2009), pp. 324–338; Tekinay et al. (1993), pp. 154–166; Tercier (2004), pp. 160–164; Tercier et al. (2016), pp. 263–280; Thévenoz and Werro (2012), arts. 19–20, and von Tuhr and Peter (1979), pp. 11, 143–144. For further explanations see Yelmen (2014).

[2] *Conditions générale des affaires, Allgemeine Geschäftsbedingungen.*

[3] Gauch et al. (2008), p. 246; Oğuzman and Öz (2015), p. 162; Eren (2015), p. 215.

İ. Helvacı, *Turkish Contract Law*, DOI 10.1007/978-3-319-60061-1_4

The provisions concerning standard terms in the Turkish Code of Obligations are also applied to contracts that are prepared by persons and institutions that perform services with the permission of a competent authority or of the law itself. Indeed, public institutions providing utility services such as natural gas, electricity, water or sewage disposal use standard terms in their contracts. Thus, these persons and institutions must comply with the provisions governing standard terms. Furthermore, the legal nature of these institutions' contracts does not affect the application of these provisions (TCO art. 20 par. 4).

In certain cases, the texts of contracts prepared with the same objective may differ. In spite of this difference, the provisions of these contracts are deemed to be standard terms (TCO art. 20 par. 2). Also, the preparing party may insert and impose certain clauses explaining that each of the standard terms has been agreed upon by negotiation. These clauses themselves do not affect the legal nature of the standard terms (TCO art. 20 par. 3). If a provision of the standard terms is not clear and understandable or is ambiguous, it is interpreted to the detriment of the drafting party (*indubio contra stipulatorem*) and to the advantage of the adhering party (TCO art. 23).

4.3 Invalid Standard Terms

4.3.1 Non-written Standard Terms

For standard terms that are contrary to the interests of the adhering party to form part of the contract, all of the following conditions must be satisfied on formation of the contract: (1) the preparing party must clearly inform the adhering party of the existence of these standard terms, (2) the preparing party must provide the opportunity for the adhering party to be informed of the content of these standard terms and (3) the adhering party must accept these standard terms. Otherwise, the standard terms are deemed to be non-written (TCO art. 21 par. 1). It should be noted that the term 'non-written' is not typical for the Turkish Code of Obligations. This term means 'non-existent'. That is to say, invalid standard terms are deemed to be non-existent.[4]

Standard terms that are unusual given the purpose of the contract and the nature of the transaction are deemed to be non-written as well (TCO art. 21 par. 2). These clauses may be defined as 'surprising' clauses in parallel with the German Civil Code § 305c. For example, if a mortgagor is not the debtor of a secured obligation and if he then unknowingly accepts being a surety[5] under the standard terms of the

[4]Oğuzman and Öz (2015), p. 164.

[5]Under the former Turkish Code of Obligations such a risk was quite possible. This is because the provisions relating to the surety have only required a simple written form for the contract to be valid. That is why it was possible for a third party mortgagor to sign a surety contract unknowingly.

mortgage contract, the clause relating to the suretyship is deemed to be non-written. This is because a mortgagor who is not the debtor of the secured debt must merely forfeit the value of the realisation of the mortgaged property in the case of non-performance of the obligation. If the money obtained from the realisation of the mortgagor's property does not meet the amount of the obligation, the creditor is not entitled to demand payment of the remaining amount from the mortgagor. However, although within the limit of the surety contract, a surety is liable for all his seizable assets for the non-performance of the obligation. Thus, standard terms of a mortgage contract that encumber a third party mortgagor with an obligation of suretyship are unusual given the nature of such a mortgage contract. Consequently, such 'surprising' clauses are deemed to be non-written.

Banks use standard terms in their loan agreements that allow them to unilaterally increase interest rates in line with inflation. Such standard terms are valid as they are not alien to the nature of loan agreements. This approach has been adopted by the Turkish Court of Cassation.[6]

4.3.2 *Partial Invalidity*

The invalidity of the standard terms does not affect the validity of the other terms of the contract. In such a case, the preparing party cannot argue that he would not have entered into the contract without the standard terms that are deemed to be non-written (TCO art. 22).

TCO art. 22 is distinct from TCO art. 27 par. 2 sent. 2 as the latter states that if it is obvious that the parties would not have concluded the contract without the invalid provisions, then the entire contract will be void. It is apparent that if the legislature had not set a special rule for partial invalidity of the contract with respect to standard terms, TCO art. 27 par. 2 sent. 2 would be applied and, thus, the judge would take into consideration the presumed intentions of the parties.

4.3.3 *Prohibition of Unilateral Amendments*

In certain cases, the preparing party may insert clauses allowing them to unilaterally amend or add new provisions to the detriment of the adhering party. Indeed, in practice, banks promote such clauses. The preparing party may insert them either in

---

However, the TCO art. 583 par. 1 states that a contract of surety must be in writing and that the date and maximum amount of the surety's liability must be indicated in the surety's own handwriting. If the surety contract is joint and several, this fact must also be included on the surety bond in the surety's handwriting. Given this qualified written form requirement of the new Code, a third party mortgagor may not readily become a joint and several surety unknowingly.

[6]Reisoğlu (2014), p. 75.

the contract containing the standard terms or in a separate contract. TCO art. 24 accepts that these clauses are deemed to be non-written. For example, a travel agency offers package tours. If in its standard terms, there is a provision that allows the travel agency to unilaterally downgrade the accommodation (such as a three-star hotel instead of a five-star hotel) without decreasing the price, then these standard terms are deemed to be non-written.

4.4 Control of Content

The drafter is not entitled to insert provisions to the standard terms that are to the detriment of the adhering party or that may aggravate the adhering party's position in a manner contrary to the principles of good faith (TCO art. 25). For example, in the standard terms, there might be a provision allowing the drafter to terminate the contract without any justifiable reason and without paying any compensation. However, the same provision allows the adhering party to terminate the contract only in specific and enumerated cases. Moreover, the same provision may require the adhering party to pay a significant penalty. This provision is non-written as it is indeed against the principles of good faith[7] and is seriously unfair or inequitable.

As has been seen, the Turkish Code of Obligations sets two stages of control.[8] The first is governed by art. 21, while the second is regulated under art. 25. In this way, the legislature has aimed to protect the adhering party. In brief, for the standard terms to be part of the contract, the preparing party must respect the rules stated under TCO art. 21, and furthermore, the content of the standard terms must not breach the rules stated in TCO art. 25.

References

Antalya OG (2012) Borçlar hukuku genel hükümler, vol 1. Legal, İstanbul
Atamer MY (1999) Sözleşme özgürlüğünün sınırlandırılması sorunu çerçevesinde genel işlem şartlarının denetlenmesi. Beta, İstanbul
Aybay A (2011) Borçlar hukuku dersleri genel bölüm. Filiz, İstanbul
Aydoğdu M (2014) Genel işlem koşullarının ve tüketici hukukunda haksız şartların denetimi. Seçkin, Ankara
Berger B (2012) Allgemeines Schuldrecht. Stämpfli, Bern
Engel P (1997) Traité des obligations en droit Suisse. Stämpfli, Bern
Eren F (2015) Borçlar hukuku genel hükümler. Yetkin, Ankara
Gauch P, Schluep WR, Schmid J (2008) Schweizerisches Obligationenrecht, Allgemeiner Teil, vol 1. Schulthess, Zürich

---

[7]Oğuzman and Öz (2015), p. 166.

[8]For further explanations, see Atamer (1999), Havutçu (2003), Aydoğdu (2014).

Havutçu A (2003) Açık içerik denetimi yoluyla tüketicinin genel işlem şartlarına karşı korunması. Güncel, İzmir
Honsell H, Vogt NP, Wiegand W (eds) (2003) Basler Kommentar zum Schweizerischen Privatrecht, Obligationenrecht 1: Art. 1-529 OR. Helbing Lichtenhahn, Basel
Kılıçoğlu AM (2013) Borçlar hukuku genel hükümler. Turhan, İstanbul
Kocayusufpaşaoğlu N (2014) Borçlar hukuku genel bölüm, vol 1 (Kocayusufpaşaoğlu/Hatemi/ Serozan/Arpacı). Filiz, İstanbul
Nomer HN (2015) Borçlar hukuku genel hükümler. Beta, İstanbul
Oğuzman K, Öz T (2015) Borçlar hukuku genel hükümler, vol 1. Vedat, İstanbul
Reisoğlu S (2014) Türk borçlar hukuku genel hükümler. Beta, İstanbul
Schwenzer I (2009) Schweizerisches Obligationenrecht, Allgemeiner Teil. Schulthess, Bern
Tekinay SS, Akman S, Burcuoğlu H, Altop A (1993) Tekinay borçlar hukuku genel hükümler. Filiz, İstanbul
Tercier P (2004) Le droit des obligations. Schulthess, Zurich
Tercier P, Pichonnaz P, Develioğlu HM (2016) Borçlar hukuku genel hükümler. On iki levha, İstanbul
Thévenoz L, Werro F (éd) (2012) Commentaire romand code des obligations 1: art. 1-529 CO. Helbing Lichtenhahn, Bâle
von Tuhr A, Peter H (1979) Allgemeiner Teil des Schweizerischen Obligationenrecht, vol 1. Schulthess, Zürich
Yelmen A (2014) Türk borçlar kanununa göre genel işlem şartları. Yetkin, Ankara

Chapter 5
Content of the Contract

5.1 Freedom of Contract[1]

The principle of freedom of contract has its basis in TCO art. 26. Pursuant to this article, the parties may freely determine the content of the contract, their obligations, duties, responsibilities, liabilities, rights, entitlements, remedies, etc. within the limits of the law. According to this principle, within the limits of the law, persons are free to conclude or not to conclude a contract and they also have freedom of choice with respect to the contracting parties.[2]

When parties intend to enter into a contract, they may agree on a type of contract regulated by law. For instance, the parties can adopt contract types that are regulated in the Turkish Code of Obligations such as sale (arts. 207–281), barter (arts. 282–284), gift (art. 285–298), lease (art. 299–378), loan (art. 379–392), employment (art. 393–447), agency (art. 502–514), work (art. 470–486), surety (art. 581–603), life annuities (art. 607–610), simple partnership (art. 620–645), etc. In addition, the parties may choose another type of contract regulated by other legislation. Moreover, the parties can freely create their own contracts within the limits of the law. While doing so, they can create *sui generis* contracts (*e.g.*, a settlement agreement) or mixed contracts (*e.g.*, a software contract related to design and maintenance of software).

[1]Antalya (2012), pp. 273–284; Aybay (2011), pp. 37–41; Becker (1941), art. 19–20; Berger (2012), pp. 58–59, 370–385; Engel (1997), pp. 94–99, 267–297; Eren (2015), pp. 297–301, 316–345; Feyzioğlu (1976), pp. 231–248, 266–273; Gauch et al. (2008), pp. 120–152; Honsell et al. (2003), art. 19–20; Kılıçoğlu (2013), pp. 75–80, 86–104; Kocayusufpaşaoğlu (2014), pp. 525–619; Nomer (2015), pp. 56–81; Oser and Schönenberger (1929), art. 19–20; Oğuzman and Öz (2015), pp. 81–90, 173–183; Özsunay (1983), pp. 55–59; Reisoğlu (2014), pp. 133–140; Schwenzer (2009), pp. 246–259; Tekinay et al. (1993), pp. 362–364, 369–407; Tercier (2004), pp. 98–111, 137–146; Tercier et al. (2016), pp. 221–236; Thévenoz and Werro (2012), art. 19–20, and von Tuhr and Peter (1979), pp. 223–233, 247–266.

[2]Such freedom has two exceptions that are considered below. See Chap. 7.

İ. Helvacı, *Turkish Contract Law*, DOI 10.1007/978-3-319-60061-1_5

5.2 Restrictions

TCO art. 27 par. 1 states that contracts that are contrary to the mandatory rules of law, morality (*boni mores*), public order, personal rights[3] or contracts in which the object is impossible to perform are void. These restrictions are elucidated in detail below.

5.2.1 Mandatory Rules of Law

Mandatory rules of law are defined as rules of law that cannot be derogated from by agreement between the contracting parties. In certain rules of law, the mandatory nature is clearly understood from the wording. For instance, the contracting parties are not entitled to agree in advance to a clause that excludes their liability for gross fault (unlawful intent or gross negligence—*culpa lata*). Such a clause will be void (TCO art. 115 par. 1). Another example: TCO art. 160 states that a party may not exclude the limitation period defence in advance.

However, in certain cases, the question of whether a rule of law is mandatory or not cannot be readily answered from the wording of the rule. In such cases, a judge must consider the objective (*ratio legis*) of the rule.[4] Rules of law that aim to protect public order, public interest, moral public values, personal rights and a socially, economically or physically weaker party in a contract, such as employees or consumers, are generally mandatory.[5]

5.2.2 Rules of Law Protecting Personal Rights

As has been pointed out, rules of law that aim to protect personal rights are mandatory. Thus, if a contract breaches a specific rule of law that protects personal rights, then the contract actually violates this mandatory rule.

However, even if there is not a specific rule in the legislation, a contract may nevertheless violate personal rights. Indeed, according to the Turkish Civil Code art. 23, no person may wholly or partially renounce his legal capacity (TCC art. 8) or his capacity to act (TCC art. 9). No person may renounce his freedom or restrict its use contrary to law and morality. Consequently, for instance, no person may promise that he will not marry or divorce or change his religion. Moreover, contracts that specify an excessively long term, such as 30 or 40 years, may be

[3]For further explanations see Helvacı (2001).

[4]Engel (1997), p. 107.

[5]von Tuhr and Peter (1979), § 31, II, pp. 250–251; Oğuzman and Öz (2015), p. 82; Reisoğlu (2014), p. 134.

deemed illegal. For example, a person cannot make a commitment not to sell a property during his lifetime.[6]

5.2.3 *Morality*[7]

Certain mandatory rules of law are based on morality. For example, TPC art. 272 imposes punishments for falsely testifying under oath (perjury). Accordingly, a contract that concerns perjury breaches this mandatory rule and is deemed immoral and illegal.[8] However, it is apparent that public moral values are not usually defined by specific rules of law. Thus, even if there is not a specific rule based on morality in the legislation if the content of the contract or the contracting parties' objectives are contrary to morality, then the content of the contract will be deemed to be immoral.

It should be kept in mind that if one of the parties aims to obtain an immoral outcome and the other party does not adopt this immoral aim, then the contract cannot be deemed immoral.[9] In order to decide whether or not the contract is moral, the judge may not take his subjective moral beliefs into consideration; instead, moral principles that are generally accepted within society at the time of judgment must be considered.

The following are examples of immoral contracts: (1) a contract concluded in order to direct a journalist to publish a false news item and (2) a partnership contract concluded to manage a disorderly house (a brothel) without having the necessary permission from the government. Nonetheless, it should be noted that a lease agreement between an owner of immovable property and a manager of a disorderly house is binding. This is due to the fact that the Turkish Court of Cassation has decided that if the management of a disorderly house is permitted by law, such a contract is valid.[10]

5.2.4 *Public Order*

Certain mandatory rules of law have their basis in concerns for public order. Even though it is not easy to define public order, it is possible to define the rules

---

[6]Oğuzman and Öz (2015) p. 84.

[7]For further explanations see Ateş (2007).

[8]In most cases illegality and immorality may overlap. Kocayusufpaşaoğlu (2014), p. 555.

[9]Kocayusufpaşaoğlu (2014), pp. 556–557, see and compare to von Tuhr and Peter (1979) § 31, V, 1, pp. 257–258; Oğuzman and Öz (2015) p. 86.

[10]Decision to Unify the Jurisprudence of the Court of Cassation, 14.01.1948, File No: 30, Decision No: 2 (Official Gazette 30.07.1948; No: 6971).

concerning public order as the rules that protect the fundamental interests of the public and the structure of social life.[11] These kinds of rules may derive from either public law[12] or private law.[13] For instance, rules concerning construction or protection of the environment result from public law, whereas rules protecting lessees of dwelling houses and business premises have their basis in private law. Another example arising from private law is TCO art. 148. According to this article, limitation periods described under the second chapter of the third title of the Turkish Code of Obligations cannot be modified by agreement between the parties.

Moreover, besides the mandatory written rules defining public order, there is an independent concept of public order based on unwritten rules.[14] In this sense, public order has social, economic, philosophical and moral content, and this content can change over time.[15] Where a contract's content is contrary to these written or unwritten rules, the contract is illegal.

5.2.5 *Initial Impossibility*[16]

The conditions for the initial impossibility of the object of a contract are as follows: (1) it must be impossible to perform the obligation at the time the contract is concluded, (2) this impossibility must be objective—that is to say, it must be the case for any person.

Whether the cause of the initial impossibility is legal or factual is not relevant. Indeed, an initial impossibility of performance can emerge due to a legal prohibition.[17] For instance, the legislature sets forth certain height restrictions for buildings and the specification in the parties' agreement exceeds these limits. An initial impossibility of performance can also be based on factual grounds.[18] For example, in a sale contract regarding specific goods, the goods have already been destroyed by the time the contract is concluded. The debtor's knowledge of the initial impossibility is not relevant.

---

[11]Kocayusufpaşaoğlu (2014), p. 546. For further explanations see Honsell et al. (2003), art. 19–20, N. 23.

[12]Becker (1941), art. 19, N. 28.

[13]Becker (1941), art. 19, N. 25.

[14]Kocayusufpaşaoğlu (2014), p. 549.

[15]Kocayusufpaşaoğlu (2014), p. 546.

[16]For further explanations see Altunkaya (2005).

[17]Thévenoz and Werro (2012), art. 19–20, N. 76; Engel (1997), p. 270; Gauch et al. (2008), p. 124; Honsell et al. (2003), art. 19–20, N. 46; Tekinay et al. (1993), p. 404; Oğuzman and Öz (2015), p. 88; Feyzioğlu (1976), p. 268.

[18]Tekinay et al. (1993), pp. 405–406; Oğuzman and Öz (2015), p. 88; Feyzioğlu (1976), pp. 267–268; Nomer (2015), pp. 80–81.

5.3 Breach of Restrictions

5.3.1 Nullity

As mentioned above, according to TCO art. 27 par. 1, contracts that are against the mandatory rules of law, morality (*boni mores*), public order, personal rights and contracts that comprise objects that are impossible to perform[19] are void. That is to say, the contract is deemed invalid by operation of law. Therefore, it is unnecessary to bring an action to establish its invalidity. However, if the validity of the contract is disputed, the party that asserts that it is invalid may file a declaratory lawsuit.[20] There is no limitation period for relying on the nullity of a contract. Furthermore, even if the parties do not assert the invalidity of the contract in a lawsuit, the judge must take this nullity into consideration *ex officio*.[21] Moreover, the ratification or good faith (*bona fides*) of the parties cannot remedy this invalidity.[22]

It should be noted that in cases of initial impossibility, the contract is void, even if the debtor does not know of the impossibility. Where the debtor has knowledge of this fact, the contract will also be void. However, in such a case, the debtor must pay compensation to the creditor for negative damage. This type of liability is an example of *culpa in contrahendo* (fault in contracting) as the fault of the debtor arises during contract negotiations.[23]

5.3.2 Partial Nullity[24]

It is possible that only some of the terms of the contract are invalid. In this case, the contract will be partially invalid. In other words, a partial nullity will occur. Indeed, according to TCO art. 27 par. 2 sent. 1, the invalidity of certain provisions of a contract does not affect the validity of other provisions. For instance, with regard to partial nullity, consider the following example: under TCC art. 949, in a pledge contract, any agreement by which the pledged chattel becomes the property of the

[19]*Impossibilium nulla obligatio est*: No-one has a legal obligation to do the impossible or there is no obligation to perform an impossible act.

[20]For further explanations see Kuru and Budak (2010).

[21]von Tuhr and Peter (1979), § 29, II, p. 225; Becker (1941), art. 20, N. 11, Gauch et al. (2008), p. 138; Tercier (2004), p. 101; Thévenoz and Werro (2012), art. 19–20, N. 94.

[22]Oğuzman and Öz (2015), p. 175; Kocayusufpaşaoğlu (2014), pp. 585–586; Nomer (2015), p. 58; Reisoğlu (2014), p. 146; Eren (2015), p. 334; Tercier et al. (2016), p. 156.

[23]See Sects. 1.10 and 22.6.

[24]For further explanations see Başpınar (1998), Üçer (2013).

pledgee in the event of non-performance of the debt is void.[25] Therefore, according to TCO art. 27 par. 2 sent. 1, if the parties to the pledge contract stipulate a provision of this nature, this provision will be void, but the other provisions of the pledge agreement will remain unaffected and valid.[26]

As mentioned above, if some of the provisions of the contract are invalid, as a rule, the other provisions of the contract remain valid. Nonetheless, under TCO art. 27 par. 2 sent. 2, if it is obvious that the parties would not have concluded the contract without the invalid provisions, then the entire contract will be void. It should be noted that, in practice, even if this is true for only one of the parties, the entire contract is considered to be void.[27] For instance, a buyer wants to purchase a loading machine and a packaging machine. The loading machine's price is €40,000 and the packaging machine costs €10,000. The buyer pays €50,000 for these specific goods. However, it is subsequently discovered that the loading machine had been destroyed at the time of formation of the contract, while the packaging machine was still merchantable. The seller argues that the provision of the contract relating to the loading machine is void due to the initial impossibility of performance, while the provision relating to the packaging machine remains valid. Accordingly, the seller keeps the €10,000; delivers the packaging machine to the buyer; and repays the loading machine's price – *i.e.*, €40,000. However, the buyer argues that the entire contract is invalid as if he had known that the loading machine was damaged at the time of formation of the contract, he would not have purchased the packaging machine. In this case, the judge will determine the extent of the invalidity of the contract by taking into consideration the presumed intentions of the parties, especially of the buyer. It should be added that if the buyer still wishes to purchase the packaging machine, the seller must comply with the contract. The seller may not argue that if he had known of this partial invalidity, he would not have sold the packaging machine. Such an assertion is against the principles of good faith (TCC art. 2 par. 2).

TCO art. 27 par. 2 sent. 2 states that if it is obvious that the parties would not have entered into the contract without the invalid provisions, then the entire contract will be void. Consequently, in such a case, the judge must take the presumed intentions of the parties into consideration in order to determine whether the contract is partially invalid. However, in certain cases, the protective aim of the violated provision or the principles of good faith do not allow the judge to take the presumed intentions of the parties into consideration. For example, in Turkish law, contracting parties may agree on a clause that excludes their liability. However, the

---

[25]It should be kept in mind that the Act on Movable Pledge on Commercial Transactions sets a specific rule. According to article 14 of this Act, in the case of non-performance of a loan agreement the creditor may demand that ownership of the pledged assets be transferred to him in lieu of performance. However, if the value of the pledged asset exceeds the amount of the secured debt, the creditor must pay this difference to the pledgor or, if there are other creditors in the subsequent rank, to them.

[26]For further explanations see Helvacı (1997), pp. 102–107.

[27]Kocayusufpaşaoğlu (2014), pp. 598–599.

provisions of an agreement in advance purporting to exclude liability for gross fault (unlawful intent or gross negligence—*culpa lata*) will be void (TCO art. 115 par. 1). In this case, the provisions of the agreement excluding liability for gross fault will be invalid but the provisions will remain valid to the extent of excluding liability for slight negligence (*culpa levis*).[28]

With this in mind, it will be helpful to mention that, pursuant to TComC art. 1530, transactions and terms prohibited by commercial provisions are invalid unless the contrary is stipulated. However, where a maximum limit is prescribed by law or by the competent authorities and a provision of a contract exceeds that limit, then the maximum prescribed limit will be deemed to apply to the contract. In that respect, TCO art. 27 par. 2 sent. 2 is not applicable. For instance, the legislature may limit interest rates in commercial loan agreements to 10% per annum. If, in these circumstances, the parties agree to an interest rate of 25% per annum, the judge will deem the contract to be concluded within the maximum limit (*i.e.*, 10%) without taking into consideration their presumed intentions.

References

Altunkaya M (2005) Edimin başlangıçtaki imkânsızlığı. Yetkin, Ankara
Antalya OG (2012) Borçlar hukuku genel hükümler, vol 1. Legal, İstanbul
Ateş D (2007) Borçlar hukuku sözleşmelerinde genel ahlaka aykırılık. Turhan, Ankara
Aybay A (2011) Borçlar hukuku dersleri genel bölüm. Filiz, İstanbul
Başpınar V (1998) Borç sözleşmelerinin kısmi butlanı. Güncel, Ankara
Becker H (1941) Kommentar zum Schweizerischen Zivilgesetzbuch, Volume VI, Obligationenrecht, 1. Abteilung: Allgemeine Bestimmungen, Art. 1-183. Stämpfli, Bern
Berger B (2012) Allgemeines Schuldrecht. Stämpfli, Bern
Engel P (1997) Traité des obligations en droit Suisse. Stämpfli, Bern
Eren F (2015) Borçlar hukuku genel hükümler. Yetkin, Ankara
Feyzioğlu FN (1976) Borçlar hukuku genel hükümler, vol 1. Fakülteler, İstanbul
Gauch P, Schluep WR, Schmid J (2008) Schweizerisches Obligationenrecht, Allgemeiner Teil, vol 1. Schulthess, Zürich
Helvacı İ (1997) Türk medenî kanununa göre lex commissoria (mürtehinin merhunu temellük) yasağı (mk. m. 788/c.2 ve mk. m. 863). Alfa, İstanbul
Helvacı S (2001) Türk ve İsviçre hukuklarında kişilik hakkını koruyucu davalar (mk. md. 24/a fıkra I/imk. md. 28a fıkra I). Beta, İstanbul
Honsell H, Vogt NP, Wiegand W (eds) (2003) Basler Kommentar zum Schweizerischen Privatrecht, Obligationenrecht 1: Art. 1-529 OR. Helbing Lichtenhahn, Basel
Kılıçoğlu AM (2013) Borçlar hukuku genel hükümler. Turhan, İstanbul
Kocayusufpaşaoğlu N (2014) Borçlar hukuku genel bölüm, vol 1 (Kocayusufpaşaoğlu/Hatemi/Serozan/Arpacı). Filiz, İstanbul
Kuru B, Budak AC (2010) Tespit davaları. On iki levha, İstanbul
Nomer HN (2015) Borçlar hukuku genel hükümler. Beta, İstanbul
Oğuzman K, Öz T (2015) Borçlar hukuku genel hükümler, vol 1. Vedat, İstanbul

[28]Kocayusufpaşaoğlu (2014), pp. 599–600, 602.

Oser H, Schönenberger W (1929) Kommentar zum Schweizerischen Zivilgesetzbuch, Volume V: Das Obligationenrecht, Erster Halbband: Art. 1-183. Schulthess, Zürich
Özsunay E (1983) Borçlar hukuku, vol I. Filiz, İstanbul
Reisoğlu S (2014) Türk borçlar hukuku genel hükümler. Beta, İstanbul
Schwenzer I (2009) Schweizerisches Obligationenrecht, Allgemeiner Teil. Schulthess, Bern
Tekinay SS, Akman S, Burcuoğlu H, Altop A (1993) Tekinay borçlar hukuku genel hükümler. Filiz, İstanbul
Tercier P (2004) Le droit des obligations. Schulthess, Zurich
Tercier P, Pichonnaz P, Develioğlu HM (2016) Borçlar hukuku genel hükümler. On iki levha, İstanbul
Thévenoz L, Werro F (éd) (2012) Commentaire romand code des obligations 1: art. 1-529 CO. Helbing Lichtenhahn, Bâle
Üçer M (2013) Roma hukukunda ve karşılaştırmalı hukukta sözleşmelerin kısmi butlanı. Yetkin, Ankara
von Tuhr A, Peter H (1979) Allgemeiner Teil des Schweizerischen Obligationenrecht, vol 1. Schulthess, Zürich

Chapter 6
Abstract Acknowledgement of Debt

6.1 General[1]

Initially, one might think that an acknowledgement of debt[2] is a unilateral legal transaction. However, this is not true; on the contrary, an acknowledgement of debt is a contract.[3] In fact, such a contract does not require any specific form.[4] Nevertheless, in practice, this kind of legal transaction is usually concluded in written form.

Within an acknowledgement of debt, the parties may state the legal ground (*causa*) of the obligation. For instance, in a deed, D acknowledges that he is obliged to pay €10,000 to C because he has bought a car from C. In this case, the acknowledgement of debt comprises its cause (legal ground); this cause is referred to as *causa credendi* (for the sake of obtaining a claim). This is because D is obliged to pay €10,000 in order to have a claim for the transfer of the ownership of the car.

[1]Antalya (2012), pp. 81, 268–273; Aybay (2011), pp. 54–55; Becker (1941), art. 17; Berger (2012), pp. 96–97; Engel (1997), pp. 156–157; Eren (2015), pp. 190–198; Feyzioğlu (1976), pp. 286–297; Gauch et al. (2008), pp. 263–265; Honsell et al. (2003), art. 17; Kılıçoğlu (2013), pp. 49–51; Kocayusufpaşaoğlu (2014), pp. 119–129; Nomer (2015), pp. 49–50; Oser and Schönenberger (1929), art. 17; Oğuzman and Öz (2015), pp. 205–210; Özsunay (1983), pp. 79–82; Reisoğlu (2014), pp. 100–102; Schwenzer (2009), pp. 19–21; Tekinay et al. (1993), pp. 137–142; Tercier (2004), pp. 69–70; Tercier et al. (2016), pp. 101–103; Thévenoz and Werro (2012), art. 17, and von Tuhr and Peter (1979), pp. 266–273.

[2]*Reconnaissance de dette*, *Schuldbekenntnis*.

[3]Honsell et al. (2003), art. 17, N. 3; Oğuzman and Öz (2015), p. 207; Tekinay et al. (1993), p. 137; Nomer (2015), p. 49; Eren (2015), p. 193, on the contrary see Thévenoz and Werro (2012), art. 17, N. 4.

[4]Honsell et al. (2003), art. 17, N. 3.

İ. Helvacı, *Turkish Contract Law*, DOI 10.1007/978-3-319-60061-1_6

6.2 Validity of Abstract Acknowledgement of Debt

It is possible that the parties may create an acknowledgement of debt without stating its reason.[5] For instance, in a deed, D acknowledges that he is obliged to pay €10,000 to C without stating the legal ground of the debt. This is an example of an abstract acknowledgement of debt. According to TCO art. 18, even if an acknowledgement of debt does not state its cause, it is nevertheless valid. The cause of the debt may be a sale contract (*causa credendi*) or a deed that constitutes a promise of a gift (*causa donandi*).

However, it is possible that an acknowledgement of debt does not have a valid legal ground. In this case, the validity of the acknowledgement of debt is contentious.

Certain scholars are influenced by FCC art. 1131 (version in force from 17th February 1804 to 1st October 2016), which states that an obligation without cause or with a false cause, or with an unlawful cause, may not have any effect. Therefore, these scholars are of the opinion that the validity of the acknowledgement of debt depends on its cause. That is to say, if there is no valid cause, then the acknowledgement of debt is invalid.[6] In accordance with this point of view, an acknowledgement of debt does not constitute a new obligation in addition to the obligation resulting from the principal obligational relationship; it only affects the burden of proof of the creditor, that is to say, the creditor may bring an action based on this acknowledgment of debt, and thus, he does not have to prove the cause of his claim. On the contrary, if there is no valid cause, the burden of proof lies with the debtor. According to this point of view, if the court establishes that the acknowledgement of debt has no valid cause, then the absence of a valid cause must be taken into consideration *ex officio*.

Other scholars, influenced by BGB § 780, accept that an acknowledgement of debt constitutes a new obligation in addition to the obligation resulting from the principal obligational relationship.[7] From this perspective, even if the acknowledgement of debt has no valid cause, it is nevertheless valid; however, it constitutes a case of unjust enrichment to the advantage of the creditor. Therefore, the court is not entitled to take into consideration the lack of legal ground (*causa*) of its own motion (*ex officio*).

In the Turkish Code of Obligations, art. 82 may be considered to support this second point of view. According to par. 2 of this article, if the enrichment consists of a claim against the impoverished party, he can refuse the demand of the enriched party in respect of performance even if the claim of unjust enrichment is time-barred. As has been seen according to TCO art. 82 par. 2, if a claim has no valid

---

[5]For further explanations see Sungurbey (1957), Karlı (2008).

[6]Oser and Schönenberger (1929), art. 17, N. 13, 19 *ff*; Tekinay et al. (1993), p. 141; Eren (2015), pp. 194–195.

[7]von Tuhr and Peter (1979), § 32, III, pp. 270–272; Sungurbey (1957), p. 40 *ff*; Oğuzman and Öz (2015), p. 208.

cause, it constitutes a case of unjust enrichment in the assets of the creditor. If it were not possible to acquire a claim in the absence of a valid cause, this article would have been unnecessary.[8]

However, this second point of view must be restricted in certain cases. If the cause of the acknowledgement of debt is unlawful or immoral, the court must take this into consideration *ex officio* and must declare that it is void. Indeed, according to TCO art. 604 par. 1, claims resulting from gambling and betting may not be sued upon and may not be enforced. In addition, TCO art. 605 par. 1 states that even if an acknowledgement of debt or a negotiable instrument (a bill of exchange, a promissory note or a cheque) signed by the gambler or the bettor to cover a gambling or betting transaction is transferred to a third party, no person may file a lawsuit or demand the enforcement of these instruments.[9] As has been seen, these provisions accept that if the legal ground of an acknowledgement of debt is gambling or betting, the acknowledgement of debt may not give rise to legal claims; in other words, it constitutes a natural obligation.[10] Therefore, the court must take this fact into consideration *ex officio* and dismiss demands based on such acknowledgements of debt. Since the legislature explicitly accepts that an acknowledgement of debt relating to gambling or betting constitutes a natural obligation, then if the cause of the acknowledgement of debt is unlawful or immoral, it must be inferred *a fortiori* that it is void.[11]

Regardless of which point of view is accepted, the burden of proof relating to the existence of the illegality or immorality of the cause is on the debtor.

References

Antalya OG (2012) Borçlar hukuku genel hükümler, vol 1. Legal, İstanbul

Aybay A (2011) Borçlar hukuku dersleri genel bölüm. Filiz, İstanbul

Becker H (1941) Kommentar zum Schweizerischen Zivilgesetzbuch, Volume VI, Obligationenrecht, 1. Abteilung: Allgemeine Bestimmungen, Art. 1-183. Stämpfli, Bern

Berger B (2012) Allgemeines Schuldrecht. Stämpfli, Bern

Engel P (1997) Traité des obligations en droit Suisse. Stämpfli, Bern

Eren F (2015) Borçlar hukuku genel hükümler. Yetkin, Ankara

Feyzioğlu FN (1976) Borçlar hukuku genel hükümler, vol 1. Fakülteler, İstanbul

Gauch P, Schluep WR, Schmid J (2008) Schweizerisches Obligationenrecht, Allgemeiner Teil, vol 1. Schulthess, Zürich

Honsell H, Vogt NP, Wiegand W (eds) (2003) Basler Kommentar zum Schweizerischen Privatrecht, Obligationenrecht 1: Art. 1-529 OR. Helbing Lichtenhahn, Basel

[8]Kocayusufpaşaoğlu (2014), pp. 124–125.

[9]The rights of third parties in good faith arising from negotiable instruments are reserved (TCO art. 605 par. 1 sent. 2).

[10]See Sect. 21.2.1.

[11]Sungurbey (1957), p. 99; Kocayusufpaşaoğlu (2014), p. 128; Feyzioğlu (1976), p. 294. See on the contrary von Tuhr and Peter (1979), § 32, III, p. 271.

Karlı Ö (2008) Sebebi gösterilmeyen borç tanıması (mücerret borç ikrarı bk. mad. 17). Vedat, İstanbul
Kılıçoğlu AM (2013) Borçlar hukuku genel hükümler. Turhan, İstanbul
Kocayusufpaşaoğlu N (2014) Borçlar hukuku genel bölüm, Volume 1 (Kocayusufpaşaoğlu/Hatemi/Serozan/Arpacı). Filiz, İstanbul.
Nomer HN (2015) Borçlar hukuku genel hükümler. Beta, İstanbul
Oğuzman K, Öz T (2015) Borçlar hukuku genel hükümler, vol 1. Vedat, İstanbul
Oser H, Schönenberger W (1929) Kommentar zum Schweizerischen Zivilgesetzbuch, Volume V: Das Obligationenrecht, Erster Halbband: Art. 1-183. Schulthess, Zürich
Özsunay E (1983) Borçlar hukuku, vol I. Filiz, İstanbul
Reisoğlu S (2014) Türk borçlar hukuku genel hükümler. Beta, İstanbul
Schwenzer I (2009) Schweizerisches Obligationenrecht, Allgemeiner Teil. Schulthess, Bern
Sungurbey İ (1957) Borç ikrarı ve borç vaadi, İstanbul
Tekinay SS, Akman S, Burcuoğlu H, Altop A (1993) Tekinay borçlar hukuku genel hükümler. Filiz, İstanbul
Tercier P (2004) Le droit des obligations. Schulthess, Zurich
Tercier P, Pichonnaz P, Develioğlu HM (2016) Borçlar hukuku genel hükümler. On iki levha, İstanbul
Thévenoz L, Werro F (éd) (2012) Commentaire romand code des obligations 1: art. 1-529 CO. Helbing Lichtenhahn, Bâle
von Tuhr A, Peter H (1979) Allgemeiner Teil des Schweizerischen Obligationenrecht, vol 1. Schulthess, Zürich

Chapter 7
Obligation to Contract

7.1 General[1]

According to the principle of freedom of contract, within the limits of the law, each person is free to enter into a contract or not. However, in certain circumstances, a person may have an obligation to contract.

The obligation to contract may arise from an agreement called a pre-contract (preliminary agreement) or by virtue of the law itself. In this section, these two bases of an obligation to contract will be analysed.

7.2 Pre-contract[2]

7.2.1 General[3]

According to TCO art. 29, a pre-contract to enter into a main contract at a later time is valid. A pre-contract (*pactum de contrahendo*) is binding and ensures the conclusion of the main contract. Its binding effect means that the parties undertake

[1]Antalya (2012), pp. 261–267; Aybay (2011), pp. 41–43; Becker (1941), art. 22; Berger (2012), p. 58; Engel (1997), pp. 99–102, 181–183; Eren (2015), pp. 301–315; Feyzioğlu (1976), pp. 273–286; Gauch et al. (2008), pp. 233–244; Honsell et al. (2003), art. 22; Kılıçoğlu (2013), pp. 75–78, 265–268; Kocayusufpaşaoğlu (2014), pp. 100–110, 505–525; Nomer (2015), pp. 50–53; Oser and Schönenberger (1929), art. 22; Oğuzman and Öz (2015), pp. 183–190; Özsunay (1983), pp. 83–85; Reisoğlu (2014), pp. 97–100, 133; Schwenzer (2009), pp. 172–177; Tekınay et al. (1993), pp. 142–148, 365–367; Tercıer (2004), pp. 109–110; Tercier et al. (2016), pp. 171–173; Thévenoz and Werro (2012), art. 19–20, 22, and von Tuhr and Peter (1979), pp. 273–285.

[2]*Précontrat, promesse de contracter, Vorvertrag.*

[3]For further explanations see Ayrancı (2006), Doğan (2006).

İ. Helvacı, *Turkish Contract Law*, DOI 10.1007/978-3-319-60061-1_7

to enter into the main contract subject to the conditions agreed in the pre-contract. In a pre-contract, one or both parties may undertake to enter into the main contract.

The reason or purpose for postponement of the main contract may be various. The economic or legal conditions at the time of the conclusion of the pre-contract may not be convenient for entering into the main contract, for example, in circumstances where prices or foreign currency rates fluctuate or a party responsible for obtaining any necessary official permission may not yet have been granted such permission, etc.

In order for there to be a pre-contract, the main contract must be of an obligatory nature.[4] In this context, the principal contract may be a sale, lease or work contract. For instance, in a sale contract, which is an obligatory legal transaction (*acte géné rateur d'obligation, Verpflichtungsgeschäft*),[5] the buyer does not acquire ownership of the property sold. With the conclusion of the sale contract, the buyer only becomes entitled to claim that the property is to be transferred to him.

However, if the main contract to be entered into does not create or constitute any obligations, then the existence of the pre-contract will not be in question.[6] For example, an assignment of a claim transfers the assignor's claim to the assignee. Consequently, if the parties promise to make an assignment of a claim, such a contract will not qualify as a pre-contract.

7.2.2 Form

Pursuant to TCO art. 29 par. 2, where the law requires a specific form for the validity of a main future contract, the pre-contract must also be made in that form. However, there are certain exceptions to this rule. According to this article, for example, since the law requires a specific form for the validity of a surety contract, a pre-contract relating to a surety contract (that is, the promise to stand surety) must also be made in that form. Indeed, TCO art. 583 par. 2 sent. 1 confirms this requirement.

As to the exceptions, the following is an example: a sale contract relating to immovable property must be concluded before a land registry officer (TCO art. 237 par. 1, LRA art. 26). Therefore, in accordance with TCO art. 29 par. 2, a pre-contract relating to the sale of real estate must be concluded in the same form. Nevertheless, according to NPA art. 89, the parties may also conclude such a pre-contract before a notary public.

---

[4]Obligatory: Imposing obligation, creating or constituting an obligation.

[5]A suggested translation for *Verpflichtungsgeschäft* is 'transaction of obligation' (Foster and Sule (2010), p. 416 fn. 22). According to certain scholars, an appropriate term that defines *Verpflichtungsgeschäft* is 'obligatory transaction' (Häcker (2013), p. 20 fn. 14). In this sense, Zekoll and Reimann (2005), p. 234; Faber and Lurger (2011), p. 563.

[6]von Tuhr and Peter (1979), § 33, I, p. 274; Oğuzman and Öz (2015), p. 188; Reisoğlu (2014), p. 98; Eren (2015), p. 311; Nomer (2015), p. 50; Kocayusufpaşaoğlu (2014), p. 100.

7.2.3 *Consequences*

If the parties fulfil their obligations to enter into a main contract arising from a pre-contract, the expectations of the parties will be satisfied. However, a party undertaking to conclude a main contract may breach the pre-contract and fail to fulfil his obligation. In such a case, the other party may seek a court order to enforce the conclusion of the main contract. The court order stands for the failing party's declaration of will (intention),[7] which is necessary for the formation of the main contract,[8] and thus, the main contract is deemed to be concluded.[9]

In practice, the most common type of obligation to contract concerns the sale of immovable property.[10] If the prospective seller does not conclude the main contract, the other party may demand a court order for its conclusion. In such cases, the court order constitutes the main contract. However, in practice, the claimants usually demand the transfer of the ownership of the immovable property as if a sale contract existed. As a result, if the court accepts the demand, then the court orders not only constitute the main contract but they also give effect to the transfer of ownership of the immovable property to the claimant (TCC art. 716 par. 1).[11] Such a result is theoretically not satisfactory because it denies the difference between a sale contract and a pre-contract for sale. Nevertheless, it is obvious that it simplifies and economises the procedure.[12]

7.3 Obligation to Contract Arising from the Law

In certain cases, a specific provision may encumber a person with the obligation to conclude a contract. According to TCPA art. 6 par. 1, the sale of goods, which are displayed in shop windows, on shelves, in electronic media or anywhere else where the goods are clearly visible, is mandatory, unless it is indicated that the goods are not for sale.

Moreover, an obligation to contract may arise from the principles of good faith (TCC art. 2).[13] Indeed, in certain cases, failing to conclude a contract may breach this article. For instance, the sole pharmacy or the sole baker in a small village is not entitled to refuse to contract without any justifiable reason.[14] Furthermore, an

[7]*Déclaration de volonté*, *Willenserklärung*.

[8]Reisoğlu (2014), p. 98; Nomer (2015), p. 51.

[9]Engel (1997), p. 182; Kocayusufpaşaoğlu (2014), p. 107.

[10]Thévenoz and Werro (2012), art. 22, N. 7.

[11]Eren (2015), p. 315; Nomer (2015), p. 51; Oğuzman and Öz (2015), p. 190, 376.

[12]Oğuzman and Öz (2015), pp. 189–190, 376; Eren (2015), pp. 314–315.

[13]Oğuzman and Öz (2015), p. 185, *Cf.* Gauch et al. (2008), p. 243.

[14]Compare to Engel (1997), p. 100.

obligation to contract may also arise out of public law.[15] Indeed, public institutions that supply utility services, such as water, electricity, telecommunications[16] and natural gas, or that supply public transportation, such as railways, subways, etc., are not entitled to refuse to contract without any justifiable reason.

If a person who is under an obligation to contract fails to conclude the contract—*i.e.*, does not declare his will, which is necessary for the formation of the contract—the claimant may file a lawsuit and the contract will be deemed to be concluded by the court order. In such a case, the court decision replaces the abstaining person's declaration of will (intention).[17]

References

Antalya OG (2012) Borçlar hukuku genel hükümler, vol 1. Legal, İstanbul
Aybay A (2011) Borçlar hukuku dersleri genel bölüm. Filiz, İstanbul
Ayrancı H (2006) Ön sözleşme. Yetkin, Ankara
Becker H (1941) Kommentar zum Schweizerischen Zivilgesetzbuch, Volume VI, Obligationenrecht, 1. Abteilung: Allgemeine Bestimmungen, Art. 1-183. Stämpfli, Bern
Berger B (2012) Allgemeines Schuldrecht. Stämpfli, Bern
Doğan G (2006) Ön sözleşme (sözleşme yapma vaadi). Yeditepe, İstanbul
Engel P (1997) Traité des obligations en droit Suisse. Stämpfli, Bern
Eren F (2015) Borçlar hukuku genel hükümler. Yetkin, Ankara
Faber W, Lurger B (eds) (2011) National reports on the transfer of movables in Europe, vol 6. Sellier, München
Feyzioğlu FN (1976) Borçlar hukuku genel hükümler, vol 1. Fakülteler, İstanbul
Foster N, Sule S (2010) German legal system and laws. Oxford Publishing, New York
Gauch P, Schluep WR, Schmid J (2008) Schweizerisches Obligationenrecht, Allgemeiner Teil, vol 1. Schulthess, Zürich
Häcker B (2013) Consequences of impaired consent transfers, a structural comparison of English and German law. Hart Publishing, Oxford and Portland, Oregon
Honsell H, Vogt NP, Wiegand W (eds) (2003) Basler Kommentar zum Schweizerischen Privatrecht, Obligationenrecht 1: Art. 1-529 OR. Helbing Lichtenhahn, Basel
Kılıçoğlu AM (2013) Borçlar hukuku genel hükümler. Turhan, İstanbul
Kocayusufpaşaoğlu N (2014) Borçlar hukuku genel bölüm, vol 1 (Kocayusufpaşaoğlu/Hatemi/Serozan/Arpacı). Filiz, İstanbul
Nomer HN (2015) Borçlar hukuku genel hükümler. Beta, İstanbul
Oğuzman K, Öz T (2015) Borçlar hukuku genel hükümler, vol 1. Vedat, İstanbul
Oser H, Schönenberger W (1929) Kommentar zum Schweizerischen Zivilgesetzbuch, Volume V: Das Obligationenrecht, Erster Halbband: Art. 1-183. Schulthess, Zürich
Özsunay E (1983) Borçlar hukuku, vol I. Filiz, İstanbul
Reisoğlu S (2014) Türk borçlar hukuku genel hükümler. Beta, İstanbul
Schwenzer I (2009) Schweizerisches Obligationenrecht, Allgemeiner Teil. Schulthess, Bern
Tekinay SS, Akman S, Burcuoğlu H, Altop A (1993) Tekinay borçlar hukuku genel hükümler. Filiz, İstanbul

[15]Tekinay et al. (1993), p. 365; Eren (2015), pp. 304–305.

[16]For further explanations see Yıldız (2012).

[17]*Déclaration de volonté*, *Willenserklärung*.

Tercier P (2004) Le droit des obligations. Schulthess, Zurich
Tercier P, Pichonnaz P, Develioğlu HM (2016) Borçlar hukuku genel hükümler. On iki levha, İstanbul
Thévenoz L, Werro F (éd) (2012) Commentaire romand code des obligations 1: art. 1-529 CO. Helbing Lichtenhahn, Bâle
von Tuhr A, Peter H (1979) Allgemeiner Teil des Schweizerischen Obligationenrecht, Volume 1. Schulthess, Zürich
Yıldız MG (2012) Son kullanıcıyla akdedilen elektronik haberleşme hizmeti sözleşmesi. On iki levha, İstanbul
Zekoll J, Reimann M (eds) (2005) Introduction to German law. Kluwer Law International, The Hague

Chapter 8
Contract Interpretation and Simulation

8.1 Interpretation of the Contract[1]

8.1.1 General

If the interpretation of the contract is not contested by the parties, then their common interpretation will be applied. However, in the event that each party interprets the text (wording) of the contract in a different manner and the parties' interpretation is contradictory, this dispute will be determined by a judge.[2]

According to TCO art. 19 par. 1, in evaluating the provisions of the contract, the judge will seek to establish the real and common intentions of the parties. When it is not possible to establish the real and common intentions of the parties, the judge will determine the presumed intentions of the parties in light of the 'trust theory' (*théorie de la confiance, Vertrauenstheorie*).[3] According to this principle, the judge must seek the meaning that the parties would have assumed, pursuant to the

[1]Antalya (2012), pp. 201–210, 354–360; Aybay (2011), pp. 46–55; Becker (1941), art. 18; Berger (2012), pp. 231–236, 386–393; Engel (1997), pp. 223–226, 235–242; Eren (2015), pp. 349–365, 466–475; Feyzioğlu (1976), pp. 187–210, 350–361; Gauch et al. (2008), pp. 217–224, 271–282; Honsell et al. (2003), art. 18; Kılıçoğlu (2013), pp. 171–180, 250–254; Kocayusufpaşaoğlu (2014), pp. 331–338, 345–363; Nomer (2015), pp. 42–45, 90–96; Oser and Schönenberger (1929), art. 18; Oğuzman and Öz (2015), pp. 127–133, 190–193; Özsunay (1983), pp. 70, 91–103; Reisoğlu (2014), pp. 102–114; Schwenzer (2009), pp. 226–228, 263–266; Tekinay et al. (1993), pp. 148–153, 407–415; Tercier (2004), pp. 115–116, 173–175; Tercier et al. (2016), pp. 182–183, 290–303; Thévenoz and Werro (2012), art. 18, and von Tuhr and Peter (1979), pp. 285–297.

[2]Oğuzman and Öz (2015), p. 190; Eren (2015), p. 466; Kocayusufpaşaoğlu (2014), p. 331; Tercier et al. (2016), p. 297; Gauch et al. (2008), p. 271.

[3]von Tuhr and Peter (1979), § 34, I, p. 287; Reisoğlu (2014), p. 102; Nomer (2015), p. 43; Tercier et al. (2016), p. 300; Tekinay et al. (1993), p. 150; Oğuzman and Öz (2015), p. 191; Eren (2015), p. 469; Feyzioğlu (1976), pp. 355–356.

İ. Helvacı, *Turkish Contract Law*, DOI 10.1007/978-3-319-60061-1_8

principles of good faith, to their reciprocal declaration of will (intention),[4] while taking into account all the circumstances.

8.1.2 Principles of Interpretation

In establishing either the real and common intentions or presumed intentions of the parties, the judge must, first, take the text (wording) of the contract into consideration.[5] That is to say, the judge will make an evaluation on the basis of the actual words and phrases used in the contract (literal construction). In that respect, the judge has to assign the ordinary and common meaning to the contract provisions.

However, the contracting parties may use expressions in a special or technical sense. In this case, the judge will consider how these expressions are normally used by persons within the relevant business or profession and interpret them in that sense.[6] The judge, in establishing the meaning of a particular provision in the contract, is not entitled to evaluate it separately. On the contrary, the provision must be analysed within the context of the entire contract.[7] When dealing with matters of interpretation, the judge must evaluate all of the circumstances that preceded or accompanied the formation of the contract.

There are additional principles relating to the interpretation of the contract. For example, the judge may take into account the parties' negotiations and conduct before the formation of the contract (drafts of the contract, exchanges of correspondence such as traditional mail and emails, etc.). The judge may also take into consideration the parties' conduct after the formation of the contract.[8]

There are also subsidiary rules for the interpretation of contracts. Where the judge cannot determine the real or presumed common intentions of the parties, the following rules can be applied: (1) an ambiguity is generally interpreted to the detriment of the drafter (*indubio contra stipulatorem*), particularly in adhesion contracts; (2) an ambiguity is interpreted in favour of the party that is under obligation (*favor debitoris*); and (3) any superfluous or meaningless provisions or terms must be interpreted in a way that supports the validity of the contract.[9]

---

[4] *Déclaration de volonté, Willenserklärung.*

[5] von Tuhr and Peter (1979), § 34, I, p. 286; Gauch et al. (2008), p. 274; Thévenoz and Werro (2012), art. 18, N. 15; Oğuzman and Öz (2015), p. 192; Tercier et al. (2016), p. 298.

[6] Gauch et al. (2008), p. 274; Tercier et al. (2016), p. 298, compare to Kocayusufpaşaoğlu (2014), p. 333.

[7] Gauch et al. (2008), p. 275; Eren (2015), p. 472; Oğuzman and Öz (2015), p. 192; Feyzioğlu (1976), p. 356; Tekinay et al. (1993), p. 151; Tercier et al. (2016), p. 301; Nomer (2015), p. 44.

[8] Eren (2015), pp. 470–471; Kocayusufpaşaoğlu (2014), pp. 334–335.

[9] Kocayusufpaşaoğlu (2014), p. 336; Oğuzman and Öz (2015), p. 193; Eren (2015), p. 473.

8.2 Common Mistake and Simulation[10]

As mentioned above, when the judge interprets a contract, he must establish the real and common intention of the parties. Indeed, the judge, first and foremost, will interpret the wording of the contract. However, the parties might have used certain expressions that are not accurate or precise. Inaccuracy in the terminology used can result from the parties' common mistake or may be intended with the objective to disguise their real intention (simulation). In the following paragraphs, the concept of common mistake and the concept of simulation will be analysed respectively.

8.2.1 Common Mistake

The parties to a contract while determining the terms and conditions of the contract might have made a common mistake. In such a case, the judge must establish the common and real intention of the parties without taking into consideration inaccurate expressions erroneously used by them (TCO art. 19 par. 1). For instance, in a car sale contract, the parties specified the subject matter of the contract as a Mercedes E 200 with the number plate 00 XX 1234, but in the contract they record the number plate of the car erroneously as 00 X 1234. In such a case, the contract is deemed to be concluded in accordance with the parties' common and real intention (*falsa demonstratio non nocet*).[11]

8.2.2 Simulation

In the case of simulation, the inaccuracy of the terms used by the parties arises from their objective to disguise their real intention.[12] Even so, in the case of simulation, the judge must establish the common and real intention of the parties without taking into consideration inaccurate or misleading expressions used by them (TCO art. 19 par. 1). The concept of simulation, which is regulated under TCO art. 19, can be divided into three types: absolute, relative and partial.

---

[10]For further explanations see Esener (1956), Aday (1992), Özmen and Özkaya (1993), Özkaya (2017).

[11]Honsell et al. (2003), art. 18, N. 46–49; Tercier (2004), p. 115; Oğuzman and Öz (2015), p. 91.

[12]Becker (1941), art. 18, N. 28.

8.2.2.1 Absolute Simulation (Simple Simulation)

In absolute simulation, although the parties make a contract, they agree that this contract will not have any legal effect.[13] The author's opinion is that an absolutely simulated contract will be void (compare to TCO art. 19 par. 1).[14]

This rule also applies to a written acknowledgement of debt. Thus, an absolutely simulated written acknowledgement of debt is void. However, even if it is absolutely simulated and therefore void, the creditor may attempt to assign his pseudo-claim to a third party. In these circumstances, this assignment is also invalid. Nevertheless, if the third party relies on this written acknowledgement of debt, the debtor cannot plead to the third party that the transaction is simulated. For example, there is a written real estate lease contract and the rent is determined at TL 100,000 per year but the contracting parties agree that this contract has no legal effect. Despite this simulation, if the creditor attempts to assign this pseudo-claim to a third party who relies on this written lease contract, the debtor cannot plead to the third party that this contract is simulated and, consequently, he must pay the amount stated in the contract (TCO art. 19 par. 2).

8.2.2.2 Relative Simulation

In relative simulation, there are two contracts between the parties: an apparent and a concealed contract. The apparent contract is agreed to have no legal effect. However, at the same time, the parties make another contract and agree that this concealed contract will be valid.[15] In such a case, scholars widely accept that the apparent contract is void as it is simulated and that the concealed contract is valid unless there are circumstances that affect its validity.[16]

At this point, it is necessary to mention three examples. Example 1: a father, who has one son and two daughters, wants to gift his real estate to his son. However, the father makes a simulated sale contract with his son before a land registry officer in order to avoid adverse reactions by his daughters. In this case, the real estate sale contract (the apparent contract) that has been concluded before the land registry officer is void since it is simulated. As to the promise to gift the real estate (the concealed contract), which has been orally concluded between the parties, it is also

[13] Honsell et al. (2003), art. 18, N. 50; Tercier (2004), p. 115; Oğuzman and Öz (2015), p. 128; Eren (2015), p. 353.

[14] Certain scholars are of the opinion that a simulated contract is void, see Oğuzman and Öz (2015), p. 130; Reisoğlu (2014), p. 106. Other scholars argue that a simulated contract is non-existent, see Eren (2015), pp. 356–357; Kocayusufpaşaoğlu (2014), pp. 354–355.

[15] Honsell et al. (2003), art. 18, N. 50; Tercier (2004), p. 115; Oğuzman and Öz (2015), p. 128; Eren (2015), p. 353.

[16] Reisoğlu (2014), p. 108; Nomer (2015), p. 91; Oğuzman and Öz (2015), p. 131; Tercier et al. (2016), p. 182; Feyzioğlu (1976), pp. 199–200; Kocayusufpaşaoğlu (2014), p. 356; Eren (2015), p. 361; Tercier (2004), p. 115; von Tuhr and Peter (1979), § 35, III, p. 293.

invalid as the contract does not satisfy the official written form requirement (TCO art. 288 par. 2).

Example 2: in the above-mentioned case, assume that the subject matter of the contract is movable property. The father makes a written sale contract with his son in order to avoid adverse reactions by his daughters. Additionally, they conclude a written promise to make a gift relating to this movable property. In this situation, the sale contract (the apparent contract) that has been concluded in written form between the parties is void since it is simulated. However, the promise to make a gift (the concealed contract) is valid since it satisfies the form requirement for promises of a gift relating to movable property (TCO art. 288 par. 1).

Example 3: in the second example, if the father had orally made a promise to make a gift to his son, this contract would have been invalid. However, even though the promise to make a gift is invalid, the father might, regardless, transfer ownership of the movable property to his son. In such a case, the promise to make a gift will be deemed valid. This is because, according to TCO art. 288 par. 3, if a promise to make a gift is invalid due to a lack of form but it is nonetheless performed by the donor, it will be treated as a gift from hand to hand. Indeed, TCO art. 289 states that a gift from hand to hand is concluded by delivering the object from the donor to the donee.

8.2.2.3 Partial Simulation

In certain cases, only certain clauses of a contract may be simulated rather than the entire contract. In such a case, there is a partial simulation.[17] The explanations relating to absolute and relative simulations are also applicable. In Turkish law, the most common example occurs in real estate sale contracts; namely, the contracting parties may appear to agree on a sale price that is higher or lower than the real sale price. For example, the real sale price is TL 100,000, whereas the contracting parties represent it as TL 50,000. In this case, the sale price determined in the apparent contract is lower than the real price. In other words, the price is simulated and the contract clause relating to the price is invalid. The real sale price determined in the concealed contract is also invalid since it does not satisfy the form requirements. Nevertheless, if claiming the invalidity of the concealed contract is contrary to the principles of good faith (TCC art. 2 par. 2), then the sale price determined in the concealed contract will be valid.[18]

---

[17]Thévenoz and Werro (2012), art. 18, N. 78; Eren (2015), p. 357; Kocayusufpaşaoğlu (2014), p. 346; Gauch et al. (2008), p. 219; Honsell et al. (2003), art. 18, N. 50.

[18]Oğuzman et al. (2016), p. 379.

References

Aday N (1992) Taşınmaz mülkiyetinin naklinde muvazaa (konuya ilişkin Yargıtay kararları ile). Kazancı, İstanbul
Antalya OG (2012) Borçlar hukuku genel hükümler, vol 1. Legal, İstanbul
Aybay A (2011) Borçlar hukuku dersleri genel bölüm. Filiz, İstanbul
Becker H (1941) Kommentar zum Schweizerischen Zivilgesetzbuch, Volume VI, Obligationenrecht, 1. Abteilung: Allgemeine Bestimmungen, Art. 1-183. Stämpfli, Bern
Berger B (2012) Allgemeines Schuldrecht. Stämpfli, Bern
Engel P (1997) Traité des obligations en droit Suisse. Stämpfli, Bern
Eren F (2015) Borçlar hukuku genel hükümler. Yetkin, Ankara
Esener T (1956) Türk hususi hukukunda muvazaalı muameleler. Fakülteler, İstanbul
Feyzioğlu FN (1976) Borçlar hukuku genel hükümler, vol 1. Fakülteler, İstanbul
Gauch P, Schluep WR, Schmid J (2008) Schweizerisches Obligationenrecht, Allgemeiner Teil, vol 1. Schulthess, Zürich
Honsell H, Vogt NP, Wiegand W (eds) (2003) Basler Kommentar zum Schweizerischen Privatrecht, Obligationenrecht 1: Art. 1-529 OR. Helbing Lichtenhahn, Basel
Kılıçoğlu AM (2013) Borçlar hukuku genel hükümler. Turhan, İstanbul
Kocayusufpaşaoğlu N (2014) Borçlar hukuku genel bölüm, vol 1 (Kocayusufpaşaoğlu/Hatemi/Serozan/Arpacı). Filiz, İstanbul
Nomer HN (2015) Borçlar hukuku genel hükümler. Beta, İstanbul
Oğuzman K, Öz T (2015) Borçlar hukuku genel hükümler, vol 1. Vedat, İstanbul
Oğuzman K, Seliçi Ö, Oktay-Özdemir S (2016) Eşya Hukuku. Filiz, İstanbul
Oser H, Schönenberger W (1929) Kommentar zum Schweizerischen Zivilgesetzbuch, Volume V: Das Obligationenrecht, Erster Halbband: Art. 1-183. Schulthess, Zürich
Özmen İ, Özkaya E (1993) Muvazaa davaları. Adalet, Ankara
Özkaya E (2017) İnançlı işlem ve muvazaa davaları. Seçkin, Ankara
Özsunay E (1983) Borçlar hukuku, vol I. Filiz, İstanbul
Reisoğlu S (2014) Türk borçlar hukuku genel hükümler. Beta, İstanbul
Schwenzer I (2009) Schweizerisches Obligationenrecht, Allgemeiner Teil. Schulthess, Bern
Tekinay SS, Akman S, Burcuoğlu H, Altop A (1993) Tekinay borçlar hukuku genel hükümler. Filiz, İstanbul
Tercier P (2004) Le droit des obligations. Schulthess, Zurich
Tercier P, Pichonnaz P, Develioğlu HM (2016) Borçlar hukuku genel hükümler. On iki levha, İstanbul
Thévenoz L, Werro F (éd) (2012) Commentaire romand code des obligations 1: art. 1-529 CO. Helbing Lichtenhahn, Bâle
von Tuhr A, Peter H (1979) Allgemeiner Teil des Schweizerischen Obligationenrecht, vol 1. Schulthess, Zürich

Chapter 9
Incomplete Contracts

9.1 Gap in the Contract[1]

As mentioned in the section concerning the formation of the contract,[2] in order to form a contract, the parties must agree on all the necessary elements of the contract. The necessary elements of a contract are divided into two categories: objectively essential elements and subjectively essential elements. Furthermore, there are also secondary elements of a contract, but, as a rule, they are not indispensable for the conclusion of the contract.

Since the objectively essential elements constitute the minimum contents of a contract in order for it to be valid, where the parties do not agree on them, the contract cannot be formed.[3] For instance, in a lease contract, a description of the leased object and the rental fee are objectively necessary elements of the contract. If the parties do not agree on these elements, the contract will not be concluded and there will be no question of a gap in the contract to be filled by a judge.

Subjectively essential elements are, in fact, subsidiary elements of the contract. Nevertheless, even if they are not *conditio sine qua non* for the formation of the contract, they are necessary by virtue of the intentions of one or both of the

[1]Antalya (2012), pp. 164–168; Aybay (2011), pp. 48–49; Berger (2012), pp. 394–397; Engel (1997), pp. 218–220, 243–244; Eren (2015), pp. 233–239, 475–480; Feyzioğlu (1976), pp. 66–67; Gauch et al. (2008), pp. 283–291; Honsell et al. (2003), art. 2, 18; Kocayusufpaşaoğlu (2014), pp. 172–179, 338–341; Nomer (2015), pp. 42–45; Oğuzman and Öz (2015), pp. 72–73, 193–196; Reisoğlu (2014), pp. 63–64; Schwenzer (2009), pp. 222–224, 266–269; Tekinay et al. (1993), pp. 74–81; Tercier (2004), pp. 176–177; Tercier et al. (2016), pp. 303–305; Thévenoz and Werro (2012), art. 2, 18, and von Tuhr and Peter (1979), pp. 189–191, 291.

[2]See Sect. 1.7.

[3]Thévenoz and Werro (2012), art. 2, N. 2; Honsell et al. (2003), art. 1, N. 44; Engel (1997), p. 219; Gauch et al. (2008), p. 288; Oğuzman and Öz (2015), p. 72; Eren (2015), p. 234; Reisoğlu (2014), p. 63; Nomer (2015), p. 42; Tekinay et al. (1993), p. 78; Kocayusufpaşaoğlu (2014), p. 173; Tercier et al. (2016), p. 179.

İ. Helvacı, *Turkish Contract Law*, DOI 10.1007/978-3-319-60061-1_9

parties.[4] For instance, a penalty clause in a contract may constitute a subjectively essential element for both of the contracting parties or for just one of them. Where the parties do not agree on such a subsidiary, but subjectively essential, element, then the contract may not be formed and consequently there will be no question of a gap in the contract to be filled by a judge.

As to the secondary elements of a contract, they do not form its core and are not a part of it. They are not objectively or subjectively *conditio sine qua non* for the formation of the contract.[5] For instance, in a sale contract, the time of performance and the place of delivery of the goods are accepted to be secondary elements. According to TCO art. 2 par. 1, if the parties have agreed on objectively or subjectively essential elements of the contract, the contract is deemed to be formed, even if they have not negotiated the secondary elements at all. Where the parties do not agree on such a secondary element, then the contract can be formed but there will be a question of a gap in the contract to be filled by a judge.

9.2 Principles of Filling Contractual Gaps[6]

As mentioned above, if the parties have agreed on the necessary elements of a contract, then the fact that they have not negotiated the secondary elements does not preclude the contract's formation. In this case, a judge will determine the secondary elements in accordance with the default rules of the Code. For instance, in a sale contract, the parties agree on the subject matter of the sale and its price, but they do not negotiate the place and the time of performance. In such a case, a judge will fill this contractual gap by relying on the default rules of the Turkish Code of Obligations. Indeed, the judge will fill the gap relating to the place of performance in accordance with TCO art. 89 and the gap relating to the time of performance in accordance with TCO art. 90 *ff*. Another example is that of parties that have only agreed that the debtor will fulfil the obligation at the beginning or at the end of a month and have not determined the exact time for the performance. In this case, a judge will fill this gap, with reference to TCO art. 91 par. 1, according to which the beginning or the end of a month means the first or last day of the stated month, respectively (TCO art. 91 par. 1).

Where the judge cannot find an applicable default rule in the law, he must fill the contractual gap according to customary law. In the absence of customary law, the judge will fill the contractual gap according to the rules that he would have laid down if he were acting as the legislature (TCC art. 1).[7]

---

[4]Engel (1997), p. 219; Gauch et al. (2008), p. 288; Eren (2015), p. 235; Kocayusufpaşaoğlu (2014), pp. 175–176; Tercier et al. (2016), 179; Tekinay et al. (1993), p. 76; Oğuzman and Öz (2015), p. 73.

[5]Engel (1997), p. 219; Thévenoz and Werro (2012), art. 2, N. 6; Oğuzman and Öz (2015), p. 73; Feyzioğlu (1976), p. 66; Eren (2015), p. 237; Reisoğlu (2014), p. 64.

[6]For further explanations see Dursun (2008).

[7]Eren (2015), p. 476 *ff*; compare to Oğuzman and Öz (2015), p. 194 *ff*.

It is also possible that the parties have agreed on the necessary elements of a contract and have negotiated the secondary elements before the formation of the contract and decide to determine the secondary elements later. In this case, there are two possibilities: (1) if the parties come to an agreement regarding these secondary elements after the formation of the contract, this agreement will be binding and there is no question of a gap to be filled by a judge; (2) where the parties are not able to come to an agreement with regard to the secondary elements after the formation of the contract, then this lack of agreement constitutes a contractual gap. Consequently, a judge will fill this gap, but he is not entitled to rely on the default rules of the Code in the filling of the gap. This is because the parties have negotiated the secondary elements before the formation of the contract. The judge will fill this gap, taking into consideration the nature of the contract, its (financial) objective and all other circumstances (TCO art. 2 par. 2).[8]

It should be kept in mind that if the parties negotiate the secondary elements of the contract during the contract negotiations and do not come to an agreement regarding them, then the contract cannot be formed. This is because a secondary element is deemed to become a subjectively necessary element of the contract due to the wishes of one or both of the parties.[9]

9.3 Reservation of Form Requirements

TCO art. 2 par. 3 states that the provisions relating to the form of contracts are reserved. Indeed, if the contract requires a specific legal form in order to be valid, even if the parties agree on the necessary elements of the contract, the contract will not be valid unless the parties comply with the form requirement.

Furthermore, even if the contract does not require a specific legal form, the parties may determine that the contract's validity will be subject to a specific form (TCO art. 17). In this case, even if the parties agree on the necessary elements of the contract, unless the parties comply with this specific form requirement, the contract is deemed not to be concluded.[10]

References

Antalya OG (2012) Borçlar hukuku genel hükümler, vol 1. Legal, İstanbul
Aybay A (2011) Borçlar hukuku dersleri genel bölüm. Filiz, İstanbul
Berger B (2012) Allgemeines Schuldrecht. Stämpfli, Bern
Dursun SA (2008) Borçlar hukukunda hâkimin sözleşmeyi tamamlaması. On iki levha, İstanbul

[8]Kocayusufpaşaoğlu (2014), pp. 178–179; Nomer (2015), p. 43.
[9]Oğuzman and Öz (2015), p. 73; Eren (2015), p. 235.
[10]See and compare to Oğuzman and Öz (2015), p. 73.

Engel P (1997) Traité des obligations en droit Suisse. Stämpfli, Bern
Eren F (2015) Borçlar hukuku genel hükümler. Yetkin, Ankara
Feyzioğlu FN (1976) Borçlar hukuku genel hükümler, vol 1. Fakülteler, İstanbul
Gauch P, Schluep WR, Schmid J (2008) Schweizerisches Obligationenrecht, Allgemeiner Teil, vol 1. Schulthess, Zürich
Honsell H, Vogt NP, Wiegand W (eds) (2003) Basler Kommentar zum Schweizerischen Privatrecht, Obligationenrecht 1: Art. 1-529 OR. Helbing Lichtenhahn, Basel
Kocayusufpaşaoğlu N (2014) Borçlar hukuku genel bölüm, vol 1 (Kocayusufpaşaoğlu/Hatemi/Serozan/Arpacı). Filiz, İstanbul
Nomer HN (2015) Borçlar hukuku genel hükümler. Beta, İstanbul
Oğuzman K, Öz T (2015) Borçlar hukuku genel hükümler, vol 1. Vedat, İstanbul
Reisoğlu S (2014) Türk borçlar hukuku genel hükümler. Beta, İstanbul
Schwenzer I (2009) Schweizerisches Obligationenrecht, Allgemeiner Teil. Schulthess, Bern
Tekinay SS, Akman S, Burcuoğlu H, Altop A (1993) Tekinay borçlar hukuku genel hükümler. Filiz, İstanbul
Tercier P (2004) Le droit des obligations. Schulthess, Zurich
Tercier P, Pichonnaz P, Develioğlu HM (2016) Borçlar hukuku genel hükümler. On iki levha, İstanbul
Thévenoz L, Werro F (éd) (2012) Commentaire romand code des obligations 1: art. 1-529 CO. Helbing Lichtenhahn, Bâle
von Tuhr A, Peter H (1979) Allgemeiner Teil des Schweizerischen Obligationenrecht, vol 1. Schulthess, Zürich

Chapter 10
Revision of the Contract (Hardship)

10.1 General[1]

In determining the terms of a contract, the parties consider the existing circumstances that constitute the basis of the contract (*e.g.*, cost, price, regulations related to performance, etc.). However, after the conclusion of the contract, a change in these circumstances may occur and significantly affect the obligations to be performed.[2] For instance, the price of the raw materials to be used in the performance of the obligations may increase substantially, and consequently a fundamental imbalance in the rights, obligations and entitlements of the parties to the contract may arise.

These cases that substantially affect the obligations of the parties to a contract and thereby create a fundamental imbalance are referred to as hardship.[3] Hardship is regulated by TCO art. 138. However, if there is a specific rule related to this issue in the applicable law, then this rule will be applied instead of the general rule (*lex specialis derogat legi generali*). For example, TCO art. 480 states[4] that in a work contract, where the exact price is fixed in advance, the contractor must perform the work for the agreed amount and is not entitled to claim a price increase even though he may incur unforeseen labour costs or other expenses. Nevertheless,

[1]Aybay (2011), p. 136; Berger (2012), pp. 397–403; Engel (1997), pp. 785–794; Eren (2015), pp. 330–331, 480–487; Feyzioğlu (1977), pp. 467–481; Gauch et al. (2008), pp. 292–297; Honsell et al. (2003), art. 18, N. 95–125; Kılıçoğlu (2013), pp. 254–265; Nomer (2015), pp. 323–327; Oğuzman and Öz (2015), pp. 196–201, 559–564; Reisoğlu (2014), pp. 413–418; Schwenzer (2009), pp. 269–272; Serozan (2014), pp. 264–278; Tekinay et al. (1993), pp. 368–369, 1004–1007; Tercier (2004), pp. 177–179; Tercier et al. (2016), pp. 233–234, 305–313; Thévenoz and Werro (2012), art. 18, N. 193–215, and von Tuhr and Escher (1974), pp. 170–172. For further explanations see Gürsoy (1950), Kaplan (1987), Burcuoğlu (1995), Arat (2006), Baysal (2017).

[2]Engel (1997), p. 786; Feyzioğlu (1977), pp. 469–470; Eren (2015), pp. 480–481.

[3]Tekinay et al. (1993), p. 1004.

[4]For further explanations see Erman (1979).

İ. Helvacı, *Turkish Contract Law*, DOI 10.1007/978-3-319-60061-1_10

extraordinary circumstances, which could not be foreseen or which were excluded by the parties, may prevent or seriously hinder the performance of the work. In this case, the contractor may demand that the contract be revised according to the new circumstances. If this revision is not possible or if it cannot be borne by the other party, the contractor may withdraw from the contract (*ex tunc*).[5] However, the principles of good faith may only allow termination (*ex nunc*)[6] but not withdrawal from the contract.

10.2 Principles of Hardship

If there is no specific rule in the law or the contract,[7] the effect of the fundamental imbalance in the rights, obligations and entitlements of the parties to the contract due to supervening circumstances will be considered according to TCO art. 138. This article states that, in cases of hardship, the disadvantaged party may apply to the court and demand variation of the contract having regard to the new circumstances. Where the judge cannot vary the contract to accommodate the new circumstances, the disadvantaged party may withdraw from the contract (*ex tunc*).[8] Nevertheless, if there is a continuing contract between the parties, the disadvantaged party, as a rule, may terminate the contract (*ex nunc*) instead of withdrawing from it.

The disadvantaged party may exercise these rights if all of the following conditions are met: (1) an extraordinary event that is not foreseen or not expected to be foreseen by the parties at the time of formation of the contract occurs; (2) the disadvantaged party is not the cause of the supervening event; (3) this event alters the circumstances as they were at the time of formation of the contract to the detriment of the debtor, to such an extent that the demand for performance would violate the principles of good faith (TCC art. 2); and (4) the debtor has not yet performed his obligation or has performed it by reserving his rights resulting from hardship.

These rules also apply to contracts that include foreign currency debts (TCO art. 138 par. 2). For example, in a sale contract, if the price is in a certain currency and it is devalued by 70–80% as a result of an unexpected economic crisis, this fact will be considered a case of hardship.

[5]Termination of the contract takes effect retroactively (*résolution, Rücktritt*).

[6]Termination of the contract takes effect prospectively (*résiliation, Kündigung*).

[7]The parties may adopt a specific rule in their contract for supervening circumstances that may affect their obligations. In such a case, this rule will be applied in order to revise the contract. Gauch et al. (2008), p. 293; Berger (2012), p. 399; Oğuzman and Öz (2015), p. 196; Eren (2015), p. 483.

[8]In this sense, von Tuhr and Escher (1974), § 74, IV, 6, p. 170.

It should be added that hardship was not regulated directly in the former Turkish Code of Obligations. At the time when the former Code was in effect, cases of hardship were considered according to the principles of good faith (TCC art. 2).

References

Arat A (2006) Sözleşmenin değişen şartlara uyarlanması. Seçkin, Ankara
Aybay A (2011) Borçlar hukuku dersleri genel bölüm. Filiz, İstanbul
Baysal B (2017) Sözleşmenin uyarlanması. On iki levha, İstanbul
Berger B (2012) Allgemeines Schuldrecht. Stämpfli, Bern
Burcuoğlu H (1995) Son mahkeme kararları ve Yargıtay kararları ışığında hukukta beklenmeyen hal ve uyarlama, taşınmaz kirası sözleşmelerinde ve dövize endeksli kira sözleşmelerinde uyarlama uygulaması. Filiz, İstanbul
Engel P (1997) Traité des obligations en droit Suisse. Stämpfli, Bern
Eren F (2015) Borçlar hukuku genel hükümler. Yetkin, Ankara
Erman H (1979) İstisna sözleşmesinde beklenilmeyen haller (bk 365/2). Fakülteler, İstanbul
Feyzioğlu FN (1977) Borçlar hukuku genel hükümler, vol 2. Fakülteler, İstanbul
Gauch P, Schluep WR, Schmid J (2008) Schweizerisches Obligationenrecht, Allgemeiner Teil, vol 1. Schulthess, Zürich
Gürsoy KT (1950) Hususi hukukta clausula rebus sic stantibus - emprevizyon nazariyesi. Ankara üniversitesi, Ankara
Honsell H, Vogt NP, Wiegand W (eds) (2003) Basler Kommentar zum Schweizerischen Privatrecht, Obligationenrecht 1: Art. 1-529 OR. Helbing Lichtenhahn, Basel
Kaplan İ (1987) Hâkimin sözleşmeye müdahalesi (sözleşmenin yorumu - sözleşmenin tamamlanması - sözleşmenin değişen hal ve şartlara uydurulması). Seçkin, Ankara
Kılıçoğlu AM (2013) Borçlar hukuku genel hükümler. Turhan, İstanbul
Nomer HN (2015) Borçlar hukuku genel hükümler. Beta, İstanbul
Oğuzman K, Öz T (2015) Borçlar hukuku genel hükümler, vol 1. Vedat, İstanbul
Reisoğlu S (2014) Türk borçlar hukuku genel hükümler. Beta, İstanbul
Schwenzer I (2009) Schweizerisches Obligationenrecht, Allgemeiner Teil. Schulthess, Bern
Serozan R (2014) Borçlar hukuku genel bölüm, vol 3 (Kocayusufpaşaoğlu/Hatemi/Serozan/Arpacı). Filiz, İstanbul
Tekinay SS, Akman S, Burcuoğlu H, Altop A (1993) Tekinay borçlar hukuku genel hükümler. Filiz, İstanbul
Tercier P (2004) Le droit des obligations. Schulthess, Zurich
Tercier P, Pichonnaz P, Develioğlu HM (2016) Borçlar hukuku genel hükümler. On iki levha, İstanbul
Thévenoz L, Werro F (éd) (2012) Commentaire romand code des obligations 1: art. 1-529 CO. Helbing Lichtenhahn, Bâle
von Tuhr A, Escher A (1974) Allgemeiner Teil des Schweizerischen Obligationenrecht, vol 2. Schulthess, Zürich

Chapter 11
Mistake, Fraud and Duress

11.1 Mistake[1]

11.1.1 General[2]

According to TCO art. 30, a party entering into a contract under a material (fundamental) mistake (error) will not be bound by such a contract. In the Turkish Code of Obligations, there are two types of mistake: the first is a mistake in declaration of will (intention), and the second is a mistake in motive.

11.1.2 Mistake in Declaration of Will (Intention)[3]

When a contracting party is declaring his will, if there is a discrepancy between his will and his declaration and such a discrepancy occurs unintentionally,[4] the

[1]Antalya (2012), pp. 218–250; Aybay (2011), pp. 63–70; Becker (1941), Vorbemerkungen zu art. 23–31, art. 23–31; Berger (2012), pp. 323–344; Engel (1997), pp. 315–368; Eren (2015), pp. 375–416; Feyzioğlu (1976), pp. 120–182; Gauch et al. (2008), pp. 161–199; Honsell et al. (2003), Vorbemerkungen zu art. 23–31, art. 23–31; Kılıçoğlu (2013), pp. 184–218; Kocayusufpaşaoğlu (2014), pp. 342–344, 393–478; Nomer (2015), pp. 81–90; Oser and Schönenberger (1929), Vorbemerkungen zu art. 23–31, art. 23–31; Oğuzman and Öz (2015), pp. 90–127; Özsunay (1983), pp. 105–119; Reisoğlu (2014), pp. 117–132; Schwenzer (2009), pp. 273–303; Tekinay et al. (1993), pp. 425–457; Tercier (2004), pp. 147–157; Tercier et al. (2016), pp. 237–257; Thévenoz and Werro (2012), art. 23–31, and von Tuhr and Peter (1979), pp. 297–342. For further explanations see Özkaya (2014).

[2]For further explanations, see Kocayusufpaşaoğlu (1968), Edis (1973), Özsunar (2005).

[3]*Erreur dans la déclaration, Erklärungsirrtum.*

[4]Where this discrepancy is created intentionally there is either a *reservatio mentalis* (mental reservation) or a declaration which is frivolous. See Sect. 1.6.

İ. Helvacı, *Turkish Contract Law*, DOI 10.1007/978-3-319-60061-1_11

declaring party is said to be mistaken. If the recipient knows or should have known that the declaring party was mistaken, in other words his real intention, then there are two possibilities with regard to the formation of the contract: (1) if the declaration of will of the recipient is consistent with the real intention of the mistaken party, then the contract is concluded according to the mistaken party's real intention, that it to say, according to the parties' mutual and consistent declarations of will; (2) if the declaration of will of the recipient is not consistent with the real intention of the mistaken party, then the contract cannot be concluded. For example, although the buyer wishes to purchase a black Opel Astra, he declares mistakenly that he wants to buy a white Opel Astra. If the seller knows or should have known that the real intention of the buyer was the purchase of a black Opel Astra and the seller's declaration of will is consistent with the buyer's real intention, then the contract is deemed to be concluded for the black Opel Astra. Even if the seller knows or should have known that the buyer wishes to purchase a black Opel Astra, if the seller's declaration of will relates to the sale of a white Opel Astra, then the contract cannot be concluded as the parties' declarations of will are not consistent.

If the recipient, according to the principles of good faith acting as a reasonable person and taking into consideration all the circumstances, does not know and should not have known the real intention of the mistaken party, then the contract is deemed to be concluded in accordance with his (objective) justifiable understanding. However, in such a case, the mistaken party may avoid the contract according to the rules relating to a material mistake (TCO art. 39).

Where the mistake is not material (fundamental), it does not affect the validity of the contract. In order to say that the mistaken party is not bound by the contract, the mistake must be material (fundamental). According to TCO art. 31, the mistake is material, in particular, in the following cases: (1) the mistaken party declares his will for a contract other than the contract that he intended (*error in negotio*); (2) the mistaken party declares his will for a subject matter other than the subject matter that he intended (*error in corpore*); (3) the mistaken party addresses his declaration of will to someone other than to the person intended (*error in persona*); (4) although the mistaken party intends to enter into a contract relating to a person who has specific qualifications, he declares his will for another person; and (5) the mistaken party declares his will for a contractual performance significantly greater than he actually intends to undertake or for a consideration significantly less than he actually intends (*error in quantitate*).

With regard to these cases, consider the following examples: (1) the owner of immovable property, who wants to conclude a lease agreement, signs a partnership contract (*i.e.*, an error in the nature of the contract); (2) although a person wants to buy a laptop on the Internet, he declares his intention to purchase a tablet computer (*i.e.*, an error in object); (3) a manager wants to enter into an employment contract with candidate X but sends the proposal to candidate Y and the latter accepts it (*i.e.*, an error in person); (4) a nurse intends to make a patient care contract with a hospital manager for an old but healthy woman X but enters into a contract for an old and paralysed woman Y; and (5) a retailer intends to buy 100 pairs of jeans from a wholesaler but offers to buy 500 pairs of jeans in his proposal (*i.e.*, an error in quantity).

Errors in calculations do not affect the contract's validity; they will be the subject of correction (TCO art. 31 par. 2).

11.1.3 Mistake in Communication

Where the declaration of will (intention)[5] with regard to the formation of the contract is wrongly conveyed by an intermediary (*e.g.*, a messenger or an interpreter) or by other means of communication, the provisions relating to mistake will apply (TCO art. 33). For instance, a Turkish nut wholesaler actually wants to export 5 tons of nuts to an Italian merchant in consideration of €14,000, but his secretary wrongly translates this intention as an importation offer and the Italian party accepts it. In this case, the validity of the importation contract is affected by the secretary's mistake.

11.1.4 Mistake in Motive[6]

If, when entering into a contract, there is a discrepancy between a party's knowledge and the actual circumstances relevant to the contract, such a discrepancy is deemed to be a mistake in motive.[7] A mistake in motive, as a rule, is not considered to be a material mistake because the one who is wrong must bear the consequences.[8]

However, in certain cases, a mistake in motive is deemed to be material. For a mistake in motive to be material and to affect the validity of the contract, all of the following conditions must be realised[9]: (1) a party must be mistaken about one or more facts that form the basis of the contract; (2) the mistake must be related to an essential component of the contract for the mistaken party (*conditio sine qua non)*—*i.e.*, if the mistaken party had known of the mistake, he would not have concluded the contract or would not have entered into it under the existing conditions; (3) it must be the case that the mistaken party's motive is known or could be

---

[5]*Déclaration de volonté, Willenserklärung.*

[6]*Erreur sur la base nécessaire du contrat, Grundlagenirrtum.*

[7]von Tuhr and Peter (1979), § 36, II, p. 300; Tercier (2004), p. 152; Thévenoz and Werro (2012), art. 23–24, N. 7; Eren (2015), p. 379; Oğuzman and Öz (2015), p. 99.

[8]von Tuhr and Peter (1979), § 36, II, p. 300; Becker (1941), art. 24, N. 31, art. 23, N. 5; Tercier (2004), p. 152; Berger (2012), p. 324; Reisoğlu (2014), p. 120; Eren (2015), p. 381.

[9]von Tuhr and Peter (1979), § 37, V, pp. 308–309; Tercier (2004), pp. 152–153; Honsell et al. (2003), art. 24, N. 20–23; Berger (2012), pp. 327–329; Oğuzman and Öz (2015), pp. 99–105.

known by the other party[10]; and (4) according to the principles of good faith in business relations, the claim that the mistake affects the validity of the contract must be justifiable.

In light of the above-mentioned conditions, the two following examples are worth considering: (1) a person buys a painting for €1,000,000, which he thinks was painted by Picasso but was not a Picasso; (2) a person thinks that the land he has bought is suitable for construction of a 20-storey building when, in fact, the maximum permissible height for the building is 10 storeys. If the above-mentioned conditions are met, the mistakes in motive will be deemed material in these examples.

11.1.5 Consequences of Material Mistake

In accordance with TCO art. 39 par. 1, in the case of a material mistake, the mistaken party may rescind (avoid) the contract. Where the mistaken party intends to rely on this right of rescission, this right needs to be exercised within 1 year. This one-year period commences from the date the error was discovered by the mistaken party.

The mistaken party must notify the rescission of the contract or demand the restitution of the performance made by him within a one-year period from the discovery of the mistake. If he fails to do so, the contract is deemed to be ratified (TCO art. 39 par. 1).

Under TCO art. 34 par. 1, the mistaken party may not rescind the contract in a manner that is contrary to the principles of good faith (TCC art. 2). In particular, where the other party accepts the formation of the contract according to the real intention of the mistaken party, the latter is not entitled to rescind the contract (TCO art. 34 par. 2). In this case, the mistaken party's rescission will be contrary to the principles of good faith. For instance, S intends to sell a mobile phone for TL 700 to B. S sets its price by mistake at TL 500 in his declaration of will, and B accepts it. Afterwards, S discovers this mistake and wants to rescind the contract. However, B declares that he is ready to pay TL 700 for the mobile phone. In this case, if S still wishes to rescind the contract relying on the mistake, such an attempt will be contrary to the principles of good faith (TCC art. 2), and thus, it must be rejected.[11]

The fact that the mistaken party has been negligent does not affect his right of rescission.[12] Even though the mistaken party has been negligent, he may rescind the contract, but in this case he must compensate the injured party for any damage resulting from the rescission (TCO art. 35 par. 1 sent. 1). Where the injured party knew or should have known of this mistake, he is not entitled to demand any

---

[10] Kocayusufpaşaoğlu (1968), p. 161; Oğuzman and Öz (2015), p. 104.

[11] Oğuzman and Öz (2015), p. 107.

[12] Engel (1997), p. 339.

compensation (TCO art. 35 par. 1 sent. 2). It should be noted that this rule cannot be applied to mistakes in declaration of will because the 'trust theory' (*théorie de la confiance, Vertrauenstheorie*) precludes its application. This is because if the other party knew or should have known of the mistake in the declaration, then the contract would be concluded according to the real intent of the mistaken party, provided that the other party's intention is consistent with it.[13]

Where, due to rescission the negligent mistaken party is required to compensate the damage of the injured party, this compensation will include the negative damage[14] of the injured party—*e.g.*, the expenses relating to the conclusion of the contract or any damage for loss of an opportunity to make another contract with better conditions.[15] For instance, A and B enter into a contract that is notarised and B pays the notary expenses, but A makes a mistake that is attributable to his own negligence and rescinds the contract. In this case, B is entitled to claim compensation for the notary expenses (negative damage) that he would not have incurred if this contract had not been entered into with A.

Where it is equitable, the judge may award further compensation to the injured party (TCO art. 35 par. 2). For instance, in the above example, if B has made a resale contract with C, which will result in a profit of €2000, and misses this opportunity because of the rescission of the contract, then B may demand compensation for this loss of profit (positive damage) provided that this demand is equitable. It should be kept in mind that the damages to be paid by the negligent mistaken party may not exceed the interest that the injured party might obtain in the event of the proper performance of the obligation (TCO art. 35 par. 2).

11.2 Fraud[16]

11.2.1 Fraud by a Contracting Party

Where a party has been induced to enter into a contract by the wilful fraud of the other party, he is not bound by the contract even though his mistake is not material (TCO art. 36 par. 1). According to this provision, the conditions relating to fraud by the contracting party are as follows[17]: (1) a party must make a mistake in motive,[18] (2) this mistake must result from the other party's conduct, (3) the other party's

---

[13]Oğuzman and Öz (2015), p. 109.

[14]For further explanations see Ergüne (2008).

[15]In this sense Oğuzman and Öz (2015) p. 106.

[16]*Dol, Absichtliche Täuschung*. For further explanations, see Yıldırım (2002), Kurşat (2003).

[17]Oğuzman and Öz (2015), pp. 110–112.

[18]Tercier (2004), p. 155; Oğuzman and Öz (2015), p. 109; von Tuhr and Peter (1979), § 38, II, 1, p. 320.

fraudulent conduct must be wilful and (4) this fraudulent conduct must lead to the formation of the contract.[19]

The fraudulent conduct of the other party may be active or passive. The fraudulent party may misrepresent or suppress the truth with false representations,[20] for instance, where a jeweller sells a worthless necklace as if it were gold. Moreover, the fraudulent conduct of the other party may be created by mere silence or by inaction (passive conduct). Where a party does not represent a fact to the other party, which requires representation according to the principles of good faith, the fraud arises from his passive conduct.[21] That is to say, if a party is aware of the other party's mistake and does not warn him, contrary to the principles of good faith, then this will constitute a case of passive fraud.[22] For instance, in a reputable art gallery, a buyer believes that a painting is by Picasso and offers a substantial amount of money for it. However, in fact, the painting is not by Picasso and is worthless. If the art gallery's owner is aware of this mistake and does not warn the buyer, this omission constitutes a passive fraud.

11.2.2 Fraud by a Third Party

Fraud may also result from a third party. Where a party has been induced to enter into a contract by the wilful fraud of a third party, he is not bound by the contract if the other contracting party knew or should have known of the fraud at the time of the formation of the contract. According to TCO art. 36 par. 2, the conditions relating to fraud by a third party are as follows[23]: (1) a party must make a mistake in motive, (2) this mistake must be a result of the third party's conduct, (3) the third party's fraudulent conduct must be wilful, (4) this fraudulent conduct must lead to the formation of the contract, and (5) the party, who is not the victim of the fraud, knew or should have known of the fraud when entering into the contract.

11.2.3 Consequences of Fraud

In accordance with TCO art. 39 par. 1, the deceived party may rescind (avoid) the contract. Where the deceived party intends to use the right of rescission, this right

---

[19]von Tuhr and Peter (1979), § 38, II, 5, p. 322; Engel (1997), p. 354; Thévenoz and Werro (2012), art. 28, N. 1.

[20]Gauch et al. (2008), p. 181; Engel (1997), p. 351; Tekinay et al. (1993), p. 446; Kurşat (2003), p. 50.

[21]von Tuhr and Peter (1979), § 38, I, 4, p. 321; Thévenoz and Werro (2012), art. 28, N. 9; Engel (1997), p. 352; Gauch et al. (2008), p. 182; Tekinay et al. (1993), p. 446; Kurşat (2003), p. 51.

[22]Oğuzman and Öz (2015), p. 110.

[23]von Tuhr and Peter (1979), § 38, II, 6, p. 323; Honsell et al. (2003), art. 28, N. 15–17; Thévenoz and Werro (2012), art. 28, N. 31–33; Oğuzman and Öz (2015), p. 112; Eren (2015), p. 400.

must be exercised within one year. This one-year period commences from the date the deceived party became aware of the fraud.

Where the deceived party does not notify the rescission of the contract or demand the restitution of performance made by him within one year from the discovery of the fraud, the contract is deemed to be ratified (TCO art. 39 par. 1).

Even though the deceived party ratifies the contract, either explicitly or implicitly, his right to compensation for damage remains unaffected. That is to say, the deceived party, despite ratification of the contract, is entitled to demand compensation for his damage (TCO art. 39 par. 2). The basis of the other party's liability is *culpa in contrahendo* (fault in contracting), whereas the third party's liability is subject to the rules of tort (TCO art. 49 *ff*).[24]

11.3 Duress[25]

11.3.1 General[26]

According to TCO art. 37 par. 1, a party that was induced to enter into a contract under duress[27] by the other contracting party or a third party is not bound by the contract.

In order to determine whether duress exists, it must be shown that[28] (1) a party must be faced with a threat; the specific form of the threat is unimportant—*e.g.*, it may or may not be verbal. The threat may also result from the behaviour of the other party or of a third party. In the case of threat by a third party, whether the advantaged party knows of the duress or not does not affect the invalidity of the contract.[29] (2) The threatened party must believe that he will suffer harm if he does not conclude the contract. This threat must be serious and imminent. If a threat is related to an insignificant or prospective risk, it does not affect the validity of the contract. (3) The threat must be directed to the threatened party himself or to persons close to him. The threat may concern personal rights (life, body, honour, etc.) or assets (house, car, etc.). (4) This threat must be unlawful, such as a threat of murder or kidnapping. Also, the threat of enforcement of a legal right or of a legal power may constitute an unlawful threat, provided that the other party extorts

[24]Eren (2015), p. 254; Ergüne (2008), pp. 172–173; Oğuzman and Öz (2015), p. 113; Kurşat (2003), p. 127 *ff*.

[25]*Crainte fondée, Furchterregung*.

[26]For further explanations see Karakocalı (2016).

[27]Where a person is forced to enter into a contract by direct physical violence there is no declaration of will (intention) made at all, and, thus, the contract cannot be formed.

[28]von Tuhr and Peter (1979), § 38, III, pp. 325–329; Gauch et al. (2008), pp. 185–187; Engel (1997), pp. 364–368; Oğuzman and Öz (2015), pp. 114–116.

[29]Oğuzman and Öz (2015), p. 114.

excessive advantages from the threatened party's distress (TCO art. 38 par. 2). (5) This threat must lead to the formation of the contract. That is to say, if there had not been an unlawful threat, the innocent party would have concluded this contract with other clauses or would not have concluded it at all.

It would be helpful to mention examples in which duress is present. For instance, B intends to buy S's house but S does not want to sell it. B tells S that if S does not accept the offer, then he will kill him or will kidnap his child or will burn the house down. Another example: B intends to buy S's car. B knows that S has committed a crime. The actual value of the car is €100,000, but B wants to pay only €5000 for it and threatens S with submitting a deposition to the public prosecutor for the crime he has committed.

11.3.2 Consequences of Duress

In accordance with TCO art. 39 par. 1, the threatened party may rescind (avoid) the contract. Where the threatened party intends to use the right of rescission, this right must be exercised within one year. This one-year period runs from the time that the effect of the duress ended.

Where the threatened party does not notify the rescission of the contract or demand the restitution of performance made by him within one year from the time that the duress ended, the contract will also be binding on him (TCO art. 39 par. 1).

The threatened party may demand compensation for damage arising from the threat.[30] The source or cause of duress is not important. Thus, a contracting party issuing threats, or a third party doing so, is liable for the damage resulting from the threats. The basis of the other party's liability is *culpa in contrahendo* (fault in contracting), whereas the third party's liability is subject to the rules of tort (TCO art. 49 *ff*).[31]

It should be noted that in the case of a threat by a third party, the threatened party may rescind the contract even if the other party did not know, or could not have known, of the existence of the duress. In this case, where equity requires, the rescinding party must compensate the damage of the other party (TCO art. 37 par. 2). However, the rescinding party who compensates the damage of the other party may have recourse to the third party for the compensation paid by him.[32]

As mentioned above, where the threatened party does not notify the rescission of the contract or demand the restitution of the performance made by him within a one-year period from the time that the duress ended, the contract is deemed to be ratified (TCO art. 39 par. 1). Even though the threatened party ratifies the contract

[30] Thévenoz and Werro (2012), art. 31, N. 41–49; Tercier (2004), p. 157; Oğuzman and Öz (2015), p. 116.

[31] Eren (2015), p. 254; Ergüne (2008), pp. 175–176; Oğuzman and Öz (2015), p. 116.

[32] Oğuzman and Öz (2015), p. 117.

either explicitly or implicitly, his claim for compensation for damage is unaffected. That is to say, the threatened party, despite the ratification of the contract, remains entitled to demand compensation for the damage (TCO art. 39 par. 2).

References

Antalya OG (2012) Borçlar hukuku genel hükümler, vol 1. Legal, İstanbul
Aybay A (2011) Borçlar hukuku dersleri genel bölüm. Filiz, İstanbul
Becker H (1941) Kommentar zum Schweizerischen Zivilgesetzbuch, Volume VI, Obligationenrecht, 1. Abteilung: Allgemeine Bestimmungen, Art. 1-183. Stämpfli, Bern
Berger B (2012) Allgemeines Schuldrecht. Stämpfli, Bern
Edis S (1973) Türk /İsviçre borçlar hukuku sistemine göre akdin lüzumlu vasıflarında hata. Ankara üniversitesi hukuk fakültesi, Ankara
Engel P (1997) Traité des obligations en droit Suisse. Stämpfli, Bern
Eren F (2015) Borçlar hukuku genel hükümler. Yetkin, Ankara
Ergüne S (2008) Olumsuz zarar. Beta, İstanbul
Feyzioğlu FN (1976) Borçlar hukuku genel hükümler, vol 1. Fakülteler, İstanbul
Gauch P, Schluep WR, Schmid J (2008) Schweizerisches Obligationenrecht, Allgemeiner Teil, vol 1. Schulthess, Zürich
Honsell H, Vogt NP, Wiegand W (eds) (2003) Basler Kommentar zum Schweizerischen Privatrecht, Obligationenrecht 1: Art. 1-529 OR. Helbing Lichtenhahn, Basel
Karakocalı A (2016) Roma Hukukunda ve Türk Hukukunda Korkutma (Metus). Seçkin, Ankara
Kılıçoğlu AM (2013) Borçlar hukuku genel hükümler. Turhan, İstanbul
Kocayusufpaşaoğlu N (1968) Güven nazariyesi karşısında borç sözleşmelerinde hata kavramı. İstanbul üniversitesi hukuk fakültesi, İstanbul
Kocayusufpaşaoğlu N (2014) Borçlar hukuku genel bölüm, vol. 1 (Kocayusufpaşaoğlu/Hatemi/Serozan/Arpacı). Filiz, İstanbul
Kurşat Z (2003) Borçlar hukuku alanında hile kavramı. Kazancı, İstanbul
Nomer HN (2015) Borçlar hukuku genel hükümler. Beta, İstanbul
Oğuzman K, Öz T (2015) Borçlar hukuku genel hükümler, vol 1. Vedat, İstanbul
Oser H, Schönenberger W (1929) Kommentar zum Schweizerischen Zivilgesetzbuch, Volume V: Das Obligationenrecht, Erster Halbband: Art. 1-183. Schulthess, Zürich
Özkaya E (2014) Yanılma, Aldatma, Korkutma Davaları (Hata-Hile-İkrah). Seçkin, Ankara
Özsunar E (2005) Roma ve Türk hukukunda hata. Turhan, Ankara
Özsunay E (1983) Borçlar hukuku, vol I. Filiz, İstanbul
Reisoğlu S (2014) Türk borçlar hukuku genel hükümler. Beta, İstanbul
Schwenzer I (2009) Schweizerisches Obligationenrecht, Allgemeiner Teil. Schulthess, Bern
Tekinay SS, Akman S, Burcuoğlu H, Altop A (1993) Tekinay borçlar hukuku genel hükümler. Filiz, İstanbul
Tercier P (2004) Le droit des obligations. Schulthess, Zurich
Tercier P, Pichonnaz P, Develioğlu HM (2016) Borçlar hukuku genel hükümler. On iki levha, İstanbul
Thévenoz L, Werro F (éd) (2012) Commentaire romand code des obligations 1: art. 1-529 co. Helbing Lichtenhahn, Bâle
von Tuhr A, Peter H (1979) Allgemeiner Teil des Schweizerischen Obligationenrecht, vol 1. Schulthess, Zürich
Yıldırım MF (2002) Borçlar hukukuna göre sözleşmenin kuruluşunda hile. Nobel, Ankara

Chapter 12
Unfair Exploitation (Lesion)

12.1 Requirements[1]

When the parties to a contract are reciprocally obliged so that the obligation of one party is correlative to the obligation of the other, this contract is called a bilateral contract. In other words, a bilateral (synallagmatic) contract is a contract formed by the exchange of mutual or reciprocal promises between the parties.[2] For example, in a sale contract, the seller has an obligation to transfer ownership of the goods specified in the contract, and the buyer is obliged to pay the agreed price. Similarly, in lease, employment or work contracts, each party undertakes reciprocal obligations.

Usually, there is equivalence between the parties' reciprocal obligations. However, in certain cases, the parties' obligations are not proportionate. This disproportion may have different causes. For example, a mother sells her car to her daughter for a price that is significantly lower than its market value. The mother's intention is to make a partial gift to her daughter, and the latter accepts it. In this case, the disadvantaged party is not exploited by the advantaged one. On the contrary, the mother knows that there is a clear disparity between the market value and the agreed price, but she intends to donate this amount to the advantaged party, and the latter has no intention to exploit the disadvantaged one. Such a contract is valid provided that there are no other reasons that affect its validity.

[1]Antalya (2012), pp. 251–260; Aybay (2011), pp. 70–71; Becker (1941), art. 21; Berger (2012); pp. 357–359; Engel (1997), pp. 298–306; Eren (2015), pp. 417–423; Feyzioğlu (1976), pp. 248–266; Gauch et al. (2008), pp. 153–161; Honsell et al. (2003), art. 21; Kılıçoğlu (2013), pp. 218–226; Koçayusufpaşaoğlu (2014), pp. 478–500; Nomer (2015), pp. 96–99; Oser and Schönenberger (1929), art. 21; Oğuzman and Öz (2015), pp. 134–138; Reisoğlu (2014), pp. 141–144; Schwenzer (2009), pp. 260–262; Tekinay et al. (1993), pp. 458–466; Tercier (2004), pp. 157–159; Tercier et al. (2016), pp. 257–262; Thévenoz and Werro (2012), art. 21, and von Tuhr and Peter (1979), pp. 342–347.

[2]Engel (1997), p. 161; Tercier (2004), p. 59; Berger (2012), p. 98.

İ. Helvacı, *Turkish Contract Law*, DOI 10.1007/978-3-319-60061-1_12

However, if the evident disparity arises from the exploitation of the distress, inexperience or improvidence (incautiousness) of the disadvantaged party, TCO art. 28 par. 1 applies.

According to TCO art. 28 par. 1, where there is an evident disproportion between the obligations of the parties in a bilateral contract[3] and such disproportionality is obtained by exploiting the disadvantaged party's distress, inexperience or improvidence,[4] an unfair exploitation (lesion)[5] is deemed to exist.[6] For there to be an unfair exploitation, the advantaged party must know and exploit the circumstances of the disadvantaged party. It should be noted that it is not important who the offeror is.[7] It may be the disadvantaged or the advantaged party.

It will be useful to explore the concepts of distress, inexperience and improvidence[8]: (1) the distress of the disadvantaged party may result from economic factors, for instance, a person sells his very valuable property for significantly less than its actual worth due to financial difficulties. Furthermore, the distress of the disadvantaged party may have psychological origins, for example, a mother agrees to the payment of a large sum of money because her child urgently needs surgery. (2) The inexperience of the disadvantaged party means that he is not knowledgeable enough to conclude the contract. For instance, a grandfather dies and leaves a very valuable stamp collection to his grandson, who has no experience of such things. The grandson sells it for considerably less than its actual value without consulting experts. (3) Improvidence means that one makes a decision without paying the necessary attention to the effects of the concluded contract, for example, where an elderly person with significantly weakened mental abilities enters into a contract that seriously affects his assets and liabilities.

12.2 Consequences

In the case of unfair exploitation, according to the circumstances, the disadvantaged party has two rights: (1) to rescind (avoid) the contract and to demand the restitution of the performed obligation[9] or (2) to elect to remain bound by the contract and to

[3]von Tuhr and Peter (1979), § 40, I, 1, pp. 343–344; Tercier (2004), p. 158; Engel (1997), p. 300; Becker (1941), art. 21, N. 1–4; Berger (2012), p. 358; Eren (2015), p. 418; Reisoğlu (2014), p. 141; Oğuzman and Öz (2015), pp. 134–135.

[4]von Tuhr and Peter (1979), § 40, I, 2, pp. 344–345; Becker (1941), art. 21, N. 5–9; Berger (2012), p. 358; Tercier (2004), p. 158; Engel (1997), p. 303; Eren (2015), p. 421; Reisoğlu (2014), p. 142; Oğuzman and Öz (2015), pp. 135–136.

[5]*Laesio enormis, lésion, Übervorteilung.*

[6]For further explanations see Elbir (1957), Aslan (2006).

[7]Oğuzman and Öz (2015), p. 136.

[8]For further explanations see Tekinay et al. (1993), p. 463; Eren (2015), p. 421.

[9]Eren (2015), p. 422; Nomer (2015), p. 97; Engel (1997), p. 305; Thévenoz and Werro (2012), art. 21, N. 15–17; von Tuhr and Peter (1979), § 40, II, p. 346; Becker (1941), art. 21, N. 10.

demand the removal of the disproportionality between performance and consideration (TCO art. 28 par. 1).[10] For instance, in the above-mentioned example of the grandson selling his grandfather's valuable stamp collection, the grandson may rescind the sale contract and demand the return of the collection. However, if the buyer has already sold the collection to a third party, it will not be possible to demand its return. In that case, the grandson will be entitled to resolve the disparity by claiming the difference between the actual price and the agreed price in the contract.

It should be noted that the disadvantaged party must exercise either of the two aforementioned rights depending on the circumstances: (1) where the disproportionality arises from his improvidence or inexperience, the disadvantaged party must notify the rescission or the removal of this disproportionality within 1 year of becoming aware of the relevant situation, but in any case, within 5 years of the formation of the contract, or (2) where the disproportionality arises from his distress, the disadvantaged party may exercise these rights within 1 year of the relief of the distress, but in any case, within 5 years of the formation of the contract (TCO art. 28 par. 2).

References

Antalya OG (2012) Borçlar hukuku genel hükümler, vol 1. Legal, İstanbul
Aslan ÇM (2006) Gabinin unsurları ve hukuki sonuçları (bk. md. 21). Yetkin, Ankara
Aybay A (2011) Borçlar hukuku dersleri genel bölüm. Filiz, İstanbul
Becker H (1941) Kommentar zum Schweizerischen Zivilgesetzbuch, vol VI, Obligationenrecht, 1. Abteilung: Allgemeine Bestimmungen, Art. 1-183. Stämpfli, Bern
Berger B (2012) Allgemeines Schuldrecht. Stämpfli, Bern
Elbir HK (1957) Türk pozitif hukukunda gabin. İstanbul
Engel P (1997) Traité des obligations en droit Suisse. Stämpfli, Bern
Eren F (2015) Borçlar hukuku genel hükümler. Yetkin, Ankara
Feyzioğlu FN (1976) Borçlar hukuku genel hükümler, vol 1. Fakülteler, İstanbul
Gauch P, Schluep WR, Schmid J (2008) Schweizerisches Obligationenrecht, Allgemeiner Teil, vol 1. Schulthess, Zürich
Honsell H, Vogt NP, Wiegand W (eds) (2003) Basler Kommentar zum Schweizerischen Privatrecht, Obligationenrecht 1: Art. 1-529 OR. Helbing Lichtenhahn, Basel
Kılıçoğlu AM (2013) Borçlar hukuku genel hükümler. Turhan, İstanbul
Kocayusufpaşaoğlu N (2014) Borçlar hukuku genel bölüm, vol 1 (Kocayusufpaşaoğlu/Hatemi/Serozan/Arpacı). Filiz, İstanbul
Nomer HN (2015) Borçlar hukuku genel hükümler. Beta, İstanbul
Oğuzman K, Öz T (2015) Borçlar hukuku genel hükümler, vol 1. Vedat, İstanbul
Oser H, Schönenberger W (1929) Kommentar zum Schweizerischen Zivilgesetzbuch, vol V: Das Obligationenrecht, Erster Halbband: Art. 1-183. Schulthess, Zürich
Reisoğlu S (2014) Türk borçlar hukuku genel hükümler. Beta, İstanbul
Schwenzer I (2009) Schweizerisches Obligationenrecht, Allgemeiner Teil. Schulthess, Bern

[10] Eren (2015), p. 422; Nomer (2015), p. 97; Engel (1997), p. 305; Thévenoz and Werro (2012), art. 21, N. 18–22.

Tekinay SS, Akman S, Burcuoğlu H, Altop A (1993) Tekinay borçlar hukuku genel hükümler. Filiz, İstanbul
Tercier P (2004) Le droit des obligations. Schulthess, Zurich
Tercier P, Pichonnaz P, Develioğlu HM (2016) Borçlar hukuku genel hükümler. On iki levha, İstanbul
Thévenoz L, Werro F (éd) (2012) Commentaire romand code des obligations 1: art. 1-529 CO. Helbing Lichtenhahn, Bâle
von Tuhr A, Peter H (1979) Allgemeiner Teil des Schweizerischen Obligationenrecht, vol 1. Schulthess, Zürich

Chapter 13
Agency

13.1 General[1]

A person (the agent) may enter into a legal transaction, especially a contract, in the name of and on behalf of another person (the principal). In the case of a contract, there may be three persons: an agent, a principal and the other party to the contract. If the agent has the authority and acts in the name of and on behalf of the principal, the contract binds the principal. The agent has neither rights nor obligations with regard to the concluded contract between the parties. Such a case is referred to as direct agency.[2] It should be noted that there are certain legal transactions that cannot be entered into by an agent such as an engagement, a marriage and a testamentary disposition.

The basis of the authority to represent the principal may be the law itself or the will of the principal.[3] For instance, parents, within the limits of their parental power, may act as agents for their children in transactions with third parties (TCC art. 342 par. 1). In this case, the parents' authority to represent arises from the law itself. This kind of representation (legal representation) is regulated under the Turkish Civil Code and is

[1]Antalya (2012), pp. 361–406; Aybay (2011), pp. 71–79; Becker (1941), Vorbemerkung zu art. 32–40 (Stellvertretung), art. 32–40; Berger (2012), pp. 273–293; Engel (1997), pp. 372–416; Eren (2015), pp. 424–459; Feyzioğlu (1976), pp. 376–439; Gauch et al. (2008), pp. 299–328; Honsell et al. (2003), art. 32–40; Kılıçoğlu (2013), pp. 226–250; Kocayusufpaşaoğlu (2014), pp. 620–772; Nomer (2015), pp. 121–135; Oser and Schönenberger (1929), Vorbemerkungen zu art. 32–40, art. 32–40; Oğuzman and Öz (2015), pp. 210–246; Özsunay (1983), pp. 132–145; Reisoğlu (2014), pp. 148–161; Schwenzer (2009), pp. 303–324; Tekinay et al. (1993), pp. 166–207; Tercier (2004), pp. 82–95; Tercier et al. (2016), pp. 121–145; Thévenoz and Werro (2012), art. 32–40, and von Tuhr and Peter (1979), pp. 347–405. For further explanations see Esener (1961), Özdemir (1994), Akyol (2009).

[2]von Tuhr and Peter (1979), § 41, I, p. 348; Thévenoz and Werro (2012), art. 32, N. 4; Engel (1997), p. 374; Eren (2015), p. 427; Oğuzman and Öz (2015), p. 212.

[3]von Tuhr and Peter (1979), § 41, I, 1, p. 349; Engel (1997), pp. 373–374; Berger (2012), p. 273; Oğuzman and Öz (2015), p. 217; Nomer (2015), p. 125.

İ. Helvacı, *Turkish Contract Law*, DOI 10.1007/978-3-319-60061-1_13

dealt with as a matter of family law. As mentioned above, the basis of the authority to represent may arise from the principal's will, and such agency is regulated under the Turkish Code of Obligations and will be analysed in this section.

13.2 Direct Agency[4]

According to the Turkish Code of Obligations, the existence of direct agency[5] requires two conditions: (1) the agent must be authorised to represent the principal; (2) the agent must act in the name of and on behalf of the principal.

13.2.1 Authority to Represent

13.2.1.1 Legal Nature

An agent may represent the principal only if he has authority to do so. The granting of the authority to represent is a unilateral legal transaction by the principal.[6] The principal's declaration of will (intention)[7] relating to the authority to represent may be express or implied. It should be directed to the agent and will come into force when it reaches the agent.[8]

An agent may act in accordance with the authority or not. That is to say, the granting of the authority to represent does not bind the agent personally. Accordingly, the principal may grant authority to represent to a person having mental capacity notwithstanding that he is a minor or a person placed under a guardianship order (TCC art. 16 par. 1 sent. 1).

13.2.1.2 Comparison with Agency Contract

At this point, it is useful to compare agency contract (mandate) and agency. Granting someone the authority to represent another is a unilateral transaction, whereas an agency contract is a bilateral transaction whereby the agent undertakes to carry out business transactions or services entrusted to him by the principal.[9]

---

[4]*Représentation directe, direkte Stellvertretung.*

[5]For further explanations see İnceoğlu (2009).

[6]Oser and Schönenberger (1929), art. 32, N. 19; Engel (1997), p. 381; Berger (2012), p. 278; Reisoğlu (2014), p. 151; Oğuzman and Öz (2015), p. 220.

[7]*Déclaration de volonté, Willenserklärung.*

[8]Engel (1997), p. 381.

[9]Eren (2015), p. 440; Oğuzman and Öz (2015), pp. 218–219.

As mentioned above, the principal may grant the authority to represent to a minor or to a person placed under a guardianship order who has mental capacity without the consent of their legal representatives. However, these persons are not entitled to enter into an agency contract as an agent without the consent of their legal representatives (TCC art. 16 par. 1 sent. 1).

Although the concepts of agency and agency contract are different, they may overlap in certain cases. Where an agency contract is concerned, if the agent's obligations include carrying out a legal transaction, then it also includes the authority to represent (TCO art. 504 par. 2).

13.2.1.3 Independence of the Authority to Represent

The authority to represent may be incorporated into other types of contract such as employment, construction or partnership contracts. Granting the authority to represent is independent of the above-mentioned contracts, that is to say, the invalidity of the contract does not affect the validity of the authority to represent.[10] For example, where the authority to represent is incorporated into a construction contract, the customer may terminate the contract but the authority to represent may remain valid. It is also possible that the customer may revoke the authority to represent but the contract may remain binding.

Moreover, as mentioned above,[11] a minor who has mental capacity may not be an agent in an agency contract without the consent of his legal representatives. If the legal representatives do not consent, then the agency contract will be invalid. However, if the principal grants the authority to represent through this agency contract, then the latter's invalidity does not affect the validity of the authority to represent.

13.2.1.4 Scope of the Authority to Represent

Where the authority to represent arises from public law provisions, its scope will be determined according to these rules. If the basis of the authority to represent is a legal transaction, its scope will be determined having regard to the content of the legal transaction (TCO art. 41 par. 1). Furthermore, the principal may inform a third party of the existence of an authority to represent. In such a case, its scope will be determined according to the terms of the communication (TCO art. 41 par. 2).

The authority to represent may be general or specific.[12] If the authority is general, the agent may conclude legal transactions of any kind within the limits

---

[10] Oser and Schönenberger (1929), art. 32, N. 26, art. 34, N. 2; von Tuhr and Peter (1979), § 42, II, p. 359; Engel (1997), p. 382; Berger (2012), p. 280; Tekinay et al. (1993), p. 176; Oğuzman and Öz (2015), p. 219.

[11] Section 13.2.1.1.

[12] von Tuhr and Peter (1979), § 42, IV, 3, p. 361; Engel (1997), p. 389; Gauch et al. (2008), p. 310; Eren (2015), pp. 441–442; Feyzioğlu (1976), p. 411.

of the authority. However, there are certain legal transactions that require a specific authority to represent, such as concluding a settlement agreement, consenting to arbitration, signing negotiable instruments (bills of exchange, promissory notes and cheques), becoming a surety, making a gift, and alienating or encumbering real estate (TCO art. 504 par. 3).

13.2.1.5 Form Requirement

Generally, the granting of the authority to represent does not require a specific form. It may be express or implied.[13] However, in certain cases, the granting of the authority to represent requires a specific form in order to be valid.[14] According to TCO art. 583 par. 1, a surety contract requires a specific form. If a surety intends to make this contract by means of an agent, he must grant the necessary specific authority in compliance with the form requirements of a surety contract (TCO art. 583 par. 2). Otherwise, the authority to represent will be void.

In addition, according to RLR art. 18 par. 4, an authority to represent, which allows the making of a transaction before a land registry officer, requires a specific form. It must be drafted before a notary (NPA art. 89). However, in the event that a principal fails to comply with these rules, the authority to represent will remain legally valid. This is due to the fact that the RLR is a regulation and, therefore, does not have the power to govern the form of the validity of the authority to represent.

13.2.2 Conduct in the Name of the Principal

As mentioned above, with regard to direct agency, the agent has the authority to represent, and he acts in the name of, and on behalf of, the principal. Accordingly, the rights and obligations arising from the contract will be attributed to the principal. Although the agent acts with the intention of representing the principal, it is possible that he may fail to disclose this to a third party. In this case, as a rule, there is no agency. However, although an agent does not disclose that he is acting as an agent, in certain circumstances, agency may exist. TCO art. 40 par. 2 regulates two exceptions in this case: (1) the third party infers or should infer from the circumstances that there is an agency relationship. For example, a supermarket customer enters into a contract with a shop assistant. Even if the shop assistant does not disclose the fact that he is an agent, the contract binds the owner of the supermarket as the customer must infer the shop assistant's agency. (2) Where

[13]Oser and Schönenberger (1929), art. 32, N. 25; von Tuhr and Peter (1979), § 42, I, p. 355; Thévenoz and Werro (2012), art. 33, N. 9; Gauch et al. (2008), p. 308.

[14]Engel (1997), p. 384; Thévenoz and Werro (2012), art. 33, N. 9; Nomer (2015), p. 126; Tekinay et al. (1993), pp. 173–174.

the identity of the contracting counter-party does not matter to a third party, *e.g.*, in a cash transaction, the identity of the party making the payment is of no importance.[15]

Apart from these exceptions, even if an agent acts in the name of and on behalf of a principal, where he does not disclose the agency, the contract is formed between the agent and the third party. However, such an agent may demand that the principal assume the rights and obligations arising from the contract. The rights will be assigned (TCO art. 183 *ff*),[16] and the obligations will be assumed (TCO art. 195 *ff*)[17] in accordance with the applicable principles (TCO art. 40 par. 3).

13.3 Agency Without Authorisation[18]

If a person does not have the authority to represent another person but nonetheless purports to act as an agent and enters into a contract in the name of the alleged principal, initially, this contract will only bind the third party (TCO art. 46 par. 1).[19] At this stage, it is not certain whether the alleged principal will be bound by the contract. With the aim of ending this uncertainty, the third party may demand that the alleged principal ratify the contract within a reasonable time. If the alleged principal ratifies this contract, he will be bound from the time of formation.[20] Otherwise, where the alleged principal does not ratify the contract within a reasonable time, the third party will no longer be bound by this contract. Thus, the contract will be void (TCO art. 46 par. 2).[21]

The alleged principal may ratify the contract expressly or impliedly.[22] If the alleged principal does not ratify the contract, then the third party may demand compensation from the unauthorised agent for the damage that is a consequence of the invalidity of the contract. However, if the unauthorised agent proves that the third party knew or should have known of the lack of authority, then he will not be liable for this damage (TCO art. 47 par. 1). It should be noted that the damage arising from the invalidity of the contract is referred to as negative damage. Where equity requires it and the unauthorised agent is at fault, the third party may demand compensation for other damage, which is referred to as positive damage[23] (TCO art. 47 par. 2).

---

[15]For further explanations see Akünal (1975).

[16]See Chap. 32.

[17]See Chap. 33.

[18]*Représentation sans pouvoir*, *Vertretung ohne Ermächtigung*.

[19]For further explanations see Kutlu Sungurbey (1988).

[20]Oğuzman and Öz (2015), p. 241; Tercier et al. (2016), p. 137.

[21]Tercier (2004), p. 91.

[22]Tercier et al. (2016), p. 137; Tercier (2004), p. 91.

[23]See Sect. 22.2.3.3.1.

It is explained above that if the alleged principal does not ratify the contract within a reasonable period of time, it will be void. However, the third party might fulfil his obligations even though the contract's validity is uncertain. In this case, if the alleged principal is unjustly enriched, then the third party may sue for this unjust enrichment. For example, a third party pays the amount determined in the contract to the alleged principal. When the contract becomes invalid because of the failure to ratify, he may demand to have this amount refunded (TCO art. 47 par. 3).

13.4 Limitation, Revocation and Termination

13.4.1 Limitation and Revocation

The principal may, at any time, limit or revoke the authority to represent arising from a legal transaction (TCO art. 42 par. 1 sent. 1). However, if there is a legal relationship between the principal and the agent such as a relationship of employment, mandate or partnership, then the rights and obligations of the parties arising from them remain unaffected (TCO art. 42 par. 1 sent. 2). For instance, in an employment contract, the employer grants the authority to represent to the employee. However, after a period of time, the employer may revoke the authority to represent, but the employment contract may remain unaffected. In effect, this rule confirms the independence (abstractness) of the authority to represent.[24]

The principal may not waive the right of limitation and revocation of the authority to represent in advance (TCO art. 42 par. 2). This rule is mandatory, and the parties are not entitled to agree to the contrary.

The principal may give notice of the authority to represent expressly or impliedly to third parties. After a period of time, he may limit or revoke it. If the principal does not give notice of this limitation or revocation, he is not entitled to claim that the authority to represent has been limited or revoked against third parties acting in good faith (TCO art. 42 par. 3).

13.4.2 Death, Incapacity and Other Circumstances

Unless otherwise agreed, or unless implied by the nature of the transaction, an authority conferred by means of a legal transaction expires when either the agent or the principal dies, is declared a missing person (TCC art. 32) or bankrupt or loses the capacity to act (TCO art. 43 par. 1). This rule is also applicable in cases of dissolution of a legal entity (TCO art. 43 par. 2).

---

[24]Eren (2015), p. 439; Tekinay et al. (1993), p. 176; Berger (2012), p. 280.

In the above-mentioned cases, the authority to represent expires automatically. However, the parties may agree to the contrary. For example, a principal may grant an authority to represent that remains effective after his death (*mandatum post mortem*).

It should be noted that where the authority to represent expires automatically, the parties' mutual rights are not thereby affected (TCO art. 43 par. 3). For instance, in an employment contract, the employer grants the authority to represent to the employee. After a period of time, the employer dies. According to TCO art. 43 par. 1, the authority to represent expires automatically, unless otherwise agreed or unless apparent from the nature of the legal transaction. However, although the authority to represent may expire, the employee's rights will not necessarily be affected—*e.g.*, he may demand the payment of wages due and owing.

13.4.3 Return of the Instrument Conferring Authority

As a general rule, the granting of the authority to represent does not need to meet any form requirements for its validity. Nevertheless, in practice, the parties may prefer to use a written form or, in certain cases, must use a written form.[25] Accordingly, the principal may give the agent a written authority to represent. In such a case, if the authority to represent expires, the agent must return the written authority to the principal or deposit it with a court (TCO art. 44 par. 1). Also, when the authority to represent expires, the principal or his successors must enforce the return or the deposit of the instrument. If they fail to do so, they are liable to pay compensation for damage sustained by third parties acting in good faith in reliance on the authority (TCO art. 44 par. 2).

13.4.4 Restriction to the Claim of Termination

Although the authority to represent expires, it is possible that the agent and the third parties do not know of this fact. In this case, the contract binds the principal or his successors. This is because TCO art. 45 states that so long as the agent does not know of the expiration of the authority to represent, the principal or his successors are bound by the legal transaction. This rule does not apply where the third parties know of the expiration of the authority to represent. In addition, in fact, TCO art. 45 does not state explicitly that the principal or his successors will be bound if the agent or third parties 'should have known' of the expiration of the authority to represent. That is to say, the said article does not clearly require that the agent or third parties act in good faith (TCC art. 3). However, certain scholars believe that

[25] TCO.art.583/par.2.

the contract does not bind the principal or his successors if the agent or the third parties should have known of the expiration of the authority to represent even though TCO art. 45 does not explicitly state this.[26]

13.5 Indirect Agency[27]

In certain cases, the agent acts in his own name and on behalf of the principal.[28] Indeed, if the agent does not disclose the agency while acting as an agent, then this is a case of an indirect agency.[29] In such cases, initially, the rights and the obligations belong to the agent himself. Later, the agent may assign his rights to the principal and the principal may assume the obligations of the agent. This indirect agency is not regulated under arts. 40–48 of the Turkish Code of Obligations. However, other articles refer to specific examples of this type of agency. For instance, according to TCO art. 532 par. 1, a buying or selling agent undertakes, in return for a commission, to buy or to sell properties or securities in his own name and on behalf of the principal.

13.6 Reservation of Special Provisions

Special provisions relating to the authority of representatives and boards of companies and commercial agencies (TCO arts. 547–554) are reserved (TCO art. 48).

References

Akünal T (1975) Türk-İsviçre borçlar kanununda ilgili için işlem teorisi. İstanbul üniversitesi, İstanbul
Akyol Ş (2009) Türk medeni hukukunda temsil. Vedat, İstanbul
Antalya OG (2012) Borçlar hukuku genel hükümler, vol 1. Legal, İstanbul
Aybay A (2011) Borçlar hukuku dersleri genel bölüm. Filiz, İstanbul
Becker H (1941) Kommentar zum Schweizerischen Zivilgesetzbuch, vol VI, Obligationenrecht, 1. Abteilung: Allgemeine Bestimmungen, Art. 1-183. Stämpfli, Bern
Berger B (2012) Allgemeines Schuldrecht. Stämpfli, Bern
Engel P (1997) Traité des obligations en droit Suisse. Stämpfli, Bern

[26]Kocayusufpaşaoğlu (2014), pp. 702–703; Nomer (2015), p. 132; Oğuzman and Öz (2015), p. 235.

[27]*Représentation indirecte, indirekte, mittelbare Stellvertretung.*

[28]Engel (1997), p. 407; Tercier (2004), p. 94; Berger (2012), p. 274; Kocayusufpaşaoğlu (2014), p. 630; Tercier et al. (2016), p. 144; Nomer (2015), p. 123.

[29]von Tuhr and Peter (1979), § 41, I, p. 348. For further explanations see Yavuz (1983).

Eren F (2015) Borçlar hukuku genel hükümler. Yetkin, Ankara
Esener T (1961) Sâlahiyete müstenit temsil. Ankara üniversitesi hukuk fakültesi, Ankara
Feyzioğlu FN (1976) Borçlar hukuku genel hükümler, vol 1. Fakülteler, İstanbul
Gauch P, Schluep WR, Schmid J (2008) Schweizerisches Obligationenrecht, Allgemeiner Teil, vol 1. Schulthess, Zürich
Honsell H, Vogt NP, Wiegand W (eds) (2003) Basler Kommentar zum Schweizerischen Privatrecht, Obligationenrecht 1: Art. 1-529 OR. Helbing Lichtenhahn, Basel
İnceoğlu MM (2009) Borçlar hukukunda doğrudan temsil. On iki levha, İstanbul
Kılıçoğlu AM (2013) Borçlar hukuku genel hükümler. Turhan, İstanbul
Kocayusufpaşaoğlu N (2014) Borçlar hukuku genel bölüm c: 1 (Kocayusufpaşaoğlu/Hatemi/Serozan/Arpacı). Filiz, İstanbul
Kutlu Sungurbey A (1988) Yetkisiz temsil özellikle culpa in contrahendo (sözleşmenin görüşülmesinde kusur) ve olumsuz zarar. İstanbul
Nomer HN (2015) Borçlar hukuku genel hükümler. Beta, İstanbul
Oğuzman K, Öz T (2015) Borçlar hukuku genel hükümler, vol 1. Vedat, İstanbul
Oser H, Schönenberger W (1929) Kommentar zum Schweizerischen Zivilgesetzbuch, Volume V: Das Obligationenrecht, Erster Halbband: Art. 1-183. Schulthess, Zürich
Özdemir E (1994) Türk hukukunda yetkiye dayanan temsil ve nam-ı müstear uygulaması. Adalet, Ankara
Özsunay E (1983) Borçlar hukuku, vol I. Filiz, İstanbul
Reisoğlu S (2014) Türk borçlar hukuku genel hükümler. Beta, İstanbul
Schwenzer I (2009) Schweizerisches Obligationenrecht, Allgemeiner Teil. Schulthess, Bern
Tekinay SS, Akman S, Burcuoğlu H, Altop A (1993) Tekinay borçlar hukuku genel hükümler. Filiz, İstanbul
Tercier P (2004) Le droit des obligations. Schulthess, Zurich
Tercier P, Pichonnaz P, Develioğlu HM (2016) Borçlar hukuku genel hükümler. On iki levha, İstanbul
Thévenoz L, Werro F (éd) (2012) Commentaire romand code des obligations 1: art. 1-529 CO. Helbing Lichtenhahn, Bâle
von Tuhr A, Peter H (1979) Allgemeiner Teil des Schweizerischen Obligationenrecht, vol 1. Schulthess, Zürich
Yavuz C (1983) Türk-İsviçre ve Fransız medeni hukuklarında dolaylı temsil. İstanbul üniversitesi, İstanbul

Part II
The Effect of Obligations, Performance, Non-Performance, the Effect on Third Parties

Chapter 14
Performance of Obligation

14.1 General[1]

A debtor may be obliged to give, to do or not to do something. The debtor must perform what he is obliged to perform. The following examples may be given for each type of obligation.

Obligation to give: if the debtor is obliged to transfer ownership of a chattel (*e.g.*, a car) or real estate (land), he must transfer ownership of these properties to the creditor. Furthermore, a pecuniary obligation is also a kind of obligation to give.

Obligation to do: if the debtor undertakes to construct a building, complete a painting, compose a song or write a book, he must perform what he is obliged to do. Other examples of obligations to do include an employee who has a duty to carry out certain work or a doctor who is obliged to treat a patient.

Obligation not to do: if the debtor is obliged not to compete, he has a duty not to start a similar company in a certain field during a fixed time period, or if he is obliged not to disclose any confidential information, he must keep it secret.

When the debtor fulfils his obligation, the obligation is extinguished. After the extinguishment of the obligation, any ancillary[2] rights, such as a mortgage, pledge, surety, etc., are also terminated.

---

[1]Aybay (2011), p. 112; Becker (1941), Vorbemerkungen zu art. 68–96; Berger (2012), pp. 417–418; Engel (1997), pp. 607–610; Eren (2015), pp. 906–914; Feyzioğlu (1977), pp. 3–9; Gauch et al. (2008), pp. 1–5; Honsell et al. (2003), Vorbemerkungen zu art. 68–74; Kılıçoğlu (2013), p. 536; Nomer (2015), pp. 265–266; Oser and Schönenberger (1929), art. 68–96; Oğuzman and Öz (2015), p. 249; Reisoğlu (2014), pp. 292–294; Schwenzer (2009), pp. 39–41, 495–498; Serozan (2014), pp. 3–22; Tekinay et al. (1993), pp. 758–761; Tercier (2004), pp. 169–172; Tercier et al. (2016), pp. 290–295, 314–320; Thévenoz and Werro (2012), Introduction aux art. 68–83, p. 627–630, and von Tuhr and Escher (1974), pp. 1–11.

[2]Although 'accessory' is widely used in European texts, the author has preferred the use of 'ancillary' throughout this book to refer to subordinate or dependent rights which cannot exist without the principal obligation.

İ. Helvacı, *Turkish Contract Law*, DOI 10.1007/978-3-319-60061-1_14

14.2 Legal Nature

As mentioned above, if the debtor undertakes to do something, he must do what has to be done. Where the debtor undertakes not to do something, he must avoid doing it. In such cases, the intention of the debtor regarding the performance of the obligation does not have any importance. Also, it is not important whether he has the capacity to act.[3]

However, if the debtor undertakes to give something, such as to transfer property or to assign a claim, his intention of performance and capacity to act are important.[4] For instance, when transferring property, if the debtor does not have mental capacity, the transfer of the property is void. Another example is that of the assignment of a claim: if the assignor is a minor who has mental capacity or a person who has mental capacity but who is under guardianship, he is not entitled to assign the claim to the assignee without the consent of his legal representatives (TCC art. 16 par. 1 sent. 1, TCC art. 451 par. 1).

At this point, it should be added that if the performance of the obligation requires a dispositive transaction[5] (*acte de disposition, Verfügungsgeschäft*)[6] with regard to the debtor, such as the transfer of property or the assignment of a claim, the debtor must also have the power of disposition (*pouvoir de disposer, Verfügungsmacht*).[7] If the debtor does not have the power of disposition, then his dispositive act is void. It is possible that a person who has the capacity to act may not have the power of disposition. For instance, a debtor may have the capacity to act, but if he is a person, such as a merchant, who is subject to bankruptcy proceedings, after the commencement of bankruptcy procedures against him by a competent judge, although he will continue to have the capacity to act, his authority to dispose of the assets that form part of his bankrupt's estate will become restricted as against his creditors (TCBE art. 191 par. 1).[8]

In certain cases, the debtor may fulfil the obligation without the participation of the creditor. For example, obligations to refrain from acting, such as an obligation not to compete or not to disclose, do not require the creditor's participation. In these

[3]Nomer (2015), p. 266; Thévenoz and Werro (2012), Introduction aux art.68–83, N. 3; von Tuhr and Escher (1974), § 55, IX, 1, p. 8, compare to Engel (1997), p. 609.

[4]Thévenoz and Werro (2012), Introduction aux art.68–83, N. 3; von Tuhr and Escher (1974), § 55, IX, 1, p. 8.

[5]Dispositive: Relating to disposal. Where a legal transaction reduces one person's assets, such as the transfer of property or assignment of a claim, this transaction can be defined as a dispositive transaction with regard to him. For further explanations see Ayiter (1953).

[6]*Verfügungsgeschäft* can be literally translated in to English as 'transaction of disposal' (Foster and Sule (2010), p. 416 fn: 23). In order to define *Verfügungsgeschäft*, a possible translation is 'dispositional transaction', Posch (1996), p. 42. Another possible translation is 'dispository transaction' (Häcker (2013), p. 20 fn: 15). The author in this book prefers 'dispositive transaction' or 'dispositive act' (in this sense, Oğuzman (1996), p. 33).

[7]von Tuhr and Escher (1974), § 55, VIII, p. 7.

[8]Oğuzman and Öz (2015), p. 256; von Tuhr and Escher (1974), § 55, IX, 2, p. 9.

cases, it is obvious that the creditor's capacity to act has no relevance to the performance of the obligation.[9]

However, in certain cases, the debtor cannot fulfil the obligation without the participation of the creditor. Indeed, with regard to obligations to do, the creditor's participation is often necessary. For instance, if the debtor is obliged to repair a machine in the factory of the creditor or to repair a demolished wall in the garden of the creditor, the latter must permit the debtor to enter the building or the garden.

The participation of the creditor is also needed for the performance of obligations to give. Moreover, the performance of certain obligations to give may require a legal transaction.[10] For example, in the transfer of ownership of movable property to a creditor, the possession of the movable property must be transferred to the creditor, and while doing so, the parties must agree on the transfer of ownership of the movable property. In other words, the parties must accept that the possession of the movable property is transferred in order to satisfy the debtor's obligation.[11]

In cases where a legal transaction is needed for the performance of the obligation, the creditor must have the capacity to act. For example, if the creditor does not have mental capacity, the debtor cannot perform the obligation. In addition, if the creditor is a minor who has mental capacity or a person having mental capacity but under guardianship, he is not entitled to accept the performance of the obligation without the consent of his legal representative (TCC art. 16 par. 1 sent. 1, TCC art. 451 par. 1).

It should be noted that performance extinguishes the obligation. That is why in cases where the participation of the creditor is needed, the creditor must have the power of disposition.[12] Otherwise, the debtor may not be discharged from the obligation. For example, according to TCBE art. 192 par. 1, after the commencement of bankruptcy procedures by the competent judge against the creditor, the creditor may no longer accept any performance of an obligation due to him.

---

[9]Eren (2015), p. 935; Oğuzman and Öz (2015), p. 265.

[10]Oğuzman and Öz (2015), pp. 265–266.

[11]The transfer of possession is of a factual nature. The material transfer of possession must be complemented by the parties' agreement concerning the transfer of ownership. This agreement is referred to as 'a real agreement'. It is a bilateral legal act and does not require any specific form. It may be formed by the parties' express or implied declarations of will (intention). Real agreement (*dinglicher Vertrag*) is a dispositive act and it is to be distinguished from the *causa* that is to say the underlying contract which constitutes the obligation to transfer ownership. Real agreements are also different from real contracts (*contractus realis*) in Roman law. In *contractus realis* the transfer of possession of the subject matter of the contract represents a constitutive component. See and compare to Kocayusufpaşaoğlu (2014), pp. 96–97; Tercier (2004), p. 131.

[12]*Pouvoir de disposer, Verfügungsmacht.*

References

Aybay A (2011) Borçlar hukuku dersleri genel bölüm. Filiz, İstanbul

Ayiter K (1953) Medeni hukukta tasarruf muameleleri. Siyasal bilgiler fakültesi, Ankara

Becker H (1941) Kommentar zum Schweizerischen Zivilgesetzbuch, vol VI, Obligationenrecht, 1. Abteilung: Allgemeine Bestimmungen, Art. 1-183. Stämpfli, Bern

Berger B (2012) Allgemeines Schuldrecht. Stämpfli, Bern

Engel P (1997) Traité des obligations en droit Suisse. Stämpfli, Bern

Eren F (2015) Borçlar hukuku genel hükümler. Yetkin, Ankara

Feyzioğlu FN (1977) Borçlar hukuku genel hükümler, vol 2. Fakülteler, İstanbul

Foster N, Sule S (2010) German legal system and laws. Oxford Publishing, New York

Gauch P, Schluep WR, Emmenegger S (2008) Schweizerisches Obligationenrecht, Allgemeiner Teil, vol 2. Schulthess, Zürich

Häcker B (2013) Consequences of impaired consent transfers, a structural comparison of English and German law. Hart Publishing, Oxford and Portland, Oregon

Honsell H, Vogt NP, Wiegand W (eds) (2003) Basler Kommentar zum Schweizerischen Privatrecht, Obligationenrecht 1: Art. 1-529 OR. Helbing Lichtenhahn, Basel

Kılıçoğlu AM (2013) Borçlar hukuku genel hükümler. Turhan, İstanbul

Kocayusufpaşaoğlu N (2014) Borçlar hukuku genel bölüm, vol 1 (Kocayusufpaşaoğlu/Hatemi/Serozan/Arpacı). Filiz, İstanbul

Nomer HN (2015) Borçlar hukuku genel hükümler. Beta, İstanbul

Oğuzman K (1996) Turkey. In: Blanpain R, Herbots J (eds) International encyclopaedia of laws. Contracts Suppl. 12, vol 5. Kluwer Law International, The Hague

Oğuzman K, Öz T (2015) Borçlar hukuku genel hükümler, vol 1. Vedat, İstanbul

Oser H, Schönenberger W (1929) Kommentar zum Schweizerischen Zivilgesetzbuch, vol V: Das Obligationenrecht, Erster Halbband: Art. 1-183. Schulthess, Zürich

Posch W (1996) Austria. In: Blanpain R, Herbots J (eds) International encyclopaedia of laws. Contracts Suppl. 13, vol 1. Kluwer Law International, The Hague

Reisoğlu S (2014) Türk borçlar hukuku genel hükümler. Beta, İstanbul

Schwenzer I (2009) Schweizerisches Obligationenrecht, Allgemeiner Teil. Schulthess, Bern

Serozan R (2014) Borçlar hukuku genel bölüm, vol 3 (Kocayusufpaşaoğlu/Hatemi/Serozan/Arpacı). Filiz, İstanbul

Tekinay SS, Akman S, Burcuoğlu H, Altop A (1993) Tekinay borçlar hukuku genel hükümler. Filiz, İstanbul

Tercier P (2004) Le droit des obligations. Schulthess, Zurich

Tercier P, Pichonnaz P, Develioğlu HM (2016) Borçlar hukuku genel hükümler. On iki levha, İstanbul

Thévenoz L, Werro F (éd) (2012) Commentaire romand code des obligations 1: art. 1-529 CO. Helbing Lichtenhahn, Bâle

von Tuhr A, Escher A (1974) Allgemeiner Teil des Schweizerischen Obligationenrecht, Volume 2. Schulthess, Zürich

Chapter 15
The Object of Performance

15.1 General[1]

A debtor must perform exactly what he is obliged to perform. If the debtor offers performance of an obligation that is different from the original, then the creditor does not have to accept it.[2] Even if the value of the debtor's proposal is higher than the original obligation, the creditor need not accept it.[3] Similarly, a creditor is not entitled to demand performance of an obligation that is different from the original.[4] In other words, the debtor does not have to accept such a proposal. Even if the value of the creditor's proposal is less than the original obligation, the debtor need not accept it either.

However, at the time of fulfilment, the contracting parties may agree that the obligation is deemed to be fulfilled by the performance of an act other than that owed pursuant to the contract. This kind of performance is referred to as 'an acceptance in lieu of performance'.[5] In the case of acceptance in lieu of performance, if the value of the given object is higher than the value of the original obligation, the debtor must bear its disadvantageous consequences. In other words, the creditor does not have to

[1] Aybay (2011), pp. 112–117; Becker (1941), art. 69–73, 84–87; Berger (2012), pp. 420–432; Engel (1997), pp. 619–622, 633–649; Eren (2015), pp. 914–924, 957–985, 1009–1010; Feyzioğlu (1977), pp. 9–75; Gauch et al. (2008), pp. 31–54; Honsell et al. (2003), art. 69–73, 84–87; Kılıçoğlu (2013), pp. 590–596, 604–613, 616–622; Nomer (2015), pp. 266–290; Oser and Schönenberger (1929), art. 69–73, 84–87; Oğuzman and Öz (2015), pp. 271–309; Reisoğlu (2014), pp. 298–323; Schwenzer (2009), pp. 48–50, 52–63, 498–504; Serozan (2014), pp. 77–119; Tekinay et al. (1993), pp. 761–766, 771–800, 811–818; Tercier (2004), pp. 180–185, 197–201; Tercier et al. (2016), pp. 314–323, 341–351; Thévenoz and Werro (2012), art. 69–73, 84–87, and von Tuhr and Escher (1974), pp. 11–17. For further explanations see İpek (2016).

[2] Engel (1997), p. 619; Tercier (2004), p. 180.

[3] Oğuzman and Öz (2015), pp. 271–272; Tekinay et al. (1993), p. 761.

[4] Feyzioğlu (1977), p. 9; Eren (2015), p. 914.

[5] *Dation en paiement*, *Zahlungsstatt*. See *Annahme an Erfüllungs statt*: BGB §364.

İ. Helvacı, *Turkish Contract Law*, DOI 10.1007/978-3-319-60061-1_15

pay any excess. In parallel, if the value of the given object is lower than the value of the original obligation, then the creditor must bear its disadvantageous consequences.[6] That is to say, the debtor does not need to compensate for the deficiency. For example, D owes €20,000 to C. At the time of fulfilment, the debtor does not perform his obligation and proposes to transfer a boat, and the creditor accepts that transfer in lieu of performance. It is irrelevant whether the boat's value is €30,000 or €10,000. Thus, in both cases, the original obligation is extinguished by the transfer of ownership of the boat to the creditor (*datio in solutum*).

Moreover, at the time of fulfilment, the debtor may propose to perform an act other than the original object of the obligation. For example, the debtor may propose to the creditor to deliver an object, which is different from the original object of the obligation, and to allow the creditor to realise it, and the creditor may accept this proposal.[7] In this case, the original obligation is not automatically extinguished by the parties' agreement. On the contrary, the original obligation is extinguished only to the extent of the money obtained from the realisation of the object. In cases where the realised value does not satisfy the value of the original obligation, the debtor must perform the remaining part of the debt. In addition, where the realised amount exceeds the value of the original debt, the creditor must return the excess amount.[8]

In the above-mentioned cases, the creditor must act as if he were an agent. That is to say, the creditor, in the realisation of the object, must act diligently and faithfully. Otherwise, the creditor is liable for the damage of the debtor.

As has been seen, it is important to determine if there is a *datio in solutum* (an acceptance in lieu of performance) or not as these kinds of agreements extinguish the original obligations. If the agreement is not clear enough, it is assumed that the parties do not agree on the *datio in solutum*; on the contrary, their agreement is made with the aim of fulfilment.

15.2 Partial Performance

15.2.1 In Principle

If the object of an obligation is indivisible by nature or by law, it is impossible for a debtor to partially perform the obligation.[9] For instance, in a sale contract relating

[6]von Tuhr and Escher (1974), § 56, I, p. 11; Engel (1997), p. 619; Berger (2012), p. 428; Reisoğlu (2014), p. 299; Serozan (2014), p. 91.

[7]*Dation en vue du paiement*, *Zahlungshalber*.

[8]von Tuhr and Escher (1974), § 56, II, pp. 13–14; Engel (1997), p. 620; Berger (2012), pp. 427–428; Feyzioğlu (1977), p. 13; Oğuzman and Öz (2015), p. 274; Tekinay et al. (1993), p. 763.

[9]Thévenoz and Werro (2012), art. 69, N. 2; Oser and Schönenberger (1929), art. 69, N. 1; Becker (1941), art. 69, N. 8.

to a car, a house or a machine, the subject matter of the contract is indivisible by nature.[10] If the subject matter of the sale contract is land, the land is divisible in principle. However, it may be indivisible in law. For example, public authorities may have restricted its partition. Thus, in such cases, the obligation cannot be partially performed.

Obligations not to do are indivisible. In principle, certain obligations to do (*e.g.*, to create an artistic work) are also indivisible. Therefore, such obligations cannot be partially performed either.[11]

If the object of an obligation is divisible, whether by nature or by law, the obligation may be partially performed. For example, generic obligations, especially pecuniary obligations, may be partially performed. However, even if the object of the obligation is divisible, the creditor does not have to accept a partial performance where the entire obligation is determined and due (TCO art. 84 par. 1). Therefore, if the creditor refuses partial performance, he does not fall into creditor's default.[12] On the contrary, the debtor falls into default for the entirety of the obligation.[13]

In cases where partial performance is possible, the creditor may demand partial performance. The debtor may accept or refuse this proposal. That is to say, notwithstanding a claim for partial performance by the creditor, the debtor is entitled to perform the obligation entirely in accordance with the contract. However, in cases where the creditor demands partial performance and the debtor accepts it, the latter is not entitled to refuse to perform the accepted part of the obligation (TCO art. 84 par. 2).

15.2.2 Exceptions

In certain cases, the creditor must accept partial performance. This necessity may result from the parties' agreement, the principles of good faith (TCC art. 2), the nature of the circumstances or specific provisions, as set out in the paragraph below.[14]

(1) The parties may specify in the contract that the creditor must accept a partial performance. Another example is related to an instalment debt. In such a case, the debtor must only perform the instalment unless the entirety of the obligation is due. (2) If the refusal of partial performance is against the principles of good faith, the creditor must accept the partial performance. For example, the amount of a loan is €344,499. The total amount is due, but the debtor pays €344,000. In this case, the creditor is not entitled to refuse the partial payment. It should be noted that the

[10]Reisoğlu (2014), p. 299.

[11]Oğuzman and Öz (2015), p. 275; Feyzioğlu (1977), p. 29; Becker (1941), art. 70, N. 2.

[12]See Chap. 20.

[13]See Chap. 23.

[14]Feyzioğlu (1977), pp. 34–35; Tekinay et al. (1993), pp. 764–765.

remaining claim of the creditor is reserved. (3) In certain cases, it may be nearly impossible or too difficult to perform the obligation in a single action. For example, if the debtor is obliged to deliver 10,000 tons of wheat, he may not be able to deliver the entirety of the order in one consignment. (4) Although the Turkish Code of Obligations, in principle, denies the right to partial performance, the Turkish Commercial Code, which is an inseparable part of the Turkish Code of Obligations, allows the debtor to make partial payment in certain cases. According to TComC art. 709 par. 2, relating to a bill of exchange, a holder is not entitled to refuse partial payment. This rule, unless it is contrary to its nature, also applies to promissory notes (TComC art. 778 par. 1 subcl. c) and to cheques (TComC art. 818 par. 1 subcl. h).

It should be noted that if a part of the obligation is disputed, the debtor may perform the undisputed part and the creditor is not entitled to refuse this partial performance. Scholars infer this outcome by way of *argumentum a contrario* from the wording of TCO art. 84 par. 1.[15]

It is worth noting that the payment of rents that arise at specific times (such as every month) is not categorised as a partial performance. Furthermore, in a contract that is successively performed, each act of fulfilment is not a partial performance. Moreover, in a pecuniary obligation, capital and interest debts are separated. Hence, the payment of interest is not a partial payment.[16]

15.3 Indivisible Obligations

If an obligation is indivisible by nature or by law and there is one debtor and one creditor, performance of the obligation has no specific features.[17] However, if an indivisible claim belongs to more than one creditor or the obligation is undertaken by more than one debtor, TCO art. 85 will apply.

If an indivisible obligation is due to several creditors, each of them may demand that performance be rendered to all of them jointly. In such a case, the debtor must perform the obligation jointly for all creditors (TCO art. 85 par. 1). If an indivisible obligation is due by several debtors, each of them must perform the entire obligation (TCO art. 85 par. 2). Unless the contrary is understood from the circumstances, the performing debtor is subrogated to the creditor and is entitled to proportional contributions from the other debtors (TCO art. 85 par. 3).

[15]Oğuzman and Öz (2015), p. 279; Reisoğlu (2014), p. 300.

[16]von Tuhr and Escher (1974), § 57, VI, p. 16; Oğuzman and Öz (2015), p. 278.

[17]Oğuzman and Öz (2015), p. 287.

15.4 Specific Obligations[18]

In specific obligations, the object of the obligation is particularly specified and cannot be substituted by another item. In other words the object of the obligation is irreplaceable because it is 'unique'. Generally, non-fungible items[19] become the object of a specific obligation.[20] For example, if a debtor is obliged to transfer ownership of an Opel Astra whose number plate is 00 XX 0000 or a painting by Picasso named *Guernica*, then the objects of the contract are individually and specifically identified.

In the above-mentioned cases, if the debtor intends to perform the obligation, then he must transfer ownership of these specifically identified objects. In other words, the debtor must perform his obligation by delivering the particular thing specified in the contract. The debtor is not entitled to offer to transfer another Opel Astra or another of Picasso's paintings in lieu of the original specific goods, unless otherwise agreed.

15.5 Generic Obligations[21]

In generic obligations, the object of the obligation is purely generic. In other words, the object of the obligation is replaceable, and it forms an undifferentiated portion or quantity of the same type of things. Generally, fungible items[22] become the object of generic obligations.[23] For instance, if a debtor is obliged to deliver 2000 litres of milk, 3 tons of wheat or 3 Opel Astras, such obligations are referred to as 'generic obligations'.

According to TCO art. 86, unless the contrary is understood from the legal relationship and the nature of the circumstances, the debtor may select which object is to be given. However, the debtor is not entitled to select an object of below average quality. Otherwise, the creditor may reject the performance as non-conforming to the contract. In such cases, the debtor must bear the consequences of the non-performance. TCO art. 86 is not mandatory. Thus, the parties

---

[18] *Obligatio in specie, dette de corps certain, Speziesschuld* or *Stückschuld.*

[19] A non-fungible item is not destroyed by use, has a specific individual value and cannot be replaced by another item. See Oğuzman et al. (2016), p. 13.

[20] However, a non-fungible item may be the object of a generic obligation, such as three Picasso paintings (without specifying which three Picasso paintings).

[21] *Obligatio in genere, obligation de genre, Gattungsschuld.*

[22] A fungible item is something which is destroyed by being used and can be replaced by equal quantities of the same quality, such as oil, wine, cotton, money, etc. See Oğuzman et al. (2016), p. 12.

[23] However, fungible items (*res fungibiles, choses fongibles, vertretbare Sachen*) may also be the object of a specific obligation. For example, a football club W won a coin toss against another football club L after their championship match ended in a draw. This coin has been displayed in the winning club's museum for years. This coin, notwithstanding being a fungible item, may be sold in an auction and become the object of a specific obligation.

may agree otherwise, or the nature of the circumstances may require that this right of selection belongs to the creditor or to a third party.

In an obligation to give, the parties may define the object of the contract in generic terms, but they may agree on certain specific features.[24] For instance, in Turkey, apples grown in Amasya have particular features. If the parties agree that the debtor must deliver 3 tons of Amasya apples, he is not entitled to deliver 3 tons of another kind of apple.

In a generic obligation, the parties may intend to restrict the object of the obligation. For example, if the parties agree that the debtor must deliver 3 tons of wheat from a particular silo or 10,000 kg of grapes from a specific vineyard, then these kinds of obligations are referred to as 'restricted generic obligations'.[25] In such a case, the debtor may not deliver any 3 tons of wheat or any 10,000 kg of grapes.[26] In addition, the debtor is not entitled to select objects below average quality from these stocks.[27]

15.6 Alternative Obligations

Where there is more than one choice for the subject matter of the obligation and either one of the different acts (prestations) is to be performed, this is referred to as an alternative obligation.[28] For example, in a contract, a debtor is obliged to deliver either a Mercedes Benz C 180 or a studio flat. In another example, the debtor is obliged to construct a house or to deliver a boat. The debtor is allowed to perform either one of these acts.

In such a case, the parties or the nature of the circumstances may grant the right to choose which act is to be performed either to the creditor or to the debtor.[29] The right of choice may also belong to a third party.[30] If the parties or the nature of the circumstances do not determine to whom this right of choice belongs, the debtor has the right of choice (TCO art. 87). Once the debtor exercises this right of choice and determines which act is to be performed, then the object of the obligation becomes definitive. Other acts are no longer possible objects of the obligation.[31]

In alternative obligations, if the debtor or the third party who has the right of choice omits to exercise this right, the creditor may file an alternative lawsuit. If the

[24]Tekinay et al. (1993), pp. 761–762.

[25]*Begrenzte Gattungsschuld.*

[26]Oser and Schönenberger (1929), art. 71, N. 6; Serozan (2014), p. 84.

[27]Oser and Schönenberger (1929), art. 71, N. 6; Serozan (2014), p. 84.

[28]von Tuhr and Peter (1979), § 11, I, p. 77; Tercier (2004), p. 184; Berger (2012), p. 422; Nomer (2015), pp. 274–275; Tercier et al. (2016), p. 321.

[29]Becker (1941), art. 72, N. 3–4.

[30]Becker (1941), art. 72, N. 5.

[31]Becker (1941), art. 72, N. 7; Oser and Schönenberger (1929), art. 72, N. 8; Oğuzman and Öz (2015), p. 284.

court accepts the claim, it can order the debtor to perform one of the alternative obligations. If the debtor does not voluntarily perform the obligation despite the court decision, then the creditor who intends to enforce the court order must elect one of the acts determined in the court order as the object of his enforcement. Despite this election, the debtor may still perform the other act (TCPC art. 112).[32]

It should be noted that an alternative obligation is distinct from a facultative obligation. In the latter, there is only one object of obligation, but the debtor has the right to substitute the object of obligation (*facultas alternativa*).[33] Therefore, the debtor does not have to obtain the creditor's permission. Furthermore, the debtor does not have to exercise this right, although he may choose to do so.

The importance of the difference between alternative obligations and facultative obligations becomes apparent in cases in which performance is impossible. For example, with regard to alternative obligations relating to two different acts, if one of them becomes impossible to perform, then the act that remains possible must constitute the object of the obligation. In contrast, in cases of *facultas alternativa* where the principal act becomes impossible, the obligation is extinguished.[34]

15.7 Pecuniary Obligations

15.7.1 General

A pecuniary obligation is a kind of obligation to give.[35] Money is a fungible thing, and pecuniary obligations are a particular type of generic obligations. Therefore, the performance of pecuniary obligations can never become impossible.[36]

15.7.2 National Currency

As a rule, pecuniary obligations must be paid in the national currency (TCO art. 99 par. 1). In Turkey, the national currency, at the present time, is the Turkish lira.[37] There is no other recognised currency.

[32] Nomer (2015), p. 275.

[33] Becker (1941), art. 72, N. 16; Tercier (2004), p. 184; Oğuzman and Öz (2015), p. 282, for further explanations see Serozan (2014), pp. 88–90.

[34] Oğuzman and Öz (2015), pp. 282–283. In this sense, Reisoğlu (2014), p. 303.

[35] Engel (1997), pp. 634–635.

[36] Eren (2015), p. 971; Serozan (2014), p. 97; Tercier et al. (2016), p. 342; Tercier (2004), p. 198.

[37] The national currency of the Turkish Republic was the Turkish Lira as of 1 June 1938. See Act on Recognition of Lira in State Accounts, No 3290 of 24 December 1937 (Official Gazette 30.12.1937; No: 3796). However, the legislature, with a specific act, erased six zeros and accepted a new currency

15.7.3 *Pecuniary Obligations in Foreign Currency*

15.7.3.1 Literal Performance

As mentioned above, in principle, pecuniary obligations must be paid in the national currency. Nevertheless, this rule is not mandatory, and thus, the parties may agree to the contrary. In this case, the debtor must perform the obligation in the specified foreign currency.[38]

15.7.3.2 Performance in the National Currency

With regard to pecuniary obligations in foreign currency, if a creditor does not want to accept performance in the national currency, the parties must agree on the literal performance of the pecuniary obligations. Otherwise, the debtor may perform the foreign pecuniary obligation in the national or in the foreign currency. In fact, with respect to pecuniary obligations in foreign currency, unless there is a clause requiring literal performance or an expression that has the same effect in the contract, the debtor may perform it in the national currency according to the rate of exchange on the due date (TCO art. 99 par. 2). However, in the above-mentioned case, if the debtor does not perform his obligation on the due date, the creditor may demand that the debtor perform literally or in the national currency according to the rate of exchange on the due date or the actual performance date (TCO art. 99 par. 3).

It is worth noting that, under TCO art. 99 par. 2, the legislature gives the right to a debtor to replace the foreign currency debts with the national currency. That is why this rule may be defined as an example of *facultas alternativa*. Nevertheless, if a debtor does not pay the pecuniary debt on the due date, the granted faculty to do so is extinguished.[39]

15.7.4 *Interest*

15.7.4.1 General

The parties may agree whether or not the pecuniary obligation involves the payment of interest. For example, in a non-commercial loan agreement, the lender may

---

as the New Turkish Lira as of 1 January 2005. Therefore, before this enactment, *e.g.*, the price of a cup of coffee was TL3,000,000 and after it the price became New TL3. See Act on the National Currency of Republic of Turkey, No 5083 of 28 January 2004 (Official Gazette 31.01.2004; No: 25363). Subsequently, following a decree of the Council of Ministers 'New' was abrogated as of 1 January 2009. In effect, *e.g.*, the price of a cup of coffee became TL3. See Decree of the Council of Ministers, No 2007/11963 of 04 April 2007 (Official Gazette 05.05.2007; No: 26513).

[38]For further explanations see Pekcanıtez (1988), Baygın (1997).

[39]Serozan (2014), p. 102.

only demand interest if so agreed (TCO art. 387 par. 1). However, in certain cases, even if the parties do not agree that interest is to be paid, payment of interest may be implied by law. Indeed, in commercial loan agreements, even if the parties do not agree to it, the lender may demand that the borrower pay interest (TCO art. 387 par. 2). In brief, the obligation to pay interest may arise from the parties' agreement or from the law itself. This kind of interest is referred to as capital interest and is different from default interest.[40]

In cases where pecuniary obligations involve the payment of interest, the parties may determine its rate. Should the contractual (*e.g.*, annual) interest rate not be determined by the parties, this rate is to be determined according to the relevant legislation at the time the interest liability arises (TCO art. 88 par. 1).

According to LIA art. 1 par. 1, in cases where payment of interest on capital is required, under the Code of Obligations and the Commercial Code, if the rate is not determined in the contract, then previously the rate was deemed to be 12% per annum.[41] However, LIA art. 1 par. 2 allows the Council of Ministers to determine a monthly rate. Further, the Council of Ministers has the authority to determine the annual rate to be as low as 10% of the rate determined by the legislation or to be as high as 100% of that rate. As of 1 January 2006, the Council of Ministers has determined this rate to be 9% per annum.[42]

It is worth noting that in non-commercial affairs, the interest rate determined by the parties may not be more than 50% greater than the legal interest rate (TCO art. 88 par. 2). Since the current legal interest rate is 9% per annum, the parties may determine the interest rate provided that it does not exceed 13.5% per annum. However, pursuant to TComC art. 8 par. 1, in commercial affairs, the parties have more freedom to determine the interest rate provided that this rate is not immoral or contrary to the rules protecting personal rights (TCO art. 27 par. 1 and TCC art. 23).

Pursuant to LIA art. 3 par. 1, compound interest (interest on the accrued interest) is prohibited. Nevertheless, LIA art. 3 par. 2 states that the provisions of the Turkish Commercial Code are reserved. Indeed, according to TComC art. 8 par. 2, a clause imposing compound interest, based on intervals of no less than three months, is allowed only in current accounts and loan agreements that qualify as a commercial transaction for both parties. Nevertheless, this paragraph only applies to contracts in which the parties are merchants. Further, the rules protecting consumers are reserved (TComC art. 8 par. 3).

The rules explained above also apply to pecuniary obligations in foreign currency. However, the legal interest rate on capital is equivalent to the maximum interest rate

[40] See below Sect. 23.3.1.

[41] See Act on the Legal Interest and Default Interest, No 3095 of 4.12.1984 (Official Gazette 19.12.1984; No: 18610) and Act on the Amendment of Certain Acts and Decree-Laws, art.14, No 5335 of 21.4.2005 (Official Gazette 27.04.2005; No: 25798).

[42] Decree of the Council of Ministers, No 2005/9831 of 19.12.2005 (Official Gazette 30.12.2005; No: 26039).

that the state banks pay on a term deposit account opened in the relevant foreign currency with a one-year maturity (see and compare to LIA art. 4 a).

15.7.4.2 Legal Nature

Interest debts are ancillary to the principal debt.[43] Thus, the interest debt requires the existence of a principal pecuniary obligation. In other words, if the principal pecuniary obligation is extinguished, the obligation to pay interest is also extinguished. This is due to the fact that when the principal pecuniary obligation is extinguished, it may no longer generate interest. As to accrued interest, it can only be claimed if such a right is reserved in the contract or is reserved by the creditor's notification, which must be made by the date of performance, or if such a reservation is inferred from the circumstances (TCO art. 131 par. 2).

Given the fact that an interest debt is an ancillary right arising out of a principal pecuniary obligation, it is worth mentioning certain specific rules as set out in the following paragraphs.

If the creditor gives a receipt for the entire performance of the principal pecuniary obligation, the interest is presumed to have also been paid (TCO art. 104 par. 2). Where the creditor assigns the claim to a third party, arrears of interest are presumed to be assigned together with the principal pecuniary claim (TCO art. 189 par. 2). Also, the assignee will be entitled to interest that accrues after assignment.

When the principal claim is time-barred, interest claims are also time-barred (TCO art. 152). However, the claim for interest is subject to a different period of limitation. Actually, unless otherwise provided by law, all claims become time-barred after 10 years (TCO art. 146), whereas interest payable on the principal becomes time-barred after 5 years (TCO art. 147 subcl. 1). Given these provisions, it can be seen that the obligation to pay interest may be time-barred before the principal claim becomes time-barred.

Although the claim for interest is an ancillary right of the principal claim, the former may be assigned[44] or sued for independently of the principal claim.[45] The interest claim does not form part of the principal claim. Therefore, the payment of interest cannot constitute a partial performance, and so the creditor is not entitled to refuse a proposal for payment of interest without payment of the principal pecuniary obligation.[46]

---

[43] Oğuzman and Öz (2015), p. 303; Tekinay et al. (1993), p. 786; von Tuhr and Peter (1979), § 10, II, p. 71; Engel (1997), p. 647; Thévenoz and Werro (2012), art. 73, N. 3; Becker (1941), art. 73, N. 3; Oser and Schönenberger (1929), art. 73, N. 14.

[44] Tercier (2004), p. 200.

[45] Feyzioğlu (1977), pp. 61–62; Eren (2015), p. 979; Thévenoz and Werro (2012), art. 73, N. 3; Oser and Schönenberger (1929), art. 73, N. 15.

[46] Oğuzman and Öz (2015), p. 277.

15.7.5 Appropriation

15.7.5.1 General

With regard to pecuniary obligations, if the debtor pays the principal debt (the capital), its interest and expenses, then appropriation is not in question. However, if the debtor's payment does not satisfy the entire obligation, the manner of allocation constitutes a legal problem. The Turkish Code of Obligations deals with this problem by setting out two possibilities, which are stated in the paragraphs below.

15.7.5.2 In the Case of Partial Payment

If the debtor is not in arrears with interest or expenses, then he is entitled to appropriate the partial payment to the principal (TCO art. 100 par. 1). It should not be forgotten that, because the interest debt is not part of the principal debt, the payment of interest does not constitute any partial performance. For example, the principal debt is €10,000 and the interest debt is €3000. If the debtor pays €13,000, that is to say, the entire debt, then there is no need for appropriation. However, where the debtor intends to pay €3000, he may only appropriate this partial payment to the principal debt provided that he is not in arrears with the interest debt. If the debtor is in arrears with the interest debt, then he may not appropriate this partial payment to the principal debt. TCO art. 100 par. 1 is a mandatory rule. Thus, the parties are not entitled to agree to the contrary (TCO art. 100 par. 1 sent. 2).

The pecuniary obligation may be secured by a surety, pledge, mortgage, etc. If the security guarantees the entire debt, the partial payment by the debtor does not create a risk for the creditor. However, if the security does not guarantee the entire debt, in cases where the debtor partially fulfils the debt, he is not entitled to appropriate this partial payment to that part of the debt that is covered by the security or by a better security (TCO art. 100 par. 2). For example, a debtor is obliged to pay €10,000 to a creditor, and there is a surety for €3000 and a pledge for €2000. In this case, if the debtor pays €5000, he is not entitled to appropriate this partial payment to the secured part of the debt.

15.7.5.3 In the Case of Several Debts

15.7.5.3.1 According to the Parties' Declarations

If a debtor is under several obligations to be performed for the same creditor, then the debtor is entitled to declare which debt he intends to satisfy at the time of performance (TCO art. 101 par. 1). If the debtor does not exercise this right, it belongs to the creditor. In this case, the payment is appropriated to the debt that the creditor acknowledges in his receipt. However, the debtor may immediately object to this appropriation (TCO art. 101 par. 2).

15.7.5.3.2 According to the Law

In certain cases, there may be no legally valid declaration or any indication in the receipt relating to the appropriation. In these cases, the payment is deemed to have been appropriated to the debt that falls due. In the event that several debts fall due, the payment is deemed to have been appropriated to the debt that has first been enforced. Where none of the debts have been enforced, the payment is deemed to have been appropriated to the debt that falls due first (TCO art. 102 par. 1).

Where several debts fall due at the same time, the payment is deemed to have been appropriated proportionately. Should none of several debts fall due, the payment is deemed to have been appropriated to the debt with the least security (TCO art. 102 par. 2).

References

Aybay A (2011) Borçlar hukuku dersleri genel bölüm. Filiz, İstanbul

Baygın C (1997) Yabancı para üzerinden borçlanmalar ve hukuki sonuçları. Kazancı, İstanbul

Becker H (1941) Kommentar zum Schweizerischen Zivilgesetzbuch, vol VI, Obligationenrecht, 1. Abteilung: Allgemeine Bestimmungen, Art. 1-183. Stämpfli, Bern

Berger B (2012) Allgemeines Schuldrecht. Stämpfli, Bern

Engel P (1997) Traité des obligations en droit Suisse. Stämpfli, Bern

Eren F (2015) Borçlar hukuku genel hükümler. Yetkin, Ankara

Feyzioğlu FN (1977) Borçlar hukuku genel hükümler, vol 2. Fakülteler, İstanbul

Gauch P, Schluep WR, Emmenegger S (2008) Schweizerisches Obligationenrecht, Allgemeiner Teil, vol 2. Schulthess, Zürich

Honsell H, Vogt NP, Wiegand W (eds) (2003) Basler Kommentar zum Schweizerischen Privatrecht, Obligationenrecht 1: Art. 1-529 OR. Helbing Lichtenhahn, Basel

İpek E (2016) Edime uygun ifa kuralı ve bu kuralın ihlaline bağlanan hukuki sonuçlar. Filiz, İstanbul

Kılıçoğlu AM (2013) Borçlar hukuku genel hükümler. Turhan, İstanbul

Nomer HN (2015) Borçlar hukuku genel hükümler. Beta, İstanbul

Oğuzman K, Öz T (2015) Borçlar hukuku genel hükümler, vol 1. Vedat, İstanbul

Oğuzman MK, Seliçi Ö, Oktay-Özdemir S (2016) Eşya Hukuku. Filiz, İstanbul

Oser H, Schönenberger W (1929) Kommentar zum Schweizerischen Zivilgesetzbuch, Volume V: Das Obligationenrecht, Erster Halbband: Art. 1-183. Schulthess, Zürich

Pekcanıtez H (1988) Medenî usûl ve icra - iflâs hukukunda yabancı para alacaklarının tahsili. Yetkin, Ankara

Reisoğlu S (2014) Türk borçlar hukuku genel hükümler. Beta, İstanbul

Schwenzer I (2009) Schweizerisches Obligationenrecht, Allgemeiner Teil. Schulthess, Bern

Serozan R (2014) Borçlar hukuku genel bölüm, vol 3 (Kocayusufpaşaoğlu/Hatemi/Serozan/Arpacı). Filiz, İstanbul

Tekinay SS, Akman S, Burcuoğlu H, Altop A (1993) Tekinay borçlar hukuku genel hükümler. Filiz, İstanbul

Tercier P (2004) Le droit des obligations. Schulthess, Zurich

Tercier P, Pichonnaz P, Develioğlu HM (2016) Borçlar hukuku genel hükümler. On iki levha, İstanbul

Thévenoz L, Werro F (éd) (2012) Commentaire romand code des obligations 1: art. 1-529 CO. Helbing Lichtenhahn, Bâle

von Tuhr A, Escher A (1974) Allgemeiner Teil des Schweizerischen Obligationenrecht, vol 2. Schulthess, Zürich
von Tuhr A, Peter H (1979) Allgemeiner Teil des Schweizerischen Obligationenrecht, vol 1. Schulthess, Zürich

Chapter 16
Performance of the Debtor

16.1 Performance in Person[1]

According to TCO art. 83, a debtor, as a rule, need not fulfil the obligation in person. However, where the debtor's specific personal skills and experience is of importance to the creditor, the obligations under the contract may not be fulfilled by a third party. In this respect, the following examples can be mentioned: (1) according to TCO art. 395, unless the contrary is understood from the contract or the circumstances, an employee must perform the work in person; (2) TCO art. 506 par. 1 states that an agent, subject to certain exceptions, must carry out the obligation in person; and (3) TCO art. 471 par. 3 sent.1 states that, subject to certain exceptions, a contractor must carry out the work in person or have it carried out under his specific direction.

Certain specific examples can be referenced for work contracts. For instance, a patient enters into a contract for plastic surgery with a highly experienced and well-known surgeon. In this case, this operation must be performed by this surgeon, and another surgeon may not carry out this operation. Other examples include the painting of a picture by a famous artist, the sewing of a dress by a well-known tailor or the undertaking of an architectural project by an award-winning architect.

Where performance by the debtor in person is necessary, the debtor is not entitled to substitute himself, but he may work with assistants.[2] Such co-operation does not breach the contract. In the example of the well-known

[1]Aybay (2011), pp. 117–119, 149–150; Becker (1941), art. 68; Berger (2012), pp. 418–419, 778–779; Engel (1997), pp. 611–615; Eren (2015), pp. 924–934; Feyzioğlu (1977), pp. 82–93; Gauch et al. (2008), pp. 7–11; Honsell et al. (2003), art. 68; Kılıçoğlu (2013), pp. 559–568; Nomer (2015), pp. 273–274, Oser and Schönenberger (1929), art. 68; Oğuzman and Öz (2015), pp. 250–264; Reisoğlu (2014), pp. 295–297; Schwenzer (2009), pp. 50–52; Serozan (2014), pp. 22–31; Tekinay et al. (1993), pp. 766–770; Tercier (2004), pp. 187–189; Tercier et al. (2016), pp. 326–329; Thévenoz and Werro (2012), art. 68, and von Tuhr and Escher (1974), pp. 23–32.

[2]Serozan (2014), p. 23; Oğuzman and Öz (2015), p. 251; von Tuhr and Escher (1974), § 59, I, p. 24; Engel (1997), p. 611; Thévenoz and Werro (2012), art. 68, N. 5.

İ. Helvacı, *Turkish Contract Law*, DOI 10.1007/978-3-319-60061-1_16

surgeon, during the operation, the surgeon may work with certain assistants such as nurses, anaesthetists, etc. In the other examples, the tailor, the famous painter or the award-winning architect may also fulfil their obligations with the assistance of third parties. Whether the debtor substitutes himself or fulfils the obligations with the help of assistants, he is liable for any damage resulting from the acts of the substitute or the assistants that are contrary to the obligations under the contract.

16.2 Performance by a Third Party

16.2.1 General

If the debtor's personal qualifications or skills are not relevant to the creditor, the obligation may be fulfilled by a third party.[3] For example, in pecuniary obligations, the personal qualifications or skills of a debtor have no importance for the creditor. Hence, the debtor may leave the payment of the pecuniary obligations to a third party. These third parties are referred to as substitute persons.[4]

It should be noted that this fact is not restricted to pecuniary obligations. For example, if a contractor's specific skills and experience are not important for the customer, then the contractor is not obliged to personally carry out the work. The contractor may leave the performance to a substitute person.

Moreover, in the case of obligations that can be performed by a third party, the latter may fulfil the obligation. The consent of the debtor is irrelevant.

16.2.2 Subrogation

As a rule, whether the debtor or a third party fulfils the obligation, the obligation is extinguished. However, in cases regulated by TCO art. 127, the fulfilment of the obligation by a third party satisfies the creditor, but the obligation is not extinguished, and the claim passes to the third party. This is referred to as subrogation.[5]

[3]Eren (2015), p. 924; Oğuzman and Öz (2015), p. 251; Tekinay et al. (1993), p. 767; Tercier et al. (2016), p. 327; Engel (1997), p. 611; Thévenoz and Werro (2012), art. 68, N. 1; von Tuhr and Escher (1974), § 59, I, p. 24; Becker (1941), art. 68, N. 4.

[4]Serozan (2014), p. 23; Oğuzman and Öz (2015), p. 251.

[5]See Sect. 24.2.

References

Aybay A (2011) Borçlar hukuku dersleri genel bölüm. Filiz, İstanbul
Becker H (1941) Kommentar zum Schweizerischen Zivilgesetzbuch, vol VI, Obligationenrecht, 1. Abteilung: Allgemeine Bestimmungen, Art. 1-183. Stämpfli, Bern
Berger B (2012) Allgemeines Schuldrecht. Stämpfli, Bern
Engel P (1997) Traité des obligations en droit Suisse. Stämpfli, Bern
Eren F (2015) Borçlar hukuku genel hükümler. Yetkin, Ankara
Feyzioğlu FN (1977) Borçlar hukuku genel hükümler, vol 2. Fakülteler, İstanbul
Gauch P, Schluep WR, Emmenegger S (2008) Schweizerisches Obligationenrecht, Allgemeiner Teil, vol 2. Schulthess, Zürich
Honsell H, Vogt NP, Wiegand W (eds) (2003) Basler Kommentar zum Schweizerischen Privatrecht, Obligationenrecht 1: Art. 1-529 OR. Helbing Lichtenhahn, Basel
Kılıçoğlu AM (2013) Borçlar hukuku genel hükümler. Turhan, İstanbul
Nomer HN (2015) Borçlar hukuku genel hükümler. Beta, İstanbul
Oğuzman K, Öz T (2015) Borçlar hukuku genel hükümler, vol 1. Vedat, İstanbul
Oser H, Schönenberger W (1929) Kommentar zum Schweizerischen Zivilgesetzbuch, Volume V: Das Obligationenrecht, Erster Halbband: Art. 1-183. Schulthess, Zürich
Reisoğlu S (2014) Türk borçlar hukuku genel hükümler. Beta, İstanbul
Schwenzer I (2009) Schweizerisches Obligationenrecht, Allgemeiner Teil. Schulthess, Bern
Serozan R (2014) Borçlar hukuku genel bölüm, vol 3 (Kocayusufpaşaoğlu/Hatemi/Serozan/Arpacı). Filiz, İstanbul
Tekinay SS, Akman S, Burcuoğlu H, Altop A (1993) Tekinay borçlar hukuku genel hükümler. Filiz, İstanbul
Tercier P (2004) Le droit des obligations. Schulthess, Zurich
Tercier P, Pichonnaz P, Develioğlu HM (2016) Borçlar hukuku genel hükümler. On iki levha, İstanbul
Thévenoz L, Werro F (éd) (2012) Commentaire romand code des obligations 1: art. 1-529 CO. Helbing Lichtenhahn, Bâle
von Tuhr A, Escher A (1974) Allgemeiner Teil des Schweizerischen Obligationenrecht, vol 2. Schulthess, Zürich

Chapter 17
Place of Performance

17.1 General[1]

A debtor must perform the obligation at the place determined for performance. If the debtor does not do so, the creditor may reject the performance. In that case, the debtor must bear the consequences of non-performance.[2] However, the creditor may also accept performance that is offered at a different place. In such a case, the obligation is deemed to be performed and, is thus, extinguished.[3]

As explained above, determining the place of performance is important. The place of performance may be determined by the law itself. For example, according to TCO art. 566, a bailed chattel must be returned at the place where it had been kept. However, this article is not mandatory; thus, the parties may change the place of performance.

Furthermore, the place of performance may be determined according to the nature of the transaction.[4] For example, dental treatment is generally performed in a dental surgery. However, the parties may amend the place of performance by agreeing that the dentist will come to the patient's house.

---

[1]Aybay (2011), pp. 119–120; Becker (1941), art. 74; Berger (2012), pp. 433–434; Engel (1997), pp. 629–632; Eren (2015), pp. 938–946; Feyzioğlu (1977), pp. 100–107; Gauch et al. (2008), pp. 14–19; Honsell et al. (2003), art. 74; Kılıçoğlu (2013), pp. 537–546; Nomer (2015), pp. 292–294; Oser and Schönenberger (1929), art. 74; Oğuzman and Öz (2015), pp. 320–324; Reisoğlu (2014), pp. 326–328; Schwenzer (2009), pp. 42–46; Serozan (2014), pp. 40–51; Tekinay et al. (1993), pp. 807–811; Tercier (2004), pp. 194–196; Tercier et al. (2016), pp. 338–340; Thévenoz and Werro (2012), art. 74, and von Tuhr and Escher (1974), pp. 39–44.

[2]Reisoğlu (2014), p. 326; Tekinay et al. (1993), pp. 807–808.

[3]Oğuzman and Öz (2015), p. 320.

[4]Eren (2015), p. 941; Serozan (2014), p. 43; Engel (1997), p. 629; Thévenoz and Werro (2012), art. 74, N. 5; Oser and Schönenberger (1929), art. 74, N. 6.

İ. Helvacı, *Turkish Contract Law*, DOI 10.1007/978-3-319-60061-1_17

Nevertheless, in certain cases, the place of performance may not be amended.[5] For instance, if a debtor undertakes to look for oil on land belonging to the creditor, the debtor, obviously, must carry out this exploration on the creditor's land.

It is evident that if a place is not mandatorily determined by law itself as the place of performance or is not the unique place for the performance of the obligation, the parties may simply specify the place of performance.

17.2 Default Rules

Apart from the above-mentioned cases, the place of performance will be determined according to TCO art. 89. This article clearly states that the parties may determine the place of performance in a manner that is express or implied. However, where the parties do not determine the place of performance, the following rules will be applied: (1) pecuniary obligations are to be paid at the creditor's place of residence at the time of payment; (2) obligations relating to specific objects are to be performed—that is to say, the specific objects are to be delivered—where the object was located when the contract was formed; (3) other obligations are to be performed at the debtor's place of residence where these obligations originated.

It should be noted that in order for TCO art. 89 par. 1 subcl. 2 to apply in cases where the specific object of an obligation is located at a place other than the debtor's place of residence, the parties must be aware of this fact.[6] For example, an American seller whose place of residence is Istanbul sells a machine, which is in Washington, D.C., to a Turkish buyer who lives in Istanbul. They negotiate and agree on the essential elements of the contract. However, they do not determine the place of performance. The American seller, according to TCO art. 89 par. 1 subcl. 2, claims that delivery of the machine must take place in Washington as it was located there when the contract was concluded. If the buyer did not know that the machine was in Washington, he may require that the machine be delivered to the seller's place of residence at the time that the obligation originated.

The creditor of an obligation, which is to be performed at his place of residence, may change this place after the obligation originates. Consequently, the performance of the obligation may become excessively difficult. In such a case, the debtor may perform the obligation at the creditor's original place of residence (TCO art. 89 par. 2).

---

[5]Tekinay et al. (1993), p. 808.

[6]von Tuhr and Escher (1974), § 61, II, p. 42; Oser and Schönenberger (1929), art. 74, N. 16; Serozan (2014), p. 43; Oğuzman and Öz (2015), p. 322, compare to Nomer (2015), p. 293.

References

Aybay A (2011) Borçlar hukuku dersleri genel bölüm. Filiz, İstanbul
Becker H (1941) Kommentar zum Schweizerischen Zivilgesetzbuch, vol VI, Obligationenrecht, 1. Abteilung: Allgemeine Bestimmungen, Art. 1-183. Stämpfli, Bern
Berger B (2012) Allgemeines Schuldrecht. Stämpfli, Bern
Engel P (1997) Traité des obligations en droit Suisse. Stämpfli, Bern
Eren F (2015) Borçlar hukuku genel hükümler. Yetkin, Ankara
Feyzioğlu FN (1977) Borçlar hukuku genel hükümler, vol 2. Fakülteler, İstanbul
Gauch P, Schluep WR, Emmenegger S (2008) Schweizerisches Obligationenrecht, Allgemeiner Teil, vol 2. Schulthess, Zürich
Honsell H, Vogt NP, Wiegand W (eds) (2003) Basler Kommentar zum Schweizerischen Privatrecht, Obligationenrecht 1: Art. 1-529 OR. Helbing Lichtenhahn, Basel
Kılıçoğlu AM (2013) Borçlar hukuku genel hükümler. Turhan, İstanbul
Nomer HN (2015) Borçlar hukuku genel hükümler. Beta, İstanbul
Oğuzman K, Öz T (2015) Borçlar hukuku genel hükümler, vol 1. Vedat, İstanbul
Oser H, Schönenberger W (1929) Kommentar zum Schweizerischen Zivilgesetzbuch, vol V: Das Obligationenrecht, Erster Halbband: Art. 1-183. Schulthess, Zürich
Reisoğlu S (2014) Türk borçlar hukuku genel hükümler. Beta, İstanbul
Schwenzer I (2009) Schweizerisches Obligationenrecht, Allgemeiner Teil. Schulthess, Bern
Serozan R (2014) Borçlar hukuku genel bölüm, vol 3 (Kocayusufpaşaoğlu/Hatemi/Serozan/Arpacı). Filiz, İstanbul
Tekinay SS, Akman S, Burcuoğlu H, Altop A (1993) Tekinay borçlar hukuku genel hükümler. Filiz, İstanbul
Tercier P (2004) Le droit des obligations. Schulthess, Zurich
Tercier P, Pichonnaz P, Develioğlu HM (2016) Borçlar hukuku genel hükümler. On iki levha, İstanbul
Thévenoz L, Werro F (éd) (2012) Commentaire romand code des obligations 1: art. 1-529 CO. Helbing Lichtenhahn, Bâle
von Tuhr A, Escher A (1974) Allgemeiner Teil des Schweizerischen Obligationenrecht, vol 2. Schulthess, Zürich

Chapter 18
Time of Performance

18.1 Obligation Without a Time Limit[1]

If the time of performance is not determined either by the parties' agreement, by the nature of the legal transaction or by the law itself, the obligation falls due immediately (TCO art. 90). Accordingly, if the obligation may be performed immediately, then immediate performance may be demanded.

18.2 Obligation with a Time Limit

The parties may specify the time of performance in the contract.[2] For example, in a work contract relating to the installation of windows in a house, the parties may determine the due date as nine months after the formation of the contract.

The parties may agree that the creditor will determine the time when the obligation falls due.[3] That is to say, they may agree on a maturity clause. In that case, the creditor is able to determine the time of performance. Moreover, the law itself may grant this right to

[1]Aybay (2011), pp. 121–125; Becker (1941), art. 75–83; Berger (2012), pp. 434–438; Engel (1997), pp. 623–628, 655–660; Eren (2015), pp. 946–957, 985–1001; Feyzioğlu (1977), pp. 108–138; Gauch et al. (2008), pp. 20–31; Honsell et al. (2003), art. 75–83; Kılıçoğlu (2013), pp. 546–559, 597–603; Nomer (2015), pp. 294–302; Oser and Schönenberger (1929), art. 75–83; Oğuzman and Öz (2015), pp. 310–320, 330–349; Reisoğlu (2014), pp. 328–335; Schwenzer (2009), pp. 46–48, 445–448; Serozan (2014), pp. 51–76; Tekinay et al. (1993), pp. 800–807, 825–837; Tercier (2004), pp. 191–194; Tercier et al. (2016), pp. 333 337; Thévenoz and Werro (2012), art. 75–83, and von Tuhr and Escher (1974), pp. 44–69. For further explanations see Yüce (2015).

[2]Thévenoz and Werro (2012), art. 75, N. 7; Tercier (2004), p. 194; Berger (2012), p. 434; Reisoğlu (2014), p. 329; Oğuzman and Öz (2015), p. 314.

[3]Thévenoz and Werro (2012), art. 75, N. 7; Serozan (2014), p. 57; Oğuzman and Öz (2015), p. 316; Feyzioğlu (1977), p. 110.

İ. Helvacı, *Turkish Contract Law*, DOI 10.1007/978-3-319-60061-1_18

the creditor. For example, TCO art. 392 states that in the absence of any stipulation for the repayment of a loan on a certain day or after a period of notice or on demand, the lender has the right to determine the time of performance. However, the borrower may not be required to repay the loan prior to the expiration of 6 weeks after the lender's first demand.

Also, the time of performance may be determined by the nature of the transaction.[4] For example, in a work contract for the design of a website, in the event that the parties fail to fix a time of performance, the nature of the legal transaction will imply a time of performance. This is because it is assumed that the contractor will require a reasonable period of time for the completion of the website.

Moreover, the law itself may determine the time of performance. For instance, TCO art. 314 states that unless otherwise agreed or unless local custom requires it, the lessee must pay the rent and, if necessary, ancillary charges at the end of each month and, at the latest, at the end of the rental period. Another example: TCO art. 406 par. 1 sent. 1 states that unless custom requires otherwise, the employer must pay the employee's salary at the end of each month.

If the time of performance is determined either by the parties, the nature of the legal transaction or the law itself, the creditor may not demand the performance of the obligation before it falls due. However, the debtor, as a rule, may perform the obligation before the due date. It should be noted that the parties may agree that the debtor cannot perform the obligation before the due date. Furthermore, this may be inferred from the nature of the contract or the circumstances (TCO art. 96 sent. 1). Indeed, in certain cases, the time limit is not only for the advantage of the debtor but also for the advantage of the creditor.[5] For example, in a work contract for the manufacture of certain furniture, the parties determine the due date as 3 months after the formation of the contract as the manufacturer requires time to complete the work. In addition, the customer also needs such a time limit to rent a store in which he will display and sell the furniture to be manufactured. In this case, it is obvious that the party ordering the work (the customer) may not demand performance before it falls due. Further, even if the contractor completes the manufacture of the furniture and wishes to give delivery before the date specified in the contract, he is not entitled to demand that the customer accept this early performance.

18.3 Calculation of the Time Limit

18.3.1 Monthly Term

Where the parties determine the beginning or the end of the month as the time of performance, these terms mean the first or last day of the month, respectively. Where the time limit is fixed as the middle of the month, the date is deemed to be the 15th day of the month (TCO art. 91 par. 1).

---

[4]Engel (1997), p. 625; Berger (2012), p. 434; Gauch et al. (2008), p. 23; Becker (1941), art. 75, N. 3; Eren (2015), p. 950; Tercier et al. (2016), p. 335; Oğuzman and Öz (2015), p. 315.

[5]Feyzioğlu (1977), p. 119; Oğuzman and Öz (2015), p. 312; Engel (1997), p. 628.

If the parties stipulate a month without specifying a certain day for performance of the obligation, the date is deemed to be the last day of that month (TCO art. 91 par. 2).

18.3.2 Other Time Limits

Where an obligation or any other responsibility is to be performed within a certain period after the conclusion of the contract, the following rules set out under TCO art. 92 par. 1 will apply.

If the time limit is fixed by days, the obligation falls due on the last day of the period. This period does not include the date on which the contract was formed. If the agreed time limit is specified as 8 or 15 days, it should not be interpreted as 1 week or 2 weeks; on the contrary, it should be interpreted exactly as it is, excluding the date of formation (subcl. 1).

If the time limit is fixed by weeks, the obligation is due on the day of the last week that corresponds to the day when the contract was formed (subcl. 2).

If the time limit is fixed by months or a period including several months such as a year, a half-year or a quarter-year, the obligation falls due in the last month of the period, on the date that corresponds to the date when the contract was formed. If there is no such corresponding day in the final month, the obligation is deemed to be due on the last day of that month (subcl. 3). For example, a contract is entered into on 31 January 2016. The parties fix a one-month time limit after the formation of the contract. In 2016, the month of February has 29 days. Therefore, the obligation falls due on the last day of February 2016—*i.e.*, 29 February.

The period of half a month is deemed to be understood as 15 days. When the time limit is determined as one or more months plus half a month, this period is determined by adding 15 days to the last month (subcl. 4). For example, in a contract entered into on 20 March, the parties fix a time limit of one and a half months. In this case, the obligation falls due on 5 May.

These rules also apply to cases where the time limit runs from a date other than that of the contract's formation (TCO art. 92 par. 2).

When a certain period is specified for the debtor to perform an obligation, the debtor must perform it before the period expires (TCO art. 92 par. 3).

18.3.3 Holidays and Performance During Working Hours

Where the time of performance or the last day of a time limit corresponds with a legally recognised holiday,[6] the time of performance or the last day of the time limit

[6]National and General Holidays Act, No 2429, 17.03.1981 (Official Gazette 19.03.1981; No: 17284).

will automatically extend to the first working day after the holiday (TCO art. 93 par. 1). This rule is not mandatory; thus, the parties may agree to the contrary (TCO art. 93 par. 2).

The performance of the obligation must be carried out and must be accepted during normal working hours (TCO art. 94). This is a default rule, and thus, the parties may agree to the contrary. For example, a concert pianist may undertake to give a recital outside of normal working hours—*e.g.*, at 9 pm.

18.3.4 Extension of the Time Limit

The parties may extend the time limit. In such a case, the new time limit begins on the first day after the expiration of the former time limit (TCO art. 95). For example, the parties determine the time limit as 5 January. If they extend this time limit for 4 days, the revised time limit will be 9 January. However, if the parties extend this time limit for a month, the revised time limit will end on 6 February. TCO art. 95 is not mandatory, and thus, the parties may agree to the contrary.

18.3.5 Early (Premature) Performance

As mentioned above, a creditor may not demand the performance of an obligation before it falls due, but a debtor, as a rule, may perform an obligation before the due date. This is because, pursuant to TCO art. 96 sent. 1, unless the terms or nature of the contract or the circumstances indicate that the parties intended otherwise, the debtor is entitled to perform the obligation before the due date.

The time limit is usually to the advantage of the debtor, and generally, the debtor will not wish to perform the obligation before it falls due. However, exceptionally, a debtor may perform the obligation before it is due. In this case, the creditor, as a rule, must accept this early performance. Nevertheless, the debtor is not entitled to a discount unless the law, the contract or custom requires it (TCO art. 96 sent. 2). For instance, in a loan contract, the borrower may not expect any discount due to early repayment.

It should be noted that in certain cases, the time limit is intended to be to the advantage of both parties. In such a case, the debtor may not perform the obligation before it falls due and the creditor does not have to accept early performance.[7]

---

[7]See mentioned example following footnote 5.

18.4 Performance of Bilateral Contracts

18.4.1 Determination of the Performance Order

A bilateral (synallagmatic) contract is a contract formed by the exchange of mutual or reciprocal promises between the parties.[8] For example, in a sale contract, the seller must transfer ownership of the goods sold to the buyer and the buyer must pay the price of the goods in return.

In a bilateral contract, the parties, the law, the nature of the transaction or custom may determine the order of performance.[9] For example, in a sale contract, the parties agree that first the seller transfers ownership of the goods sold and then the buyer pays the price, which is the consideration. In such a case, the seller is not entitled to claim payment without transferring ownership of the goods. Another example relating to the order of performance is regulated by TCO art. 406 par. 1, according to which, unless custom requires otherwise, an employer must pay his employee's salary at the end of each month.

As mentioned above, the order of performance may be determined by the nature of the transaction.[10] For example, in the case of services rendered by a public utility such as those supplying water, electricity and natural gas, first, the service provider renders these services to consumers and then the consumers pay for them. It is obvious that the price of the services is proportionate to their usage.[11]

The order of performance may also be determined by custom.[12] For instance, in a self-service restaurant, customers pay the price of the food in advance. However, in other types of restaurant, the customers pay for the meals after they have finished their meal.[13]

18.4.2 Uncertainty of the Performance Order

18.4.2.1 Simultaneous Performance

In a bilateral contract, it is possible that the order of performance is not determined. In such a case, neither party must perform his obligation in advance of the other. That is to say, the parties' reciprocal obligations must be performed simultaneously. For example, in a contract of sale, according to TCO art. 207 par. 2, unless

[8]Tercier (2004), p. 59; Engel (1997), p. 655; Becker (1941), art. 82, N. 7.

[9]Reisoğlu (2014), p. 332; Nomer (2015), p. 298; Oğuzman and Öz (2015), p. 333.

[10]Oğuzman and Öz (2015), p. 333; Tekinay et al. (1993), p. 827.

[11]Reisoğlu (2014), p. 332; Oğuzman and Öz (2015), p. 333.

[12]von Tuhr and Escher (1974), § 64, I, p. 58.

[13]Oğuzman and Öz (2015), p. 334.

otherwise provided by the agreement or by custom, transfer of the ownership of the property and payment must be made simultaneously.

It should be noted that this rule relating to simultaneous performance will readily apply if the places of the mutual obligations' performance are the same. However, if these places are different, the application of this rule becomes difficult. That is why, in such a case, one of the parties may have to perform his obligation in advance of the other.[14]

18.4.2.2 *Exceptio non Adimpleti Contractus*

In a bilateral contract, if the performance order is not determined, the party who claims that the counter-party's obligation must be performed should first perform his own obligation or offer to do so (TCO art. 97). Otherwise, the counter-party may raise the fact that the claimant party has not performed his own obligation or offered its performance (*exceptio non adimpleti contractus*).[15]

Exceptio non adimpleti contractus is a dilatory defence.[16] It can be raised, as a rule, in bilateral contracts and only applies to reciprocal primary obligations.[17] This defence allows the defendant to withhold his own performance and gives him a right to ward off a claim for performance until the claimant has duly performed or offered to perform his obligation.[18]

It should be noted that this kind of defence may not be taken into consideration by the judge *ex officio*.[19] Therefore, if the defendant intends to ward off a claim for performance, he must raise this defence. For the defendant to raise this defence: (1) there must be a bilateral contract, (2) the reciprocal obligations must not be extinguished, (3) the reciprocal obligations must be simultaneously performed; (4) the reciprocal obligations must have fallen due and (5) the claimant must not have performed or offered to perform his obligation.[20]

The defence of *exceptio non adimpleti contractus* may be applied by analogy to imperfect bilateral contracts.[21] For example, in an agency contract, without remuneration, related to a sale agreement, the (indirect) agent may become the owner of the goods. In such a case, the latter must transfer ownership of the property to the principal (TCO art. 508 par. 1). Even if the principal is not obliged to pay any

---

[14]von Tuhr and Escher (1974), § 64, II, pp. 58–59; Oğuzman and Öz (2015), p. 334.

[15]For further explanations see Kaneti (1962).

[16]von Tuhr and Escher (1974), § 64, IV, p. 61; Berger (2012), p. 436; Engel (1997), p. 656; Thévenoz and Werro (2012), art. 82, N. 3.

[17]Feyzioğlu (1977), p. 134; Oğuzman and Öz (2015), p. 339; Thévenoz and Werro (2012), art. 82, N. 5.

[18]Eren (2015), p. 986.

[19]Eren (2015), p. 986; Tekinay et al. (1993), p. 827.

[20]Kaneti (1962), p. 46 *ff.*

[21]Tercier et al. (2016), p. 336; Thévenoz and Werro (2012), art. 82, N. 9.

remuneration, he must pay the price of the sold goods, the expenses and advances, with interest, paid by the agent (TCO art. 510 par. 1). As has been seen, the legal relationship between the obligations of the agent and the principal is similar to the relationship between the obligation and its equivalent in a bilateral contract. Therefore, if the principal demands that the agent transfer ownership of the goods sold to him without performing or offering to perform his obligations, the agent may raise the defence of *exceptio non adimpleti contractus*.[22]

Moreover, the defence of *exceptio non adimpleti contractus* may also be applied, by analogy, to obligations arising from the invalidity or rescission of a bilateral contract.[23] For instance, in a contract of sale relating to immovable property that is invalid due to the lack of form, the seller transfers possession of the immovable property to the buyer and the buyer pays its price in return. However, the seller does not transfer ownership of the property to the buyer. In such a case, the seller must reimburse the paid amount and the buyer must return possession of the immovable property.[24] As has been seen, the relationship between the parties' obligations is similar to the reciprocal obligations arising from a bilateral contract. Therefore, if the seller demands that the buyer transfer possession of the immovable property without performing or offering to perform his obligation related to the reimbursement, the buyer may raise the defence of *exceptio non adimpleti contractus*.[25] The Turkish Court of Cassation, in its decisions, accepts this approach as raised by scholars.[26]

In brief, when the defendant raises the *exceptio non adimpleti contractus*, the counter-party will have to offer to perform or will have to perform his obligation. Unless he does so, the defendant may withhold the performance of his own obligation. It is obvious that this defence provides a kind of security by allowing the defendant to withhold his own performance until the other party duly performs the obligation or offers its performance.

18.4.3 One Party's Insolvency

In a bilateral contract, the party who has to perform the obligation later may become insolvent after the conclusion of the contract. Clearly, this fact may jeopardise the party who is required to perform his own obligation first. That is why the legislature has aimed to protect the first performer and enacted TCO art. 98. According to this article, in a bilateral contract, if one party's claim is jeopardised by the counter-party's

---

[22]Kaneti (1962), pp. 85–86.

[23]Feyzioğlu (1977), p. 137; Thévenoz and Werro (2012), art. 82, N. 5; Kaneti (1962), pp. 86–87.

[24]See and compare to Sect. 3.5.

[25]Kaneti (1962), pp. 86–87.

[26]Kaneti (1962), p. 99 *ff*; Decision to Unify the Jurisprudence of the Turkish Court of Cassation, 10.07.1940, File No: 1939/2, Decision No: 1940/77 (Official Gazette 01.02.1941; No: 4723). In this decision, the Court of Cassation seems to apply this defence without analogy.

insolvency and, in particular, as a result of bankruptcy or an unsuccessful execution, then the jeopardised party may withhold performance until the insolvent party's prospective performance has been secured (TCO art. 98 par. 1). Moreover, the party whose rights are jeopardised may withdraw from the contract (*ex tunc*)[27] unless his claim for security is satisfied within a reasonable time (TCO art. 98 par. 2).

It is worth noting that if the debtor was insolvent at the time of the formation of the contract and the counter-party was not aware of this fact, then he may rescind the contract provided that the conditions of material mistake or fraud[28] are satisfied.[29]

TCO art. 98 does not explicitly state that the jeopardised party must perform his own obligation first. However, if the jeopardised party does not have to perform his obligation first, then he may simply raise the defence of *exceptio non adimpleti contractus*, without referring to TCO art. 98. That is why the rights regulated by TCO art. 98 are especially important in cases where the jeopardised party must perform the obligation first.[30]

TCO art. 98 gives three rights to the party whose rights are jeopardised: (1) he may withhold performance until the necessary security is provided. This defence arising from the said article must be raised by the jeopardised party. The judge may not take it into consideration *ex officio*. When the necessary securities such as a mortgage or suretyship are provided, the defendant may no longer withhold performance. (2) He may demand that the debtor provide security for performance. In this case, he should grant a reasonable time to the debtor. These securities may be provided either directly by the debtor or by third parties. For example, a mortgage or a pledge may be provided. Furthermore, a suretyship or a guarantee may be provided by a third party. (3) He may withdraw from the contract (*ex tunc*) if the necessary security is not provided within a reasonable time.[31] If there is a continuing contract between the parties, according to TCO art. 126 applied by analogy, the debtor may terminate the contract (*ex nunc*)[32] instead of withdrawing from it.

It should be noted that there are certain specific rules in the Turkish Code of Obligations that are similar to art. 98. For instance, according to art. 332, if a lessee becomes bankrupt, then the lessor may demand security for the rents that will fall due in the future. With this objective, the lessor grants a reasonable period of time to the lessee and to the bankrupt's estate. If the necessary security is not provided within that period, the lessor is entitled to terminate the contract immediately. Another example is TCO art. 436, according to which if an employer becomes

---

[27]Termination of the contract takes effect retroactively (*résolution*, *Rücktritt*).

[28]Thévenoz and Werro (2012), art. 83, N. 7.

[29]See Chap. 11.

[30]Oğuzman and Öz (2015), p. 346; Serozan (2014), pp. 65–66.

[31]The jeopardised party is not entitled to bring an action in order for the necessary securities to be provided. Consequently if security is not offered voluntarily by the debtor then the only option for the claimant is to withdraw from the contract.

[32]Termination of the contract takes effect prospectively (*résiliation*, *Kündigung*).

insolvent, then the employee may immediately terminate the employment contract unless the employer provides the necessary securities within a reasonable time with respect to the employee's rights arising from the contract, such as wages. These specific rules override TCO art. 98, which is a general rule (*lex specialis derogat legi generali*).[33]

References

Aybay A (2011) Borçlar hukuku dersleri genel bölüm. Filiz, İstanbul
Becker H (1941) Kommentar zum Schweizerischen Zivilgesetzbuch, vol VI, Obligationenrecht, 1. Abteilung: Allgemeine Bestimmungen, Art. 1-183. Stämpfli, Bern
Berger B (2012) Allgemeines Schuldrecht. Stämpfli, Bern
Engel P (1997) Traité des obligations en droit Suisse. Stämpfli, Bern
Eren F (2015) Borçlar hukuku genel hükümler. Yetkin, Ankara
Feyzioğlu FN (1977) Borçlar hukuku genel hükümler, vol 2. Fakülteler, İstanbul
Gauch P, Schluep W R, Emmenegger S (2008) Schweizerisches Obligationenrecht, Allgemeiner Teil, vol 2. Schulthess, Zürich
Honsell H, Vogt NP, Wiegand W (eds) (2003) Basler Kommentar zum Schweizerischen Privatrecht, Obligationenrecht 1: Art. 1-529 OR. Helbing Lichtenhahn, Basel
Kaneti S (1962) Akdin ifa edilmediği def'i. İstanbul üniversitesi hukuk fakültesi, İstanbul
Kılıçoğlu AM (2013) Borçlar hukuku genel hükümler. Turhan, İstanbul
Nomer HN (2015) Borçlar hukuku genel hükümler. Beta, İstanbul
Oğuzman K, Öz T (2015) Borçlar hukuku genel hükümler, vol 1. Vedat, İstanbul
Oser H, Schönenberger W (1929) Kommentar zum Schweizerischen Zivilgesetzbuch, Volume V: Das Obligationenrecht, Erster Halbband: Art. 1-183. Schulthess, Zürich
Reisoğlu S (2014) Türk borçlar hukuku genel hükümler. Beta, İstanbul
Schwenzer I (2009) Schweizerisches Obligationenrecht, Allgemeiner Teil. Schulthess, Bern
Serozan R (2014) Borçlar hukuku genel bölüm, vol 3 (Kocayusufpaşaoğlu/Hatemi/Serozan/Arpacı). Filiz, İstanbul
Tekinay SS, Akman S, Burcuoğlu H, Altop A (1993) Tekinay borçlar hukuku genel hükümler. Filiz, İstanbul
Tercier P (2004) Le droit des obligations. Schulthess, Zurich
Tercier P, Pichonnaz P, Develioğlu HM (2016) Borçlar hukuku genel hükümler. On iki levha, İstanbul
Thévenoz L, Werro F (éd) (2012) Commentaire romand code des obligations 1: art. 1-529 CO. Helbing Lichtenhahn, Bâle
von Tuhr A, Escher A (1974) Allgemeiner Teil des Schweizerischen Obligationenrecht, vol 2. Schulthess, Zürich
Yüce MB (2015) Alacaklı ve borçlu açısından ifa zamanı. Vedat, İstanbul

[33]Oğuzman and Öz (2015), p. 346 fn. 345.

Chapter 19
Proof of Performance

19.1 General[1]

The Turkish Code of Obligations sets out three specific provisions relating to proof of performance of pecuniary obligations. However, these specific provisions are also applicable to other types of obligation.[2]

19.2 Forms of Proof

19.2.1 A Receipt

A debtor who fulfils his obligation either partially or entirely is entitled to request a receipt (TCO art. 103 par. 1). If the debtor requests a receipt during the course of fulfilling the obligation but the creditor does not agree to this request, the debtor may abstain from performing the obligation. Further, in this case, the creditor is deemed to be in default and the debtor may exercise his rights as regulated by the provisions relating to the creditor's default (TCO art. 107 *ff*).[3]

[1]Aybay (2011), pp. 125–126; Becker (1941), art. 88–90; Berger (2012), pp. 438–439; Engel (1997), pp. 650–654; Eren (2015), pp. 1002–1009; Feyzioğlu (1977), pp. 75–82; Gauch et al. (2008), pp. 57–60; Honsell et al. (2003), art. 88–90; Kılıçoğlu (2013), pp. 631–636; Nomer (2015), pp. 290–292; Oser and Schönenberger (1929), art. 88–90; Oğuzman and Öz (2015), pp. 324–330; Reisoğlu (2014), pp. 323–325; Schwenzer (2009), pp. 504–505; Serozan (2014), pp. 119–123; Tekinay et al. (1993), pp. 818–825; Tercier (2004), p. 251; Tercier et al. (2016), p. 437; Thévenoz and Werro (2012), art. 88–90, and von Tuhr and Escher (1974), pp. 32–39.

[2]Thévenoz and Werro (2012), art. 88, N. 2; Engel (1997), p. 650; Eren (2015), p. 1003; Oğuzman and Öz (2015), pp. 324–325; Serozan (2014), p. 119.

[3]See Chap. 20.

İ. Helvacı, *Turkish Contract Law*, DOI 10.1007/978-3-319-60061-1_19

19.2.2 Return of a Document Acknowledging the Debt

In certain cases, a debtor might give a document to the creditor acknowledging the debt. In such a case, where the debtor fulfils the entire debt, he is entitled to demand the return of this document or its cancellation (TCO art. 103 par. 1). However, if the debtor does not fulfil the entire debt or the document acknowledging the debt grants other rights to the creditor, the debtor may only demand a receipt and the record of the payment on such a document (TCO art. 103 par. 2).

19.2.3 Cancellation of the Document Acknowledging the Debt

Although the debtor is entitled to demand the return of the document acknowledging the debt, the document might be lost. If the creditor asserts that the document is lost, the debtor may demand that the creditor declare, by an authenticated or duly legalised deed, that the lost document is cancelled and the debt is extinguished (TCO art. 105 par. 1). In this case, these transactions are carried out by a notary public.

The provisions relating to the cancellation of lost negotiable instruments are reserved (TCO art. 105 par. 2). Indeed, the specific provisions of the Turkish Commercial Code require a court decision.

19.3 Presumptions of Performance

If the creditor returns the document acknowledging the debt to the debtor, the debt that is stated on it is presumed to be performed (TCO art. 104 par. 3). However, if the creditor proves the contrary, this presumption is refuted. For instance, the creditor might give the document to the debtor because it has been superseded by a new document.[4]

If a creditor gives a receipt for the principal (capital), he is presumed to have received the interest on it (TCO art. 104 par. 2).

In certain cases, there may be periodical acts (prestations). For example, in a lease contract, in a loan agreement with interest or in a sale by instalments, the obligations of the debtor are periodical. In such cases, if the creditor gives a receipt for a later payment, without reservation, then the previous payments that fall due are assumed to have been performed (TCO art. 104 par. 1). For instance in a one-year lease agreement, the lessee does not pay the rent for the first three months

[4]Oğuzman and Öz (2015), p. 328.

and then wishes to pay the rent for the fourth month, without paying the previous rents. In this case, if the lessor gives a receipt for the last month's rent, which is paid, without reserving his previous claims, then it is presumed that the previous rents were paid. It should be noted that the creditor may refute this presumption.

References

Aybay A (2011) Borçlar hukuku dersleri genel bölüm. Filiz, İstanbul

Becker H (1941) Kommentar zum Schweizerischen Zivilgesetzbuch, vol VI, Obligationenrecht, 1. Abteilung: Allgemeine Bestimmungen, Art. 1-183. Stämpfli, Bern

Berger B (2012) Allgemeines Schuldrecht. Stämpfli, Bern

Engel P (1997) Traité des obligations en droit Suisse. Stämpfli, Bern

Eren F (2015) Borçlar hukuku genel hükümler. Yetkin, Ankara

Feyzioğlu FN (1977) Borçlar hukuku genel hükümler, vol 2. Fakülteler, İstanbul

Gauch P, Schluep WR, Emmenegger S (2008) Schweizerisches Obligationenrecht, Allgemeiner Teil, vol 2. Schulthess, Zürich

Honsell H, Vogt NP, Wiegand W (eds) (2003) Basler Kommentar zum Schweizerischen Privatrecht, Obligationenrecht 1: Art. 1-529 OR. Helbing Lichtenhahn, Basel

Kılıçoğlu AM (2013) Borçlar hukuku genel hükümler. Turhan, İstanbul

Nomer HN (2015) Borçlar hukuku genel hükümler. Beta, İstanbul

Oğuzman K, Öz T (2015) Borçlar hukuku genel hükümler, vol 1. Vedat, İstanbul

Oser H, Schönenberger W (1929) Kommentar zum Schweizerischen Zivilgesetzbuch, vol V: Das Obligationenrecht, Erster Halbband: Art. 1-183. Schulthess, Zürich

Reisoğlu S (2014) Türk borçlar hukuku genel hükümler. Beta, İstanbul

Schwenzer I (2009) Schweizerisches Obligationenrecht, Allgemeiner Teil. Schulthess, Bern

Serozan R (2014) Borçlar hukuku genel bölüm, vol 3 (Kocayusufpaşaoğlu/Hatemi/Serozan/Arpacı). Filiz, İstanbul

Tekinay SS, Akman S, Burcuoğlu H, Altop A (1993) Tekinay borçlar hukuku genel hükümler. Filiz, İstanbul

Tercier P (2004) Le droit des obligations. Schulthess, Zurich

Tercier P, Pichonnaz P, Develioğlu HM (2016) Borçlar hukuku genel hükümler. On iki levha, İstanbul

Thévenoz L, Werro F (éd) (2012) Commentaire romand code des obligations 1: art. 1-529 CO. Helbing Lichtenhahn, Bâle

von Tuhr A, Escher A (1974) Allgemeiner Teil des Schweizerischen Obligationenrecht, vol 2. Schulthess, Zürich

Chapter 20
Default of the Creditor

20.1 General[1]

In certain cases, a debtor may fulfil an obligation without the participation of the creditor. In this context, for an obligation not to do, such as an obligation not to compete, the creditor's participation is not needed. In such a case, the default of the creditor is not in question.[2]

However, in certain cases, the debtor cannot fulfil the obligation without the participation of the creditor. Indeed, in obligations to do, the creditor's participation is often necessary. For instance, if the debtor is obliged to repair a machine in a factory belonging to the creditor, the latter must permit the debtor to enter the building. The participation of the creditor may also be needed for the performance of obligations to give. For example, in the transfer of ownership of movable property to the creditor, the participation of the creditor is indispensable.[3] In the event that the participation of the creditor is necessary for the performance of an obligation, his failure to cooperate constitutes the creditor's default (*mora creditoris*)[4] provided that the requirements, which will be examined below, are met.

[1]Aybay (2011), pp. 126–129; Becker (1941), Vorbemerkungen zu art. 91–96, art. 91–96; Berger (2012), pp. 440–449, 542–543; Engel (1997), pp. 661–668; Eren (2015), pp. 1010–1026; Feyzioğlu (1977), pp. 140–159; Gauch et al. (2008), pp. 60–68, 92–93; Honsell et al. (2003), Vorbemerkungen zu Art. 91–96, art. 91–96; Kılıçoğlu (2013), pp. 672–683; Nomer (2015), pp. 302–305; Oser and Schönenberger (1929), Vorbemerkungen zu Art. 91–96, art. 91–96; Oğuzman and Öz (2015), pp. 349–365; Reisoğlu (2014), pp. 336–343; Schwenzer (2009), pp. 481–490; Serozan (2014), pp. 142–162; Tekinay et al. (1993), pp. 837–850; Tercier (2004), pp. 250–255; Tercier et al. (2016), pp. 435–442; Thévenoz and Werro (2012), art. 91–96, and von Tuhr and Escher (1974), pp. 69–85. For further explanations see Koç (1992).

[2]Eren (2015), p. 1011; Oğuzman and Öz (2015), p. 350.

[3]See explanations made p. 120 and fn. 11.

[4]*Demeure du créancier, Verzug des Gläubigers.*

İ. Helvacı, *Turkish Contract Law*, DOI 10.1007/978-3-319-60061-1_20

20.2 Requirements

According to TCO art. 106 par.1, for a creditor to be in default, all of the following requirements must be met: (1) the debtor must propose the performance of the obligations to do or to give as required, (2) the creditor must refuse to accept it or fail to carry out any preparations that must be performed by him and (3) the refusal or the failure of the creditor must not be justifiable.

The creditor is deemed to have refused the properly offered performance only when the debtor has proposed the performance of the obligation and his proposition is in accord with the obligation in terms of place, time, quantity and quality. Indeed, if the debtor's proposition for fulfilment is not consistent with proper performance, then the creditor may simply refuse it.[5] Further, the proposition for proper fulfilment must be actual.[6] In principle, an oral proposition is not sufficient. However, if the creditor has already declared that he will not accept performance, then an oral proposal may be sufficient.[7]

The creditor is deemed to have failed to carry out preparations that must be performed by him only when[8] (1) the debtor has an obligation to give or to do and (2) the debtor needs the participation of the creditor for the performance of the obligation and (3) the creditor fails to provide such participation, for example, if a debtor is obliged to repair a machine in the factory of the creditor and the latter does not give permission to the debtor to enter the building. Another example, regarding alternative obligations, is when the creditor does not exercise his right of choice.[9]

The creditor must not have any justifiable reason for non-acceptance of performance or his failure to perform. In other words, if the creditor's non-acceptance or failure is justifiable, then he is not in default.[10] This can be illustrated by the following case. In the 'fixing a machine in a factory' example, the debtor wishes to fix the broken machine and his proposal for performance is consistent with the obligation. However, the creditor refuses the proposal as there is a strike in the factory. It is rather difficult for even the creditor to enter the factory because of the workers' industrial action. In such a case, the non-acceptance of the creditor is justifiable. It should be noted that for the creditor's default, his fault is not necessary.[11]

---

[5]Engel (1997), p. 663; von Tuhr and Escher (1974), § 65, II, 1, p. 70; Thévenoz and Werro (2012), art. 91, N. 14–16.

[6]Engel (1997), p. 663; von Tuhr and Escher (1974), § 65, II, 2, p. 70.

[7]Engel (1997), p. 663; Tekinay et al. (1993), p. 839; Oğuzman and Öz (2015), p. 352; Feyzioğlu (1977), p. 143; Nomer (2015), p. 302.

[8]Berger (2012), pp. 442–443.

[9]Engel (1997), p. 663; Berger (2012), p. 442.

[10]von Tuhr and Escher (1974), § 65, IV, p. 72; Berger (2012), pp. 441–442; Thévenoz and Werro (2012), art. 91, N. 11–13.

[11]Reisoğlu (2014), p. 338; Serozan (2014), p. 145.

If the creditor is in default against one of the joint and several debtors, he is deemed to be in default against the other joint and several debtors (TCO art. 106 par. 2).

20.3 Consequences

20.3.1 *General*

In principle, the obligation is not extinguished by the default of the creditor. However, in a surety contract, if the creditor is in default, the obligation will be extinguished solely due to this fact. Indeed, where the creditor refuses to accept the surety's proposal of payment, without just cause, the surety is released from his obligations (TCO art. 593 par. 2).

Furthermore, as a rule, the default of the creditor does not give rise to the creditor's liability. In other words, the creditor is not liable to pay any compensation.[12] However, in certain cases, the creditor's acceptance of the debtor's performance is not only a preliminary act but also an obligation with regard to the creditor.[13] For instance, in a sale contract relating to movable property, the buyer is obliged to accept the seller's performance; that is to say, the buyer must accept delivery of the goods (TCO art. 232 par. 1). Therefore, in this case, if the buyer does not accept the seller's performance, then the buyer fails to fulfil his obligation. Thus, the seller may rely on the provisions relating to either the creditor's default or non-performance of the obligation.[14]

20.3.2 *In Obligations Relating to Delivery*

20.3.2.1 Right of Deposit

If the debtor is obliged to deliver movable property to the creditor and the latter is in default, then the debtor is entitled to perform his obligation by depositing the movable property at a specific place at the creditor's risk and expense (TCO art. 107 par. 1). Pursuant to TCO art. 107 par. 2 sent. 1, the place of deposit is determined by a court whose jurisdiction includes the place where the obligation is to be performed. The court is not required to consider whether the debtor has the

[12]Eren (2015), p. 1017; Thévenoz and Werro (2012), art. 91, N. 2; Engel (1997), p. 665; von Tuhr and Escher (1974), § 65, V, p. 73.

[13]Thévenoz and Werro (2012), art. 91, N. 2, fn. 2.

[14]Oğuzman and Öz (2015), p. 355; Nomer (2015), p. 302, compare to Serozan (2014), pp. 146–147.

right of deposit; it has only to determine the place of deposit. Further, commercial goods may be deposited in a warehouse without the decision of a judge (TCO art. 107 par. 2 sent. 2).

When the debtor deposits the object of the performance, he makes an agreement of bailment with the bailee, and this contract must be made for the benefit of the creditor in accordance with TCO art. 129.[15] When the debtor deposits the object of the performance, he is discharged from his obligation. Consequently, the securities that are ancillary to the claim, such as a surety, a pledge or a mortgage, will also be extinguished.

20.3.2.2 Right of Taking Back Deposited Objects

Unless the creditor declares that he accepts the deposited object or unless the deposit of the object gives rise to the redemption of a pledge, the debtor is entitled to take back the deposited object (TCO art. 109 par. 1). In the event that the debtor exercises his right to take back the deposited object, the claim stands with all ancillary rights (TCO art. 109 par. 2). In this regard, the deposit is distinct from the performance of the obligation. That is to say, a deposit may be revocable, but the performance of an obligation is irrevocable in nature.[16]

20.3.2.3 Right of Sale

The characteristics of the object of the contract or the nature of the transaction may preclude the deposit of the object; the object may be perishable (*e.g.*, milk, meat, fresh vegetables, etc.) or its maintenance, protection or deposit may require substantial expense.[17] For instance, where the object of a sale contract is a circus animal such as a tiger, an elephant or a lion, their maintenance or deposit requires substantial expense. In such cases, after a warning, the debtor may deposit the sale proceeds.

The sale of the object, as a rule, can only take place with the permission of a judge and by public auction (TCO art. 108 par. 1). The judge must consider whether or not the conditions of the creditor's default have been fulfilled, the necessity of the sale and the presence of a warning. The judge's order for sale does not resolve the dispute relating to the creditor's default and is not binding for any future court that will settle the case.[18]

---

[15]See. Sect. 24.4.

[16]Oğuzman and Öz (2015), p. 359.

[17]Engel (1997), p. 667.

[18]von Tuhr and Escher (1974), § 66, II, p. 83 fn. 62; Oğuzman and Öz (2015), p. 361.

Where the object to be delivered is quoted on the stock exchange or has a market price or has a small value in proportion to the expense of selling it at auction, the judge may permit an ordinary sale. Moreover, the judge may permit the sale without requiring a previous notification to have been made (TCO art. 108 par. 2).

The debtor, after the deposit of the sale price, is released from his obligation. However, according to TCO art. 109 par. 1, it is possible for the debtor to revoke this deposit. If the debtor revokes this deposit, it is reasonable to accept that his obligation to give becomes an obligation to pay the sale proceeds.[19]

20.3.3 In Other Obligations

In the case of obligations other than those concerning the delivery of objects, such as in obligations to do, if the creditor falls into default, the debtor may withdraw from the contract (*ex tunc*)[20] according to the provisions relating to the debtor's default.[21]

As a rule, the debtor must grant a reasonable period of time to the creditor for the acceptance of the performance or the fulfilment of any preliminary stages of performance. Furthermore, the debtor may demand that the court determine this period of time (TCO art. 123). If the creditor does not meet these demands, the debtor may withdraw from the contract (*ex tunc*) by immediate notification to the creditor (TCO art. 125 par. 2).

In cases that are regulated by TCO art. 124, the debtor does not have to grant a period of time to the creditor. For instance, where the creditor's conduct indicates that granting such a period of time would be useless, the debtor may withdraw from the contract (*ex tunc*) without granting such a period.

It should be noted that certain scholars accept that, as a rule, the withdrawing debtor is not entitled to demand compensation for his negative damage.[22] Certain other scholars argue that the defaulting creditor must pay damages to the debtor for his negative damage.[23]

Furthermore, if there is a continuing contract between the parties, according to TCO art. 126 applied by analogy, the debtor may terminate the contract (*ex nunc*)[24] instead of withdrawing from it.

---

[19]Oğuzman and Öz (2015), p. 361.

[20]Termination of the contract takes effect retroactively (*résolution, Rücktritt*).

[21]See Sect. 23.4.2.

[22]Oğuzman and Öz (2015), p. 362; Serozan (2014), p. 151.

[23]See Tekinay et al. (1993), p. 846; Eren (2015), pp. 1025–1026; von Tuhr and Escher (1974), p. 84.

[24]Termination of the contract takes effect prospectively (*résiliation, Kündigung*).

20.4 Other Reasons Preventing Performance[25]

In certain cases, the debtor, through no fault of his own, cannot perform the obligation for the creditor or for his agent, for instance, where the debtor does not have knowledge of the creditor's identity—*i.e.*, the person to whom the claim belongs. Furthermore, the debtor may fail to perform his obligation because of the personal circumstances of the creditor. In such a case, the debtor is entitled to deposit or to withdraw from the contract as in the case of a creditor's default (TCO art. 111). The following are examples of such cases: the creditor passes away, and the debtor does not know the identity of his heirs; the creditor assigns the claim, but the assignment is disputed; or the creditor has neither mental capacity nor a legal representative.

20.5 Impossibility of Performance Due to the Creditor

Even if the debtor wishes to perform his obligation, the performance of the obligation may be impossible due to the creditor's circumstances or conduct. For instance, if a traveller who buys a plane ticket misses the flight, then the obligation of the airline becomes impossible on account of the conduct of the creditor. The general provisions of the Turkish Code of Obligations (arts. 1–206) do not regulate such possibilities. Therefore, there is a lacuna (*praeter legem*). Indeed, the fact that BGB § 326 subs. 2 regulates such circumstances supports this thesis. It is possible to fill this gap by considering certain specific provisions. Indeed, in the second division of the Turkish Code of Obligations, relating to types of contractual relationship, there are certain specific provisions that are relevant to some extent to the type of situations under consideration. These specific provisions will be evaluated in the following paragraphs.

In a lease contract, the lessor is obliged to deliver the leased object in a fit condition for the use agreed in the contract and to maintain it in this condition during the contract. Assume that the lessor performs his obligations but the lessee does not use the leased object or uses it in a restricted manner as a result of his own circumstances. According to TCO art. 324, in such a case, the lessee must pay the rent. However, if the lessor saves some expenses, the latter must permit their deduction from the rental fee.

Similarly, an employee might wish to perform his obligations, but the employer's conduct may preclude it. In such a case, according to TCO art. 408, the employer must pay the employee's salary. However, if the employee saves some expenses because he was prevented from working, this amount will be deducted from the salary payable.

[25]For further explanations see Akkanat (1996).

If it is accepted that there is a gap in the Turkish Code of Obligations relating to the impossibility of the performance due to the creditor, then it is possible to fill this gap by considering the above-mentioned specific provisions. Consequently, in the event of performance of an obligation becoming impossible due to the creditor, it is proper to accept that the debtor will be released from his obligation. Furthermore, in a bilateral contract, he may demand performance in return; in addition, if the debtor is relieved of some expenses or if he gains a benefit or intentionally fails to gain a benefit, these amounts are to be deducted.[26]

References

Akkanat H (1996) Alacaklı temerrüdü dışında alacaklı yüzünden borcun ifa edilemediği başlıca durumlar ve sonuçları. Filiz, İstanbul

Aybay A (2011) Borçlar hukuku dersleri genel bölüm. Filiz, İstanbul

Becker H (1941) Kommentar zum Schweizerischen Zivilgesetzbuch, vol VI, Obligationenrecht, 1. Abteilung: Allgemeine Bestimmungen, Art. 1-183. Stämpfli, Bern

Berger B (2012) Allgemeines Schuldrecht. Stämpfli, Bern

Engel P (1997) Traité des obligations en droit Suisse. Stämpfli, Bern

Eren F (2015) Borçlar hukuku genel hükümler. Yetkin, Ankara

Feyzioğlu FN (1977) Borçlar hukuku genel hükümler, vol 2. Fakülteler, İstanbul

Gauch P, Schluep WR, Emmenegger S (2008) Schweizerisches Obligationenrecht, Allgemeiner Teil, vol 2. Schulthess, Zürich

Honsell H, Vogt NP, Wiegand W (eds) (2003) Basler Kommentar zum Schweizerischen Privatrecht, Obligationenrecht 1: Art. 1-529 OR. Helbing Lichtenhahn, Basel

Kılıçoğlu AM (2013) Borçlar hukuku genel hükümler. Turhan, İstanbul

Koç N (1992) İsviçre-Türk hukukunda alacaklının temerrüdü. Dokuz eylül üniversitesi, Ankara

Nomer HN (2015) Borçlar hukuku genel hükümler. Beta, İstanbul

Oğuzman K, Öz T (2015) Borçlar hukuku genel hükümler, vol 1. Vedat, İstanbul

Oser H, Schönenberger W (1929) Kommentar zum Schweizerischen Zivilgesetzbuch, Volume V: Das Obligationenrecht, Erster Halbband: Art. 1-183. Schulthess, Zürich

Reisoğlu S (2014) Türk borçlar hukuku genel hükümler. Beta, İstanbul

Schwenzer I (2009) Schweizerisches Obligationenrecht, Allgemeiner Teil. Schulthess, Bern

Serozan R (2014) Borçlar hukuku genel bölüm, vol 3 (Kocayusufpaşaoğlu/Hatemi/Serozan/ Arpacı). Filiz, İstanbul

Tekinay SS, Akman S, Burcuoğlu H, Altop A (1993) Tekinay borçlar hukuku genel hükümler. Filiz, İstanbul

Tercier P (2004) Le droit des obligations. Schulthess, Zurich

Tercier P, Pichonnaz P, Develioğlu HM (2016) Borçlar hukuku genel hükümler. On iki levha, İstanbul

Thévenoz L, Werro F (éd) (2012) Commentaire romand code des obligations 1: art. 1-529 CO. Helbing Lichtenhahn, Bâle

von Tuhr A, Escher A (1974) Allgemeiner Teil des Schweizerischen Obligationenrecht, vol 2. Schulthess, Zürich

[26]Oğuzman and Öz (2015), p. 365; Serozan (2014), pp. 154–158.

Chapter 21
Natural Obligations

21.1 General[1]

It is not easy to give an exact definition that encompasses all types of natural obligations (*obligatio naturalis*). That is why, in this section, each type of natural obligation will be analysed individually. However, a common characteristic of natural obligations, except for time-barred obligations, is that when a creditor seeks an order against a debtor to perform the obligation, the court must dismiss the case.[2] As to time-barred obligations, the court may not take into consideration *ex officio* the fact that the obligation is time-barred (TCO art. 161).[3] If the debtor raises the fact that the obligation is time-barred, then the court must dismiss the case. In addition, there is a further attribute that all natural obligations share; namely, if a debtor performs the obligation voluntarily, then it may not be recovered.[4]

[1]Antalya (2012), pp. 24–27; Aybay (2011), p. 9; Becker (1941), Allgemeine Bestimmungen, N. 5–15; Berger (2012), p. 22; Engel (1997), pp. 43–53; Eren (2015), pp. 88–95; Feyzioğlu (1976), pp. 764–774; Gauch et al. (2008), p. 21; Honsell et al. (2003), art. 63; Kılıçoğlu (2013), pp. 32–36; Kocayusufpaşaoğlu (2014), pp. 44–58; Nomer (2015), pp. 24–25; Oser and Schönenberger (1929), Vorbemerkungen zum ersten Titel (art. 1-67), pp. 10–12; Oğuzman and Öz (2015), pp. 18–20; Reisoğlu (2014), pp. 38–39; Schwenzer (2009), p. 33; Tekinay et al. (1993), pp. 23–30; Tercier (2004), pp. 67–68; Tercier et al. (2016), pp. 97–99; Thévenoz and Werro (2012), art. 63, and von Tuhr and Peter (1979), pp. 32–39.

[2]Eren (2015), p. 88; Tercier et al. (2016), p. 98; Engel (1997), p. 43; Kocayusufpaşaoğlu (2014), pp. 44–46; Oğuzman and Öz (2015), p. 18; von Tuhr and Peter (1979), § 4, p. 32; Becker (1941), Allgemeine Bestimmungen, N. 5.

[3]See Sect. 26.1.

[4]Tekinay et al. (1993), p. 24; Engel (1997), p. 45; Kocayusufpaşaoğlu (2014), p. 58.

İ. Helvacı, *Turkish Contract Law*, DOI 10.1007/978-3-319-60061-1_21

21.2 Types of Natural Obligations

21.2.1 Obligations Resulting from Gambling and Betting

According to TCO art. 604 par. 1, claims resulting from gambling and betting may not be sued upon and enforced. In addition, TCO art. 605 par. 1 states that even if an acknowledgement of debt or a negotiable instrument signed by the gambler or the bettor for a gambling or betting transaction is transferred to a third party, no person may bring an action or demand the enforcement of these instruments.[5] However, pursuant to TCO art. 605 par. 2 sent. 1, payments effected voluntarily for obligations resulting from gambling and betting may not be recovered.

It should be noted that an obligation resulting from gambling or betting cannot be secured by a surety, a mortgage or a pledge.[6] This is because these securities are ancillary to the principal obligation. Indeed, in the event that the obligation is secured by a surety contract, the surety may plead that the obligation has resulted from gambling or betting even if he was aware of this fact at the time that the surety contract was concluded (TCO art. 591 par. 4).

21.2.2 Obligations Resulting from Marriage Brokerage

Pursuant to TCO art. 524, an obligation resulting from marriage brokerage may not be sued upon and enforced. Nevertheless, if the debtor voluntarily pays his debt, the paid fee may not be recovered. These obligations cannot be secured by a surety, a mortgage or a pledge, as in the case of obligations resulting from gambling or betting. This is because these securities are ancillary to the principal obligation.[7]

21.2.3 Time-Barred Obligations

The expiration of the limitation period does not give rise to the extinguishment of the obligation. Thus, the creditor may demand its performance or enforcement. Nevertheless, if the debtor pleads that the obligation is time-barred, then the court must dismiss the action. It should be noted that the court is not entitled to take into consideration *ex officio* that the obligation is time-barred (TCO art. 161).

---

[5]The rights of third parties in good faith arising from negotiable instruments are reserved (TCO art. 605 par. 1 sent. 2).

[6]Ergüne (2002), p. 113.

[7]Ergüne (2002), p. 113.

If the debtor performs a time-barred obligation voluntarily, it does not constitute a case of unjust enrichment. However, the legislature, for the sake of clarity, states that its restitution is excluded (TCO art. 78 par. 2).

A time-barred obligation, in contrast with other types of natural obligation, may be secured by ancillary securities, such as a surety, mortgage or pledge.[8] It should be noted that if the surety knows that the obligation is time-barred, he is not entitled to plead this fact (TCO art. 591 par. 1 sent. 2).

21.2.4 Promise Concerning the Performance of a Moral Duty

A moral duty is distinct from an obligation. A moral duty may not be sued upon and enforced. Nevertheless, if a person voluntarily performs a moral duty, its restitution is excluded (TCO art. 78 par. 2). Furthermore, the performance of a moral duty is not considered to be a donation (TCO art. 285 par. 3). A promise concerning the performance of a moral duty may be secured by ancillary securities, such as a surety, mortgage or pledge.[9]

21.2.5 Another Case of Natural Obligation

An engagement to be married may not give rise to an action to enforce the marriage. Where a penalty or a forfeiture clause has been agreed by the parties, it may not be sued upon. However, if the promisor has paid the penalty or forfeit money, then he is not entitled to reclaim it (TCC art. 119).

References

Antalya OG (2012) Borçlar hukuku genel hükümler, vol 1. Legal, İstanbul

Aybay A (2011) Borçlar hukuku dersleri genel bölüm. Filiz, İstanbul

Becker H (1941) Kommentar zum Schweizerischen Zivilgesetzbuch, vol VI, Obligationenrecht, 1. Abteilung: Allgemeine Bestimmungen, Art. 1-183. Stämpfli, Bern

Berger B (2012) Allgemeines Schuldrecht. Stämpfli, Bern

Engel P (1997) Traité des obligations en droit Suisse. Stämpfli, Bern

Eren F (2015) Borçlar hukuku genel hükümler. Yetkin, Ankara

Ergüne MS (2002) Hukukumuzda taşınır rehninin, özellikle teslime bağlı taşınır rehninin kuruluşu. Filiz, İstanbul

[8]Ergüne (2002), p. 113.

[9]Ergüne (2002), p. 113.

Feyzioğlu FN (1976) Borçlar hukuku genel hükümler, vol 1. Fakülteler, İstanbul
Gauch P, Schluep WR, Schmid J (2008) Schweizerisches Obligationenrecht, Allgemeiner Teil, vol 1. Schulthess, Zürich
Honsell H, Vogt NP, Wiegand W (eds) (2003) Basler Kommentar zum Schweizerischen Privatrecht, Obligationenrecht 1: Art. 1-529 OR. Helbing Lichtenhahn, Basel
Kılıçoğlu AM (2013) Borçlar hukuku genel hükümler. Turhan, İstanbul
Kocayusufpaşaoğlu N (2014) Borçlar hukuku genel bölüm, vol 1 (Kocayusufpaşaoğlu/Hatemi/Serozan/Arpacı). Filiz, İstanbul
Nomer HN (2015) Borçlar hukuku genel hükümler. Beta, İstanbul
Oğuzman K, Öz T (2015) Borçlar hukuku genel hükümler, vol 1. Vedat, İstanbul
Oser H, Schönenberger W (1929) Kommentar zum Schweizerischen Zivilgesetzbuch, Volume V: Das Obligationenrecht, Erster Halbband: Art. 1-183. Schulthess, Zürich
Reisoğlu S (2014) Türk borçlar hukuku genel hükümler. Beta, İstanbul
Schwenzer I (2009) Schweizerisches Obligationenrecht, Allgemeiner Teil. Schulthess, Bern
Tekinay SS, Akman S, Burcuoğlu H, Altop A (1993) Tekinay borçlar hukuku genel hükümler. Filiz, İstanbul
Tercier P (2004) Le droit des obligations. Schulthess, Zurich
Tercier P, Pichonnaz P, Develioğlu HM (2016) Borçlar hukuku genel hükümler. On iki levha, İstanbul
Thévenoz L, Werro F (éd) (2012) Commentaire romand code des obligations 1: art. 1-529 CO. Helbing Lichtenhahn, Bâle
von Tuhr A, Peter H (1979) Allgemeiner Teil des Schweizerischen Obligationenrecht, vol 1. Schulthess, Zürich

Chapter 22
Non-performance of the Obligation

22.1 Specific Performance[1]

22.1.1 General[2]

If a debtor fails to perform an obligation, in principle, as long as the performance of the obligation is possible, the creditor may only demand and sue for specific performance[3] of that obligation.[4] If the court accepts a lawsuit filed by a creditor against a debtor for performance of an obligation, then two possibilities arise: (1) the debtor may comply with the court order, fulfil the obligation and thereby extinguish it or (2) the debtor may fail to obey the court order, and the obligation will remain unfulfilled. In the latter case, the creditor is entitled to enforce the court order according to the provisions of the Turkish Code of Bankruptcy and Enforcement.

[1]Aybay (2011), pp. 130–142; Becker (1941), Vorbemerkungen zu art. 97–109, art. 97–101; Berger (2012), pp. 503–541, 556–562, 607–616, 624–630, 689–692; Engel (1997), pp. 697–724; Eren (2015), pp. 1027–1089, 1128–1139; Feyzioğlu (1977), pp. 160–219; Gauch et al. (2008a), pp. 203–208; Gauch et al. (2008b), pp. 69–105, 137–185; Honsell et al. (2003), Einleitung zu art. 97–109, art. 97–101; Kılıçoğlu (2013), pp. 80–86, 636–672; Nomer (2015), pp. 307–333, 376–379; Oser and Schönenberger (1929), Vorbemerkungen zum zweiten Abschnitt (97–109), art. 97–101; Oğuzman and Öz (2015), pp. 366–455; Reisoğlu (2014), pp. 344–368; Schwenzer (2009), pp. 338–345, 439–461, 474–481; Serozan (2014), pp. 130–141, 198–215, 246–263, 278–301; Tekinay et al. (1993), pp. 851–911, 972–983; Tercier (2004), pp. 203–229; Tercier et al. (2016), pp. 353–398; Thévenoz and Werro (2012), Introduction aux articles 97–109 CO, art. 97–101; von Tuhr and Escher (1974), pp. 86–131, and von Tuhr and Peter (1979), pp. 192–193.

[2]For further explanations see Başoğlu (2012).

[3]Performance in kind, *exécution en nature*.

[4]Oğuzman and Öz (2015), p. 371.

İ. Helvacı, *Turkish Contract Law*, DOI 10.1007/978-3-319-60061-1_22

22.1.2 Specific Provisions for Obligations to Give

In cases where an obligation to give is not performed by the debtor, the creditor may bring an action and demand performance of the obligation. If the court accepts the demand and the debtor, honouring the court order, fulfils his obligation to give, then the obligation is performed and, thus, extinguished.

In the event of the debtor failing to comply with the court order, the dispute should be resolved in accordance with the characteristics of the subject matter of the obligation to give, such as movable property, immovable property or a claim. For example, assume that the debtor is obliged to deliver movable property to the creditor but does not perform his obligation. The creditor sues and the court accepts the demand, but the debtor does not comply with the court order. In this case, the creditor may have the court order executed through the debt enforcement office. This office is entitled to take the movable property from the debtor's possession and deliver it to the creditor (TCBE art. 24).[5]

In certain cases of non-performance, it is not necessary for the court order to be executed. This is because when the court order becomes final, the creditor automatically becomes the owner of the subject matter of the order. For instance, a seller is obliged to transfer ownership of immovable property to a buyer, but the seller does not fulfil his obligation. The buyer brings an action, and the court accepts the demand. In this case, it is not necessary for the court order to be executed. This is because the buyer automatically becomes the owner of the immovable property when the court order becomes final (TCC art. 716 par. 1).[6]

A similar provision is that of TCO art. 185. According to this article, where a creditor is obliged to assign a claim to an assignee but does not perform his obligation, the assignee may bring an action against the assignor. If the court accepts the demand of the assignee, the claim sued upon automatically transfers to the assignee when the court order becomes final. Thus, it is not necessary for the court order to be executed.[7]

22.1.3 Specific Provisions for Obligations to Do

In cases where an obligation to do is not performed by the debtor, the creditor may bring an action and demand performance of the obligation. If the court accepts the demand and the debtor, honouring the court order, fulfils his obligation to do, then the obligation is performed and, thus, extinguished.

---

[5]Oğuzman and Öz (2015), p. 374. For further explanations see Kuru (2016), pp. 412–414; Pekcanıtez et al. (2013), pp. 477–478.

[6]Oğuzman and Öz (2015), p. 374. For further explanations see Oğuzman et al. (2016), pp. 407–408; Steinauer (2002), p. 61.

[7]Oğuzman and Öz (2015), p. 374; Oğuzman and Öz (2016), p. 596.

In the event the debtor fails to comply with the court order, the dispute should be resolved in accordance with the characteristics of an obligation to do. This is because obligations to do are of two types: (1) obligations that must be fulfilled by the debtor in person and (2) obligations that do not have to be fulfilled by the debtor in person.[8]

Certain obligations to do may only be fulfilled by the debtor himself. For instance, when a famous composer is obliged to compose a concerto or when a well-known painter undertakes to complete a painting, other persons cannot fulfil these obligations. If the court order is related to an obligation that only the debtor can fulfil and he does not obey the court order, without a justifiable cause, then the creditor may demand that the debtor be sentenced to prison according to TCBE art. 343. However, despite the threat of imprisonment, of which the maximum duration is 3 months, it is possible that the debtor fails to fulfil his obligation to do. In such a case, the creditor cannot obtain performance of the obligation.[9] He must be content with compensation for damage according to TCO art. 113 par. 1.[10]

Certain obligations to do may be performed by the debtor or by other persons. For example, when a debtor is obliged to paint a wall or to fix a hedge, the personal qualifications of the debtor are irrelevant. In cases where the obligation to do may be performed by other persons and the debtor does not comply with the court order, the creditor may demand its enforcement.[11] First, an expert nominated by the debt enforcement official determines the costs of the third party's prospective performance. Thereafter, there are two alternatives: (1) the creditor may pay the necessary expenses in advance, and after a third party fulfils the obligation to do, under the direction of the debt enforcement office, the creditor may then demand that the debtor pay the expenses for the performance of the obligation, or (2) the creditor may refuse to pay the necessary expenses in advance and demand that the debtor pay them. In such a case, if the debtor does not pay these expenses, then the seizable assets of the debtor that are sufficient for the performance of the obligation can be seized and realised. With the proceeds obtained from the realisation of the debtor's assets, the debt enforcement office will authorise a third party to carry out the obligation to do (TCBE art. 30).

In cases where the obligation to do may be performed by other persons, the creditor may rely on TCO art. 113 par. 1, rather than the above-mentioned general provisions and the specific provision of TCBE art. 30. According to TCO art. 113 par. 1, where a debtor does not fulfil an obligation to do, the creditor is entitled to demand from the court the authority to fulfil the performance of the obligation himself or to have a third party fulfil it at the debtor's expense. Further, the creditor may demand compensation for damage.[12]

---

[8]See Chap. 16.

[9]Kuru (2016), p. 421; Pekcanıtez et al. (2013), p. 484; Oğuzman and Öz (2015), p. 375.

[10]Tekinay et al. (1993), p. 921; Oğuzman and Öz (2015), p. 375.

[11]Kuru (2016), p. 421; Pekcanıtez et al. (2013), p. 484.

[12]For further explanations see Aydıncık (2013).

22.1.4 Specific Provisions for Obligations Not to Do

The debtor may be obliged not to perform certain acts, in other words, to refrain from certain acts. For instance, a debtor may be obliged not to compete or not to disclose a trade secret (*e.g.*, a formula, a practice, a design, a patent, etc.). As long as the fulfilment of the obligation not to do is possible, in principle, the creditor may only demand its performance. For instance, the debtor is obliged not to compete for 5 years from the conclusion of the contract but breaches this obligation in the second year. In this case, the creditor may bring an action, and the court may accept his demand. Then there are two possibilities: (1) the debtor may comply with the court order. In this case, the dispute is resolved by the honouring of the court order. However, if the non-performance of the debtor has caused damage to the creditor, the latter may also demand compensation for the damage arising from the breach of the non-competition agreement. (2) the debtor may fail to comply with the court order without a justifiable cause. In this case, the creditor may demand that the debtor be sentenced to prison according to TCBE art. 343.[13] However, despite the threat of imprisonment, the maximum duration of which is 3 months, the debtor may continue to breach his obligation not to do (*e.g.*, in a non-competition agreement, he may continue competing). In such a case, the creditor cannot procure performance of the obligation. He must be content with compensation for damage according to TCO art. 113 par. 2. This article states that where a debtor who is under an obligation not to perform certain acts violates this obligation, he is then liable to compensate the creditor for damage.[14]

It should be added that the non-performance of the debtor might result in certain consequences that must be remedied. For instance, a debtor builds a wall blocking the view of a neighbour despite an obligation not to do so. Another example is where a debtor, obliged by a non-disclosure agreement not to reveal a trade secret, such as a formula, nonetheless discloses the trade secret on a website. In these cases, it is evident that the wall must be demolished and that the information published on the website must be removed. Therefore, the creditor may demand that the situation created by the debtor is remedied, or he may demand authorisation to remedy it at the debtor's expense (TCO art. 113 par. 3).[15]

22.1.5 Specific Provisions for Pecuniary Obligations

The performance of pecuniary obligations may not become impossible. As mentioned above, as long as the performance of the obligation is possible, the debtor

[13]Kuru (2016), pp. 421–422; Pekcanıtez et al. (2013), p. 484.

[14]Tekinay et al. (1993), pp. 923–924; Eren (2015), p. 1034; Oğuzman and Öz (2015), pp. 377–378, pp. 428–429.

[15]Eren (2015), p. 1034; Tekinay et al. (1993), p. 924; Oğuzman and Öz (2015), p. 429.

must fulfil it. Therefore, when a debtor does not pay his pecuniary obligation, the creditor is entitled to bring an action. If the court accepts the demand and the debtor, in compliance with the court order, pays the debts, then the dispute is resolved. However, if the debtor does not obey the court order, the creditor may demand its enforcement. In such a case, as a general rule,[16] the seizable assets of the debtor that are sufficient for the performance of the obligation are seized and realised under the authority of the debt enforcement office.[17] With the proceeds obtained from the realisation of the debtor's assets, the obligation is fulfilled and, thus, the creditor's claim is satisfied.[18]

In addition to the general provisions, the legislature gives the creditor the right to commence enforcement proceedings without a court order (TCBE art. 42).[19] Indeed, the creditor can initiate execution proceedings by submitting an enforcement request to the competent debt enforcement office. In this case, the enforcement office must issue a summons to pay and serve it on the debtor. When the debtor receives this summons to pay, he may pay the debt within 7 days, thereby resolving the dispute. On the other hand, the debtor might not pay the debt and might not object to the summons to pay. In such a case, the summons to pay becomes enforceable and the creditor may request that the enforcement proceedings be continued. Consequently, the seizable assets of the debtor are seized and realised under the authority of the debt enforcement office. With the proceeds obtained from the realisation of the debtor's assets, the obligation is fulfilled and, thus, the creditor's claim is satisfied. A third possibility is that the debtor might not pay the debt and might object to the order. In such a case, the execution proceedings are suspended, and if the creditor wishes to continue the execution, there are two alternatives: (1) the creditor must bring an action before a civil court within 1 year of the debtor's objection (TCBE art. 67), or (2) the creditor must commence proceedings before a court of enforcement within 6 months (TCBE arts. 68–70). The debtor's objection may be dismissed by the civil court or annulled by the court of enforcement. In these cases, the creditor can request continuation of the enforcement proceedings.

22.2 Action for Damages in Lieu of Specific Performance

22.2.1 Subsequent Impossibility[20]

In the event that the performance of the obligation becomes impossible after the formation of the contract, clearly, the creditor may no longer demand its specific

[16]The specific rules relating to the bankruptcy are reserved.

[17]Pekcanıtez et al. (2013), pp. 476–477. For further explanations see Kuru (2016), pp. 400–404.

[18]Oğuzman and Öz (2015), p. 373; Reisoğlu (2014), p. 347.

[19]For further explanations see Kuru (2016), p. 107 *ff*; Pekcanıtez et al. (2013), p. 182 *ff*.

[20]For further explanations see Gündoğdu (2014).

performance.[21] If performance of an obligation cannot be obtained through the debt enforcement office, then performance of the obligation is deemed to have become impossible. In this case, the creditor may only demand compensatory damages provided that the debtor is responsible for the impossibility of performance.[22] As a general rule, if the debtor is at fault for the subsequent impossibility, then he will be liable for compensation for the creditor's damage (TCO art. 112). However, even if the debtor is not at fault for the subsequent impossibility, he may be held liable for compensation for the creditor's damage provided that the law itself or the agreement of the parties imposes a liability of this nature.[23]

At this point, it should be remembered that impossibility of performance, which is analysed under this section, is distinct from initial impossibility. In the case of initial impossibility, the performance of the obligation is impossible when the contract is formed and this impossibility is objective; that is to say, the performance of the obligation by any person is not possible. The initial impossibility results in the nullity of the contract (TCO art. 27 par. 1).[24] In the case of subsequent impossibility, the performance of the obligation becomes impossible after the formation of the contract. Moreover, according to certain scholars, it is irrelevant whether the impossibility of performance is objective or subjective.[25] In either case, the performance of the obligation becomes impossible.

22.2.2 Other Causes of Action for Damages

In certain cases, although performance of the obligation is possible, the creditor may instead demand compensation for damage resulting from non-performance of the obligation.

This right may be granted to the creditor by the contract.[26] For instance, the parties may agree that a penalty in lieu of performance must be paid in the event of the debtor failing to perform his obligation (TCO art. 179 par. 1).[27]

This right may also be granted to the creditor by the law itself.[28] Indeed, in bilateral contracts, if the debtor does not perform his obligation and falls into

---

[21] *Impossibilium nulla obligatio est*: No-one has a legal obligation to do the impossible or there is no obligation to perform an impossible act.

[22] If the debtor is not responsible for the impossibility of the performance, then the debtor is released from his obligation (TCO art. 136). Cases in which the debtor is not responsible for the impossibility of performance will be analysed below under Sect. 25.5.

[23] Oğuzman and Öz (2015), pp. 411–412; Oser and Schönenberger (1929), art. 99, N. 12, N. 13.

[24] See Sect. 5.2.5.

[25] See Sect. 25.5.1.

[26] Oğuzman and Öz (2015), p. 372.

[27] See Sect. 31.3.2.

[28] Oğuzman and Öz (2015), p. 372.

default (TCO art. 117), the creditor may grant a reasonable time period for the performance of the obligation to the debtor or demand the court to set such time period (TCO art. 123). If the debtor does not cure his default by the end of this time period, then the creditor may demand compensation for damage in lieu of specific performance (TCO art. 125 par. 2).[29]

Moreover, in certain cases, the nature of the circumstances may entail an action for damages in lieu of specific performance. This is the case, for example, in obligations to do if the obligation may not be performed by a third party. In other words, if the debtor must perform his obligation in person and refuses to perform it, it is reasonable to assume that the creditor may demand that the debtor compensate him for damage.[30]

Finally, even if performance of the obligation is possible and the creditor is not entitled to bring an action for compensation for damage in lieu of specific performance, he may still file a lawsuit with this objective. In such a case, if the debtor does not defend himself or prove that the performance of the obligation is still possible, the court may decide that the debtor must pay compensation, provided that the debtor is responsible for non-performance of the obligation.[31]

22.2.3 *Requirements of Action for Damages*

In order for the debtor to be liable for non-performance of the obligation, the following conditions are necessary: (1) the debtor must fail to fulfil his obligation; (2) the debtor must be responsible for the non-performance of the obligation; (3) the creditor must incur certain damage, which can be moral or pecuniary; and (4) there must be an adequate causal link between the non-performance and the damage.

22.2.3.1 Non-performance

In principle, as long as the performance of the obligation is possible, a creditor is not entitled to demand compensation in lieu of specific performance. Therefore, as a rule, in order for the debtor to be required to pay compensation to the creditor for non-performance of the obligation, the performance of the obligation must have become impossible (subsequent impossibility).[32] However, in certain cases, although the performance of the obligation is possible, the creditor may instead demand compensation for damage resulting from the non-performance provided

[29]See Sect. 23.4.2.

[30]Compare to Oğuzman and Öz (2015), p. 375 and fn. 36 and pp. 426–427.

[31]Oğuzman and Öz (2015), p. 371.

[32]See Sect. 22.2.1.

that this right is given to him by the contract, by the law itself or by the nature of the circumstances as referred to above (other causes of action for damages).[33]

22.2.3.2 Responsibility of the Debtor for Non-performance

22.2.3.2.1 Presumption of Fault

According to TCO art. 112, if a debtor fails to fulfil the obligation, then he is liable for damage, unless he proves that there is no fault on his part. A debtor is presumed to be at fault in the event of non-performance of the obligation. However, the debtor may refute this presumption of fault.

If the debtor is at fault for non-performance, then he is liable to compensate the creditor's damage. For example, in a sale contract relating to a specific object, if the seller is responsible for the object being destroyed, then he is liable to compensate the buyer for damage. Where the debtor is not at fault, he is not liable to pay damages to the creditor. For instance, in a sale contract relating to a specific object, if, after the formation of the contract, the object is destroyed by a lightning strike, then the debtor is not at fault regarding the non-performance. In this case, the obligation is extinguished due to subsequent impossibility, and thus, the debtor is released from his obligation (TCO art. 136 par. 1).[34]

The conduct of the debtor resulting in non-performance may be intentional or negligent. The negligence of the debtor may be gross or slight. The degree of the debtor's fault is irrelevant. In other words, the debtor is generally liable for any fault (TCO art. 114 par. 1 sent. 1).[35]

The parties may mitigate the liability of the debtor. By *argumentum a contrario*, as set out in TCO art. 115 par. 1, the parties may agree that the debtor is not liable to pay damages in cases where he is at slight fault (*culpa levis*).[36] Furthermore, the law itself may mitigate the responsibility of the debtor. For instance, according to TCO art. 294 par. 1, a donor is not liable to a donee for any damage arising from a gift except where he has caused this damage by gross fault (*culpa lata* – intentionally or by gross negligence).[37]

---

[33]See Sect. 22.2.2.

[34]See Sect. 25.5.

[35]Oğuzman and Öz (2015), p. 403.

[36]See Sect. 22.4.

[37]For further explanations see Tercier (2003), p. 239; Thévenoz and Werro (2012), art. 248, N. 9; Tandoğan (1990), p. 374; Yavuz (2014), p. 351.

22.2.3.2.2 Refutation of Presumption

The debtor may prove that he is not at fault for the non-performance of the obligation, and thus, he may be released from his liability. For instance, the non-performance might result from a force majeure, a fortuitous event (such as an accident)[38] or the creditor's or a third party's fault. It is also possible that the debtor does not have mental capacity (capacity of discernment). In such cases, no fault can be attributed to the debtor.[39] The debtor may also refute this presumption of culpability proving that he fulfilled his duty of care objectively as required by law, by the contract and by the principles of good faith for the performance of the obligation.

A debtor who permanently lacks mental capacity (capacity of discernment) cannot be considered culpable and, thus, cannot be held liable for his breach of contract. Nevertheless, where equity requires, the court may order a debtor who does not have mental capacity to pay total or partial compensation for the damage he has caused (TCO art. 65).[40] If a debtor has temporarily lost his mental capacity and has caused damage to the creditor, he must pay compensation to the creditor. However, where the debtor proves that he has lost this capacity without fault, he can be released from such liability (TCO art. 59).[41] Indeed, according to TCO art. 114 par. 2, provisions relating to tort liability are applied by analogy to contractual breaches.

It is worth elaborating upon force majeure and fortuitous events. Fortuitous events (*casus fortuitus*, unavoidable accidents) are events that are proximate to the parties or the object of the obligation,[42] for example, a boiler explosion in a factory.[43] On the other hand, force majeure (*vis major*) covers extraordinary events or circumstances—for example, natural disasters such as hurricanes, floods, earthquakes, volcanic eruptions, lightning strikes, etc. or social or commercial disruptions such as war, strikes, riots, interdictions of importation or exportation that are beyond the control of the debtor and therefore prevent the performance of the obligation.[44] A fortuitous event is any event that was not foreseen but if it had been foreseen, it could have been avoided; on the other hand, force majeure is any event that is beyond the control of the parties, whether or not it is foreseen.

---

[38]For further explanations see Gözübüyük (1957).

[39]Oğuzman and Öz (2015), pp. 403–405.

[40]von Tuhr and Escher (1974), § 69, IV, p. 117; Becker (1941), art. 97, N. 58; Oğuzman and Öz (2015), p. 412.

[41]von Tuhr and Escher (1974), § 69, IV, p. 117; Oğuzman and Öz (2015), p. 404.

[42]von Tuhr and Escher (1974), § 69, VII, pp. 120–121; Engel (1997), p. 467; Thévenoz and Werro (2012), art. 43, N. 33, art. 103, N. 7.

[43]Reisoğlu (2014), p. 359; Oğuzman and Öz (2015), p. 405.

[44]Tekinay et al. (1993), pp. 1002–1004; Feyzioğlu (1977), p. 226; Engel (1997), p. 468; Thévenoz and Werro (2012), art. 41, N. 46, art. 103, N. 7; von Tuhr and Escher (1974), § 69, VII, pp. 121–122.

In certain cases, the parties may exacerbate the responsibility of the debtor and agree that the debtor will be liable for his non-performance even in cases of force majeure or fortuitous events.[45] Alternatively, the parties may agree that the performance of the obligation will be suspended as long as the circumstances remain.

Further, the law itself may exacerbate the responsibility of the debtor. Pursuant to TCO art. 563 par. 2, without a bailor's consent, a bailee must not use the bailed chattel. Otherwise, the bailee is responsible for any accidental damage that occurs, unless he proves that the chattel would nevertheless have been damaged in the same accident.[46]

22.2.3.3 The Creditor's Damage

22.2.3.3.1 Pecuniary Losses

The creditor must prove both the existence of any damage and its amount. If the creditor fails to prove the exact amount of the damage, the extent of liability of the debtor will be determined in accordance with the provisions relating to tort liability. This is because TCO art. 114 par. 2 states that the rules relating to tort liability[47] apply by analogy to cases of breach of contract. Therefore, TCO art. 50 par. 2 will be applicable in such cases. According to this provision, if the exact amount of the damage is not proven, then it is determined by the court at its discretion; the court must take into consideration the ordinary course of events and the measures taken by the creditor.[48]

Damage resulting from the non-performance of the obligation is referred to as 'positive damage', and this includes both actual damage (*damnum emergens*) and the deprivation of the opportunity to obtain a benefit (*lucrum cessans*) and avoid a loss.[49] For example, a bailee is obliged to return the bailed object (*e.g.*, a car) to the bailor. However, the bailed car is destroyed due to the fault of the bailee. In this case, the bailor (creditor) may demand that the bailee (debtor) pay damages for the market value of the car (*damnum emergens*). The difference between the value of the creditor's assets in the event of performance and non-performance represents the creditor's damage, and the debtor must compensate for that diminution in value.[50]

In a car sale contract, assume that the buyer has made a resale agreement for the car, according to which the car would be sold to a third party resulting in a profit of

---

[45] *Cf.* Oğuzman and Öz (2015), p. 412.

[46] Oğuzman and Öz (2015), p. 411.

[47] For further explanations see Nomer (1996).

[48] Oğuzman and Öz (2015), p. 390; Oser and Schönenberger (1929), art. 42, N. 3–7; Becker (1941), art. 42, N. 4–5.

[49] Oğuzman and Öz (2015), p. 387; Becker (1941), art. 97, N. 34–45.

[50] Becker (1941), art. 97, N. 34; Oğuzman and Öz (2015), p. 387.

€20,000. However, the car is destroyed due to the fault of the seller. In this case, where the buyer proves that there was such a prospective sale, he may demand that the seller compensate for this damage (loss of profit—*lucrum cessans*).[51]

22.2.3.3.2 Non-pecuniary Losses[52]

Non-performance of the obligation may give rise to the infringement of the creditor's personal rights and may thus cause moral damage. In such a case, the creditor is entitled to demand that his moral damage be compensated. For instance, a television star has breast cancer and wishes to be operated on by a well-known plastic surgeon. In fact, surgeons are not permitted to reveal any medical information about their patients without their permission. Despite this fact, the surgeon describes the patient's surgery in a book. In this case, the non-performance of the obligation—that is to say, the disclosing of the patient's condition and treatment—infringes the personal rights of the patient, and so she may demand that the surgeon compensate her moral damage. Indeed, TCO art. 114 par. 2 states that the rules relating to tort liability apply by analogy to cases of breach of contract. Therefore, TCO art. 58 will be applicable in such cases.[53]

It should be noted that, since TCO art. 114 par. 2 states that the rules relating to tort liability apply by analogy to cases of breach of contract, pursuant to TCO art. 56 par. 1, if a breach of a contract causes personal injury to a creditor, he may demand moral compensation for his injuries. As a consequence of TCO art. 114 par. 2, if the breach of the contract results in either the death or serious injury of the creditor, persons in a close relationship with him may be entitled to moral damages (TCO art. 56 par. 2).

22.2.3.4 Causation (Adequate Causal Link)

The debtor must compensate the creditor's damage resulting from non-performance. Nevertheless, a mere causal link between the non-performance of the debtor and the creditor's damage is not sufficient. Indeed, the debtor does not have to compensate all damage resulting from non-performance. There must be an adequate (proximate) causal link[54] between the non-performance of the debtor and the creditor's damage. In other words, the debtor is liable solely for the normal, expected results of his non-performance.[55] For instance, according to a contract between a car owner and a

---

[51] Becker (1941), art. 97, N. 37–39; Oğuzman and Öz (2015), p. 387.

[52] For further explanations see Genç Arıdemir (2008).

[53] Becker (1941), art. 97, N. 26; Oğuzman and Öz (2015), pp. 388–389; Tekinay et al. (1993), p. 857; Reisoğlu (2014), p. 356.

[54] For further explanations see Eren (1985).

[55] Oğuzman and Öz (2015), p. 380.

mechanic, the latter is obliged to fix the brakes of the car. However, the mechanic returns it without fixing the brakes. The car owner has an accident and misses his flight and catches the following flight, but the airplane crashes and the car owner dies. In this case, it is obvious that the mechanic is liable for the car accident. This is due to the fact that there is an adequate causal link between the non-performance and the car accident. However, the mechanic is not liable for the car owner's death.

It is obvious that there is a causal link between the non-performance of the obligation and the car owner's fate. One may say that if the car had been fixed as required, then the car owner would not have had the car accident, would not have missed the flight and, thus, would not have died. However, there is no adequate (proximate) causal link between the non-performance of the obligation and the plane crash. This is because, in the course of life, not fixing a car's brakes is quite likely to give rise to a car accident but does not normally give rise to death in a plane crash. In other words, the causal link must be foreseeable in order to be considered adequate.

22.2.3.5 The Extent of Compensation

The extent of the debtor's liability depends on the special nature of the legal transaction. In particular, where the transaction does not provide any benefit to the debtor, his liability is assessed less severely (TCO art. 114 par. 1 sents. 2 and 3).

The maximum limit of the compensation is the extent of the creditor's damage.[56] Within this limit, the judge may determine the extent and the form of the compensation (TCO art. 51 par. 1). This is due to the fact that the provisions relating to tort liability are applied by analogy to breaches of contract (TCO art. 114 par. 2). In this regard, the liability of the debtor is determined taking into consideration the circumstances and the degree of the debtor's fault (TCO art. 51). Therefore, if the debtor is at gross fault—in other words, if he breaches the obligation intentionally or by gross negligence (*culpa lata*), then his liability is more severe in comparison to a debtor who is at slight fault (*culpa levis*).[57]

The court, while determining the extent of the compensation, must also take into account the aggrieved party's fault[58] (TCO art. 52 par. 1). If the injured party consented to the breach of the contract or caused or increased the damage or exacerbated the debtor's position, then the judge may reduce the compensation or may dismiss the claim.[59] For instance, there is an employment agreement between a car owner and his driver. The car crashes due to the fault of the driver, and the car

[56]Tekinay et al. (1993), p. 855; Eren (2015), p. 1069; Reisoğlu (2014), p. 361; Oğuzman and Öz (2015), p. 425.

[57]Tekinay et al. (1993), pp. 870–872; Eren (2015), p. 1064; Reisoğlu (2014), p. 361; Oğuzman and Öz (2015), p. 425.

[58]For further explanations see Baysal (2012); Altınok Ormancı (2016).

[59]Reisoğlu (2014), p. 361; Oğuzman and Öz (2015), p. 425.

owner is injured. However, the owner refuses to be treated for tetanus and, thus, dies needlessly. In this case, the debtor (driver) may not be held liable for the death of the creditor; he is only liable for the creditor's other injuries resulting from the car crash.

Moreover, the judge may reduce the compensation in cases where the debtor would be impoverished were he to pay the full compensation, provided that the debtor is at slight fault and equity requires it (TCO art. 52 par. 2).

22.3 Improper Performance of the Obligation

The debtor fulfils his obligation; nevertheless, the performance may be improper. That is to say, the debtor's performance may be inconsistent with the obligation in terms of the quantity, the quality, the place of performance or the time of performance, etc. In such cases, the creditor may refuse this improper performance and may demand the performance to be as required by the contract.[60] As explained above, as long as the performance of the obligation is possible, the creditor may demand performance in accordance with the contract. Therefore, the author's explanations regarding specific performance are also applicable in this case.[61]

However, it is possible that the creditor will accept the improper performance of the obligation and demand compensation for damage.[62] In order for the debtor to be liable for the compensation for the creditor's damage resulting from improper performance, the following conditions are necessary: (1) the debtor must fail to fulfil the obligation as required; (2) the debtor must be responsible for the improper performance of the obligation; (3) the creditor must incur certain damage, which can be pecuniary or non-pecuniary; and (4) there must be an adequate causal link between the improper performance and the damage. The author's explanations regarding an action for damages in lieu of specific performance are also applicable in this case.[63]

It is worth noting that late performance of an obligation is a specific case of improper performance. Consequently, the legislature sets out specific provisions for the default of the debtor.[64]

[60] Oğuzman and Öz (2015), p. 467.

[61] See Sect. 22.1.

[62] Oğuzman and Öz (2015), pp. 467–468.

[63] See Sect. 22.2.3.

[64] See Chap. 23.

22.4 Contractual Exclusion of Liability[65]

22.4.1 General

If the debtor does not perform his obligation, he will be liable for the damage arising from non-performance of the obligation. Nevertheless, the parties may agree in advance that the debtor will not be liable for such damage. An agreement for the non-liability of the debtor may be included by the parties as a clause in the contract. Such clauses are referred to as 'exemption clauses'. Further, the parties may also make a separate agreement that excludes the debtor's liability. Such agreements are referred to as 'non-liability agreements' or 'agreements excluding the debtor's liability'. The term 'non-liability agreement' includes both exemption clauses and separate agreements.[66]

The Turkish Code of Obligations accepts the validity of such agreements. However, the Code sets certain restrictions on the contractual exclusion of liability. These restrictions are analysed in the following paragraphs.

22.4.2 Restrictions

The first restriction is that, according to TCO art. 115 par. 1, any agreement in advance purporting to exclude liability for unlawful intent or gross negligence (*culpa lata*) is void. This is a case of partial nullity. Thus, the other terms of the contract, apart from the clause relating to the exclusion of the debtor's liability, remain valid. That is to say, the debtor is not entitled to claim that if the exemption clause had not existed, he would not have concluded the contract.[67]

The second restriction arises from TCO art. 115 par. 2. As a rule, according to the first paragraph of the said article, an agreement that excludes the debtor's liability for his slight fault (*culpa levis*) is valid. However, the legislature accepts that, in certain cases, such agreements are also void. Pursuant to TCO art. 115 par. 2, any agreement concluded in advance that accepts that a debtor will not be liable for any obligations arising from an employment contract is void. Nevertheless, at this point, it should be noted that the paragraph referred to above is written in a manner that exceeds the *ratio legis* of the provision. In fact, pursuant to the terms of this paragraph, the agreement that excludes the employee's liability for slight fault will also be void. However, such an interpretation is considered unfair as an employer is almost never in a position to be unfairly exploited by an employee.

---

[65]For further explanations see Akman (1976), Başalp (2011).

[66]The parties to a contract are also entitled to make an agreement in advance that restricts the debtor's liability instead of excluding it. The rules concerning non-liability agreements are also applied to these kinds of agreements.

[67]See Sect. 5.3.2.

On the contrary, it is more likely that an employer would be in a position to unfairly exploit an employee. That is why it should be accepted that there is a *lacuna sensu lato*. Indeed, the text of the corresponding article of the former Code of Obligations (art. 99 par. 2) supported this thesis as it required the waiving party to be employed by the other party at the time of the formation of the agreement excluding liability. Therefore, TCO art. 115 par. 2 must be understood in the sense that a provision in an employment contract that exempts the liability of the employer for slight fault is void. However, a provision in an employment contract that exempts the liability of the employee for slight fault will be deemed to be valid.[68]

The third restriction is a consequence of TCO art. 115 par. 3, according to which if a service or profession requires proficiency that can only be undertaken with the permission of competent authorities or the law, then any agreement concluded in advance that accepts that the debtor will not be liable for his slight fault (*culpa levis*) is void. For example, being a doctor, an attorney-at-law or an architect requires proficiency and can only be exercised with the permission of competent authorities or the law.[69] Therefore, any agreements excluding liabilities for slight fault on the part of these persons are void.[70]

22.5 Debtor's Liability for Assistants

22.5.1 General[71]

A debtor may perform a contractual obligation himself or with the help of assistants. Furthermore, provided that a specific debtor is not determined in the contract, a debtor may replace himself with a substitute for the performance of an obligation. Moreover, the debtor may exercise the rights arising from the contract or allow assistants, such as the people who live with or work for him, to exercise these rights. If the debtor is not permitted to do so, he will be liable for breaching the obligation (TCO art. 112).[72] However, even if the debtor is permitted to do so, he will be liable for any conduct of his assistants that is contrary to the obligation. Indeed, according to TCO art. 116 par. 1, a debtor who delegates the performance of an obligation or the exercise of a right resulting from an obligational relationship to assistants is liable to compensate the damage that they may cause to the other party while they carry out such tasks, even if their delegation was lawful.

---

[68]Oğuzman and Öz (2015), p. 409.

[69]Oser and Schönenberger (1929), art. 100, N. 5.

[70]Oğuzman and Öz (2015), p. 410.

[71]For further explanations see Şenocak (1995).

[72]Eren (2015), p. 1079; Reisoğlu (2014), pp. 364–365; Oğuzman and Öz (2015), p. 419.

22.5.2 Conditions

In order for a debtor to be liable for his assistants, the following conditions must be met: (1) the debtor must delegate the performance of an obligation or the exercise of a right resulting from an obligational relationship to assistants; (2) this delegation must not be contrary to the obligation; (3) the assistants' conduct must breach the debtor's obligation and cause damage to the creditor; (4) it must be the case that if the debtor had performed the obligation himself, he would have been liable; and (5) there must not be an agreement excluding liability of the debtor for the conduct of the assistants.

The first condition required for the debtor's liability for assistants is that the debtor must delegate the performance of an obligation or the exercise of a right resulting from an obligational relationship to his assistants.[73] For instance, assume that a moving company is obliged to transport a piano belonging to a virtuoso. The performance of the obligation will be carried out by its employees who are deemed to be its assistants. As another example, consider that a woman leases a car from a rental company. She is entitled to drive this car herself, but she may also allow her driver or spouse to drive it. In this case, the driver or the spouse would be considered an assistant.

An assistant may be any person. For a person to be considered an assistant, a superior–subordinate relationship between the debtor and the assistant is not necessary. Furthermore, any person who is participating in the performance of the obligation or the exercise of the right, with the consent of the debtor, is an assistant.[74] In the 'piano' example, even if a passer-by helps the employee to move the piano with the consent of the debtor, he is considered to be an assistant. The consent of the debtor may be express or implied. If the debtor does not give his consent to a third party to participate in the performance of the obligation or to exercise the rights, then he is not liable for the conduct of the third party.[75] This is due to the fact that the third party cannot be deemed to be an assistant. It should be noted that the managing boards of legal entities are also not deemed to be assistants.[76]

The second condition required for the debtor's liability for his assistants is that the delegation of the performance of the obligation or the exercise of the rights arising from the obligational relationship must not be contrary to the obligation. Otherwise, the debtor will not be liable according to TCO art. 115; on the contrary, his liability will be based on TCO art. 112.[77] For example, a well-known architect promises to design a project himself, without the use of assistants. If he acts contrary to the agreement and makes use of assistants, he will be liable for breaching the obligation.

---

[73]von Tuhr and Escher (1974), § 70, I, 122; Tekinay et al. (1993), p. 892; Oğuzman and Öz (2015), p. 413; Eren (2015), p. 1073; Feyzioğlu (1977), pp. 192–193.

[74]von Tuhr and Escher (1974), § 70, II, 123; Becker (1941), art. 101, N. 9; Engel (1997), p. 740; Oğuzman and Öz (2015), pp. 414–415; Eren (2015), p. 1074.

[75]Oğuzman and Öz (2015), p. 415; Reisoğlu (2014), p. 364.

[76]Tekinay et al. (1993), p. 896; Oğuzman and Öz (2015), p. 417; Reisoğlu (2014), p. 364.

[77]Oğuzman and Öz (2015), p. 419.

The third condition required for the debtor's liability for assistants is that the assistant must breach the debtor's obligation and cause damage to the creditor.[78] In the 'piano' example, if the employees damage the piano while moving it, the debtor, that is to say, the moving company, is liable for the damage. In the 'rental car' example, if the lessee's spouse causes damage to the car while driving it, the lessee is liable for this damage.

At this point, it should be noted that the conduct of the assistants must be contrary to the obligation of the debtor. If not, the debtor is not liable.[79] For instance, in the 'piano' example, an employee of the moving company steals a wallet from one of the virtuoso's guests. In such a case, it is obvious that the employee is liable for the theft, but the moving company is not liable. This is because the moving company is not obliged to protect the assets or personal rights of third parties, for example, the guests of the virtuoso.

The fourth condition required for the debtor's liability for assistants is that it must be the case that if the debtor had performed the obligation himself, he would have been liable.[80] The debtor's liability for assistants does not require fault on the part of either the debtor or the assistants.[81] Furthermore, the debtor will not be released from his liability even if he proves that he exercised all due care while choosing (*cura in eligendo*), instructing (*cura in instruendo*) and supervising (*cura in custodiendo*) his assistants.[82] However, this does not mean that the debtor is liable in every case. This is because the liability of the debtor is not based solely on the fact that he used an assistant. Therefore, in the event that the damage arises from the fault of a third party, from the fault of the creditor, from a force majeure (*vis major*) or from a fortuitous event (*casus fortuitus*), the debtor may claim that if he had performed the obligation himself, he would not have been liable and, consequently, may be released from liability.[83] For instance, in the 'piano' example, if there is an earthquake while the employees move the piano and the stairs collapse and, thus, the piano is destroyed, the debtor will not be liable for the damage incurred.

The fifth condition required for the debtor's liability for assistants is that there must not be an agreement excluding liability of the debtor for the conduct of his assistants. If there is such an agreement, the debtor will not be held liable.[84] Indeed, according to TCO art. 116 par. 2, the liability of the debtor for the assistants may be

[78]Engel (1997), p. 742; Oğuzman and Öz (2015), p. 419; Reisoğlu (2014), p. 365; Tekinay et al. (1993), p. 896; Eren (2015), p. 1079.

[79]Oğuzman and Öz (2015), p. 420.

[80]von Tuhr and Escher (1974), § 70, III, p. 129; Becker (1941), art. 101, N. 14; Oğuzman and Öz (2015), p. 422; Serozan (2014), p. 286, *Cf.* Thévenoz and Werro (2012), art. 101, N. 25–30.

[81]Engel (1997), p. 743; Oğuzman and Öz (2015), p. 422; Nomer (2015), p. 312.

[82]von Tuhr and Escher (1974), § 70, I, p. 122; Engel (1997), pp. 743–744; Oğuzman and Öz (2015), p. 422; Nomer (2015), p. 312; Tercier et al. (2016), pp. 391–392.

[83]Engel (1997), p. 744; Nomer (2015), p. 312.

[84]Tekinay et al. (1993), pp. 899–900; Eren (2015), p. 1085; Oğuzman and Öz (2015), p. 423; Reisoğlu (2014), pp. 366–367.

excluded wholly or partially in advance by an agreement. However, according to TCO art. 116 par. 3, if a service or profession requires proficiency, which can only be undertaken with the permission of competent authorities or the law, then any agreement concluded in advance that purports to exclude the debtor's liability for the conduct of assistants is void.

In the event of the debtor being liable for the conduct of assistants, the creditor, as a rule, is not entitled to demand that the assistants compensate the damage. This is due to the fact that there is no contractual relationship between the creditor and the assistants. However, if the assistants' conduct, which breaches the debtor's obligation, constitutes a tort against the creditor, the latter may demand that the assistants compensate for the damage, according to the provisions relating to tort (TCO art. 49 *ff*).[85]

If a debtor who is liable for his assistants' conduct compensates the creditor's damage, he may have recourse to the assistants. In such a case, there are two possibilities: (1) if there is an agreement between the debtor and the assistants and the assistants' conduct breaches this agreement, the debtor may have recourse to the assistants based on this contractual relationship; (2) if there is no agreement between the debtor and the assistants, then the debtor may have recourse to the assistants provided that the latter's conduct constitutes a tort against the creditor. In such a case, according to TCO art. 62, in considering the apportionment of the compensation among the people who are jointly and severally liable for the same damage, the judge must take into consideration all the circumstances—particularly the degree of fault attributed to each and the severity of the risk created by each.

22.6 Pre-contractual Liability (*Culpa in Contrahendo*)[86]

As analysed in the formation of the contract, the negotiating parties must protect each other's assets and personal rights.[87] If one of the negotiating parties breaches this duty of care, resulting from the principles of good faith (TCC art. 2), and the other party suffers certain damage, the breaching party must compensate for the injured party's damage.

As a rule, in order for the breaching party to be liable for the other's damage, he must be at fault. However, if the breaching party's legal position requires that he be held liable without fault, then he must compensate the other party's damage arising from the contractual negotiations even if he is not at fault.

The breaching party's pre-contractual liability does not require the conclusion of the contract.[88] In other words, even if negotiations between the parties do not result

[85]von Tuhr and Escher (1974), § 70, V, p. 130; Oser and Schönenberger (1929), art. 101, N. 13.

[86]For further explanations see Yalman (2006).

[87]See Sect. 1.10.

[88]von Tuhr and Peter (1979), § 24, VII, p. 193.

in the formation of a contract or if the contract is void, the breaching party may still be held liable.[89] At this point, it is worth noting that if persons do not intend to negotiate a contract, the fact that they are in social contact is not sufficient for the principles of good faith to give rise to an obligation to protect each other's assets and personal rights.[90]

Since there is no specific rule for the pre-contractual liability of negotiating parties in the Turkish Code of Obligations, the basis of this liability is contentious. Certain scholars are of the opinion that the breaching party should be held liable in accordance with the provisions relating to tort (TCO art. 49 *ff*).[91] Other scholars argue that the liability of the breaching party is based on the provisions pertaining to non-performance of the obligation (TCO art. 112 *ff*).[92] The latter opinion is to the advantage of the party who has incurred the damage, especially with regard to the period of limitation and the burden of proof. Indeed, in tort law, pursuant to TCO art. 72 par. 1, the claim for compensation becomes time-barred after 2 years from the date when the injured party has become aware of the damage and of the person liable, but in any case, after 10 years from the date when the act causing the injury occurred. However, the claim for damages resulting from a breach of contract becomes time-barred after 10 years. Furthermore, if the bases of pre-contractual liability are the provisions relating to tort, then the damaged party must prove that the defendant is at fault (TCO art. 50 par. 1), whereas if the bases of pre-contractual liability are the provisions pertaining to non-performance of an obligation, then the injured party does not have to prove that the defendant is at fault (TCO art. 112).

Even if there is no specific provision governing pre-contractual liability (*culpa in contrahendo*, fault in contracting) in the Turkish Code of Obligations,[93] there are certain provisions relating to this type of liability. For instance, TCO art. 35 states that if the mistaken party is at fault and rescinds the contract because of the material mistake, then he must compensate the other party's damage resulting from the rescission.[94] Another example is TCO art. 47 par. 1 sent. 1, which states that if a person attempts to conclude a contract in the name of another without the authority of agency and the alleged principal does not ratify the contract, then the alleged agent must compensate the third party's damage resulting from the nullity of the contract.[95]

---

[89]Reisoğlu (2014), p. 345; Oğuzman and Öz (2015), p. 38; Tercier (2004), p. 125.

[90]Oğuzman and Öz (2015), pp. 39–40, *Cf.* Kocayusufpaşaoğlu (2014), pp. 10–11.

[91]Kılıçoğlu (2013), pp. 85–86; Oser and Schönenberger (1929), art. 26, art. 39.

[92]Schwenzer (2009), p. 345; Tekinay et al. (1993), pp. 205, 979; Eren (2015), pp. 1131–1132; Ergüne (2008), pp. 115–116; von Tuhr and Peter (1979), pp. 193, 318, 404; Serozan (2014), pp. 252–255.

[93]There is a specific rule in BGB relating to pre-contractual liability (See BGB § 311 subs. 2, 3).

[94]See Sect. 11.1.5.

[95]See Sect. 13.3.

References

Akman GS (1976) Sorumsuzluk anlaşması. Sulhi garan matbaası, İstanbul
Altınok Ormancı P (2016) Zararı azaltma külfeti. On iki levha, İstanbul
Aybay A (2011) Borçlar hukuku dersleri genel bölüm. Filiz, İstanbul
Aydıncık Ş (2013) Yapma borçlarının ifa edilmemesi ve hukuki sonuçları özellikle tbk m. 113/I kapsamında nama ifa. Vedat, İstanbul
Başalp N (2011) Sorumsuzluk anlaşmaları. On iki levha, İstanbul
Başoğlu B (2012) Türk hukukunda ve mukayeseli hukukta aynen ifa talebi. On iki levha, İstanbul
Baysal B (2012) Zarar görenin kusuru (müterafik kusur). On iki levha, İstanbul
Becker H (1941) Kommentar zum Schweizerischen Zivilgesetzbuch, vol VI, Obligationenrecht, 1. Abteilung: Allgemeine Bestimmungen, Art. 1-183. Stämpfli, Bern
Berger B (2012) Allgemeines Schuldrecht. Stämpfli, Bern
Engel P (1997) Traité des obligations en droit Suisse. Stämpfli, Bern
Eren F (1985) Sorumluluk hukuku açısından uygun illiyet bağı teorisi. Ankara üniversitesi hukuk fakültesi, Ankara
Eren F (2015) Borçlar hukuku genel hükümler. Yetkin, Ankara
Ergüne MS (2008) Olumsuz zarar. Beta, İstanbul
Feyzioğlu FN (1977) Borçlar hukuku genel hükümler, vol 2. Fakülteler, İstanbul
Gauch P, Schluep WR, Emmenegger S (2008a) Schweizerisches Obligationenrecht, Allgemeiner Teil, vol 2. Schulthess, Zürich
Gauch P, Schluep WR, Schmid J (2008b) Schweizerisches Obligationenrecht, Allgemeiner Teil, vol 1. Schulthess, Zürich
Genç Arıdemir A (2008) Sözleşmeye aykırılıktan doğan manevi tazminat. On iki levha, İstanbul
Gözübüyük AP (1957) Hukuki mesuliyet bakımından mücbir sebepler ve beklenmeyen haller. Kazancı, Ankara
Gündoğdu F (2014) Borca aykırılık hallerinden kusurlu ifa imkânsızlığı ve hukuki sonuçları. On iki levha, İstanbul
Honsell H, Vogt NP, Wiegand W (eds) (2003) Basler Kommentar zum Schweizerischen Privatrecht, Obligationenrecht 1: Art. 1-529 OR. Helbing Lichtenhahn, Basel
Kılıçoğlu AM (2013) Borçlar hukuku genel hükümler. Turhan, İstanbul
Kocayusufpaşaoğlu N (2014) Borçlar hukuku genel bölüm, vol 1 (Kocayusufpaşaoğlu/Hatemi/Serozan/Arpacı). Filiz, İstanbul
Kuru B (2016) İstinaf sistemine göre yazılmış icra ve iflas hukuku. Legal, İstanbul
Nomer HN (1996) Haksız fiil sorumluluğunda maddi tazminatın belirlenmesi. Beta, İstanbul
Nomer HN (2015) Borçlar hukuku genel hükümler. Beta, İstanbul
Oğuzman K, Öz T (2015) Borçlar hukuku genel hükümler, vol 1. Vedat, İstanbul
Oğuzman K, Öz T (2016) Borçlar hukuku genel hükümler, vol 2. Vedat, İstanbul
Oğuzman K, Seliçi Ö, Oktay Özdemir S (2016) Eşya hukuku. Filiz, İstanbul
Oser H, Schönenberger W (1929) Kommentar zum Schweizerischen Zivilgesetzbuch, Volume V: Das Obligationenrecht, Erster Halbband: Art. 1-183. Schulthess, Zürich
Pekcanıtez H, Atalay O, Sungurtekin Özkan M, Özekes M (2013) İcra ve iflas hukuku. Yetkin, Ankara
Reisoğlu S (2014) Türk borçlar hukuku genel hükümler. Beta, İstanbul
Schwenzer I (2009) Schweizerisches Obligationenrecht, Allgemeiner Teil. Schulthess, Bern
Serozan R (2014) Borçlar hukuku genel bölüm, vol 3 (Kocayusufpaşaoğlu/Hatemi/Serozan/Arpacı). Filiz, İstanbul
Şenocak Z (1995) Borçlunun ifa yardımcılarından dolayı sorumluluğu. Dayınlarlı, Ankara
Steinauer PH (2002) Les droits réels, vol 2. Stämpfli, Bern
Tandoğan H (1990) Borçlar hukuku özel borç ilişkileri, vol I/1. Evrim, İstanbul
Tekinay SS, Akman S, Burcuoğlu H, Altop A (1993) Tekinay borçlar hukuku genel hükümler. Filiz, İstanbul
Tercier P (2004) Le droit des obligations. Schulthess, Zurich

Tercier P, Pichonnaz P, Develioğlu HM (2016) Borçlar hukuku genel hükümler. On iki levha, İstanbul
Tercier P (2003) Les contrats spéciaux. Schulthess, Zurich
Thévenoz L, Werro F (éd) (2012) Commentaire romand code des obligations 1: art. 1-529 CO. Helbing Lichtenhahn, Bâle
von Tuhr A, Escher A (1974) Allgemeiner Teil des Schweizerischen Obligationenrecht, vol 2. Schulthess, Zürich
von Tuhr A, Peter H (1979) Allgemeiner Teil des Schweizerischen Obligationenrecht, vol 1. Schulthess, Zürich
Yalman S (2006) Türk-İsviçre hukukunda sözleşme görüşmelerinden doğan sorumluluk. Seçkin, Ankara
Yavuz C (2014) Türk borçlar hukuku özel hükümler. Beta, İstanbul

Chapter 23
Default of the Debtor

23.1 Requirements[1]

When an obligation becomes due, the fact that the debtor does not perform the obligation creates a delay in performance of the obligation. As a general rule, a delay in performance of the obligation does not automatically constitute the debtor's default[2] by itself. According to TCO art. 117 par. 1, in order for a debtor to fall into default, the obligation must be due, the debtor must fail to perform the obligation and the creditor must give notice for performance.

Even if TCO art. 117 par. 1 seems not to require any other conditions for the debtor to be in default, the following requirements must be met:[3] (1) the obligation must have fallen due. Since the creditor cannot demand the performance of the obligation before it falls due, the debtor cannot be in default earlier than this. (2) The debtor must have failed to perform the obligation; in other words, the debtor must have been delayed in the performance of his obligation. (3) The performance of the obligation must still be possible. As mentioned above, if the performance of the obligation becomes impossible after the formation of the contract, then the provisions pertaining to the default of the debtor cannot be

[1] Aybay (2011), pp. 142–148; Becker (1941), art. 102–09; Berger (2012), pp. 570–595; Engel (1997), pp. 684–696, 725–738; Eren (2015), pp. 1089–1128; Feyzioğlu (1977), pp. 229–266; Gauch et al. (2008), pp. 106–136; Honsell et al. (2003), Vorbemerkungen zu art. 102–109, art. 102–109; Kılıçoğlu (2013), pp. 683–737; Nomer (2015), pp. 334–375; Oser and Schönenberger (1929), Vorbemerkungen zu art. 102–109, art. 102–109; Oğuzman and Öz (2015), pp. 455–467, 479–530; Reisoğlu (2014), pp. 369–392; Schwenzer (2009), pp. 461–474; Serozan (2014), pp. 216–246; Tekinay et al. (1993), pp. 911–972; Tercier (2004), pp. 230–240; Tercier et al. (2016), pp. 399–420; Thévenoz and Werro (2012), art. 102–109, and von Tuhr and Escher (1974), pp. 135–160.

[2] *Demeure du débiteur*, *Verzug des Schuldners*.

[3] Engel (1997), pp. 684–690; Thévenoz and Werro (2012), art. 102, N. 10–32; Eren (2015), pp. 1092–1099; Oğuzman and Öz (2015), pp. 456–465; Tekinay et al. (1993), pp. 911–919.

İ. Helvacı, *Turkish Contract Law*, DOI 10.1007/978-3-319-60061-1_23

applied. On the contrary, the provisions relating to the impossibility of performance—*i.e.*, the provisions concerning subsequent impossibility[4]—must be applied. For example, a pianist is obliged to give a concert on a specific date—*e.g.*, during the opening ceremony of the Olympics. If she does not perform the obligation on this date, it is obvious that the performance of the obligation becomes impossible. Depending on the circumstances, she may be responsible for any damage resulting from the impossibility of the obligation. (4) The creditor must be able to accept performance of the obligation. If the creditor is not able or willing to accept performance of the obligation, then the debtor cannot be in default. For instance, in an alternative obligation, the parties agree that the right of choice belongs to the creditor. If the creditor does not elect which obligation is to be performed, the debtor cannot be in default. Finally, (5) the creditor must give notice to the debtor demanding the performance of the obligation. A notice of default is a notification given to a debtor stating that he must fulfil the obligation. The notice of default comes into force when it reaches the debtor. As a rule, the validity of the notice of default does not require any particular form. However, according to the TComC art. 18 par. 3, notices of default between merchants must be made by means of a formal notice from a notary, a registered letter, a telegram or a registered electronic mail system using a secure electronic signature.[5]

In certain cases, the giving of notice of default is not necessary: (1) the parties may determine the time of performance of the obligation by agreement or (2) one of the parties may determine the time of performance using a right granted to him by virtue of the parties' agreement; in these cases, the relevant principle is *dies interpellat pro homine*—that is to say, no express demand need be made as the date acts as the demand—or (3) for a tortfeasor, or for a person acting in bad faith who is unjustly enriched, giving a notice of default is not necessary. However, if the unjustly enriched person acts in good faith, notice of default is nevertheless necessary (TCO art. 117 par. 2).[6]

If giving a notice of default is necessary for the debtor's default, he falls into default when the notice reaches him. In the event that the date acts as the demand (*dies interpellat pro homine)*, the debtor falls into default as soon as the time of performance has passed. The tortfeasor is in default when he commits the tortious act. Further, a person unjustly enriched acting in bad faith is in default as of the time of enrichment.

[4]See Sect. 22.2.1.

[5]It is worth noting that even if the creditor does not comply with this article, the claim for performance may be valid and enforceable as these form requirements relate not to the validity of the notification but to proof.

[6]Oğuzman and Öz (2015), p. 460; Nomer (2015), p. 339; Reisoğlu (2014), p. 372.

23.2 General Consequences

When the debtor is in default, the creditor may simply continue to demand specific performance of the obligation. Indeed, a specific performance demand is the normal consequence of the obligational relationship. The consequences of the debtor's default are as follows[7]: (1) the creditor may demand compensation for damage resulting from the debtor's default (TCO art. 118), and (2) the debtor is liable for force majeure or fortuitous events that occur following his default (TCO art. 119).

23.2.1 Compensation for Damage

As mentioned above, where the debtor's default results in certain damage, the creditor may demand that the debtor compensate for the damage (TCO art. 118). The creditor must prove both the existence and the extent of the damage. If he fails to prove the exact amount of the damage, the extent of liability of the debtor will be determined in accordance with the provisions relating to tort liability. This is because TCO art. 114 par. 2 states that the rules relating to tort liability[8] apply by analogy to cases of breach of contract. Therefore, according to TCO art. 50 par. 2, if the exact amount of the damage is not proven, it is determined by the court at its discretion; the court must take into consideration the ordinary course of events and the mitigating measures taken by the creditor.

The default of the debtor does not require that the debtor be at fault.[9] Nevertheless, where the debtor is not at fault in falling into default, then he is not liable to pay damages (TCO art. 118 par. 1). It is worth remembering that, as a rule, the debtor is presumed to be at fault, but he may refute this presumption of fault (TCO art. 112).[10] However, if the debtor cannot prove that he is not at fault, he must compensate for the creditor's damage resulting from his default.[11]

Such damage is referred to as positive damage, and this includes both actual damage (*damnum emergens*) and the loss of opportunity to obtain a benefit (*lucrum cessans*) and avoid a loss.[12] For instance, a lessor is obliged to lease a car to a travel agency, and the travel agency is obliged to pay a lease fee of €400 per day. If the car is not delivered on the due date and the travel agency is required to lease another car

[7]Tekinay et al. (1993), pp. 920–929; Oğuzman and Öz (2015), pp. 480–485; Tercier et al. (2016), pp. 405–406.

[8]For further explanations see Nomer (1996).

[9]von Tuhr and Escher (1974), § 72, V, p. 141; Feyzioğlu (1977), p. 241; Tekinay et al. (1993), p. 919; Oğuzman and Öz (2015), pp. 465–466; Eren (2015), pp. 1098–1099; Nomer (2015), p. 340.

[10]See Sect. 22.2.3.2.2.

[11]Eren (2015), p. 1102; Oğuzman and Öz (2015), p. 482; Reisoğlu (2014), p. 374.

[12]Becker (1941), art. 103, N. 14 *ff.*; Feyzioğlu (1977), p. 243; Tekinay et al. (1993), p. 925; Oğuzman and Öz (2015), pp. 480–481; Eren (2015), pp. 1103–1104.

from a rental company for €500 per day, then the difference between the two rates is the quantum of the lessee's damage, and this is referred to as actual damage. Furthermore, the travel agency subleases the car to a tourist for €600 per day for one week. Thus, it expects to obtain a profit of €200 per day and €1400 in total. In addition, there is a penalty clause[13] in the agreement that states that in the event of the travel agency failing to deliver the car, it will pay €1000. Due to the lessor's default, the travel agency is not able to deliver the car to the sublessee. Consequently, the travel agency pays a penalty of €1000 (actual damage) to the sublessee and, in addition, is deprived of the opportunity to obtain a profit of €1400 (loss of profit). The lessor must compensate this damage resulting from his default. However, the lessor is discharged from this liability if he can prove that the delay is, in no respect, his fault.

23.2.2 Liability for Force Majeure and Fortuitous Events

The second consequence of the debtor's default is liability for any accidents that occur following the default. The debtor is discharged from this liability by proving that (1) he is not at fault in falling into default or (2) even if he had performed the obligation in a timely manner, the accident would have affected the subject matter of the obligation (TCO art. 119).[14]

For instance, a car repair company is obliged to fix a car, and the parties set the specific date by which the car is to be repaired and delivered. However, the debtor fails to fix the car and deliver it in the required time and, thus, falls into default (TCO art. 117 par. 2). Afterwards, the car is completely destroyed in a fire that arises from a lightning strike while in the possession of the defaulting debtor. In this case, even if the fire is not the fault of the debtor, he is nevertheless liable for the damage suffered by the car owner. However, where the debtor proves that he is not at fault[15] for falling into default or that punctual performance would not have prevented the car from being burned in the same fire,[16] then he is released from this liability.

---

[13]See Sect. 31.3.2.

[14]Tekinay et al. (1993), pp. 927–928; Oğuzman and Öz (2015), pp. 483–485; Eren (2015), pp. 1105–1106; Nomer (2015), p. 346.

[15]See Sect. 22.2.3.2.2.

[16]Becker (1941), art. 103, N. 22; Oser and Schönenberger (1929), art. 103, N. 12; Tekinay et al. (1993), p. 928; Oğuzman and Öz (2015), p. 485. See on the contrary, von Tuhr and Escher (1974), § 73, I, pp. 145–146 fn. 18; Thévenoz and Werro (2012), art. 104, N. 14; Eren (2015), p. 1106.

23.3 Consequences In Pecuniary Obligations

23.3.1 *Interest for Default*

The first consequence of the debtor's default concerning pecuniary obligations is that the creditor may demand that the debtor pay default interest.[17] The debtor may not be discharged from the payment of default interest even if he is not at fault in his default.[18] Further, for the payment of default interest, the creditor's damage is irrelevant—*i.e.*, the default interest must be paid even if the creditor has not incurred any damage. In other words, the creditor does not have to prove his damage.[19]

23.3.2 *Contractual Default Interest Rate*

The parties may determine the default interest rate. However, in non-commercial affairs, the annual default interest rate determined by the parties may not exceed twice the amount of the legal interest rate (TCO art. 120 par. 2). Since the legal interest rate for non-commercial affairs is 9% per annum,[20] the parties may determine the default interest rate as up to but not more than 18% per annum.[21]

It is worth noting that pursuant to TComC art. 8 par. 1, in commercial affairs, the parties are free to determine the default interest rate, provided that this rate is not immoral and is not contrary to the provisions protecting personal rights (TCO art. 27 par. 1 and TCC art. 23).[22]

23.3.3 *Legal Default Interest Rate*

In the event of the parties failing to determine the default interest rate, it is determined according to the legislation at the time that the liability for the default interest arises (TCO art. 120 par. 1).

[17]For further explanations see Öçal (1965), Barlas (1992), Helvacı (2000).

[18]von Tuhr and Escher (1974), § 73, II, p. 146; Thévenoz and Werro (2012), art. 104, N. 4; Eren (2015), p. 1100; Oğuzman and Öz (2015), p. 486; Serozan (2014), p. 224.

[19]von Tuhr and Escher (1974), § 73, II, p. 146; Thévenoz and Werro (2012), art. 104, N. 4; Eren (2015), p. 1100; Oğuzman and Öz (2015), p. 486; Tekinay et al. (1993), p. 930; Reisoğlu (2014), p. 376; Tercier et al. (2016), p. 406.

[20]See Sect. 15.7.4.

[21]Oğuzman and Öz (2015), p. 488; Nomer (2015), p. 350.

[22]Eren (2015), p. 1101; Oğuzman and Öz (2015), p. 489.

According to LIA art. 2 par. 1, the legal default interest rate is determined according to the capital interest rate indicated in LIA art. 1. Since the legal capital interest rate is 9% per annum,[23] according to this article, the legal rate of the default interest is also 9% per annum, but only in non-commercial affairs.[24]

As to commercial affairs, if the interest rate for short-term advances set by the Turkish Central Bank on 31 December of the preceding year is higher than the rate indicated in LIA art. 1—*e.g.*, 9% per annum, then, even if there is no contractual relationship between the parties, the creditor may demand that this higher rate be applied. If there is a difference of five or more points between the said advance interest rate set on 31 December of the preceding year and the advance interest rate set on 30 June, then the latter is applied for the second part of the year (LIA art. 2 par. 2).[25]

It should be noted that even if the parties do not determine the default interest rate, they may determine the capital interest rate. Should the capital interest rate be higher than the default interest rate as determined with regard to LIA art. 2 par. 1 and par. 2, then the default interest rate cannot be lower than the capital interest rate (LIA art. 2 par. 3). This principle is applicable in both commercial and non-commercial affairs. Indeed, TCO art. 120 par. 3 supports this view. According to the said article, if the parties have not determined the default interest rate, but they have determined the capital interest rate, and the capital interest rate is higher than the legal default interest rate, then the contractual capital interest rate applies as the default interest rate.[26]

The rules explained above also apply to pecuniary obligations in foreign currency. However, the legal default interest rate will be equivalent to the maximum interest rate that the state banks pay on a term deposit account opened in the relevant foreign currency with a one-year maturity (compare to LIA art. 4 a).

23.3.4 Legal Nature

A default interest debt is an ancillary right of a principal pecuniary obligation. Thus, a default interest debt requires the existence of a principal pecuniary obligation. Consequently, if the principal pecuniary obligation is extinguished, the default interest debt will also be extinguished.[27] Where the debtor has paid the pecuniary obligation, then the default interest debt can only be claimed if such a right is reserved in the contract or is reserved by the creditor's notification, which must be made by the date of performance, or if such a reservation is inferred from the circumstances (TCO art. 131 par. 2).

---

[23]See Sect. 15.7.4.

[24]Reisoğlu (2014), p. 375; Oğuzman and Öz (2015), pp. 487–488; Nomer (2015), p. 354.

[25]Oğuzman and Öz (2015), pp. 488–489; Nomer (2015), p. 354; Reisoğlu (2014), p. 375.

[26]Tercier et al. (2016), p. 407; Oğuzman and Öz (2015), p. 488; Nomer (2015), p. 356.

[27]Oğuzman and Öz (2015), p. 494; Nomer (2015), p. 284.

Although the default interest debt is an ancillary right of the principal pecuniary obligation, a claim relating to the former may be assigned or sued upon independently of the latter.[28]

23.3.5 In Case of Interest, Annuities and Gifts

Where a debtor does not fulfil a pecuniary obligation, the creditor is entitled to demand that the debtor pay default interest. In principle, on the demand of the creditor, the debtor must pay default interest from the time when he falls into default until the pecuniary obligation is discharged or extinguished.[29]

However, in certain cases, the creditor may only demand interest from the day that enforcement proceedings were initiated or the lawsuit was filed. Pursuant to TCO art. 121 par. 1, where a debtor is in default with the payment of interest, pension or donated sum, he need only pay default interest commencing from the date on which the enforcement is initiated or the lawsuit is filed. An agreement that is contrary to the said article is subject to the provisions concerning penalties (TCO art. 121 par. 2). Thus, if a penalty is considered to be excessively high by a judge, it may be reduced at the judge's discretion *ex officio* (TCO art. 182 par. 3).[30]

It should be noted that compound interest (default interest charged on accrued default interest) is prohibited (TCO art. 121 par. 3).

23.3.6 Further Damage[31]

In certain cases, default interest is not sufficient for the reparation of the creditor's damage. In other words, the creditor's damage is higher than the default interest paid by the debtor. In these cases, the creditor may demand that the debtor compensate the damage that is not satisfied by the payment of the default interest.

For any demand relating to additional damage to be accepted, the creditor must prove that such damage was actually incurred.[32] However, if the debtor proves that there is no fault on his part,[33] then he is released from the demand to pay compensation for the creditor's further damage (TCO art. 122 par. 1).[34]

[28]Oğuzman and Öz (2015), p. 494; Nomer (2015), pp. 283–284; Eren (2015), p. 1102.

[29]von Tuhr and Escher (1974), § 73, fn. 23, p. 146; Becker (1941), art. 104, N. 7; Engel (1997), p. 692; Oğuzman and Öz (2015), p. 492; Reisoğlu (2014), p. 376.

[30]Oğuzman and Öz (2015), p. 492; Eren (2015), p. 1101; Reisoğlu (2014), p. 377.

[31]For further explanations see Domaniç (1993), Ayrancı (2006).

[32]Engel (1997), p. 694; Thévenoz and Werro (2012), art. 106, N. 6; Oğuzman and Öz (2015), p. 495; Eren (2015), p. 1108; Tercier et al. (2016), p. 408; Feyzioğlu (1977), p. 252.

[33]See Sect. 22.2.3.2.2.

[34]Engel (1997), p. 694; Eren (2015), p. 1108.

If the additional damage can be determined in advance in a pending lawsuit, then, upon demand by the creditor, the court may award the quantum of the additional damage in its judgment for payment of the principal claim (TCO art. 122 par. 2).

23.4 Consequences In Bilateral Contracts

23.4.1 General

As a general rule, a creditor may demand performance of an obligation as long as performance is possible. This demand is a natural consequence of the obligational relationship (contract). The default of a debtor has two general consequences: (1) the creditor may demand compensation for damage resulting from the debtor's default (TCO art. 118), and (2) the debtor is liable for any force majeure or fortuitous events subsequent to the default (TCO art. 119).

Where bilateral contracts are concerned, the Turkish Code of Obligations grants particular rights to the creditor, which will be considered in this section. In order for the creditor to exercise these rights, he must grant a certain period of time to the defaulting debtor, and this period of time must be reasonable. Furthermore, the creditor may demand that the court determine this period of time (TCO art. 123). In the latter case, the court decision precludes prospective disputes relating to the reasonableness of the period of time.[35]

In certain cases, the creditor is not obliged to grant a period of grace to the debtor for performance. Pursuant to TCO art. 124, granting a period of time is not necessary in the following cases: (1) if it is inferred from the circumstances or from the conduct of the debtor that granting a period of grace would be futile—*e.g.*, if the debtor declares that he will not perform his obligation[36]; (2) if the performance of the obligation has become meaningless for the creditor due to the default of the debtor—*e.g.*, a mother orders a birthday cake for her daughter's birthday and prepares a big celebration party but the baker does not deliver the cake on time[37]; and (3) if it is inferred from the contract that performance is no longer acceptable for the creditor after a fixed time or after a certain period of time—*e.g.*, in a contract pertaining to a specific machine, the machine is to be delivered on a precise date and

[35]Oğuzman and Öz (2015), p. 502; Eren (2015), p. 1111; Reisoğlu (2014), p. 384.

[36]von Tuhr and Escher (1974), § 73, IV, 1, p. 150; Becker (1941), art. 108, N. 3; Engel (1997), p. 729; Thévenoz and Werro (2012), art. 108, N. 4–5; Oğuzman and Öz (2015), p. 523; Tekinay et al. (1993), p. 950; Serozan (2014), p. 230.

[37]von Tuhr and Escher (1974), § 73, IV, 2, pp. 150–151; Engel (1997), p. 730; Thévenoz and Werro (2012), art. 108, N. 6–8; Becker (1941), art. 106, N. 8; Oğuzman and Öz (2015), p. 523; Tekinay et al. (1993), p. 950; Eren (2015), p. 1113; Feyzioğlu (1977), p. 257.

the parties agree that late performance will not be acceptable. In that case, the debtor may not deliver it after the due date.[38]

If the debtor fulfils his obligation by the end of the granted period of time, the obligation is extinguished by performance. Where the debtor fails to fulfil his obligation by the end of this period of time or where it is not necessary to grant a period of time to the debtor, the creditor may exercise one of two additional rights arising from TCO art. 125. These rights will be analysed in the following paragraphs. At this point, it should be noted that, as a rule, the creditor may have these additional rights only when the debtor's default relates to his primary obligations (main duty). For instance, in a sale contract, the primary obligation (main duty) of the seller is to transfer ownership of the subject matter of the contract to the buyer. The seller may also be under certain subsidiary obligations (subsidiary duties), along with the primary obligation, such as packing the goods or giving necessary information or instructions for their proper use. In such a case, if the debtor's default relates to his primary obligation, that is to say the transfer of ownership, then the creditor may have these additional rights, whereas if the debtor's default relates to his subsidiary obligations, such as giving necessary information, then the creditor may not have these additional rights.[39]

23.4.2 Additional Alternative Rights

According to TCO art. 125 par. 2, if a creditor waives the right to specific performance and compensation for damage arising from the debtor's default, then the creditor may, in lieu thereof, demand compensation for damage for non-performance of the obligation[40] or may withdraw from the contract (*ex tunc*). If the creditor intends to exercise these rights, he must declare his intention immediately.[41]

23.4.2.1 Right to Compensation

If the creditor intends to demand compensation for damage arising from non-performance of the obligation, then he must give notice of this intention to the debtor. As a rule, this notification does not require a form, and this right may be exercised orally or in writing. Nevertheless, in certain cases, T.Com.C art. 18 par.

[38]Engel (1997), pp. 730–731; Thévenoz and Werro (2012), art. 108, N. 9–14; Oğuzman and Öz (2015), p. 524; Tekinay et al. (1993), p. 952; Eren (2015), p. 1114; Serozan (2014), p. 231; Nomer (2015), p. 364; von Tuhr and Escher (1974), § 73, IV, 3, p. 151

[39]Oğuzman and Öz (2015), p. 499. However, where the non-performance of a subsidiary obligation is so fundamental that performance of the main obligation cannot be performed as required, in those circumstances the creditor may rely on these alternative rights.

[40]For further explanations see Havutçu (1995).

[41]Engel (1997), p. 732; Thévenoz and Werro (2012), art. 107, N. 17; Tercier et al. (2016), p. 411; Reisoğlu (2014), p. 387; Oğuzman and Öz (2015), p. 504.

3 requires a specific form for this notification. Pursuant to this article, between merchants, the demand for compensation for damage must be notified through a notary public or in a registered letter or in a telegram or through a registered electronic mail system using a secured electronic signature.[42]

When the creditor demands compensation for damage arising from non-performance of the obligation, the debtor must pay compensation for this damage unless he proves that he is not at fault[43] in respect of the default (TCO art. 112).

In the event of the creditor demanding compensation for damage resulting from non-performance of the obligation, as a rule, he must still perform his own obligation. However, according to the difference theory (*Differenztheorie*),[44] the creditor will be released from his obligation. Assume, for example, a contract under which H is obliged to transfer ownership of immovable property to C, and in return C is obliged to transfer ownership of a car to H. However, H does not perform his obligation in due time determined by the agreement of the parties, and thus, he falls into default (TCO art. 117 par. 2). C grants a period of time in order for H to perform his obligation (TCO art. 123). But when the period of time has passed, H has still not transferred ownership to C. Subsequently, C wishes to claim compensation for the non-performance of the obligation. In such a case, his obligation to transfer the car to H stands. However, certain scholars argue that C does not have to transfer ownership of the car to H and, being released from the obligation, C may demand the difference in value between the two acts (prestations).[45] For instance, if the value of the immovable property is €100,000 and the value of the car is €80,000, C may demand that H pay €20,000.

23.4.2.2 Right to Withdraw

As mentioned above, the creditor also has the right to withdraw from the contract.[46] If the debtor does not perform his obligation by the end of the granted time period or in cases where granting an additional period of time is not necessary, the creditor may withdraw from the contract (*ex tunc*).[47] In such a case, the creditor must give notice of this intention immediately.[48]

The creditor's notification relating to withdrawal does not require a specific form. As a rule, he may exercise this right orally or in writing. Nevertheless, in

---

[42] It is worth noting that even if the creditor does not comply with this article, the claim for compensation may be valid and enforceable as these form requirements relate not to the validity of the notification but to proof.

[43] See Sect. 22.2.3.2.2.

[44] Oğuzman and Öz (2015), p. 391 *ff*.; Eren (2015), p. 1068; Tekinay et al. (1993), pp. 869–870.

[45] Oğuzman and Öz (2015), p. 393.

[46] For further explanations see Buz (1998), Serozan (2007).

[47] Termination of the contract takes effect retroactively (*résolution*, *Rücktritt*).

[48] Oğuzman and Öz (2015), p. 506.

certain cases, T.Com.C art. 18 par. 3 requires a specific form. Pursuant to this article, between merchants, the declaration of withdrawal must be notified through a notary public or in a registered letter or in a telegram or through a registered electronic mail system using a secured electronic signature.[49]

Where a creditor withdraws from the contract, as a rule, the contract is extinguished *ex tunc*, which is to say, from the date of the formation of the contract. Indeed, in a contract in which obligations are to be performed at one time ('instantaneous' contracts), such as a sale contract, the contract is extinguished as though it had never come into existence. Therefore, both parties are reciprocally released from their responsibilities to perform their obligations and must restitute the acts (prestations) received under the contract (TCO art. 125 par. 3 sent. 1). For instance, if the creditor performs his obligation under the contract by, say, paying the price of the counter-act (counter-prestation) and withdraws from the contract, then he may demand restitution of the money paid. In other words, the debtor must reimburse the money received under the contract.

In cases where a creditor withdraws from the contract (*ex tunc*), he may incur damage due to the withdrawal. This is referred to as negative damage.[50] That is to say, the creditor may demand compensation for damage that he would not have incurred if the contract had not been formed, such as expenses paid towards the conclusion of the contract. When the creditor demands compensation for damage arising out of withdrawal from the contract, the debtor must pay these damages unless he proves that the default is not his fault[51] (TCO art. 125 par. 3 sent. 2).

It should be noted that negative damage does not only consist of the expenses incurred in the course of the formation of the contract.[52] Another example of negative damage is the expenses incurred by the creditor in the expectation that the obligation would be performed. For instance, the creditor rents a warehouse for a machine to be delivered under a contract but subsequently withdraws from said contract upon default by the debtor. In this case, the rent paid for the warehouse is an example of negative damage. A second example is when the creditor is deprived of an opportunity to benefit from another contract offer. For example, the buyer buys a car for €10,000, but the seller does not deliver it. At the same time, another seller offers a similar car for €12,000. The buyer refuses this offer, believing that the first seller would transfer ownership of the car. Afterwards, the first seller falls into default, and the buyer, withdrawing from the sale contract, is forced to enter into a contract with the second seller. However, the second seller has already sold the car to a third party, and the buyer must now pay €14,000 to purchase a similar

---

[49]It is worth noting that even if the creditor does not comply with this article, the declaration of withdrawal may be valid as these form requirements relate not to the validity of the notification but to proof.

[50]For further explanations see Ergüne (2008).

[51]See Sect. 22.2.3.2.2.

[52]von Tuhr and Escher (1974), § 73, VII, p. 156; Becker (1941), art. 109, N. 9; Engel (1997), pp. 734–736; Thévenoz and Werro (2012), art. 109, N. 14; Nomer (2015), pp. 373–374; Reisoğlu (2014), pp. 390–391.

car from a third seller. In this case, the difference of €2000 between the prices of the second and third offers constitutes an example of negative damage.[53]

As to contracts in which obligations are to be performed over a period of time—*i.e.*, continuing contracts—the creditor is not entitled to terminate the contract retroactively, but he may terminate it *ex nunc*;[54] in other words, he may terminate it from the moment that the notification of termination reaches the debtor.[55] TCO art. 126 states that in continuing contracts, on condition that the parties have already begun to perform the obligations, if the debtor is in default, then the creditor may demand performance of the obligation and compensation for damage resulting from default by the debtor. Further, he may, contemporaneously with terminating the contract, demand compensation for damage arising from early (premature) termination of the contract.

23.4.3 Certain Specific Provisions

The legislature has set certain specific provisions regarding the debtor's default in relation to certain types of contract. In the following paragraphs, only the specific provisions relating to the default of a seller or buyer in the sale of movable property are analysed.

According to TCO art. 212 par. 1, in the event that a seller falls into default, the general provisions relating to the default of the debtor will apply. However, in commercial sale contracts, if the parties determine a period of time for the transfer of possession of the goods sold and the seller falls into default, it is assumed that the buyer renounces delivery and claims compensation for the damage arising out of non-performance (TCO art. 212 par. 2). Where the buyer intends to demand delivery, he must notify the seller of this demand immediately after the expiration of the agreed period of time (TCO art. 212 par. 3).

Pursuant to TCO art. 235, if a buyer falls into default in cases where the sold goods are to be delivered after or at the time of payment, the seller may withdraw from the sale contract without further formality, provided that the seller immediately notifies the buyer of this intention. Where the goods have passed to the possession of the buyer prior to payment, the buyer's default does not entitle the seller to withdraw from the contract and to claim the return of the goods, unless he has explicitly reserved such a right in the contract.

[53]Oğuzman and Öz (2015), p. 384.

[54]Termination of the contract takes effect prospectively (*résiliation*, *Kündigung*).

[55]For further explanations see Seliçi (1977).

References

Aybay A (2011) Borçlar hukuku dersleri genel bölüm. Filiz, İstanbul

Ayrancı H (2006) Türk borçlar hukukunda munzam zarar, bk.m.105. Yetkin, Ankara

Barlas N (1992) Para borçlarının ifasında borçlunun temerrüdü ve bu temerrüt açısından düzenlenen genel sonuçlar. İstanbul

Becker H (1941) Kommentar zum Schweizerischen Zivilgesetzbuch, vol VI, Obligationenrecht, 1. Abteilung: Allgemeine Bestimmungen, Art. 1-183. Stämpfli, Bern

Berger B (2012) Allgemeines Schuldrecht. Stämpfli, Bern

Buz V (1998) Borçlunun temerrüdünde sözleşmeden dönme. Yetkin, Ankara

Domaniç H (1993) Faizle karşılanamayan zararların giderilmesini sağlayan bk. 105 ve diğer hükümler. Beta, İstanbul

Engel P (1997) Traité des obligations en droit Suisse. Stämpfli, Bern

Eren F (2015) Borçlar hukuku genel hükümler. Yetkin, Ankara

Ergüne MS (2008) Olumsuz zarar. Beta, İstanbul

Feyzioğlu FN (1977) Borçlar hukuku genel hükümler, vol 2. Fakülteler, İstanbul

Gauch P, Schluep WR, Emmenegger S (2008) Schweizerisches Obligationenrecht, Allgemeiner Teil, vol 2. Schulthess, Zürich

Havutçu A (1995) Tam iki tarafa borç yükleyen sözleşmelerde temerrüt ve müsbet zararın tazmini. İzmir

Helvacı M (2000) Para borçlarında faiz kavramı. Beta, İstanbul

Honsell H, Vogt NP, Wiegand W (eds) (2003) Basler Kommentar zum Schweizerischen Privatrecht, Obligationenrecht 1: Art. 1-529 OR. Helbing Lichtenhahn, Basel

Kılıçoğlu AM (2013) Borçlar hukuku genel hükümler. Turhan, İstanbul

Nomer HN (1996) Haksız fiil sorumluluğunda maddi tazminatın belirlenmesi. Beta, İstanbul

Nomer HN (2015) Borçlar hukuku genel hükümler. Beta, İstanbul

Oğuzman K, Öz T (2015) Borçlar hukuku genel hükümler, vol 1. Vedat, İstanbul

Oser H, Schönenberger W (1929) Kommentar zum Schweizerischen Zivilgesetzbuch, vol V: Das Obligationenrecht, Erster Halbband: Art. 1-183. Schulthess, Zürich

Öçal A (1965) Türk hususi hukukunda gecikme faizi. Eskişehir iktisadi ve ticari ilimler akademisi, İstanbul

Reisoğlu S (2014) Türk borçlar hukuku genel hükümler. Beta, İstanbul

Schwenzer I (2009) Schweizerisches Obligationenrecht, Allgemeiner Teil. Schulthess, Bern

Seliçi Ö (1977) Borçlar kanununa göre sözleşmeden doğan sürekli borç ilişkilerinin sona ermesi. İstanbul üniversitesi, İstanbul

Serozan R (2007) Sözleşmeden dönme. Vedat, İstanbul

Serozan R (2014) Borçlar hukuku genel bölüm, vol 3 (Kocayusufpaşaoğlu/Hatemi/Serozan/Arpacı). Filiz, İstanbul

Tekinay SS, Akman S, Burcuoğlu H, Altop A (1993) Tekinay borçlar hukuku genel hükümler. Filiz, İstanbul

Tercier P (2004) Le droit des obligations. Schulthess, Zurich

Tercier P, Pichonnaz P, Develioğlu HM (2016) Borçlar hukuku genel hükümler. On iki levha, İstanbul

Thévenoz L, Werro F (éd) (2012) Commentaire romand code des obligations 1: art. 1-529 CO. Helbing Lichtenhahn, Bâle

von Tuhr A, Escher A (1974) Allgemeiner Teil des Schweizerischen Obligationenrecht, vol 2. Schulthess, Zürich

Chapter 24
Effects of the Obligation on Third Parties

24.1 Privity of the Obligational Relationship[1]

24.1.1 General

An obligational relationship is a legal bond (*vinculum iuris*) solely between a debtor and a creditor. Thus, as a general rule, an obligational relationship may not give rights to third parties.[2] This principle is referred to as privity of the obligational relationship.

The first consequence of this principle is that third parties are not entitled to demand performance of the obligation.[3] However, in certain cases, the legislature allows a third party to demand performance of the obligation (TCO art. 129).

The second consequence of the said principle is that third parties are not obliged to perform the obligation and are not liable for the non- or improper performance of the obligation. For instance, a seller S is obliged to transfer ownership of a chattel to a buyer B, but S breaches his obligation and transfers ownership of the subject matter of the sale contract to a third party. In this case, B does not have any rights

---

[1]Antalya (2012), p. 138; Aybay (2011), pp. 10–12, 149–151; Becker (1941), art. 110–113; Berger (2012), pp. 25, 802–811, 826–836; Engel (1997), pp. 10, 417–436, 613–615; Eren (2015), pp. 52–56, 1141–1160; Feyzioğlu (1976), pp. 22–23; Feyzioğlu (1977), pp. 267–291; Gauch et al. (2008), pp. 324–339; Honsell et al. (2003), art. 110–113; Kocayusufpaşaoğlu (2014), pp. 15–26; Kılıçoğlu (2013), pp. 564–587; Nomer (2015), pp. 14–24, 411–417; Oser and Schönenberger (1929), Vorbemerkungen zum dritten Abschnitt (art. 110–113), art. 110–113; Oğuzman and Öz (2015), pp. 21–23, 27–29; Oğuzman and Öz (2016), pp. 411–458; Reisoğlu (2014), pp. 34–36, 394–402; Schwenzer (2009), pp. 22–25, 535–546; Serozan (2014), pp. 28–31; Tekinay et al. (1993), pp. 60, 208–239; Tercier (2004), pp. 188–191, 245–246; Tercier et al. (2016), pp. 42–44, 328–332, 426–427; Thévenoz and Werro (2012), art. 110–113, and von Tuhr and Escher (1974), pp. 28–32, 236–254.

[2]von Tuhr and Peter (1979), § 2, p. 9; Engel (1997), p. 10; Kocayusufpaşaoğlu (2014), p. 18.

[3]Tercier (2004), p. 38; Tercier et al. (2016), p. 43; Oğuzman and Öz (2015), p. 21.

İ. Helvacı, *Turkish Contract Law*, DOI 10.1007/978-3-319-60061-1_24

against the third party. In the same example, assume that after the formation of the contract between S and B, but before B becomes the owner, a third party causes damage to the subject matter of the contract. In this case, B is not entitled to demand any compensation from the third party.[4] At this point, it should be noted that, if the third party buys the object aiming to cause damage to B in an immoral manner (*contra bonos mores*), then he is liable to compensate for B's damage (TCO art. 49 par. 2).[5]

The third consequence of the aforementioned principle is that if the debtor does not perform the obligation at all or as required, he is only obliged to compensate for the creditor's damage, even if the third party has also incurred damage.[6] For instance, a yacht contractor C is obliged to construct and deliver a yacht to a buyer B. There is a contract between C and E according to which E must deliver the yacht's engines. In addition, the buyer B enters into a lease contract with L. However, E does not deliver the engines in due time. Subsequently, C is not able to deliver the yacht to B in due time. As a result, B is not able to fulfil the lease contract, and thus, the lessee L is forced to lease another yacht, for which the rental fee is higher than that of B. In this case, even though L's damage arises from E's late performance, it is not possible for L to demand compensation for his damage directly from E. This is due to the fact that there is no contractual relationship between L and E.

However, where the debtor's non- or improper performance constitutes a tort against a third party, the latter, even if he is not entitled to demand compensation from the debtor based on the obligational relationship between the debtor and the creditor, may demand compensation based on tort.[7] For example, a yacht owner O leases his yacht to a lessee L, and during the lease contract, L enters into a mooring contract with the manager of a marina, M. The employees of M, in performing their duties, cause damage to the yacht. In this case, even if there is no contractual relationship between O and M, O may nevertheless demand that M compensate for the damage. Since M owes a duty of care in tort with regard to his employees' conduct, he is liable to pay damages for their unlawful actions (TCO art. 66 par. 1).[8] It should be noted that M can be released from this liability if he can prove that he exercised all due care (*cura in eligendo, cura in instruendo, cura in custodiendo*) to prevent the damage or that the damage would have occurred regardless of his precautions (TCO art. 66 par. 2).[9]

---

[4]Kocayusufpaşaoğlu (2014), p. 16; Feyzioğlu (1976), p. 23; Oğuzman and Öz (2015), p. 21; Eren (2015), p. 54.

[5]Oser and Schönenberger (1929), art. 41, N. 99; Kocayusufpaşaoğlu (2014), p. 17; Oğuzman and Öz (2015), p. 21; Nomer (2015), p. 15; Eren (2015), p. 55. For further explanations see Kapancı (2016).

[6]Oğuzman and Öz (2015), pp. 21–22.

[7]Oğuzman and Öz (2015), pp. 21–22.

[8]For further explanations see Reisoğlu (1958).

[9]Thévenoz and Werro (2012), art. 55, N. 17 *ff*; Engel (1997), pp. 537–538.

24.1.2 *Exceptions*

24.1.2.1 Annotation of Personal Rights in the Land Register

The legislature allows for only a limited number (*numerus clausus*) of personal rights (rights *in personam*) to be noted in the land register.[10] By the annotation of these personal rights, they become enforceable as against holders of any right subsequently acquired over the land.[11] For instance, a landowner enters into a lease contract with a lessee but subsequently transfers ownership of this land to a third party. In such a case, due to the privity of the contractual relationship, it is apparent that the lessee is not entitled to demand that the new owner be bound by the lease contract. However, according to TCO art. 312, the right of the lessee may be noted in the land register. In the above-mentioned example, had the right of the lessee been noted, the new owner would have been bound by the lease contract.

The following examples may also be given for rights that can be noted in the land register[12]: a pre-contract for the sale of real estate (TCC art. 1009), a donor's right of reversion (TCO art. 292 par. 2), an agreement providing for the advancement in rank of a mortgagee (TCC art. 871 par. 3), a construction agreement in return for a land share (TCC art. 1009), a usufructuary lease (TCO art. 358), a right of emption (TCC art. 736), a right of pre-emption resulting from a contract (TCC art. 735) and a right of repurchase (TCC art. 736).

24.1.2.2 Contracts with the Effect of Protecting Third Parties[13]

As mentioned above, since the obligational relationship exists between the debtor and the creditor, even if the debtor's non- or improper performance causes damage to a third party, the latter is not entitled to demand that the debtor compensate for this damage according to the provisions relating to non- or improper performance of the obligation (TCO art. 112).

However, certain scholars are of the opinion that third parties who are proximate to the performance of the obligation should be entitled to demand that the debtor compensate for their damage according to the provisions relating to non- or improper performance of the obligation.[14] This is because, according to the principles of good faith (TCC art. 2), the debtor is obliged to protect the creditor and third parties who are proximate to the performance of the obligation. In other

---

[10]For further explanations see Sungurbey (1963), Gümüş (2003).

[11]Steinauer (2007), p. 280; Oğuzman et al. (2016), pp. 249–251; Nomer and Ergüne (2016), pp. 131–137; Oğuzman and Öz (2015), pp. 27–29.

[12]For further explanations see Oğuzman et al. (2016), pp. 213–216; Nomer and Ergüne (2016), pp. 129–130.

[13]For further explanations see Karabağ Bulut (2009).

[14]Eren (2015), p. 1152; Kocayusufpaşaoğlu (2014), pp. 20–21.

words, according to TCC art. 2, there is an obligational relationship between the debtor and third parties whose rights may be jeopardised by the performance of the obligation.[15] Indeed, if, by the nature of the obligational relationship, the risks relating to performance affect third parties as much as they affect the creditor, then the former should be able to sue the debtor according to the provisions relating to non- or improper performance of the obligation. For instance, a woman gets into a taxi with her three-year-old daughter. Subsequently, the taxi driver is at fault in an accident in which the mother and daughter are injured. In this case, the injured woman may demand that the taxi driver compensate her for damage, according to the provisions relating to non- or improper performance of the obligation (TCO art. 112). This is because there is a contractual relationship between the woman and the taxi driver. However, the three-year-old is not in a contractual relationship with the taxi driver. Despite this fact, certain scholars argue that the three-year-old may also demand compensation for damage, based on the same provisions.[16]

Another example is as follows: a seller installs a machine in a factory but, contrary to his obligations, does not give instructions on how it is to be used. Subsequently, a factory worker is injured due to the lack of instructions. In this case, despite the fact that there is no contractual obligational relationship between the seller and the factory worker, the latter is, according to the above-mentioned scholars' opinion, entitled to demand compensation for damage based on the provisions relating to non -or improper performance of the obligation. Nevertheless, in this example, if the injured third party is a visitor of the factory worker, then he is not entitled to demand compensation for damage from the seller. This is because the visitor is not sufficiently proximate to the performance of the obligation.

As mentioned above, a contract for the benefit of third parties is one of the most common exceptions to the principle of privity of the obligational relationship. Other exceptions are subrogation, assignment of claim and assumption of debt. Due to their importance, these concepts are individually analysed.[17]

24.2 Subrogation[18]

24.2.1 Requirements

In cases where the debtor's personal skills are not important for the creditor, such as in a pecuniary obligation, then the obligation may be performed by a third party.[19]

[15]Oğuzman and Öz (2015), p. 39; Oğuzman and Öz (2016), pp. 443–445. For further explanations Kocayusufpaşaoğlu (2014), pp. 20–25.

[16]Serozan (2014), pp. 246–247; Oğuzman and Öz (2016), pp. 443–445; Eren (2015), p. 1058.

[17]See Sect. 24.4, Chaps. 32 and 33.

[18]For further explanations see Kılıçoğlu (1979).

[19]Becker (1941), art. 68, N. 4; Oğuzman and Öz (2015), p. 251.

As a rule, regardless of whether the debtor or a third party fulfils the obligation, the obligation is extinguished. However, in cases regulated by TCO art. 127, the fulfilment of the obligation by a third party satisfies the creditor, but the obligation is not extinguished, and thus, the claim passes to the third party.[20] This is referred to as subrogation. TCO art. 127 par. 1 regulates two possibilities giving rise to subrogation. According to TCO art. 127 par. 1, the performing third party subrogates the creditor's rights to the extent of his performance in the circumstances set out in the following paragraphs.

Pursuant to TCO art. 127 par. 1 subcl. 1, subrogation arises where a third party redeems an object pledged for another's debt and where he is the owner or has a limited right *in rem* to it. For example, the owner pledges his goods to secure the debtor's obligations, and the debtor does not fulfil his obligation. The creditor intends to realise the pledge, but if he does so, the owner of the pledged goods will lose his right of ownership. The owner fulfils the obligation in order to prevent the realisation of the pledge, and he thereby subrogates the creditor's rights. That is to say, the creditor's rights pass to the third party who fulfils the obligation.[21]

At this point, it is useful to mention TCC art. 884, according to which where a third party mortgages his immovable property for another person's obligation and fulfils the obligation under the mortgage on the same conditions as required by the debtor, then the third party may demand the discharge of the mortgage. In this case, the claim passes to the owner who fulfils the obligation. As has been seen, TCC art. 884 applies only to immovable property and merely regulates the rights of the owner who fulfils the debt. In comparison to TCO art. 127 par. 1 subcl. 1, its regulation is quite restricted. Taking into consideration this fact, it is accepted that TCO art. 127 par. 1 subcl. 1 may be applied to movable and immovable property.[22]

According to TCO art. 127 par. 1 subcl. 2, subrogation arises where the debtor notifies the creditor that a third party will fulfil the obligation and will replace him. This notification must be done before the third party's performance and does not require any particular form.[23]

24.2.2 Consequences

Subrogation means that the claim, to which the creditor is entitled, legally and automatically passes to the extent of his performance to the fulfilling third party. As

[20] Thévenoz and Werro (2012), art. 110, N. 1; Engel (1997), p. 613.

[21] Thévenoz and Werro (2012), art. 110, N. 14; Oğuzman and Öz (2015), pp. 262–263; Tekinay et al. (1993), p. 209; Serozan (2014), p. 28.

[22] Thévenoz and Werro (2012), art. 110, N. 23; Oğuzman and Öz (2015), p. 263; Tekinay et al. (1993), p. 210.

[23] Engel (1997), p. 614; Thévenoz and Werro (2012), art. 110, N. 31; Oğuzman and Öz (2015), p. 263; Tekinay et al. (1993), p. 211; Reisoğlu (2014), p. 297; Eren (2015), p. 932.

the claim passes to the third party, all privileges and ancillary rights pass as well, except those that are inseparable from the creditor's person.[24]

24.2.3 *Specific Provisions*

The Turkish Code of Obligations regulates other instances of subrogation. Consequently, art. 127 par. 2 states that these cases are reserved. For example, according to TCO art. 168 par. 1, a joint and several debtor who is entitled to have recourse against other debtors is subrogated to the rights of the creditor to the extent that he fulfils the obligation.[25] Another example is related to surety contracts. A surety is subrogated to the rights of the creditor to the extent of the fulfilment of his own obligation (TCO art. 596 par. 1).

Further, the Turkish Commercial Code, which is an inseparable part of the Turkish Civil Code, regulates certain subrogation cases. One of these cases is related to insurer's subrogation. TComC art. 1472 par. 1 sent.1 states that when the insurer pays the insurance indemnity, the insurer legally replaces the assured.

24.3 Guarantee of Performance by a Third Party[26]

24.3.1 *General*[27]

According to TCO art. 128 par. 1, a person (the guarantor) who warrants a third party's performance to another party (the creditor) is liable for damage resulting from the non-performance of the third party. Since the third party is not a party to the contract between the creditor and the guarantor, he does not have any rights and does not undertake any obligations arising from this contract.[28]

A guarantee of performance by a third party may be provided by a separate contract or by a clause in a contract.[29] Such contracts are generally concluded in order to provide a guarantee to the creditor. The most common example of such a contract is a performance bond.[30] In such a relationship, there are two parties: the

[24]von Tuhr and Escher (1974), § 59, III, p. 28; Oğuzman and Öz (2015), p. 263; Serozan (2014), p. 28; Tekinay et al. (1993), p. 214 *ff.*

[25]See Sect. 27.5.2.

[26]*Porte-fort, Vertrag zu Lasten eines Dritten.*

[27]For further explanations see Tandoğan (1959), Reisoğlu (1963), Yüce (2007).

[28]Feyzioğlu (1977), p. 286; Oğuzman and Öz (2016), p. 419; Tekinay et al. (1993), p. 230.

[29]Oğuzman and Öz (2016), p. 418.

[30]For further explanations see Reisoğlu (1977), Reisoğlu (1983), Barlas (1986), Kahyaoğlu (1996), Reisoğlu (1997), Doğan (2002).

bank (guarantor) and the creditor. In a performance bond, the guarantor promises that if the third party fails to perform his obligation at all or as required, the guarantor will be liable for the non-performance of the third party. That is to say, the guarantor irrevocably and unconditionally undertakes to pay a determined amount of money to the creditor on first demand.

24.3.2 Legal Nature

The author's opinion is that a contract relating to a guarantee of performance by a third party is a type of guarantee contract.[31]

The obligation of the guarantor is independent of the third party's obligation. If the third party fails to perform his obligation, then the guarantor may not be required to perform that obligation. On the contrary, the guarantor performs his own obligation, which is generally pecuniary.[32]

At this point, it will be useful to draw an analogy with a suretyship:[33] (1) the obligation of the surety is of an ancillary nature. Therefore, if the principal obligational relationship secured by a surety is void, then the surety is also void. However, a guarantee of performance by a third party is not ancillary in nature. Consequently, even if the principal obligational relationship is void, the guarantee stands. (2) In a suretyship contract, the surety has the right to raise the defences that can be brought by the principal debtor against the creditor. Moreover, he is obliged to raise them (TCO art. 591 par. 1).[34] On the other hand, the guarantor, as a rule, is not entitled to raise the defences resulting from the principal obligational relationship between the creditor and the debtor. (3) In a suretyship contract, when the surety performs his own obligation, the creditor's rights pass to the surety. In contrast, a guarantor does not have a right of recourse based on the subrogation. (4) Another difference is that a suretyship contract requires a qualified written form,[35] whereas a guarantee contract, which is executed by legal entities, does not require a particular form (TCO art. 603).

---

[31]Engel (1997), p. 430; Becker (1941), art. 111, N. 2; Oğuzman and Öz (2016), p. 414; Tekinay et al. (1993), p. 228; Eren (2015), p. 1153; Reisoğlu (2014), p. 395; Feyzioğlu (1977), pp. 286–287.

[32]Oğuzman and Öz (2016), p. 415; Eren (2015), p. 1153.

[33]Engel (1997), p. 435; Thévenoz and Werro (2012), art. 111, N. 19–25; Feyzioğlu (1977), pp. 288–289; Tekinay et al. (1993), pp. 233–238; Eren (2015), pp. 1155–1156; Oğuzman and Öz (2016), pp. 415–418.

[34]For further explanations see Elçin Grassinger (1996), Özen (2016).

[35]See Sect. 3.2.2.2.

24.3.3 Consequences

As mentioned above, in a contract relating to the guarantee of performance by a third party, the obligation of the guarantor becomes due and he becomes liable when the third party fails to perform his obligation (TCO art. 128 par. 1). In other words, until the third party fails to perform the obligation, the creditor has only an expectant right against the guarantor. Therefore, as long as the creditor has the power of disposition[36] in respect of this right, he may assign it or may discharge the guarantor from obligations arising out of the contract. It is worth remembering that in cases where the creditor assigns his expectant right, the assignee may only demand compensation for the assignor's damage rather than for his own damage.[37]

When the guarantor's obligation becomes due, he must perform his obligation. As mentioned above, this obligation is generally pecuniary and aims to compensate the creditor for damage resulting from the non-performance of the third party. Even if the principal obligational relationship secured by the guarantee is void, the guarantor may not raise this defence against the creditor. This is because the guarantee is independent of the secured principal obligational relationship. However, if the guarantee contract is invalid, then the guarantor may raise this invalidity with the creditor.

As a rule, the guarantor undertakes a pecuniary obligation in order to secure the third party's performance. However, in exceptional cases, the guarantor undertakes the same obligation as the third party but as a type of compensation in kind. For example, a third party is obliged to deliver 3 tons of tea leaves to C, and G guarantees that if the third party fails to perform, then he will become obliged to deliver 3 tons of tea leaves to C instead.[38]

In practice, the amount to be paid by the guarantor is generally determined in the guarantee contract. This is almost always true for performance bonds issued by banks. However, if this amount is not determined in the guarantee contract,[39] in the event of the non-performance of the third party's obligation, the guarantor must compensate the creditor for damage arising from that non-performance. Consequently, the guarantor must compensate the creditor's positive damage. In other words, the guarantor must compensate the difference between the value of the creditor's assets had the obligation been performed as required and the value of the

[36] *Pouvoir de disposer, Verfügungsmacht.*

[37] Oğuzman and Öz (2016), p. 426.

[38] Engel (1997), p. 430; Oğuzman and Öz (2016), p. 429; Eren (2015), p. 1159; Reisoğlu (2014), p. 394.

[39] It should be kept in mind that if the guarantor is a natural person, then the maximum amount of the guarantor's liability must be indicated in the guarantor's own handwriting. This is because the TCO art. 583 par. 1 states that a surety contract must be in writing and that the date and maximum amount of the surety's liability must be indicated in the surety's own handwriting. These rules are applied by analogy to guarantees provided by natural persons (TCO art. 603). Consequently, in such a case, if the maximum amount of the guarantor's liability is not indicated in the guarantor's own handwriting, then the guarantee contract is void.

creditor's assets resulting from non-performance. This difference constitutes the creditor's positive damage, and the guarantor is liable to compensate for it.[40]

24.3.4 Recourse

Where the guarantor compensates the creditor for damage, the issue of recourse arises. If the guarantor and the third party make an agreement concerning recourse, then the guarantor will have recourse to the third party in accordance with this agreement. In banking, the legal consequences of the bank's performance are almost always determined by a general loan agreement.[41]

In certain cases, there is no specific agreement between the third party and the guarantor concerning recourse. In such cases, the guarantor may have recourse to the third party in the following instances: (1) if the compensation for the creditor's damage by the guarantor discharges the third party, and this is to the advantage of the third party, and the latter has not validly prohibited the payment of compensation, then the guarantor may have recourse to the third party according to TCO art. 529 par. 1. Consequently, the guarantor may demand that the third party repay the amount paid by way of compensation. (2) if it is not possible to apply TCO art. 529 par. 1—for example, due to a valid prohibition by the third party—then the guarantor may have recourse to the third party according to the rules pertaining to unjust enrichment (TCO arts. 77–82) or TCO art. 530.[42]

24.3.5 Duration

In a contract relating to the guarantee of a third party's performance, the parties may determine the duration of the contract.[43] When this time limit passes, the contract is terminated, and thus, the obligation of the guarantor is extinguished by operation of law.[44]

Even if the parties do not determine the duration of the guarantee contract, they may nevertheless determine a time limit for non-performance by the third party. In such a case, if non-performance by the third party does not occur within this specified duration, the guarantor's liability will also be terminated.[45]

---

[40] Becker (1941), art. 111, N. 14; Oser and Schönenberger (1929), art. 111, N. 10; Engel (1997), p. 435; Oğuzman and Öz (2016), p. 429; Nomer (2015), p. 412; Eren (2015), p. 1159.

[41] *Cf.* Oğuzman and Öz (2016), p. 431.

[42] Oğuzman and Öz (2016), pp. 431–432.

[43] Engel (1997), p. 434; Reisoğlu (2014), p. 399; Eren (2015), p. 1160.

[44] Oğuzman and Öz (2016), p. 433.

[45] Eren (2015), p. 1160; Oğuzman and Öz (2016), p. 433.

24.3.6 Limitation Period

The limitation period runs from the maturity of the obligation (TCO art. 149 par. 1). As mentioned above, the obligation of the guarantor becomes due when the third party fails to perform his obligation and the creditor incurs damage.[46] Consequently, the limitation period commences at that time. According to TCO art. 146, unless otherwise set by law, all claims are subject to a limitation period of 10 years.[47]

If the parties specify only the duration for non-performance by the third party, then the obligation of the guarantor will be subject to a limitation period of 10 years, provided that the non-performance by the third party occurs within this specified duration.[48] If the parties specify the duration for both non-performance by the third party and for demand by the creditor, the obligation of the guarantor is terminated at the expiration of that period of time. Indeed, according to TCO art. 128 par. 2, in such cases, the parties may agree that if the creditor does not demand performance from the guarantor in written form until the expiration of the specified period of time, then the guarantor's obligation will be terminated.[49]

24.4 Contracts in Favour of Third Parties[50]

24.4.1 General[51]

A contract, as a general rule, gives rights only to the parties. However, it is possible that a contract may grant certain rights to a third party. In such a case, the components of this legal relationship are as follows: a promisor,[52] a promisee[53] and a beneficiary.[54] The contract in favour of the third party is concluded between the promisor and the promisee.[55] For instance, a lessee makes a lease contract pertaining to certain immovable property with a lessor, and the parties agree that the leased property will be used by the lessee's daughter. In this case, the parties have the following characteristics: the lessee is the promisee, the lessor is the promisor and the daughter is the beneficiary.

---

[46]Eren (2015), p. 1160; Oğuzman and Öz (2016), p. 434.

[47]Engel (1997), p. 434.

[48]Reisoğlu (2014), p. 400; Oğuzman and Öz (2016), p. 435; Eren (2015), p. 1160.

[49]Oğuzman and Öz (2016), p. 435–436; Eren (2015), p. 1160; Reisoğlu (2014), p. 399.

[50]*Stipulation pour autrui, Vertrag zugunsten eines Dritten.*

[51]For further explanations see Akyol (2008).

[52]*Promettant, Promittent.*

[53]*Stipulant, Promissar, Versprechensempfänger.*

[54]*Tiers, Dritte; Bénéficiaire, Begünstigte.*

[55]Engel (1997), p. 417; Tercier (2004), p. 190; Oğuzman and Öz (2016), p. 438; Feyzioğlu (1977), p. 271; Becker (1941), art. 112, N. 1.

In a contract in favour of a third party, generally, the third party is determined by the contracting parties. However, at the time of the formation of the contract, the beneficiary may not be determined. In such cases, it is sufficient that the beneficiary is determinable.[56]

In a contract in favour of a third party, the legal position of the beneficiary may differ: (1) only the promisee may have the right to demand performance for the beneficiary (TCO art. 129 par. 1), or (2) the beneficiary may also have the right to demand performance for himself (TCO art. 129 par. 2).

It should be noted that the promisee enters into a contract only on behalf of himself. That is why the promisee cannot be described as the agent of the beneficiary.[57] In addition, the promisor is not only authorised to but also must perform the obligation for the beneficiary. The beneficiary accepts the performance on behalf of himself. As a result, the beneficiary does not act as the agent of the promisee.[58]

The parties to a contract cannot encumber a third party.[59] Nevertheless, the promisee and the promisor may agree that the beneficiary is only able to demand performance of the obligation if he performs a specified obligation or duty.[60]

Furthermore, the parties to a contract are not entitled to make a dispositive legal transaction[61] in favour of a third party. For instance, a claim may not be transferred to a third party by agreement between the assignor and the assignee.[62]

Moreover, the beneficiary may not preclude formation of the contract in favour of himself. The beneficiary may only refuse or accept performance.[63]

24.4.2 *Consequences*

24.4.2.1 Where Only the Promisee May Demand Performance

In certain cases, the beneficiary is not a creditor. That is to say, he is not entitled to demand performance of the obligation and is only authorised to accept performance.[64] Since the beneficiary does not hold the right to claim, he does not have the

[56]Engel (1997), p. 420; Thévenoz and Werro (2012), art. 112, N. 7; Tekinay et al. (1993), p. 219; Oğuzman and Öz (2016), p. 449; Reisoğlu (2014), p. 401.

[57]Thévenoz and Werro (2012), art. 112, N. 5; Eren (2015), p. 1142; Oğuzman and Öz (2016), p. 438; Tekinay et al. (1993), p. 227; Becker (1941), art. 112, N. 4.

[58]Eren (2015), p. 1142; Oğuzman and Öz (2016), p. 438.

[59]Oğuzman and Öz (2016), pp. 446–447

[60]Oğuzman and Öz (2016), p. 447.

[61]*Acte de disposition, Verfügungsgeschäft*. See Chap. 14, fn. 5–6.

[62]Engel (1997), p. 421; Oğuzman and Öz (2016), pp. 447–448.

[63]Oğuzman and Öz (2016), pp. 448–449.

[64]Tercier (2004), p. 190; Engel (1997), p. 419; Thévenoz and Werro (2012), art. 112, N. 10; Tekinay et al. (1993), p. 220; Nomer (2015), p. 414.

power of disposition[65] and, thus, may not dispose of it.[66] For example, an assignment by the beneficiary is void.

In cases where the beneficiary is not a creditor, if the promisor fails to perform the obligation, the beneficiary is not entitled to demand that the promisor compensate his damage. The right to demand compensation belongs solely to the promisee, but this compensation must be paid to the beneficiary.[67]

As the promisee is the holder of the right to claim, he is the one who may dispose of it. Therefore, the promisee may discharge the promisor. The promisee may also set off his claim against his obligation to the promisor. The beneficiary may not intervene in this type of legal transaction.[68]

24.4.2.2 Where the Beneficiary May Also Demand Performance

In certain cases, the beneficiary becomes a creditor at the time of the conclusion of the contract between the promisor and the promisee.[69] In order for the beneficiary to become a creditor, his consent is not necessary. Even if the beneficiary does not know of the contract, he may become a creditor.[70]

In cases where the beneficiary becomes a creditor, he may, along with the promisee, also demand performance of the obligation. The successors of the beneficiary—*e.g.*, heirs or assignees—may also demand that the obligation be performed for their benefit (TCO art. 129 par. 2 sent. 1).

It is evident that the promisee and the beneficiary are not joint and several creditors.[71] This is because regardless of whether the promisee or the beneficiary demands performance of the obligation, the promisor must perform the obligation for the beneficiary.[72]

The beneficiary's right to demand performance may result from the contracting party's intentions (*e.g.*, when a mother deposits money into her daughter's bank account)[73] or from custom (*e.g.*, customarily it is the lessee, not the lessor, who pays a concierge's monthly fee).[74] The right of the beneficiary may also arise from the law itself. For instance, TCO art. 130 par. 1 states that if an employer was insured

[65]*Pouvoir de disposer, Verfügungsmacht.*

[66]Oğuzman and Öz (2016), p. 451.

[67]von Tuhr and Escher (1974), § 82, I, 1, p. 237; Engel (1997), p. 419–420; compare to Becker (1941), art. 112, N: 23, 24, *cf.* Oğuzman and Öz (2016), p. 451 fn. 123.

[68]von Tuhr and Escher (1974), § 82, I, 1, p. 237; Tekinay et al. (1993), p. 226; Oğuzman and Öz (2016), pp. 451–452.

[69]Tercier (2004), p. 190; Engel (1997), p. 420; Thévenoz and Werro (2012), art. 112, N. 16.

[70]von Tuhr and Escher (1974), § 83, I, p. 246; Oğuzman and Öz (2016), p. 452.

[71]See Chap. 28.

[72]Becker (1941), art. 112. N. 27; Oğuzman and Öz (2016), p. 453.

[73]Engel (1997), p. 422; Oğuzman and Öz (2016), p. 441.

[74]Oğuzman and Öz (2016), p. 442.

against the consequences of legal liability provided by law, the rights resulting from the insurance contract belong exclusively to the employee. It should be noted that the insurance benefits will be deducted from the compensation to be paid according to the general provisions (TCO art. 130 par. 2).

Moreover, legislative provisions pertaining to other civil liability insurances are reserved (TCO art. 130 par. 3). For example, according to TComC art. 1454 par. 1, in insurance contracts in favour of a third party, the rights resulting from the insurance contract belong to the insured party. Unless otherwise agreed by the parties, the latter may demand that the insurer pay the insurance indemnity to him.

In cases where the beneficiary becomes a creditor, the promisee will lose the power of disposition[75] on the claim when the beneficiary or his successors notify the promisor (debtor) of their intention to exercise their right to demand performance. The notification does not require a specific form. After this notification, the promisee (creditor) may no longer discharge the promisor (debtor) or change the quality or content of the obligation (TCO art. 129 par. 2 sent. 2).

In cases where the beneficiary is a creditor, if the promisor fails to perform the obligation, then the beneficiary may demand that the promisor compensate him for damage.[76]

References

Akyol Ş (2008) Tam üçüncü şahıs yararına sözleşme. Vedat, İstanbul
Antalya OG (2012) Borçlar hukuku genel hükümler, vol 1. Legal, İstanbul
Aybay A (2011) Borçlar hukuku dersleri genel bölüm. Filiz, İstanbul
Barlas N (1986) Türk hukuk sisteminde banka teminat mektupları. İstanbul
Becker H (1941) Kommentar zum Schweizerischen Zivilgesetzbuch, vol VI, Obligationenrecht, 1. Abteilung: Allgemeine Bestimmungen, Art. 1-183. Stämpfli, Bern
Berger B (2012) Allgemeines Schuldrecht. Stämpfli, Bern
Doğan V (2002) Banka teminat mektupları. Savaş, Ankara
Elçin Grassinger G (1996) Borçlar kanununa göre kefilin alacaklıya karşı sahip olduğu savunma imkânları. Alfa, İstanbul
Engel P (1997) Traité des obligations en droit Suisse. Stämpfli, Bern
Eren F (2015) Borçlar hukuku genel hükümler. Yetkin, Ankara
Feyzioğlu FN (1976) Borçlar hukuku genel hükümler, vol 1. Fakülteler, İstanbul
Feyzioğlu FN (1977) Borçlar hukuku genel hükümler, vol 2. Fakülteler, İstanbul
Gauch P, Schluep W R, Emmenegger S (2008) Schweizerisches Obligationenrecht, Allgemeiner Teil, vol 2. Schulthess, Zürich
Gümüş MA (2003) Türk medeni kanununun getirdiği yeni şerhler. Vedat, İstanbul
Honsell H, Vogt NP, Wiegand W (eds) (2003) Basler Kommentar zum Schweizerischen Privatrecht, Obligationenrecht 1: Art. 1-529 OR. Helbing Lichtenhahn, Basel
Kahyaoğlu EC (1996) Banka garantileri. İstanbul
Kapancı KB (2016) Ahlaka aykırı bir fiille kasten verilen zararın tazmini. Vedat, İstanbul
Karabağ Bulut N (2009) Üçüncü kişiyi koruyucu etkili sözleşme. On iki levha, İstanbul

[75] *Pouvoir de disposer*, *Verfügungsmacht*.

[76] Oğuzman and Öz (2016), p. 455.

Kılıçoğlu A (1979) Türk borçlar hukukunda kanuni halefiyet. Ankara üniversitesi, Ankara
Kılıçoğlu AM (2013) Borçlar hukuku genel hükümler. Turhan, İstanbul
Kocayusufpaşaoğlu N (2014) Borçlar hukuku genel bölüm, vol 1 (Kocayusufpaşaoğlu/Hatemi/Serozan/Arpacı). Filiz, İstanbul
Nomer HN (2015) Borçlar hukuku genel hükümler. Beta, İstanbul
Nomer HN, Ergüne S (2016) Eşya hukuku. On iki levha, İstanbul
Oğuzman K, Öz T (2015) Borçlar hukuku genel hükümler, vol 1. Vedat, İstanbul
Oğuzman K, Öz T (2016) Borçlar hukuku genel hükümler, vol 2. Vedat, İstanbul
Oğuzman K, Seliçi Ö, Oktay-Özdemir S (2016) Eşya hukuku. Filiz, İstanbul
Oser H, Schönenberger W (1929) Kommentar zum Schweizerischen Zivilgesetzbuch, Volume V: Das Obligationenrecht, Erster Halbband: Art. 1-183. Schulthess, Zürich
Özen B (2016) 6098 sayılı Türk borçlar kanunu çerçevesinde kefalet sözleşmesi. Vedat, İstanbul
Reisoğlu K (1958) İstihdam edenlerin mesuliyeti. Ankara
Reisoğlu S (1963) Garanti mukavelesi. Ajans-Türk, Ankara
Reisoğlu S (1977) Banka teminat mektupları ve uygulamada ortaya çıkan sorunlar. Ankara
Reisoğlu S (1983) Türk hukukunda ve bankacılık uygulamasında teminat mektupları - kontrgarantiler. Ankara
Reisoğlu S (1997) Banka teminat mektupları ve kontrgarantiler. Ankara
Reisoğlu S (2014) Türk borçlar hukuku genel hükümler. Beta, İstanbul
Schwenzer I (2009) Schweizerisches Obligationenrecht, Allgemeiner Teil. Schulthess, Bern
Serozan R (2014) Borçlar hukuku genel bölüm, Volume 3 (Kocayusufpaşaoğlu/Hatemi/Serozan/Arpacı). Filiz, İstanbul
Steinauer PH (2007) Les droits réels, vol 1. Stämpfli, Bern
Sungurbey İ (1963) Kişisel hakların tapu kütüğüne şerhi. İstanbul
Tandoğan H (1959) Garanti mukavelesi. Ankara
Tekinay SS, Akman S, Burcuoğlu H, Altop A (1993) Tekinay borçlar hukuku genel hükümler. Filiz, İstanbul
Tercier P (2004) Le droit des obligations. Schulthess, Zurich
Tercier P, Pichonnaz P, Develioğlu HM (2016) Borçlar hukuku genel hükümler. On iki levha, İstanbul
Thévenoz L, Werro F (éd) (2012) Commentaire romand code des obligations 1: art. 1-529 CO. Helbing Lichtenhahn, Bâle
von Tuhr A, Peter H (1979) Allgemeiner Teil des Schweizerischen Obligationenrecht, vol 1. Schulthess, Zürich
von Tuhr A, Escher A (1974) Allgemeiner Teil des Schweizerischen Obligationenrecht, vol 2. Schulthess, Zürich
Yüce MB (2007) Garanti sözleşmesinin bir türü olarak üçüncü kişinin fiilini taahhüt sözleşmesi. Vedat, İstanbul

Part III
Extinguishment of Obligations and Limitation Period

Chapter 25
Extinguishment of Obligations

25.1 General[1]

There are several causes of extinguishment of obligations. The normal manner of extinguishment of an obligation is its performance as required.[2] The other causes are set out in the Turkish Code of Obligations in the following order: discharge by agreement, constitution of a new obligation (novation), merger, impossibility of performance and set-off.

Before analysing these causes, it is useful to first consider the consequences of the extinguishment of obligations. For whichever reason the obligation is extinguished, the debtor is released from the obligation, and any right to demand performance of the obligation by the creditor comes to an end. According to TCO art. 131 par. 1, where an obligation is extinguished by its performance or for other reasons, the ancillary rights, such as any pledge or surety, are also extinguished automatically. As a rule, when an obligation is extinguished, the right to demand accrued interest and the performance of any penalty clause are extinguished simultaneously. These rights are also ancillary to the principal obligation. However, according to TCO art. 131 par. 2, the creditor's rights relating to liability for payment of any accrued interest and performance of any penalty clause may be reserved in the contract or may be reserved by the creditor's notification, which must be made by the date of performance. Moreover, this kind of

[1] Aybay (2011), pp. 152–162; Becker (1941), Vorbemerkung zu art. 114–142, art. 114–126; Berger (2012), pp. 450–472; Engel (1997), pp. 669–681, 761–784; Eren (2015), pp. 1257–1281, 1299–1307; Feyzioğlu (1977), pp. 409–517; Gauch et al. (2008), pp. 187–216; Honsell et al. (2003), Vorbemerkungen zu art. 114–142, art. 114–126; Kılıçoğlu (2013), pp. 835–866; Nomer (2015), pp. 381–391; Oser and Schönenberger (1929), Vorbemerkungen zum dritten Titel (art. 114–142), art. 114–126; Oğuzman and Öz (2015), pp. 531–579; Reisoğlu (2014), pp. 404–423; Schwenzer (2009), pp. 506–518; Tekinay et al. (1993), pp. 984–1030; Tercier (2004), pp. 257–279; Tercier et al. (2016), pp. 444–479; Thévenoz and Werro (2012), art. 114–126, and von Tuhr and Escher (1974), pp. 161–211.

[2] von Tuhr and Escher (1974), § 74, I, p. 161; Tercier (2004), p. 259.

İ. Helvacı, *Turkish Contract Law*, DOI 10.1007/978-3-319-60061-1_25

reservation may be inferred from the circumstances. In such cases, the creditor, despite performance of the obligation, may still demand payment of accrued interest and performance of the penalty clause. For instance, in a work contract relating to the construction of a house, the parties agree that if the contractor falls into default, he will, as a penalty, pay €10,000 for every delayed month. The builder delivers the house 4 months late. If the customer accepts the delivery of the house without any reservation, since the obligation to construct the house will have been performed and, thus, extinguished, then the ancillary debt of €40,000 arising from the penalty clause will also be extinguished (TCO art. 131 par. 2, TCO art. 179 par. 2)[3].

The provisions relating to any mortgage, negotiable instruments[4] or composition agreements are reserved. In fact, when an obligation secured by a mortgage is extinguished, the latter is extinguished as well. However, the entry on the land register stands. That is why if a debt secured by a mortgage is extinguished, then the mortgagor may demand the creditor authorise the removal of the entry from the land register (TCC art. 883).[5]

25.2 Discharge by Agreement[6]

25.2.1 The Concept and Legal Nature[7]

Although the debtor does not perform the obligation, the parties may agree that the obligation is extinguished through a discharge agreement.[8] In a discharge agreement, the creditor waives his claim to the performance of the obligation and releases the debtor. It is worth noting that the creditor's waiver, by itself, is insufficient for the extinguishment of the obligation. In order for the obligation to be extinguished, the debtor must accept the creditor's waiver.[9]

A discharge agreement may extinguish the obligation wholly or partially.[10] Obviously, where the discharge agreement is partial, the non-discharged part of the obligation stands and must be performed.

[3]Eren (2015), p. 1185; Reisoğlu (2014), p. 459; Oğuzman and Öz (2015), pp. 535–536.

[4]Although the principal obligation is extinguished, the liability for interest connected to any coupons that are independent of the principal deed is not extinguished. Oğuzman and Öz (2015), p. 535.

[5]For further explanations Helvacı (2008), pp. 402–404; Steinauer (2003), p. 177.

[6]*Remise conventionnelle*, *Aufhebung durch Übereinkunft*.

[7]For further explanations see Turanboy (1998), Gümüş (2015).

[8]von Tuhr and Escher (1974), § 75, I, p. 173; Reisoğlu (2014), p. 405; Nomer (2015), p. 382; Eren (2015), p. 1270; Oğuzman and Öz (2015), p. 536.

[9]Tercier (2004), p. 266; Thévenoz and Werro (2012), art. 115, N. 2; Oğuzman and Öz (2015), pp. 538–539; Tekinay et al. (1993), p. 986; Feyzioğlu (1977), p. 426.

[10]Engel (1997), p. 765; Thévenoz and Werro (2012), art. 115, N. 2; Berger (2012), p. 452.

A discharge agreement is a dispositive legal transaction[11] with regard to the creditor.[12] Consequently, in order for a discharge agreement to be validly formed, the creditor must have the capacity to act and the power of disposition[13] in relation to the claim.[14] Otherwise, the discharge agreement is void.

It is worth noting that the discharge agreement is distinct from a *pactum de non petendo*, which is an agreement whereby a creditor promises not to enforce an obligation. This is due to the fact that in a *pactum de non petendo*, the obligation is not extinguished but the creditor is obliged not to demand performance of the obligation, generally for a specific duration, whereas in a discharge agreement, it is evident that the obligation is extinguished.[15]

It should be noted that in certain cases, the creditor and debtor require the consent of a third party to form a discharge agreement. For instance, according to TCC art. 820, for a discharge agreement relating to a usufruct claim, the consent of the usufructuary is also necessary. Similarly, the consent of the pledgee is also necessary for a discharge agreement relating to a pledged debt (TCC art. 961).[16]

25.2.2 Form Requirements

According to TCO art. 132, even if the legal transaction creating the obligation requires a specific form whether arising from the agreement of the parties or the law, the discharge agreement itself does not require any specific form.[17] Consequently, the parties may make a discharge agreement in oral or written form. Moreover, the parties' declaration of will (intention)[18] relating to a discharge agreement may be express or implied.[19] However, if the discharge agreement is concluded orally, then certain evidentiary difficulties may arise. In order to avoid this potential problem, it is recommended that the discharge agreement be made in written form.

---

[11]*Acte de disposition, Verfügungsgeschäft*. See Chap. 14, fn. 5–6.

[12]Tercier (2004), p. 266; Thévenoz and Werro (2012), art. 115, N. 11; Tekinay et al. (1993), p. 987.

[13]*Pouvoir de disposer, Verfügungsmacht.*

[14]Tercier (2004), p. 266; Thévenoz and Werro (2012), art. 115, N. 11; Oğuzman and Öz (2015), pp. 538–539; Eren (2015), p. 1271.

[15]Thévenoz and Werro (2012), art. 115, N. 7; Tercier (2004), p. 266; Gauch et al. (2008), p. 194; von Tuhr and Escher (1974), § 75, IV, pp. 177–178; Oğuzman and Öz (2015), p. 540; Feyzioğlu (1977), p. 427.

[16]Oğuzman and Öz (2015), p. 540.

[17]Berger (2012), pp. 452–453; Becker (1941), art. 115, N. 3.

[18]*Déclaration de volonté, Willenserklärung.*

[19]Reisoğlu (2014), p. 405; Tercier et al. (2016), p. 456; Oğuzman and Öz (2015), p. 537.

25.2.3 *Consequences*

As mentioned above, with a discharge agreement, the obligation is extinguished. The natural consequence of the extinguishment of the obligation is that ancillary rights are also extinguished (TCO art. 131 par. 1).[20] For instance, consider a loan agreement between a borrower and a lender where the lender enters into a surety contract with a third party. When a discharge agreement is formed between the borrower and the lender, the third party is released from his obligation arising from the surety contract. This is because the right arising from the surety contract is an ancillary right to the principal obligation.

25.3 Novation[21]

25.3.1 *General*[22]

Novation is the extinguishment of an existing obligation by the creation of a new obligation.[23] In novation, an existing obligation is extinguished without being performed,[24] and the extinguishment of the existing obligation is dependent upon the creation of the new obligation. In the case of extinguishment of an existing obligation by agreement, there is no presumption of novation. This is due to the fact that the parties' clear intentions are an essential element of novation (TCO art. 133 par. 1).

In novation, the parties may change the object of the obligation.[25] For example, D is obliged to transfer ownership of a car to C. After a period of time, the parties make an agreement whereby they agree that D is obliged to pay €100,000 to C in lieu of transferring ownership of the car. Furthermore, the parties may change the cause (*causa*) of the obligation.[26] For instance, assume there is a sale agreement between the parties according to which the buyer must pay €10,000. Subsequently the parties make a new agreement according to which the cause of the buyer's obligation becomes a loan agreement.

[20]Engel (1997), p. 765; Tercier (2004), p. 267.

[21]*Novation, Neuerung.*

[22]For further explanations see Koyuncuoğlu (1972), Önay (2016).

[23]Oser and Schönenberger (1929), art. 116, N. 2; Gauch et al. (2008), p. 195; Tercier (2004), p. 261; Thévenoz and Werro (2012), art. 116, N. 1; Tekinay et al. (1993), p. 989; Oğuzman and Öz (2015), p. 540.

[24]Nomer (2015), p. 389.

[25]Oser and Schönenberger (1929), art. 116, N. 9; Engel (1997), p. 769; Reisoğlu (2014), p. 407; Oğuzman and Öz (2015), p. 542.

[26]Oğuzman and Öz (2015), p. 542; Tekinay et al. (1993), p. 992, *cf.* Eren (2015), p. 1265.

The parties may agree to substitute parties to the obligation. If the parties agree that the creditor is to be substituted, then the transaction is similar to the assignment of a claim. However, in novation, an existing obligation is extinguished and a new obligation is created, whereas in the assignment of a claim, the obligation is not extinguished, only the creditor is substituted.[27] Furthermore, the parties may agree that the debtor is to be substituted; in this case, the transaction is similar to the assumption of a debt. Nevertheless, in novation, an existing obligation is extinguished and a new obligation is created, whereas in the assumption of a debt, the obligation does not extinguish, only the debtor is substituted.[28]

It should be noted that novation is distinct from renewal. In the latter, an expiring obligation is renewed and its duration is extended.[29] For example, according to TCO art. 347, in fixed term lease agreements concerning dwelling houses and business premises, unless the lessee gives at least 15 days' notice prior to the expiration of the agreement, the agreement is deemed to be extended with the same provisions for 1 year. In contrast, in novation, the new obligation extinguishes the former one.

25.3.2 Conditions

Novation requires the agreement of the parties. In order for this agreement to be valid, the creditor must have both the capacity to act and the power of disposition.[30] In order for a novation to exist, the following conditions must be met: (1) there must be a valid obligation, (2) a new valid obligation must be created and (3) the parties must have the intention to novate.[31]

The most important element of this agreement is the parties' clear intentions relating to novation.[32] If there are no such intentions, then it is inferred that the parties' intent is to amend the contract without extinguishing the original obligations (TCO art. 133 par. 1). Regarding the intention to novate, TCO art. 133 par. 2 states that, in particular, the signing of negotiable instruments (bills of exchanges, promissory notes and cheques) in respect of an existing obligation or the issue of a new document establishing an acknowledgement of obligation or a new surety bond does not create novation, unless the parties have a clear intention to novate.

---

[27]Engel (1997), p. 769; Feyzioğlu (1977), p. 437; Reisoğlu (2014), p. 407; Oğuzman and Öz (2015), p. 542.

[28]Engel (1997), p. 769; Feyzioğlu (1977), p. 437; Reisoğlu (2014), p. 407; Oğuzman and Öz (2015), p. 542.

[29]Feyzioğlu (1977), p. 434; Oğuzman and Öz (2015), p. 541.

[30]*Pouvoir de disposer*, *Verfügungsmacht*.

[31]Tercier (2004), p. 261; Thévenoz and Werro (2012), art. 116, N. 1.

[32]Eren (2015), p. 1265; Oğuzman and Öz (2015), p. 542; Reisoğlu (2014), p. 408.

25.3.3 *Consequences*

As mentioned above, in the case of novation, an existing obligation is extinguished. Consequently, ancillary rights relating to the existing obligation, such as pledges and sureties, are also extinguished (TCO art. 131 par. 1). A new obligation arises and is independent of the extinguished obligation. If the creditor wishes to secure this new obligation, new securities, such as a pledge or a surety, must be provided.[33] A new limitation period will arise in respect of the new obligation.[34]

25.3.4 *Current Account*

Pursuant to TComC art. 89 par. 1, in a current account, both parties may reciprocally waive any possible claims arising for any legal reason or from the legal relationship individually and separately and may record their claims and debts and demand the balance after the account is drawn down.[35]

The Turkish Code of Obligations sets out a specific provision relating to current accounts, according to which the mere entry of various items in a current account does not constitute a novation (TCO art. 134 par. 1). However, in certain cases, the holder of a current account may draw the balance and notify the other party. In this case, the receiving party's acknowledgement of the drawn balance constitutes a novation. Thus, the existing obligation is extinguished, and a new obligation arises (TCO art. 134 par. 2).

It should be noted that, pursuant to TCO art. 134 par. 3, in the event that there is security for one of the items, the acknowledgement of the drawn balance does not extinguish the security unless otherwise agreed upon. For instance, S sells smartphones to L, and L sells laptops to S. In addition, there is a current account agreement between S and L, and L pledges certain chattels to S for a specific smartphone purchase. During the course of this commercial relationship, L becomes obliged to pay €10,000, whereas S is obliged to pay €8000. Then S draws down the balance and notifies L that the balance is €2000. L acknowledges the balance. In this case, even if L's specific obligation arising from the particular smartphone purchase is extinguished, the pledge constituted by L remains valid and secures this new obligation unless otherwise agreed upon.

[33]Feyzioğlu (1977), p. 451; Tekinay et al. (1993), p. 996; Oğuzman and Öz (2015), p. 544.

[34]Reisoğlu (2014), p. 409.

[35]For further explanations see Toksal (1956).

25.4 Merger[36]

25.4.1 General

In certain cases, the capacities of the debtor and the creditor may merge in the same person. For example, a mother is obliged to pay a certain amount of money to her daughter; subsequently, the mother dies, and her daughter becomes her sole heir.[37] In this case, the creditor has also become the debtor in respect of this obligation.[38] Similarly, a creditor may transfer his claim to his debtor, making the debtor also the creditor of the obligation.[39]

In the above-mentioned cases, according to TCO art. 135 par. 1 sent. 1, when the capacities of the creditor and the debtor are merged in the same person, the obligation is extinguished by the merger. Indeed, an obligation is a legal tie whereby a debtor is obliged to render performance of an act to a creditor. When the debtor and the creditor are the same person, since no one is able to be bound to render a performance to himself, the obligation comes to an end.[40]

Even if the obligation is extinguished, a third party might have had certain rights in respect of the claim, such as usufructuary rights or pledges. In such a case, according to TCO art. 135 par. 1 sent. 2, the existing rights of third parties in relation to the claim are not affected by the merger. For instance, D is obliged to pay €10,000 to C, and C grants a right of usufruct to U. Subsequently, D becomes entitled to the claim, or C becomes the debtor in respect of this obligation. In both cases, U's right of usufruct stands.[41]

Even if the obligation is extinguished by the merging of the capacities of the debtor and the creditor in the same person, this extinguishment may be negated. Indeed, according to TCO art. 135 par. 2, if the merger is terminated retroactively, the obligation is deemed to have never been extinguished. For example, if the sole heir, who is the creditor of the deceased, disclaims the inheritance (TCC art. 605 par. 1), the merger is extinguished retroactively.

25.4.2 Specific Provisions

According to TCO art. 135 par. 3, specific provisions pertaining to a mortgage and negotiable instruments are reserved. In fact, when an obligation secured by a

---

[36] *Confusion*, *Vereinigung*.

[37] Engel (1997), p. 778.

[38] Oser and Schönenberger (1929), art. 118, N. 2; von Tuhr and Escher (1974), § 77, I, p. 187.

[39] Tekinay et al. (1993), p. 997; Oğuzman and Öz (2015), p. 547.

[40] Tercier (2004), p. 262.

[41] Oğuzman and Öz (2015), p. 548; Reisoğlu (2014), p. 409; Eren (2015), p. 1269.

mortgage is extinguished, the mortgage is extinguished as well. However, the entry on the land register still stands. That is why if the debt that is secured by a mortgage is extinguished, then the mortgagor may demand that the creditor authorise the removal of the entry from the land register (TCC art. 883).[42]

Regarding negotiable instruments, there are several specific rules in the Turkish Code of Commerce. According to these specific rules, if a negotiable instrument payable to order is endorsed in favour of the debtor or if a negotiable instrument payable to the bearer, such as a cheque, is delivered to the debtor, the obligations that are inherent in them are not extinguished. On the contrary, the rights may be transferred again to a third party.[43]

25.5 Impossibility for Which the Debtor Is Not Responsible[44]

25.5.1 Subsequent Impossibility

It is worth remembering that subsequent impossibility of performance, which is analysed under this section, is distinct from initial impossibility of the obligation. Indeed, in the case of initial impossibility, the performance of the obligation is impossible at the time the contract is formed, and this impossibility is objective—that is to say, it must be the case for any person. Initial impossibility results in the nullity of the contract (TCO art. 27 par. 1). For instance, in a sale contract relating to a specific object, *e.g.*, Picasso's painting *Guernica*, if the object has been completely destroyed before the formation of the contract, then the contract is void.[45]

In the case of subsequent impossibility, the performance of the obligation becomes impossible after the formation of the contract. According to TCO art. 136 par. 1, if the debtor is not responsible for the subsequent impossibility, then his

---

[42]Helvacı (2008), pp. 402–404. On the contrary Oğuzman and Öz (2015), p. 549.

[43]The Turkish Commercial Code sets certain specific rules relating to the transfer of negotiable instruments. For example, any bill of exchange may be transferred by endorsement and the delivery of possession of it even if it is not expressly made out to order (TComC art. 681 par. 1, compare to SCO art. 1001). The endorsement may be made out to the drawee, regardless of whether he has accepted the bill or not, to the drawer or to any other person liable for it. These persons may re-endorse the bill (TComC art. 681 par. 3); Pursuant to the TComC art. 778 par. 1, subcl. a, these rules, unless they are contrary to its nature, also apply to promissory notes. Moreover, a cheque made payable to a specific person with or without the explicit comment 'to order' may be transferred by endorsement and the delivery of possession of it (TComC art. 788 par. 1; compare to SCO art. 1108). The endorsement may be made out to the drawer or to any other person liable for it. These persons may re-endorse the cheque (TComC art. 788 par. 3).

[44]For further explanations see Dural (1976), Kurt (2016).

[45]See Sect. 5.2.5.

obligations are extinguished. For instance, in a sale contract relating to a specific object, if, after conclusion of the contract, the specific object is destroyed by a fire for which the debtor is not responsible, then the obligation is extinguished.

It is pivotal that, as a general rule, responsibility of the debtor requires fault. According to TCO art. 112, the debtor is presumed to be at fault; unless the debtor proves that he is not at fault,[46] then he will be held responsible for the impossibility of the performance. However, in certain cases, the debtor may nevertheless be held responsible even if he is not at fault, for example, in the case of a debtor's liability for his assistants (TCO art. 116).[47]

Subsequent impossibility for which the debtor is not responsible may result from either factual or legal reasons.[48] For example, a seller is obliged to transfer ownership of immovable property, but after formation of the contract, the subject matter is expropriated (legal impossibility); in a sale contract pertaining to a specific object, the object is destroyed by fire after the formation of the contract due to a lightning strike (factual impossibility). As seen, in both cases, the debtors are not responsible for the impossibility of performance. Therefore, the obligations are extinguished; in other words, the debtors are released from their obligations.

According to certain scholars, it is irrelevant whether the impossibility of performance is objective or subjective. In either case, the performance of the obligation becomes impossible.[49]

However, certain other scholars believe that for subsequent impossibility, for which the debtor is not responsible, to give rise to the extinguishment of the obligation, the impossibility must be objective.[50] The examples of the object destroyed due to a lightning strike and the expropriation of the immovable property are examples of objective subsequent impossibility. According to these scholars, in cases where subsequent impossibility of performance is subjective, the obligation is not extinguished.[51] However, if the personal skills of the debtor are important for the creditor, the fact that the debtor becomes unable to perform the obligation will extinguish that obligation.[52] For example, a renowned composer is commissioned to compose a national anthem. Subsequently, the composer becomes deaf due to an illness. In such a case, the national anthem may be composed by another composer. However, since the object of the contract was not the composition of a national anthem but its composition by this specific composer, the obligation will be extinguished.

---

[46]See Sect. 22.2.3.2.2.

[47]See Sect. 22.5.

[48]Oser and Schönenberger (1929), art. 20, N. 4; Tercier (2004), p. 269; Reisoğlu (2014), p. 411; Tekinay et al. (1993), p. 999.

[49]Oğuzman and Öz (2015), p. 549; Reisoğlu (2014), p. 411.

[50]Tercier (2004), p. 269; Eren (2015), p. 1300; Dural (1976), p. 89, 114.

[51]Eren (2015), p. 1300; Dural (1976), p. 89.

[52]Tercier (2004), p. 269; Honsell et al. (2003), art. 19/20, N. 46.

Performance of generic obligations[53] cannot become impossible (*genus non perit*). However, if the obligation to be performed is a restricted generic obligation, performance may become impossible. For example, if the debtor is obliged to supply 3 tons of tea leaves from a specific stock and these tea leaves are destroyed due to a flood, then the obligation of the debtor is extinguished.[54]

It should be noted that in certain cases, the impossibility of the performance may be temporary, and it may be unknown when the circumstances giving rise to this impossibility will come to an end. If the parties' presumed intentions allow the performance of the obligation to be postponed until the performance becomes possible again, then the obligation is not extinguished. If the performance of the obligation may not be postponed, it is reasonable to accept the extinguishment of the obligation.[55]

25.5.2 In Bilateral Contracts

If there is a unilateral contract between the parties and the debtor's obligation becomes impossible to perform without responsibility on his part, then the debtor's obligation is extinguished, and he is discharged. However, if there is a bilateral contract between the parties and the debtor's obligation is extinguished due to subsequent impossibility for which he is not responsible, then the question of whether the counter-party's obligation will be extinguished arises. According to TCO art. 136 par. 2, the counter-party's obligation is also extinguished. Therefore, if the party, whose performance of the obligation has become impossible without responsibility on his part, has already obtained the performance of the counter-party, then this constitutes a case of unjust enrichment. Thus, the discharged party must make restitution in accordance with the provisions relating to unjust enrichment (TCO arts. 77–82). Moreover, it is apparent that since the obligations to be performed by the counter-party are also extinguished, then the party whose performance of the obligation has become impossible without responsibility on his part may not demand their performance.

However, according to TCO art. 136 par. 2 sent. 2, this provision does not apply to cases where the risk passes, either by law or by agreement, to the creditor before the performance of the obligation. Indeed, the parties may agree that even if the performance of the debtor's obligation becomes impossible without responsibility on his part, he may nevertheless demand the performance of the counter-obligation. Moreover, the law itself may regulate such a consequence. For example, according to the former TCO art. 183 par.1, in a sale contract relating to a specific object, subject to particular circumstances or agreements, the benefit and the risk relating to

[53]See Sect. 15.5.

[54]Serozan (2014), p. 84; Oğuzman and Öz (2015), p. 551; Eren (2015), p. 1301.

[55]Oğuzman and Öz (2015), p. 551, compare to Eren (2015), pp. 1300–1301.

the property pass to the buyer when the contract is formed. Pursuant to this now abolished rule, even if the sold property was destroyed after the formation of the sale contract without responsibility on the seller's part, the buyer nevertheless would have had to pay the purchase price.[56]

If the debtor does not immediately notify the creditor of the subsequent impossibility of the performance or does not take necessary measures to mitigate the resulting damage, he is liable to pay compensation for damage arising from this omission (TCO art. 136 par. 3).

In certain cases of subsequent impossibility of an obligation for which the debtor is not responsible, he may obtain certain benefits in lieu of the extinguished obligation. For example, the debtor may receive insurance indemnity for the specific object that was destroyed, or he may obtain a price through expropriation. In such cases, the question of whether the debtor must give these pecuniary benefits to the creditor arises. There is no specific provision in the Turkish Code of Obligations regarding this question. There is a lacuna (*praeter legem*).[57] Indeed, the fact that BGB § 285 and FCC art. 1303 (version in force from 17th February 1804 to 1st October 2016) regulate such circumstances supports this thesis. In the author's opinion, in the above-mentioned examples, if the counter-party wishes to receive these pecuniary benefits, the debtor must pass them on to the creditor, and thus, the creditor must perform his counter-obligation.[58]

25.5.3 *Partial Impossibility*[59]

If the performance of the obligation becomes partially impossible due to factors for which the debtor may not be held responsible, then the debtor is released only from that part of the obligation that has become impossible to perform (TCO art. 137 par. 1 sent. 1). However, if it is clearly understood that such a contract would not have been formed had one or both of the parties foreseen this partial impossibility, then the debtor is released from the entire obligation (TCO art. 137 par. 1 sent. 2).

In bilateral contracts, if a party's obligation becomes partially impossible to perform and the creditor consents to partial performance, then the counter-obligation will also be performed to that extent. However, if the creditor does not accept partial performance or the counter-obligation is indivisible, then TCO art. 136 par. 2 will apply (TCO art. 137 par. 2).

---

[56]Engel (1997), p. 783; Tercier (2004), p. 272; Tandoğan (1990), pp. 104–118; Nomer and Engin (2017), art. 208, N. 23.

[57]Thévenoz and Werro (2012), art. 119, N. 20.

[58]Thévenoz and Werro (2012), art. 119, N. 20; Eren (2015), pp. 1304–1305; Oğuzman and Öz (2015), pp. 556–557.

[59]For further explanations see Ercoşkun Şenol (2016).

25.6 Hardship

According to TCO art. 138, in cases of hardship,[60] the disadvantaged party may apply to the court and demand the variation of the contract having regard to the new circumstances. Where the judge cannot vary the contract to accommodate the new circumstances, the disadvantaged party may withdraw from the contract (*ex tunc*).[61] Nevertheless, if there is a continuing contract between the parties, then the disadvantaged party, as a rule, may terminate the contract (*ex nunc*)[62] instead of withdrawing from it.

In the case of withdrawal from a contract, all obligations, whether already performed or not, are extinguished. Pursuant to TCO art. 77 par. 2, the obligations that have already been performed by the debtor create a case of unjust enrichment in the assets of the creditor (*condictio ob causam finitam*).[63] Thus, the enriched party must restitute this performance upon the retroactive termination of the contract, in accordance with the provisions pertaining to unjust enrichment (TCO arts. 79–82).[64]

On the other hand, in the case of termination, the obligations that have already been performed are not affected. The termination will end only the obligations to be performed.

25.7 Set-Off[65]

25.7.1 General[66]

In general terms, where two persons are obliged to each other and their obligations are due and are of a similar kind, each party may set off his obligation against his claim, provided that he has not waived the right of set-off.[67] For instance, D is obliged to pay €10,000 to C, and C is obliged to pay €8000 to D. In this case, it is possible that D pays €10,000 to C and expects C to pay €8000, or in lieu of these payments, D may set off his obligation against his claim. Thus, the parties' mutual obligations are discharged to the amount of the lesser obligation, and D becomes

---

[60]See Chap. 10.

[61]Termination of the contract takes effect retroactively (*résolution*, *Rücktritt*).

[62]Termination of the contract takes effect prospectively (*résiliation*, *Kündigung*).

[63]Tekinay et al. (1993), pp. 742–743.

[64]*Cf.* Öz (1990), pp. 108–111.

[65]*Compensation*, *Verrechnung*.

[66]For further explanations see Aral (1994), Develioğlu (2012).

[67]Tercier et al. (2016), p. 469; Nomer (2015), p. 385; Oğuzman and Öz (2015), p. 564.

obliged to pay only €2000. It should be noted that, in this example, C may also exercise the right of set-off, provided that he has not waived this right.

As has been seen, the right of set-off helps to preclude unnecessary transactions relating to performance.[68] Moreover, the right of set-off provides a form of security to the party who exercises this right. In the above-mentioned example, if D, not exercising this right, performs his obligation, he undertakes the risk of C's non-performance.[69]

According to TCO art. 143 par. 1 sent. 1, the right of set-off is exercised by a unilateral declaration of will (intention).[70] In other words, acceptance by the counter-party is not required. However, it should be borne in mind that for certain obligations, the legislature requires the creditor's consent to the set-off (TCO art. 144).

Within the limits of freedom of contract, it is possible that the parties may set off their obligations by agreement.[71] Furthermore, the parties may agree that their future mutual obligations will automatically be set off.[72]

25.7.2 Conditions

In order for a party to exercise a right of set-off, the following conditions must be met: (1) each party must have a claim against the other; (2) the claims must be of the same kind; (3) the setting-off party's claim must be due, and his obligation must be able to be performed; (4) the setting-off party must not have waived his right of set-off; and (5) the party who intends to exercise the right of set-off must declare his intention to do so.

25.7.2.1 Mutuality of Obligations

The first condition of the right of set-off is that the parties must have a claim against each other.[73] In order for a party to exercise his right of set-off, he must be obliged to the counter-party and must have a claim against the counter-party.

[68]Oğuzman and Öz (2015), p. 565; Eren (2015), p. 1274; Feyzioğlu (1977), pp. 482–483.

[69]Tekinay et al. (1993), p. 1012; Oğuzman and Öz (2015), p. 565.

[70]*Déclaration de volonté, Willenserklärung.*

[71]Engel (1997), p. 670; Tercier et al. (2016), p. 470; Eren (2015), p. 1275; Nomer (2015), p. 385; Oğuzman and Öz (2015), p. 565.

[72]von Tuhr and Escher (1974), § 79, III, pp. 208–209; Oğuzman and Öz (2015), p. 566; Eren (2015), p. 1275.

[73]Tercier et al. (2016), p. 472; Eren (2015), p. 1275; Oğuzman and Öz (2015), p. 566; Thévenoz and Werro (2012), art. 120, N. 2; Tercier (2004), p. 275; Gauch et al. (2008), p. 206.

The obligations to be set off do not have to arise from the same obligational relationship; they may also arise from different obligational relationships.[74] For instance, the lessee D is obliged to pay €10,000 to the lessor C with respect to a lease contract. However, C must pay a tort compensation of €12,000 to D. In this case, even though the parties' mutual obligations arise from different obligational relationships, these obligations may be set off by a unilateral declaration by one party.

In the above-mentioned example, consider that the lessor C assigns his claim against D to a third party. In this case, neither C nor D may exercise the right of set-off. This is because the condition relating to the mutuality of the claims is no longer met. It should be noted that for the same reason, a surety is not entitled to set off his obligation arising from the surety contract against the principal debtor's obligation to the creditor. However, pursuant to TCO art. 140, so long as the principal debtor has a right of set-off against the creditor, the surety may refuse to perform his obligation.

In certain cases, a party may have contracted for the benefit of a third party. For instance, in a sale contract, the parties agree that the buyer pays €10,000 for the price of goods sold to a third party. In this case, even if the seller is obliged to pay €8000 to the buyer, the buyer is not entitled to set off his obligation against the third party with his claim relating to the seller (TCO art. 141).

If one of the parties who are mutual debtors and creditors assigns his claim to a third party, neither party to the original obligational relationship may exercise the right of set-off against the other. This is due to the fact that, with the assignment of the claim, the condition relating to the mutuality of the claims is no longer met. However, TCO art. 188 par. 2 must be considered. Assume that D is obliged to pay €10,000 to C and C is obliged to pay €12,000 to D. Subsequently, C assigns his claim to a third party T. In this case, D may no longer exercise the right of set-off against C. Nevertheless, according to TCO art. 188 par. 2, if the debtor D's counter-claim was not yet due at the time he became aware of the assignment by C, he may set off the counter-claim on the condition that it becomes due before or simultaneously with the assigned claim.[75]

25.7.2.2 Obligations of the Same Kind

The second condition of the right of set-off is that the claims must be of the same kind.[76] Pecuniary obligations are of the same kind, and thus, they may be set off. Indeed, in practice, generally pecuniary obligations are set off. However,

---

[74]Feyzioğlu (1977), pp. 496–497; Oğuzman and Öz (2015), p. 567; Eren (2015), p. 1277.

[75]See Sect. 32.2.3.3.

[76]Tercier (2004), p. 276; Thévenoz and Werro (2012), art. 120, N. 11; Oğuzman and Öz (2015), p. 568; Feyzioğlu (1977), p. 494; Oser and Schönenberger (1929), art. 120, N. 7; Gauch et al. (2008), p. 207.

obligations other than pecuniary obligations may also be set off, provided that they are of the same kind or nature.[77] For instance, D is obliged to transfer 2 tons of wheat to C, and C is obliged to transfer 3 tons of wheat to D. In this case, these obligations may be set off as they are of the same kind.

At this point, it is worth discussing whether or not pecuniary obligations in national currency and foreign currency are considered to be of the same kind. For example, consider that D is obliged to pay €10,000 to C and C is obliged to pay TL 12,000 to D. If the parties have agreed that D must perform his obligation literally, the parties' obligations are not deemed to be of the same kind. However, if the contract does not require literal performance, then D may perform the obligation in the national currency (TCO art. 99 par. 2). If D elects this alternative, then he may set off the obligation with his claim against C.[78]

25.7.2.3 Maturity and Performability of the Obligations

The third condition of the right of set-off is that the setting-off party's claim must be due and his obligation must be able to be performed.[79] According to TCO art. 139 par. 1, the parties' mutual obligations of the same kind must be due. However, in cases where the time limit is to the advantage of the debtor, even if the debtor's obligation is not due, he may exercise the right of set-off, provided that his counter-claim is due. This is because in cases where the time limit is to the advantage of the debtor, early performance is possible (TCO art. 96).[80] Since the debtor may perform his obligation before it becomes due, it is reasonable to accept that he may exercise the right of set-off prior to the due date.

Pursuant to TCO art. 142, where the debtor has become bankrupt, the creditors may set off their claims, even if they are not yet due, against the debts that are owed to the bankrupted party.

It should be acknowledged that it is possible for the setting-off party's claim to be disputed. Even if this is the case, he may still set off his obligation against his counter-claim (TCO art. 139 par. 2). If the legislature had not enacted this provision, the debtor could intentionally create a dispute in order to preclude the counterparty exercising his right of set-off. However, if it is subsequently discovered that the setting-off party's disputed claim had never existed or is extinguished, then the set-off is void.[81]

---

[77]Feyzioğlu (1977), p. 494; Oğuzman and Öz (2015), p. 568.

[78]Engel (1997), pp. 672–673; Eren (2015), p. 1276, *cf.* Oğuzman and Öz (2015), p. 569.

[79]Thévenoz and Werro (2012), art. 120, N. 8; Tercier (2004), p. 277; Eren (2015), p. 1278; Tekinay et al. (1993), p. 1017; Oğuzman and Öz (2015), p. 570; Oser and Schönenberger (1929), art. 120, N. 8; Gauch et al. (2008), pp. 208–209.

[80]See Sect. 18.3.5.

[81]Feyzioğlu (1977), p. 496; Oğuzman and Öz (2015), pp. 571–572.

25.7.2.4 Non-existence of a Waiver

The fourth condition of the right of set-off is that the setting-off party must not have waived his right of set-off.[82] According to TCO art. 145, a debtor may waive his right of set-off in advance.[83] In such a case, it is evident that the debtor no longer has the right of set-off and, thus, may not exercise it.

It should be kept in mind that a debtor or creditor may waive this right after the other conditions for set-off have been met. In such a case, he may not exercise the right of set-off either.[84]

25.7.2.5 Declaration of Set-off

The fifth condition of the right of set-off is that the party who intends to exercise the right of set-off must declare his intention to do so.[85] This declaration does not require a specific form.[86] The setting-off party must have both the capacity to act and the authority to dispose[87] of his claim.[88] The declaration of set-off must be addressed to the counter-party, and it becomes effective when it reaches him (TCO art. 143 par. 1 sent. 1). The declaration of set-off may also be raised in a pending case.

In certain cases, in order for a debtor to exercise the right of set-off, the creditor's consent is necessary. According to TCO art. 144, the following claims may not be set off without the creditor's consent:

1. Claims relating to the return of or the value of bailed objects. If the subject matter of the bailment is a specific item, this provision may not be relied upon. This is because in such a case, the second condition of set-off, which requires claims to be of the same kind, cannot be satisfied. Therefore, this provision may only be applied to fungible goods or the value of specific objects.[89]
2. Claims relating to the return of or the value of objects unlawfully obtained or retained by fraud. The legislature disapproves of a creditor who is a victim of tort or fraud being faced with a set-off without his consent.

---

[82] Engel (1997), p. 680; Tercier (2004), p. 278; Oğuzman and Öz (2015), p. 573; Reisoğlu (2014), p. 422; Gauch et al. (2008), pp. 209–210.

[83] A waiver is an agreement between the debtor and creditor (*pactum de non compensando*), and not a unilateral legal transaction by either party. Gauch et al. (2008), p. 210; Tercier (2004), pp. 278–279, on the contrary see Engel (1997), p. 680.

[84] Oğuzman and Öz (2015), p. 573.

[85] Tercier (2004), p. 274; Engel (1997), p. 675; Nomer (2015), p. 385; Tercier et al. (2016), p. 471; Oğuzman and Öz (2015), p. 573.

[86] Tercier et al. (2016), p. 471; Oğuzman and Öz (2015), p. 574.

[87] *Pouvoir de disposer, Verfügungsmacht.*

[88] Oğuzman and Öz (2015), p. 574.

[89] Oğuzman and Öz (2015), p. 575.

3. Claims that are necessary for the subsistence of the debtor and his family and that must be paid directly to the creditor due to their nature, such as alimony and wages. If the legislature had not set out this provision, certain creditors with low incomes would be deprived of the minimum amount necessary for their and their families' subsistence, on account of the debtors' declaration of set-off.

In addition, according to TCO art. 407 par. 2, an employer is not entitled to set off a claim on his employee against the employee's salary without the latter's consent. However, if the employee has intentionally caused damage to the employer, which has been determined by a decision of a court, the employer's claim for compensation may be set off against the employee's salary but only to the extent of the seizable part of his salary as determined by law.

It is relevant to note that claims relating to life annuities, compensation for loss of support and a grantee's claims arising from a life-long support agreement may also not be set off without the creditor's consent.[90]

25.7.3 *Consequences*

When a declaration of set-off reaches the counter-party, the parties' mutual obligations are discharged to the extent of the lesser obligation. Moreover, these obligations are deemed to be discharged at the earliest possible time that they could have been set off (TCO art. 143 par. 1 sent. 2). For instance, S sells a car to B for €10,000, and B's obligation becomes due on 1 July 2016 in accordance with the parties' agreement. Furthermore, S is also obliged to pay €7000 to B, and this obligation becomes due on 1 August 2016. Consider that B exercises his right of set-off on 1 December 2016. In such a case, it is apparent that S's obligation is discharged completely, whereas B's obligation is discharged partially, being reduced to €3000. In this case, even though B exercised his right of set-off on 1 December 2016, this has a retroactive effect and extinguishes the parties' obligations at the earliest possible time B could have exercised his right of set-off. That is to say, B's set-off is effective as of 1 August 2016. Clearly, the conditions of B's right of set-off are met on this date because that is when S's obligation falls due.

Moreover, it is worth analysing certain cases in order to examine the retroactive effect of set-off:

1. In the above-mentioned example, it is evident that if B does not perform his obligation on 1 July 2016, then he falls into default (TCO art. 117 par. 2) and becomes liable for default interest. However, even though B exercises his right of set-off on 1 December 2016, due to the retroactive effect of set-off, his default is extinguished as of 1 August 2016 and his obligation to pay default interest on

[90] Engel (1997), p. 679; Feyzioğlu (1977), pp. 510–511; Eren (2015), p. 1279; Oğuzman and Öz (2015), p. 576.

the sum of €10,000 is extinguished. Thereafter he will be liable for the default interest only on the balance of €3000.

2. Consider that S pledges his claim to a third party or S's creditors seize this claim against B on 1 October 2016. When B exercises his right of set-off on 1 December 2016, and since this set-off is effective retroactively as of 1 August 2016, the pledge constituted by S on the claim on 1 October 2016 is partially extinguished to the extent of the sum of €7,000. The same also holds true for the seizure by S's creditors on 1 October 2016.[91]
3. Special customs governing commercial current accounts are reserved (TCO art. 143 par. 2). In fact, the time when the set-off of mutual claims entered in a current account becomes effective is determined, first and foremost, according to special customs. In the absence of such special customs, the provisions of the Turkish Commercial Code will apply (TComC art. 90).[92]
4. If a creditor brings an action for a time-barred claim, the debtor may raise as a defence that the claim is time-barred. Therefore, a creditor may not set off his time-barred claim against the debtor's counter-claim. However, due to the retroactive effect of set-off, a time-barred claim may be set off on the condition that it was not time-barred at the time when the conditions of the right of set-off were first met (TCO art. 139 par. 3).

References

Aral F (1994) Türk borçlar hukukunda takas. Savaş, Ankara

Aybay A (2011) Borçlar hukuku dersleri genel bölüm. Filiz, İstanbul

Becker H (1941) Kommentar zum Schweizerischen Zivilgesetzbuch, vol VI, Obligationenrecht, 1. Abteilung: Allgemeine Bestimmungen, Art. 1-183. Stämpfli, Bern

Berger B (2012) Allgemeines Schuldrecht. Stämpfli, Bern

Develioğlu HM (2012) Takas. Vedat, İstanbul

Dural M (1976) Borçlunun sorumlu olmadığı sonraki imkânsızlık (bk. 117). İstanbul

Engel P (1997) Traité des obligations en droit Suisse. Stämpfli, Bern

Ercoşkun Şenol HK (2016) Borçlar hukukunda kısmi imkânsızlık. On iki levha, İstanbul

Eren F (2015) Borçlar hukuku genel hükümler. Yetkin, Ankara

Feyzioğlu FN (1977) Borçlar hukuku genel hükümler, vol 2. Fakülteler, İstanbul

Gauch P, Schluep WR, Emmenegger S (2008) Schweizerisches Obligationenrecht, Allgemeiner Teil, vol 2. Schulthess, Zürich

Gümüş MA (2015) Türk-İsviçre borçlar hukukunda ibra sözleşmesi. Vedat, İstanbul

Helvacı İ (2008) Eski medenî kanunumuzla karşılaştırmalı olarak Türk medenî kanununa göre sözleşmeden doğan ipotek hakkı. On iki levha, İstanbul

Honsell H, Vogt NP, Wiegand W (eds) (2003) Basler Kommentar zum Schweizerischen Privatrecht, Obligationenrecht 1: Art. 1-529 OR. Helbing Lichtenhahn, Basel

Kılıçoğlu AM (2013) Borçlar hukuku genel hükümler. Turhan, İstanbul

Koyuncuoğlu T (1972) Türk ve İsviçre hukukunda borcun yenilenmesi (novatio). İstanbul

[91] Oğuzman and Öz (2015), pp. 577–578.

[92] Eren (2015), p. 1281; Reisoğlu (2014), p. 423; Oğuzman and Öz (2015), p. 578.

Kurt LM (2016) Borçlunun sorumlu olmadığı sonraki imkânsızlık. Yetkin, Ankara

Nomer HN (2015) Borçlar hukuku genel hükümler. Beta, İstanbul

Nomer HN, Engin Bİ (2017) Türk borçlar kanunu şerhi, özel borç ilişkileri, Volume 1: satış sözleşmesi. Seçkin, Ankara

Oğuzman K, Öz T (2015) Borçlar hukuku genel hükümler, vol 1. Vedat, İstanbul

Oser H, Schönenberger W (1929) Kommentar zum Schweizerischen Zivilgesetzbuch, Volume V: Das Obligationenrecht, Erster Halbband: Art. 1-183. Schulthess, Zürich

Önay I (2016) Yenileme. On iki levha, İstanbul

Öz T (1990) Sebepsiz zenginleşme. Kazancı, İstanbul

Reisoğlu S (2014) Türk borçlar hukuku genel hükümler. Beta, İstanbul

Schwenzer I (2009) Schweizerisches Obligationenrecht, Allgemeiner Teil. Schulthess, Bern

Serozan R (2014) Borçlar hukuku genel bölüm, vol 3 (Kocayusufpaşaoğlu/Hatemi/Serozan/Arpacı). Filiz, İstanbul

Steinauer PH (2003) Les droits réels, vol 3. Stämpfli, Bern

Tandoğan H (1990) Özel borç ilişkileri, vol I/1. Evrim, İstanbul

Tekinay SS, Akman S, Burcuoğlu H, Altop A (1993) Tekinay borçlar hukuku genel hükümler. Filiz, İstanbul

Tercier P (2004) Le droit des obligations. Schulthess, Zurich

Tercier P, Pichonnaz P, Develioğlu HM (2016) Borçlar hukuku genel hükümler. On iki levha, İstanbul

Thévenoz L, Werro F (éd) (2012) Commentaire romand code des obligations 1: art. 1-529 CO. Helbing Lichtenhahn, Bâle

Toksal BM (1956) Hukuki cephesiyle hesabı cari. İstanbul

Turanboy KN (1998) İbra sözleşmesi. Ankara

von Tuhr A, Escher A (1974) Allgemeiner Teil des Schweizerischen Obligationenrecht, vol 2. Schulthess, Zürich

Chapter 26
Limitation Period

26.1 General[1]

As a rule, claims are subject to limitation periods.[2] When an obligation becomes time-barred, it remains valid but becomes a natural obligation.[3] Thus, the debtor may perform the time-barred obligation or raise a defence that the claim is time-barred. When the debtor asserts that the obligation is time-barred, the court must dismiss the case provided that this defence is not contrary to the principles of good faith (TCC art. 2 par. 2).[4]

As mentioned above, even if the obligation is time-barred, the debtor may nevertheless fulfil it, and this fulfilment will not constitute an unjust enrichment (TCO art. 78 par. 2). Essentially, a time-barred obligation is a type of natural obligation.[5] Furthermore, even if the debtor does not know that the obligation is time-barred and fulfils the obligation, the debtor is not entitled to assert that he fulfilled the obligation in the erroneous belief that he was obliged to do so. This is because a time-barred obligation is not an extinguished obligation.[6]

---

[1]Aybay (2011), pp. 162–169; Becker (1941), Vorbemerkungen zu art. 127-142, art. 127-142; Berger (2012), pp. 478–496; Engel (1997), pp. 795–824; Eren (2015), pp. 1281–1298; Feyzioğlu (1977), pp. 518–606; Gauch et al. (2008), pp. 217–239; Honsell et al. (2003), Vorbemerkungen zu art. 127-142, art. 127-142; Kılıçoğlu (2013), pp. 866–898; Nomer (2015), pp. 391–410; Oser and Schönenberger (1929), Vorbemerkung zu art. 127-142, art. 127-142; Oğuzman and Öz (2015), pp. 579–606; Reisoğlu (2014), pp. 424–440; Schwenzer (2009), pp. 519–533; Tekinay et al. (1993), pp. 1030–1076; Tercier (2004), pp. 280–288; Tercier et al. (2016), pp. 480–495; Thévenoz and Werro (2012), art. 127-142, and von Tuhr and Escher (1974), pp. 211–235.

[2]*Prescription, Verjährung*. For further explanations see Akçay (2010), Erdem (2010).

[3]Tekinay et al. (1993), p. 1030.

[4]Eren (2015), p. 1298; Oğuzman and Öz (2015), pp. 602–603.

[5]See Sect. 21.2.3.

[6]Tercier (2004), p. 288; Berger (2012), p. 478; Oğuzman and Öz (2015), p. 598.

İ. Helvacı, *Turkish Contract Law*, DOI 10.1007/978-3-319-60061-1_26

The judge may not take into consideration *ex officio* the fact that an obligation has become time-barred. This defence may only be raised by the debtor (TCO art. 161).

26.2 Limitation Periods

26.2.1 Ten Years

According to TCO art. 146, unless otherwise provided by law, all claims become time-barred after 10 years.

26.2.2 Five Years

In certain cases, the legislature determines the limitation period to be 5 years. Pursuant to TCO art. 147, the following claims become time-barred after 5 years:

(1) periodic payments such as rent, capital interest and wages. However, if the rental fee is to be paid non-periodically or if the capital interest is to be added to the capital, these claims become time-barred after 10 years.[7] Furthermore, default interest is not covered by this article[8];
(2) accommodation fees at such places as hotels, motels, bed and breakfasts and resorts and food and beverage costs at restaurants and other such places;
(3) claims arising from small-scale retail sales and work performed by artisans on a small scale;
(4) in a partnership, claims arising out of the partnership contract, which are between partners or between partners and the partnership; claims arising between the directors, agents or auditors of the partnership and the partnership or the partners;
(5) claims arising from agency contracts, commission and agent contracts or brokerage contracts except those relating to commercial brokerage fees; and
(6) claims arising from work contracts, except those relating to non- or improper performance by the contractor based on gross fault (*culpa lata*).

[7]Oğuzman and Öz (2015), p. 586.
[8]Tercier et al. (2016), p. 485; Nomer (2015), p. 398; Oğuzman and Öz (2015), p. 586.

26.2.3 Mandatory Limitation Periods

The limitation periods regulated under the second chapter of the third title of the Turkish Code of Obligations are mandatory. Thus, they cannot be amended by agreement between the parties. Even if such an amendment is agreed upon, it will be void (TCO art. 148).

26.2.4 Commencement of Limitation Periods

26.2.4.1 General

The limitation period commences when the obligation becomes due (TCO art. 149 par. 1). It is useful to remember that in cases where the time of performance is determined, the claim becomes due when the time limit expires. In such cases, immediate performance may not be claimed. In other words, the creditor must wait for the obligation to become due.[9] Therefore, it is evident that the limitation period does not begin until the claim falls due.

In contrast, according to TCO art. 90, if the time of performance is not determined either by the parties' agreement, by the nature of the legal transaction or by the law itself, the obligation falls due immediately. Accordingly, immediate performance may be demanded.[10] Therefore, in cases in which the time of performance is not determined, the limitation period commences as soon as the obligation arises.[11]

It is possible that the taking effect of the obligation may depend upon the occurrence of a future uncertain event. In such a case, the obligation takes effect only when and if the event occurs. This is referred to as a suspensive condition (condition precedent).[12] In cases where there is a suspensive condition, the limitation period starts when the condition is fulfilled.[13]

In certain cases, the maturity of the claim depends on the giving of notice by the creditor. Thus, if the creditor does not give notice, then the claim will not become due, and the limitation period will not commence.[14] That is why the legislature accepts that where an obligation falls due on the giving of notice by the creditor, the limitation period commences as soon as such notice is able to be given (TCO art.

[9]See Sect. 18.2.

[10]See Sect. 18.1.

[11]Engel (1997), p. 803; Thévenoz and Werro (2012), art. 130, N. 6; Feyzioğlu (1977), p. 537; Oğuzman and Öz (2015), p. 587; Reisoğlu (2014), p. 431, compare to Tekinay et al. (1993), pp. 1044–1045.

[12]See Sect. 29.2.

[13]Feyzioğlu (1977), pp. 538–539; Oğuzman and Öz (2015), p. 587; Reisoğlu (2014), p. 432.

[14]See Sect. 18.2.

149 par. 2). Essentially, if the legislature had not set this provision, the creditor could preclude the maturity of the claim and, thus, the commencement of the limitation period.[15]

If the maturity of the claim depends on the giving of notice by the debtor, then TCO art. 149 par. 2 will not apply.[16] Consequently, in such a case, the limitation period will commence when the obligation falls due. If TCO art. 149 par. 2 were to be applied to such cases, the debtor, by failing to give notice on maturity of the obligation, could preclude the creditor from demanding performance. As a result, the debtor could also cause the obligation to become time-barred.[17]

26.2.4.2 In Case of Annuities

In the case of life annuities and similar periodic obligations, the limitation period begins to run in respect of the entire obligation when the first act of performance that is delayed falls due (TCO art. 150 par. 1). Where the entire obligation is time-barred, the individual obligations that have not been performed are also deemed to be time-barred (TCO art. 150 par. 2).

26.2.5 Calculation of Limitation Periods

The day on which the limitation period commences is not included in the calculation of the limitation period, and the limitation period only expires when the last day of the period lapses without the right, that is subject to the limitation period, being exercised (TCO art. 151 par. 1). In the calculation of limitation periods, the provisions relating to the time limits for the performance of obligations are also applicable (TCO art. 151 par. 2).

If the last day of the limitation period corresponds to a legally recognised holiday, then the limitation period ends on the first working day following the holiday (TCO art. 93 par. 1).

---

[15] Engel (1997), pp. 804–805; Tekinay et al. (1993), p. 1043; Oğuzman and Öz (2015), pp. 588–589.

[16] Thévenoz and Werro (2012), art. 130, N. 7.

[17] Oğuzman and Öz (2015), p. 588; Reisoğlu (2014), p. 432.

26.3 Effects on Ancillary Claims

When the principal claim is time-barred, the interest and other ancillary claims also become time-barred (TCO art. 152). This article refers to both capital and default interest.[18] However, it should be noted that in cases where a claim for interest has already been time-barred, then this article is of no relevance. Indeed, according to TCO art. 146, the general limitation period is 10 years, whereas the limitation period for interest on capital is 5 years (TCO art. 147). Thus, this article only applies to claims for interest that have not become time-barred after 5 years.[19]

TCO art. 152 also applies to penalties. This is because penalties are ancillary claims. Assume, for example, in a contract that includes a penalty clause that the principal claim becomes time-barred. In such a case, if the creditor attempts to demand that the debtor pay the penalty, then the debtor may defend the claim on the basis that the penalty claim is time-barred due to the fact that the principal claim is time-barred.

It should be noted that ancillary securities *in rem*, such as pledges or mortgages, do not become time-barred. According to TCO art. 159, if a claim is secured by a pledge, this does not preclude the claim from becoming time-barred. However, even if the secured claim becomes time-barred, the creditor may demand that the pledge be realised under the authority of the debt enforcement office. The importance of this provision is demonstrated in the following example: a debtor is obliged to pay TL 10,000, and this obligation is secured by a pledge. After a period of time, the principal claim becomes time-barred. In spite of this, the creditor demands realisation of the pledge and receives TL 8000 from the debt enforcement office. In such a case, if the creditor demands that the debtor pay the balance of TL 2000, the debtor may at that time raise the fact that the principal claim is time-barred.

Moreover, according to TCC art. 864, when an obligation is secured by a mortgage or other security that is entered in the land register, the limitation period does not commence, or is suspended if it has already commenced, until after the discharge of the mortgage or security.[20]

26.4 Prevention and Suspension of Limitation Periods

In certain cases, an action cannot reasonably be initiated. For instance, spouses cannot readily sue each other given the emotions that are involved. Moreover, it is extremely difficult for a person under guardianship to file a lawsuit against his

[18] Thévenoz and Werro (2012), art. 133, N. 2; Feyzioğlu (1977), p. 605; Oğuzman and Öz (2015), p. 602, on the contrary see Nomer (2015), pp. 398–399.

[19] Feyzioğlu (1977), pp. 604–605; Oğuzman and Öz (2015), p. 601.

[20] For further explanations see Helvacı (2008), pp. 305–310.

guardian. That is why the legislature accepts that the limitation period will not commence or will be suspended in order to protect the creditor in such cases.[21]

According to TCO art. 153, the limitation period does not commence or, if it has commenced, will be suspended in the following cases:

(1) In relation to claims by children against their parents for so long as they are under parental power. The difficulty with a child suing his parent/parents is evident.
(2) In relation to claims by wards against their guardians or against the state in relation to guardianship, for so long as they are under guardianship. The reason for this provision is also due to the great difficulty of the ward suing his guardian or the state.
(3) In relation to claims by spouses against each other during their marriage. This is because should spouses have to bring an action against each other fearing that the obligation will become time-barred, it would lead to conflicts within their marriage.
(4) In relation to claims by household employees against their employers, during the period of their employment. If household employees were required to bring an action under the pressure of the obligation becoming time-barred, it would jeopardise the continuing relationship with their employers. This provision applies whether the employee's claim arises from an employment contract or from another obligational relationship.[22]
(5) In relation to a usufructuary right, as long as the debtor enjoys that right. Indeed, in such a case, even if the creditor brings an action and the court accepts it, as long as the debtor enjoys the usufructuary right, the creditor cannot benefit from the court decision. This is due to the fact that the debtor retains the usufruct for the money that he has paid. For this reason, the legislature considers this kind of arrangement as a factor for the postponement or suspension of the limitation period.[23]
(6) In circumstances where the claim cannot be brought before the Turkish courts. For example, in cases of force majeure, such as earthquakes, war, riots, it may be impossible to bring an action for the time being. That is why the legislature considers such circumstances to be valid reasons for the postponement or suspension of the limitation period.
(7) In relation to cases where the capacities of the debtor and the creditor are merged in the same person. Where this merger is terminated retroactively, the limitation period will be suspended until the time of termination.

It should be added that there are other factors that preclude the commencement or the continuation of the limitation period. For example, as mentioned above,

---

[21]Thévenoz and Werro (2012), art. 134, N. 1; Tekinay et al. (1993), p. 1052; Oğuzman and Öz (2015), p. 589; Eren (2015), p. 1291.

[22]Feyzioğlu (1977), pp. 571–572; Oğuzman and Öz (2015), p. 591.

[23]Feyzioğlu (1977), p. 572; Oğuzman and Öz (2015), p. 592.

according to TCC art. 864, while an obligation is secured by a mortgage or other security entered in the land registry, the limitation period does not commence, or is suspended if it has already commenced.[24]

The period of limitation begins or continues from the end of the day on which the circumstances that preclude the commencement or the continuation of the limitation period cease to have effect (TCO art. 153 par. 2).

It should be kept in mind that in cases where an obligation is secured by the debtor's mortgage or by a third party's mortgage with the consent of the debtor, even if the mortgage is discharged, a new limitation period starts to run. This is due to the fact that when the debtor or a third party grants a mortgage with the consent of the debtor, the continuity of the limitation period will be interrupted (TCO art. 154 par. 1 subcl. 1). When the circumstances that interrupted the limitation period are terminated, a new limitation period commences *ab initio* (TCO art. 156 par. 1).

26.5 Interruption of Limitation Periods

26.5.1 Causes of Interruption

Pursuant to TCO art. 154, the limitation period is interrupted in the following cases[25]:

(1) where the debtor acknowledges the debt, particularly if he pays interest, partially fulfils the obligation, gives a pledge or mortgage or provides a surety. The debtor's acknowledgement of debt may be in oral or written form. In any case, the declaration of will (intention)[26] relating to the acknowledgement of debt must be directed to the creditor.[27] In addition, the debtor's acknowledgement of debt may be implicit. For example, as mentioned above, where the debtor provides a surety or pledges a chattel or mortgages immovable property, these legal transactions are considered to be acknowledgements of debt. Further, if the debtor exercises a right of set-off and thus, partially extinguishes the obligation, this is also considered to be an implicit acknowledgement of debt.[28] It should be kept in mind that if a third party performs the obligation wholly or partially, pays interest, gives a pledge or a mortgage or provides a surety, these may only interrupt the limitation period subject to the consent of the debtor[29]; and

[24]For further explanations see Helvacı (2008), pp. 305–310.

[25]For further explanations see Ergenekon (1960).

[26]*Déclaration de volonté*, *Willenserklärung*.

[27]Feyzioğlu (1977), p. 581; Oğuzman and Öz (2015), p. 594; Tercier et al. (2016), p. 491.

[28]Feyzioğlu (1977), pp. 580–581; Eren (2015), p. 1293; Oğuzman and Öz (2015), p. 594; Tercier et al. (2016), p. 491.

[29]Oğuzman and Öz (2015), p. 594; Reisoğlu (2014), p. 434; Feyzioğlu (1977), p. 581.

(2) where the creditor brings an action, or raises a defence before a court or an arbitration tribunal, initiates enforcement proceedings or files a claim in bankruptcy proceedings.

In cases where the limitation period is interrupted, a new limitation period commences, and, in principle, this new period has the same duration as the previous period. In other words, if the interrupted limitation period is 10 years, then the new period will also be 10 years, or if the interrupted limitation period is 5 years, then the new period will also be 5 years (*cf.* TCO art. 156 par. 1).[30]

26.5.2 Effects of Interruption Among Co-debtors

In certain cases, several debtors may be jointly and severally liable for an obligation. Where the limitation period is interrupted for one person who is jointly and severally liable for an obligation, it is also interrupted for the other joint and several debtors (TCO art. 155 par. 1).

In addition, an indivisible obligation may be owed by several debtors. In this case, each debtor is liable to carry out the entire obligation (TCO art. 85 par. 2).[31] Where the limitation period is interrupted for one debtor who is liable to perform an indivisible obligation, it is also interrupted for the other debtors (TCO art. 155 par. 1).

In obligations secured by a suretyship contract, if the limitation period for the principal debtor is interrupted, then it is also interrupted for the surety (TCO art. 155 par. 2). However, where the limitation period for the surety is interrupted, it is not interrupted for the principal debtor (TCO art. 155 par. 3).

26.5.3 Commencement of a New Limitation Period

26.5.3.1 In Case of Acknowledgement of Debt or Judgment

When a limitation period is interrupted, the new limitation period has the same duration as the previous period (TCO art. 156 par. 1). Actually, this is not explicitly stated in this article. However, it can be inferred by way of *argumentum a contrario* from the second paragraph of the said article as it states that when the obligation has been acknowledged by the issue of a document or determined by a court or arbitration tribunal decision, the new limitation period will be 10 years.[32]

---

[30]See Sect. 26.5.3.1.

[31]See Sect. 15.3.

[32]Tekinay et al. (1993), p. 1062; Oğuzman and Öz (2015), p. 596; Reisoğlu (2014), p. 437.

26.5.3.2 In Case of Acts by the Creditor

Where the limitation period is interrupted by the filing of a lawsuit or any pleading, a new limitation period commences on any action taken by the parties relating to the proceedings or any decision or ruling by the court during the litigation (TCO art. 157 par. 1).

Where the limitation period is interrupted by enforcement proceedings, a new limitation period commences after each act during enforcement of the claim (TCO art. 157 par. 2).

Where the limitation period is interrupted by the filing of a claim in a bankruptcy, a new limitation period commences as of the time when the claim can be reasserted according to the provisions relating to bankruptcy (TCO art. 157 par. 3).

26.6 Extension of the Limitation Period

Only a duly brought action or defence may interrupt the limitation period. However, an action or a defence may be dismissed on account of (1) a court having no jurisdiction in relation to the subject matter or having no territorial jurisdiction, (2) a defect that can be corrected or (3) prematurity. In addition, the limitation period may expire during these proceedings. In such a case, the legislature grants an additional period of 60 days to the creditor for reasserting the claim (TCO art. 158).

It should be noted that in the Turkish legal system, certain rights must be exercised within a specific time period.[33] For instance, legal and nominated heirs have the right to disclaim the inheritance that has accrued to them (TCC art. 605 par. 1). The heirs must exercise this right within 3 months (TCC art. 606 par. 1).[34] If an heir does not make his declaration to the court within this period of time, then he will be deprived of the right to disclaim the inheritance. In addition, the court must take into consideration *ex officio* whether or not the period of time to disclaim the inheritance has expired. That is why this period of time is distinct from a limitation period.[35] However, TCO art. 158 may also be applied in cases where the exercise of a right is subject to a period of time.

[33]*Péremption, Verwirkung.*

[34]In the case of a legal heir, the period runs from the date the heirs become aware of the death of the deceased, unless they can prove that they were not aware of their entitlement until a later time; and, in the case of a nominated heir, the period runs from the date on which they were officially notified of the disposition in their favour (TCC art. 606 par. 2). For further explanations see Helvacı (2014), p. 73 *ff.*

[35]Engel (1997), p. 798.

26.7 Waiver[36]

A debtor may not waive his right of defence arising from a limitation period in advance (TCO art. 160 par. 1). The fact that a debtor who is jointly and severally liable[37] has waived the limitation period may not be asserted against the other debtors (TCO art. 160 par. 2). The same provision applies to several debtors of an indivisible obligation[38] (TCO art. 160 par. 3). The principal debtor's waiver may not be asserted against a surety (TCO art. 160 par. 4).

However, after expiration of the limitation period, the debtor may waive this defence. The waiver may be express or implied. For an implied waiver, it is necessary that the debtor has knowledge of the fact that the obligation has become time-barred. The debtor's acknowledgement of debt or the debtor's provision of security will constitute an implicit waiver only under these circumstances. Moreover, even if the debtor raises the fact that the obligation is time-barred, he may later withdraw this defence and perform his obligation.[39]

References

Akçay E (2010) Türk borçlar kanunu'na göre zamanaşımı. On iki levha, İstanbul
Aybay A (2011) Borçlar hukuku dersleri genel bölüm. Filiz, İstanbul
Becker H (1941) Kommentar zum Schweizerischen Zivilgesetzbuch, Volume VI, Obligationenrecht, 1. Abteilung: Allgemeine Bestimmungen, Art. 1-183. Stämpfli, Bern
Berger B (2012) Allgemeines Schuldrecht. Stämpfli, Bern
Engel P (1997) Traité des obligations en droit Suisse. Stämpfli, Bern
Erdem M (2010) Özel hukukta zamanaşımı. On iki levha, İstanbul
Eren F (2015) Borçlar hukuku genel hükümler. Yetkin, Ankara
Ergenekon Y (1960) Türk borçlar hukukunda müruruzamanın kat'ı. Ankara
Feyzioğlu FN (1977) Borçlar hukuku genel hükümler, vol 2. Fakülteler, İstanbul
Gauch P, Schluep WR, Emmenegger S (2008) Schweizerisches Obligationenrecht, Allgemeiner Teil, vol 2. Schulthess, Zürich
Helvacı İ (2008) Eski medenî kanunumuzla karşılaştırmalı olarak Türk medenî kanunu'na göre sözleşmeden doğan ipotek hakkı. On iki levha, İstanbul
Helvacı İ (2014) Eski medenî kanunumuzla karşılaştırmalı olarak Türk medenî kanunu'na göre mirasın reddi, (mk. m. 605 - mk. m.618). Filiz, İstanbul
Honsell H, Vogt NP, Wiegand W (eds) (2003) Basler Kommentar zum Schweizerischen Privatrecht, Obligationenrecht 1: Art. 1-529 OR. Helbing Lichtenhahn, Basel
Kılıçoğlu AM (2013) Borçlar hukuku genel hükümler. Turhan, İstanbul
Nomer HN (2015) Borçlar hukuku genel hükümler. Beta, İstanbul
Oğuzman K, Öz T (2015) Borçlar hukuku genel hükümler, vol 1. Vedat, İstanbul

[36]For further explanation see Paksoy (2012).

[37]See Chap. 27.

[38]See Sect. 15.3.

[39]Oğuzman and Öz (2015), p. 600, see and compare to, Oser and Schönenberger, Art. 141, N: 4.

Oser H, Schönenberger W (1929) Kommentar zum Schweizerischen Zivilgesetzbuch, Volume V: Das Obligationenrecht, Erster Halbband: Art. 1-183. Schulthess, Zürich

Paksoy MS (2012) Zamanaşımından feragat (tbk 160). On iki levha, İstanbul

Reisoğlu S (2014) Türk borçlar hukuku genel hükümler. Beta, İstanbul

Schwenzer I (2009) Schweizerisches Obligationenrecht, Allgemeiner Teil. Schulthess, Bern

Tekinay SS, Akman S, Burcuoğlu H, Altop A (1993) Tekinay borçlar hukuku genel hükümler. Filiz, İstanbul

Tercier P (2004) Le droit des obligations. Schulthess, Zurich

Tercier P, Pichonnaz P, Develioğlu HM (2016) Borçlar hukuku genel hükümler. On iki levha, İstanbul

Thévenoz L, Werro F (éd) (2012) Commentaire romand code des obligations 1: art. 1-529 CO. Helbing Lichtenhahn, Bâle

von Tuhr A, Escher A (1974) Allgemeiner Teil des Schweizerischen Obligationenrecht, vol 2. Schulthess, Zürich

Part IV
Joint and Several Debtors and Creditors, Conditions, Earnest and Forfeit Money, and Penalty

Chapter 27
Joint and Several Debtors

27.1 General[1]

In certain cases, there may be several debtors liable to perform the same obligation.[2] If the creditor has the right to demand that each debtor perform the entire obligation, then these debtors are referred to as joint and several debtors.[3] This situation may only arise from a legal transaction, generally a contract, or the law itself.

27.2 Reasons for Joint and Several Liabilities

27.2.1 Legal Transactions

According to TCO art. 162 par. 1, if each of several debtors declares that he will be liable for the performance of the entire obligation, then they are joint and several

[1]Aybay (2011), pp. 170–174; Becker (1941), Vorbemerkung zu art. 143-150, art. 143-149; Berger (2012), pp. 837–848; Engel (1997), pp. 836–845; Eren (2015), pp. 1195–1216; Feyzioğlu (1977), pp. 302–337; Gauch et al. (2008), pp. 295–305; Honsell et al. (2003), art. 143-149; Kılıçoğlu (2013), pp. 740–754; Nomer (2015), pp. 417–423; Oser and Schönenberger (1929), Vorbemerkungen zum ersten Abschnitt (art. 143-150), art. 143-149; Oğuzman and Öz (2016), pp. 458–492; Özsunay (1983), pp. 176–182; Reisoğlu (2014), pp. 442–447; Schwenzer (2009), pp. 546–560; Tekinay et al. (1993), pp. 285–327; Tercier (2004), pp. 289–297; Tercier et al. (2016), pp. 497–510; Thévenoz and Werro (2012), art. 143-149, and von Tuhr and Escher (1974), pp. 290–321.

[2]For further explanations see Akıntürk (1971), Canyürek (2003), Dağdelen (2011), Özdoğan (2015).

[3]*Débiteurs solidaires*, *Solidarschuldnern*.

İ. Helvacı, *Turkish Contract Law*, DOI 10.1007/978-3-319-60061-1_27

debtors. In other words, the creditor may demand the performance of the entire obligation from all or any of them.[4]

If there is no such agreement between the debtors and the creditor, the latter may only demand proportional performance from the debtors. For example, if D_1 and D_2 are obliged to pay €10,000 to C and there is no agreement for their joint and several liability, then C may only demand that each debtor pay €5000 towards the total sum owing of €10,000. However, it is not absolutely necessary that the liability of the debtors is explicitly stated to be joint and several. Such liability may be inferred from the interpretation of the legal transaction.[5]

Moreover, according to TComC art. 7 par. 1 sent. 1, if two or more persons are obliged to another person on account of a transaction that is of a commercial nature in respect of only one or all of them, then they are jointly and severally liable, unless otherwise agreed upon by the parties or stipulated by law.

Another type of joint and several liability is created by TCO art. 201. This article defines a cumulative assumption of debt as an agreement formed between a new debtor and the creditor, and as a result of this agreement, the new debtor becomes liable jointly and severally along with the existing debtor.[6]

Specifically, joint and several liability generally arises from contracts.[7] However, it may also arise from a unilateral legal transaction, such as a testamentary disposition,[8] for instance, a testator declares that all of his legatees will be jointly and severally liable against a third party for the payment of a certain sum of money.

27.2.2 *The Law*

Joint and several liability may arise from the law itself (TCO art. 162 par. 2). For instance, according to TCC art. 641 par. 1, heirs are jointly and severally liable for the obligations of the deceased. Furthermore, according to TCC art. 681 par. 1, heirs will remain jointly and severally liable to the extent of their entire seizable personal assets for the obligations of the estate even after its partition, provided that the creditors have not explicitly or implicitly consented to the division of the liability among the heirs or to its delegation to one or more of them. This liability continues for a period of 5 years. This time limit starts on the date of partition in respect of the debts that are due; for debts that are not yet due, the time limit starts on the date they become due (TCC art. 681 par. 2).[9]

---

[4]Feyzioğlu (1977), p. 311; Oğuzman and Öz (2016), p. 458; Nomer (2015), p. 311.

[5]Tekinay et al. (1993), p. 293; Feyzioğlu (1977), p. 305; Oğuzman and Öz (2016), p. 465.

[6]See Sect. 33.3.

[7]Tercier (2004), p. 293.

[8]Oser and Schönenberger (1929), art. 143, N. 3; Tekinay et al. (1993), p. 294; Eren (2015), p. 1204; Oğuzman and Öz (2016), p. 468; Thévenoz and Werro (2012), art. 143, N. 6.

[9]Dural and Öz (2015), p. 526.

For joint and several liabilities that arise from the Turkish Code of Obligations, the following may be given as examples: where several persons have jointly borrowed an object (art. 382) or where an agent has been appointed by several persons (art. 511) or where several bailees jointly receive a chattel (art. 567). In each case, they become jointly and severally liable. Moreover, in an ordinary partnership, if the partners have jointly or through an agent undertaken a certain obligation towards a third party within the scope of the partnership, then they become jointly and severally liable, unless otherwise agreed (art. 638 par. 3).

27.3 Relationship Between the Debtors and the Creditor

27.3.1 Liability of the Debtors

According to TCO art. 163, a creditor may demand partial or full performance from one or all of the debtors. As long as the obligation is not entirely fulfilled, the debtors' liability stands.[10] For instance, D_1 and D_2 are jointly and severally obliged to pay €10,000 to C. C may bring an action against either D_1 or D_2 for the payment of the entire obligation, or C may bring an action against both D_1 and D_2 for the payment of the entire obligation. However, C may not collect more than €10,000. Moreover, C may demand that D_1 pay €5000 and that D_2 pay €5000.[11]

In the aforementioned example, even if C demands that D_1 pay the entire obligation, D_2 may nevertheless perform the obligation. Furthermore, whether or not the creditor brings an action against only one of the debtors is irrelevant. In other words, until the obligation is fulfilled entirely, even if C has brought an action against one of the debtors, the other debtor may nevertheless fulfil the obligation.[12]

Moreover, even if the creditor brings an action against one of the joint and several debtors, he still has the right to bring an action against the other debtors.[13] The other debtors may not raise as a defence that the creditor has already commenced proceedings against one of the other debtors, even if the court has accepted the case.[14]

It is evident that if the creditor brings an action against one of the joint and several debtors, the court decision may not bind the other debtors and may not be enforceable against them.

---

[10] Thévenoz and Werro (2012), art. 144, N. 1; Engel (1997), p. 839.

[11] Feyzioğlu (1977), p. 317; Tekinay et al. (1993), p. 285; Oğuzman and Öz (2016), p. 471; Nomer (2015), p. 417.

[12] Tekinay et al. (1993), p. 286; Oğuzman and Öz (2016), p. 470; Eren (2015), p. 1205.

[13] Oser and Schönenberger (1929), art. 144, N. 3; Engel (1997), p. 839; Berger (2012), p. 842.

[14] Feyzioğlu (1977), p. 318; Oğuzman and Öz (2016), p. 471.

27.3.2 *Defences of the Debtors*

27.3.2.1 Personal Defences

According to TCO art. 164 par. 1, one of the joint and several debtors may raise a defence that results from his personal relationship with the creditor. The reason for this provision is that if an ordinary debtor loses the right to rely on certain personal defences as a result of becoming a joint and several debtor, then this will be unfair to him. Therefore, if one of the joint and several debtors becomes a party to the contract due to mistake, fraud or duress or has performed his obligation or has set off his obligation with a counter-claim he has against the creditor, then he may raise these defences in an action with the creditor.[15]

However, there is an exception to the aforementioned rule. Pursuant to TCO art. 155 par. 1, where the limitation period is interrupted for one person who is jointly and severally liable to perform an obligation, it is also interrupted for the other joint and several debtors. Consequently, even if the limitation period of only one of the joint and several debtors has been interrupted, this interruption will cause the other debtors to lose their limitation period defences and will exacerbate their position.[16]

27.3.2.2 Common Defences

According to TCO art. 164 par. 1, a joint and several debtor may raise defences arising from the cause or contents of the joint and several liability. These defences are referred to as common defences. For example, if a contract that establishes joint and several liability is void due to lack of form, breach of mandatory rules or immorality, then the joint and several debtors may raise these as common defences.[17]

In certain cases, reasons for the nullity of a contract may arise from the circumstances relating to only some of the joint and several debtors. For example, only one of them may lack mental capacity (capacity of discernment) or may be represented by an unauthorised agent at the time of the formation of the contract. In these cases, in order to ascertain whether or not the other debtors may raise these defences, it is necessary to determine the presumed intention of the other debtors. That is to say, if it is presumed that the other debtors would not have concluded the contract if they had known of this nullity, then they may raise these defences. If the contrary is presumed, then they are not entitled to raise these defences.[18]

---

[15]Eren (2015), p. 1207; Oğuzman and Öz (2016), p. 472; Reisoğlu (2014), p. 445.

[16]Feyzioğlu (1977), pp. 323–324; Oğuzman and Öz (2016), p. 472; Reisoğlu (2014), p. 445, *cf.* Tekinay et al. (1993), pp. 299, 1057–1059; Tercier et al. (2016), p. 505.

[17]Oğuzman and Öz (2016), p. 473; Eren (2015), p. 1206; Tercier et al. (2016), p. 506.

[18]Tekinay et al. (1993), p. 313; Oğuzman and Öz (2016), p. 473.

In cases where a joint and several debtor has the right to rescind a contract, for example due to mistake, fraud or duress, this right of rescission cannot be raised by the other debtors in lieu of the vitiated party. However, if the party who has been subject to, for example fraud or duress, rescinds the contract, then the other debtors may raise this common defence.[19]

It should be kept in mind that if the obligation of one of the joint and several debtors is extinguished, then this constitutes a common defence. Raising common defences is not only a right but a duty for joint and several debtors. Pursuant to TCO art. 164 par. 2, if a joint and several debtor does not raise common defences, then he becomes liable against the other joint and several debtors. For instance, D_1 and D_2 are jointly and severally obliged to pay €10,000 to C. The debtors decide to apportion the obligation to pay the total amount equally between them. D_1 sets off his obligation against his counter-claim of €5000 from C. Therefore, the joint and several obligation is reduced to €5000. Despite this fact, C demands that D_2 pay the full amount of €10,000 and the latter, not raising the defence that the obligation is reduced to €5000 because of D_1's set-off, pays it. In this case, if D_2 is at fault for not raising this common defence and attempts to seek recourse against D_1 for his share of the obligation, then D_1 may refuse this demand.[20]

27.3.3 Personal Conduct of Individual Debtors

27.3.3.1 General

According to TCO art. 165, one of the joint and several debtors may not prejudice the position of the other debtors by his personal conduct, unless otherwise provided by agreement or by law. Pursuant to this article, if a joint and several debtor does not raise a common defence in the course of litigation and loses the case, this fact will not affect the other debtors' positions. In other words, the creditor will have to bring an action against the other debtors, and they remain entitled to raise common defences.[21]

If some of the joint and several debtors, agreeing with the creditor, wish to accept a penalty clause, increase the amount of the obligation or shorten the period for maturity of the obligation, these terms will only bind those who accept them. The creditor is not entitled to rely on his rights resulting from this variation of the contract as against the other debtors. It is evident that if a joint and several debtor, for example, pays the penalty or pays the increased amount, then he may not have recourse to the remaining debtors who have not concluded any additional obligations under the contract.[22]

---

[19]Oğuzman and Öz (2016), p. 473.

[20]Eren (2015), p. 1206; Oğuzman and Öz (2016), p. 475.

[21]Oğuzman and Öz (2016), p. 480; Eren (2015), pp. 1207–1208.

[22]Reisoğlu (2014), p. 445; Oğuzman and Öz (2016), p. 481; Nomer (2015), p. 419.

If one of the joint and several debtors fails to perform an obligation and becomes liable for payment of compensation for the creditor's damage, then this liability will not affect the other debtors.[23] The creditor may only demand compensation from the debtor in breach.[24]

27.3.3.2 Exceptions

There is an exception to TCO art. 165. According to TCO art. 155 par. 1, where the limitation period is interrupted for one person who is jointly and severally liable for an obligation, it is also interrupted for the other joint and several debtors. If only one of the joint and several debtors acknowledges the debt, partially performs the obligation, pays a certain amount of interest or provides certain securities, then this conduct interrupts the limitation period, and the other debtors will be affected by this interruption. Consequently, the other debtors are not entitled to raise TCO art. 165 as a defence.[25]

As mentioned above, at the time of the formation of the contract that gives rise to joint and several liability, the parties may agree that the conduct of one of the joint and several debtors can exacerbate the position of the other debtors. For instance, the parties may agree that if one of the joint and several debtors breaches the contract, all joint and several debtors will be liable for compensation for the damage suffered by the creditor.

27.4 Extinguishment of the Obligation

According to TCO art. 166 par. 1, if one of the joint and several debtors extinguishes the obligation wholly or partially by performance or by set-off, the other debtors will also be discharged to that extent. For instance, D_1 and D_2 are jointly and severally obliged to pay €10,000 to C. D_1 sets off his obligation against his counter-claim of €5000 from C. In this case, the creditor may only demand the remaining €5000 from the debtors.[26]

Pursuant to TCO art. 166 par. 2, if one of the joint and several debtors is discharged from an obligation without performance, then the other debtors may benefit from this fact only to the extent that the circumstances or the nature of the obligation allows. For example, if the performance of the obligation becomes

[23]von Tuhr and Escher (1974), § 90, V, 2, p. 307; Thévenoz and Werro (2012), art. 146, N. 3; Tercier (2004), p. 294.

[24]Tercier et al. (2016), p. 505; Nomer (2015), p. 419.

[25]Oğuzman and Öz (2016), pp. 481–482; Reisoğlu (2014), p. 445; Nomer (2015), pp. 418–419.

[26]Tekinay et al. (1993), p. 297; Eren (2015), p. 1213; Oğuzman and Öz (2016), p. 477; Tercier et al. (2016), p. 505; Feyzioğlu (1977), p. 328.

impossible without any fault on the part of any of the joint and several debtors, then all debtors will be discharged from the obligation.[27] It should be noted that if the obligation becomes impossible to perform by all joint and several debtors due to fault on the part of one of them, then only the debtor who is at fault will be liable for non-performance of the obligation.

If the creditor makes a discharge agreement with one of the joint and several debtors, this agreement discharges the other joint and several debtors to the extent of the discharged party's share of the obligation (TCO art. 166 par. 3).

27.5 Relationship Between the Debtors Themselves[28]

27.5.1 Apportionment and Right of Recourse

According to TCO art. 167 par. 1, unless otherwise agreed by the joint and several debtors or unless inferred from the nature of the legal relationship between them, each debtor must assume an equal share of the performance carried out in favour of the creditor. In light of this provision, joint and several debtors may determine their share of the performance when they have recourse to each other in the future, or this determination may arise from the nature of the legal relationship between the debtors. Furthermore, if there is no such determination, then it is presumed that their shares will be equal.[29]

If one of the joint and several debtors performs the obligation partially or wholly, then he does not have to bear the consequences of this performance; he may have recourse to the other debtors. However, in order for a joint and several debtor to have recourse to the other debtors, he must have performed more than his share, and he may only have recourse to the other debtors in accordance with the apportionment of the obligation between them (TCO art. 167 par. 2).

It is worth considering examples in order to analyse these provisions. For instance, D_1 and D_2 are jointly and severally obliged to pay €10,000 to C. The debtors decide that D_1's share will be 25% and D_2's share will be 75% of the obligation. In this case, if D_1 pays the entire obligation, he may have recourse to D_2 for his share of the obligation. That is to say, D_2 will have to pay €7500 to D_1. In another example, D_1 and D_2 are jointly and severally obliged to pay €10,000 to C. However, they do not determine how they will share the obligation between them. In such a case, if D_1 pays the entire obligation, he may have recourse to D_2 in respect of only half of the obligation (TCO art. 167 par. 1). In order for the debtor who performs the obligation to have the right of recourse against the other debtors, it is not necessary that he performs the entire obligation. In the above-mentioned

[27] Oğuzman and Öz (2016), p. 478; Eren (2015), p. 1214.

[28] For further explanations see Kapancı (2015).

[29] Feyzioğlu (1977), p. 331; Eren (2015), pp. 1209–1210; Oğuzman and Öz (2016), p. 485.

example, if D_1 pays €6000 to C, he may have recourse to D_2 for the excess amount of €1000.

As mentioned above, the apportionment of the liability between the joint and several debtors may also arise from the nature of the legal relationship. For example, several persons are co-owners of immovable property (TCC art. 688), and they are jointly and severally liable to a creditor but do not determine their shares as between themselves. If one of the co-owners performs the entire obligation and wishes to have recourse to the others, then their liability will be determined according to their share in the co-ownership.[30]

It should be kept in mind that pursuant to TCO art. 164 par. 2, if a joint and several debtor does not raise common defences, then he loses the right to seek recourse as against the other debtors.

In cases where a joint and several debtor has recourse against the other debtors but cannot recover one of the joint and several debtors' shares as against him, the amount that cannot be recovered must be equally distributed among the other debtors (TCO art. 167 par. 3). In order to apply this provision, the debtor from whom the amount cannot be recovered must be insolvent in accordance with the provisions of the Turkish Code of Bankruptcy and Enforcement.[31] For instance, D_1, D_2 and D_3 are jointly and severally obliged to pay €300,000 to C. The debtors decide to apportion the total amount of the obligation equally between them. D_1 pays the entire obligation and subsequently has recourse to D_2 and D_3. However, D_3 is insolvent. In this case, D_3's share will be assumed equally by D_1 and D_2. Consequently, D_2 will pay first his share of €100,000 and half of D_3's share, €50,000.

27.5.2 Subrogation

Pursuant to TCO art. 168 par. 1, a joint and several debtor who has the right of recourse against the other debtors is subrogated to the creditor's rights to the extent of his performance. The legislature aims to protect the joint and several debtor who has performed more than his share by providing him with the right of recourse. In addition, the legislature gives a right of subrogation to him.[32] For example, D_1 and D_2 are jointly and severally obliged to pay €100,000 to C. The debtors decide to apportion the obligation equally between them. A third party P pledges certain movable properties, and another third party S provides surety. If D_1 performs the entire obligation, it is evident that he may have recourse against D_2. In addition,

[30] Tekinay et al. (1993), p. 315; Oğuzman and Öz (2016), p. 485.

[31] Oğuzman and Öz (2016), p. 490; Tekinay et al. (1993), p. 319; Reisoğlu (2014), p. 446; Nomer (2015), p. 422.

[32] Oğuzman and Öz (2016), p. 491.

according to TCO. art. 168 par. 1, D_1 is subrogated to the creditor's rights and, thus, becomes entitled to the benefit of the pledge and the surety.

It is worth adding a second possibility. In the above-mentioned case, if D_1 pays €70,000, then he may have recourse against D_2 only for €20,000. In addition, as he is subrogated to the creditor's rights to the extent of his performance, he will also obtain the benefit from the pledge and the surety to that extent. That is to say, the securities provided by P and S continue to secure C's remaining claim of €30,000 while also securing D_1's claim by way of recourse against D_2 for €20,000. It should be noted that C will be the primary beneficiary of the securities.[33]

According to TCO art. 168 par. 2, if the creditor improves the legal position of one of the joint and several debtors to the detriment of the other debtors, he must bear its consequences. This provision especially aims to preclude the creditor from releasing the securities to the detriment of the other debtors. For example, D_1 and D_2 are jointly and severally obliged to pay €100,000 to C. The debtors decide to share the obligation equally between them. A third party M provides a mortgage. Subsequently, C releases M's mortgage and then brings an action against D_1. D_1 performs the entire obligation and wishes to have recourse to D_2. However, D_2 cannot pay his share. In this case, since D_1 has lost his entitlement in respect of M's mortgage due to C's act, he may demand that C compensate him for damage arising from the release of the mortgage. This is due to the fact that if C had not released the mortgage when D_1 had recourse to D_2, then he would have been in a position to realise the mortgage and recover D_2's share of the obligation.

References

Akıntürk T (1971) Müteselsil borçluluk. Ankara

Aybay A (2011) Borçlar hukuku dersleri genel bölüm. Filiz, İstanbul

Becker H (1941) Kommentar zum Schweizerischen Zivilgesetzbuch, Volume VI, Obligationenrecht, 1. Abteilung: Allgemeine Bestimmungen, Art. 1-183. Stämpfli, Bern

Berger B (2012) Allgemeines Schuldrecht. Stämpfli, Bern

Canyürek M (2003) Müteselsil borçlulukta iç ve dış ilişkiler. Vedat, İstanbul

Dağdelen AH (2011) 818 ve 6098 sayılı borçlar kanunlarında borçlular arasında teselsül. On iki levha, İstanbul

Dural M, Öz T (2015) Miras hukuku. Filiz, İstanbul

Engel P (1997) Traité des obligations en droit Suisse. Stämpfli, Bern

Eren F (2015) Borçlar hukuku genel hükümler. Yetkin, Ankara

Feyzioğlu FN (1977) Borçlar hukuku genel hükümler, vol 2. Fakülteler, İstanbul

Gauch P, Schluep WR, Emmenegger S (2008) Schweizerisches Obligationenrecht, Allgemeiner Teil, vol 2. Schulthess, Zürich

Honsell H, Vogt NP, Wiegand W (eds) (2003) Basler Kommentar zum Schweizerischen Privatrecht, Obligationenrecht 1: Art. 1-529 OR. Helbing Lichtenhahn, Basel

Kapancı KB (2015) Birlikte borçlulukta borçlular arası ilişkiler. Vedat, İstanbul

[33]Feyzioğlu (1977), pp. 336–337, fn. 58; Tekinay et al. (1993), p. 321; Oğuzman and Öz (2016), pp. 491–492.

Kılıçoğlu AM (2013) Borçlar hukuku genel hükümler. Turhan, İstanbul
Nomer HN (2015) Borçlar hukuku genel hükümler. Beta, İstanbul
Oğuzman K, Öz T (2016) Borçlar hukuku genel hükümler, vol 2. Vedat, İstanbul
Oser H, Schönenberger W (1929) Kommentar zum Schweizerischen Zivilgesetzbuch, Volume V: Das Obligationenrecht, Erster Halbband: Art. 1-183. Schulthess, Zürich
Özdoğan N (2015) Müteselsil sorumluluk. Seçkin, Ankara
Özsunay E (1983) Borçlar hukuku I. Filiz, İstanbul
Reisoğlu S (2014) Türk borçlar hukuku genel hükümler. Beta, İstanbul
Schwenzer I (2009) Schweizerisches Obligationenrecht, Allgemeiner Teil. Schulthess, Bern
Tekinay SS, Akman S, Burcuoğlu H, Altop A (1993) Tekinay borçlar hukuku genel hükümler. Filiz, İstanbul
Tercier P (2004) Le droit des obligations. Schulthess, Zurich
Tercier P, Pichonnaz P, Develioğlu HM (2016) Borçlar hukuku genel hükümler. On iki levha, İstanbul
Thévenoz L, Werro F (éd) (2012) Commentaire romand code des obligations 1: art. 1-529 CO. Helbing Lichtenhahn, Bâle
von Tuhr A, Escher A (1974) Allgemeiner Teil des Schweizerischen Obligationenrecht, vol 2. Schulthess, Zürich

Chapter 28
Joint and Several Creditors

28.1 General[1]

In certain cases, there are several creditors of the same obligation.[2] As long as the obligation is divisible, each creditor may only demand partial performance.[3] However, if any of these creditors have the right to demand the entire performance of the obligation and the debtor can be discharged by performing the obligation for one of the creditors, then there is a joint and several claim.[4]

According to TCO art. 169 par. 1, such joint and several claims may arise from a legal transaction or from the law itself. The legal transaction may be a contract or a unilateral one. A contract between the creditors and the debtor may explicitly state that there is a joint and several claim, or this fact may be inferred from the circumstances.[5] In practice, the most common example of joint and several creditors that arises from a contract is joint accounts in banking.[6]

In addition to contracts, unilateral legal transactions may also give rise to joint and several claims. For example, in a testamentary disposition, a testator may

[1]Aybay (2011), pp. 171–172; Becker (1941), art. 150; Berger (2012), pp. 848–854; Engel (1997), pp. 832–836; Eren (2015), pp. 1217–1222; Feyzioğlu (1977), pp. 338–342; Gauch et al. (2008), pp. 291–295; Honsell et al. (2003), art. 150; Kılıçoğlu (2013), pp. 754–757; Nomer (2015), pp. 423–424; Oser and Schönenberger (1929), art. 150; Oğuzman and Öz (2016), pp. 492–501; Özsunay (1983), pp. 174–175; Reisoğlu (2014), pp. 447–450; Schwenzer (2009), pp. 560–563; Tekinay et al. (1993), pp. 327–328; Tercier (2004), pp. 298–300; Tercier et al. (2016), pp. 511–514; Thévenoz and Werro (2012), art. 150, and von Tuhr and Escher (1974), pp. 321–325.

[2]For further explanations see Acar (2003).

[3]von Tuhr and Escher (1974), § 91, I, p. 321; Eren (2015), p. 1218; Feyzioğlu (1977), p. 340.

[4]*Solidarité entre plusieurs créanciers*, *Solidarität unter mehreren Gläubigern*.

[5]Thévenoz and Werro (2012), art. 150, N. 3; Oğuzman and Öz (2016), p. 495.

[6]Engel (1997), p. 837.

İ. Helvacı, *Turkish Contract Law*, DOI 10.1007/978-3-319-60061-1_28

bequeath a sum of money to several creditors and may indicate that any of them may demand the entire performance.[7]

As mentioned above, joint and several claims may also arise from the law itself. According to TCO art. 322 par. 3, if a lessee subleases the leased property and the sublessee does not use the subject matter of the sublease in accordance with the head lease, then the lessor and the lessee may demand that the sublessee use the leased property in accordance with the terms of the lease.[8]

It should be noted that a joint and several claim may also arise from the fact that a new creditor becomes a party to an existing contract, according to TCO art. 206 par. 2. Pursuant to this provision, unless the parties agree to the contrary, the existing party and the added party who has joined become joint and several creditors.[9]

In cases of joint and several claims, the debtor may perform the obligation for one of the creditors and consequently be fully discharged from the obligation (TCO art. 169 par. 2).

28.2 Consequences

Each joint and several creditor may demand the entire performance of the obligation from the debtor. In addition, the debtor may voluntarily perform the obligation for any of the joint and several creditors. However, according to TCO art. 169 par. 3, if a joint and several creditor brings an action or initiates enforcement procedures, unless notice of this fact is served on the debtor, the latter will continue to hold the right to perform the obligation in respect of any of the joint and several creditors.

If the debtor's obligation becomes impossible as a consequence of the debtor's fault, then he must compensate the creditors for damage. In such a case, the claim for compensation also constitutes a joint and several claim.[10]

Each joint and several creditor has the right to amend the conditions of the claim by entering into an agreement with the debtor. However, this agreement and, thus, this amendment binds only the parties who accept the variation. Moreover, a joint and several creditor may conclude a discharge agreement with the debtor, but this agreement may not extinguish the claim of the other joint and several creditors.[11]

Each joint and several creditor may assign his claim to a third party. As a result, the assignee becomes a new joint and several creditor.[12]

[7]Feyzioğlu (1977), p. 339; Oğuzman and Öz (2016), p. 495.

[8]Engel (1997), p. 833; Oğuzman and Öz (2016), p. 496; Eren (2015), p. 1219; Tercier et al. (2016), p. 513; Nomer (2015), p. 423.

[9]See Sect. 34.2.

[10]Oğuzman and Öz (2016), p. 496.

[11]Engel (1997), p. 834; Berger (2012), p. 853; Oğuzman and Öz (2016), pp. 499–500; Nomer (2015), p. 424.

[12]Engel (1997), p. 834; Oğuzman and Öz (2016), p. 497; Eren (2015), p. 1220.

If a security is provided for all joint and several creditors, unless otherwise agreed, then all joint and several creditors may benefit from the security.[13]

Unless otherwise agreed upon or inferred from the nature of the legal transaction between the creditors, each joint and several creditor has equal rights with regard to the performance of the obligation (TCO art. 169 par. 4). If a joint and several creditor obtains more than his share, he is obliged to pay the excess amount to the other joint and several creditors (TCO art. 169 par. 5). For instance, C_1 and C_2 are joint and several creditors of a claim against D. The amount of D's obligation is €10,000. D pays the entire obligation to C_1. In such a case, unless otherwise agreed or inferred from the nature of the legal transaction between the creditors, C_1 is obliged to pay the excess amount of €5000 to C_2.[14]

References

Acar F (2003) Türk - İsviçre medenî hukukunda alacaklılar arası teselsül. Seçkin, Ankara

Aybay A (2011) Borçlar hukuku dersleri genel bölüm. Filiz, İstanbul

Becker H (1941) Kommentar zum Schweizerischen Zivilgesetzbuch, Volume VI, Obligationenrecht, 1. Abteilung: Allgemeine Bestimmungen, Art. 1-183. Stämpfli, Bern

Berger B (2012) Allgemeines Schuldrecht. Stämpfli, Bern

Engel P (1997) Traité des obligations en droit Suisse. Stämpfli, Bern

Eren F (2015) Borçlar hukuku genel hükümler. Yetkin, Ankara

Feyzioğlu FN (1977) Borçlar hukuku genel hükümler, vol 2. Fakülteler, İstanbul

Gauch P, Schluep WR, Emmenegger S (2008) Schweizerisches Obligationenrecht, Allgemeiner Teil, vol 2. Schulthess, Zürich

Honsell H, Vogt NP, Wiegand W (eds) (2003) Basler Kommentar zum Schweizerischen Privatrecht, Obligationenrecht 1: Art. 1-529 OR. Helbing Lichtenhahn, Basel

Kılıçoğlu AM (2013) Borçlar hukuku genel hükümler. Turhan, İstanbul

Nomer HN (2015) Borçlar hukuku genel hükümler. Beta, İstanbul

Oğuzman K, Öz T (2016) Borçlar hukuku genel hükümler, vol 2. Vedat, İstanbul

Oser H, Schönenberger W (1929) Kommentar zum Schweizerischen Zivilgesetzbuch, Volume V: Das Obligationenrecht, Erster Halbband: Art. 1-183. Schulthess, Zürich

Özsunay E (1983) Borçlar hukuku I. Filiz, İstanbul

Reisoğlu S (2014) Türk borçlar hukuku genel hükümler. Beta, İstanbul

Schwenzer I (2009) Schweizerisches Obligationenrecht, Allgemeiner Teil. Schulthess, Bern

Tekinay SS, Akman S, Burcuoğlu H, Altop A (1993) Tekinay borçlar hukuku genel hükümler. Filiz, İstanbul

Tercier P (2004) Le droit des obligations. Schulthess, Zurich

Tercier P, Pichonnaz P, Develioğlu HM (2016) Borçlar hukuku genel hükümler. On iki levha, İstanbul

Thévenoz L, Werro F (éd) (2012) Commentaire romand code des obligations 1: art. 1-529 CO. Helbing Lichtenhahn, Bâle

von Tuhr A, Escher A (1974) Allgemeiner Teil des Schweizerischen Obligationenrecht, vol 2. Schulthess, Zürich

[13]Oğuzman and Öz (2016), p. 497.

[14]Engel (1997), p. 834.

Chapter 29
Conditional Contracts

29.1 General[1]

As a rule, most legal transactions, whether they are unilateral or bilateral, may be made conditional.[2] Contracts in particular, whether obligatory[3] or dispositive,[4] may be made dependent on the occurrence or non-occurrence of a future uncertain event. There are two types of condition: suspensive (precedent) and resolutive (subsequent).

In the following paragraphs, conditional contracts are analysed. However, before considering these types of contracts, it is worth stating that certain transactions cannot be made conditional. Especially, legal transactions pertaining to family law or the law of persons, such as marriage or the recognition of a child, cannot be made dependent on a condition.[5] Moreover, certain transactions relating to the law of inheritance, such as disclaimer of an inheritance, may also not be made conditional (TCC art. 609 par. 2).[6]

It should be kept in mind that there are certain exceptions in family law and the law of inheritance. For instance, engagements, prenuptial agreements, testamentary

[1]Aybay (2011), pp. 174–179; Becker (1941), Vorbemerkung zu art. 151-157, art. 151-157; Berger (2012), pp. 259–269; Engel (1997), pp. 846–859; Eren (2015), pp. 1161–1179; Feyzioğlu (1977), pp. 343–372; Gauch et al. (2008), pp. 340–353; Honsell et al. (2003), Vorbemerkungen zu art. 151-157, art. 151-157; Kılıçoğlu (2013), pp. 758–771; Nomer (2015), pp. 424–432; Oser and Schönenberger (1929), Vorbemerkungen zum zweiten Abschnitt (art. 151-157), art. 151-157; Oğuzman and Öz (2016), pp. 501–529; Özsunay (1983), pp. 154–160; Reisoğlu (2014), pp. 451–455; Schwenzer (2009), pp. 63–71; Tekinay et al. (1993), pp. 328–338; Tercier (2004), pp. 166–167; Tercier et al. (2016), pp. 283–287; Thévenoz and Werro (2012), art. 151-157, and von Tuhr and Escher (1974), pp. 254–277.

[2]For further explanations see Pulaşlı (1989), Sirmen (1992)

[3]*Acte générateur d'obligation*, *Verpflichtungsgeschäft*. See Chap. 7 fn. 5.

[4]*Acte de disposition*, *Verfügungsgeschäft*. See Chap. 14 fn. 5–6.

[5]Oser and Schönenberger (1929), Vorbemerkungen zum zweiten Abschnitt art. 151-157, N. 17; Oğuzman and Öz (2016), p. 510.

[6]For further explanations see Helvacı (2014), pp. 56–62.

İ. Helvacı, *Turkish Contract Law*, DOI 10.1007/978-3-319-60061-1_29

dispositions (wills) and nominations of heirs may be made dependent on a condition.[7]

29.2 Suspensive Conditions (Conditions Precedent)[8]

29.2.1 General

A condition is an uncertain future event.[9] The parties to a contract may agree that the contract takes effect in the event that an uncertain future event occurs or fails to occur. Moreover, one or several obligations arising from a contract may be dependent on the occurrence or non-occurrence of an uncertain future event, which is referred to as a suspensive condition or a condition precedent (TCO art. 170 par. 1). In this book, the author prefers to use the term 'suspensive condition'.

According to TCO art. 170 par. 2, unless otherwise agreed upon, a contract dependent on a suspensive condition takes effect from the time the condition is fulfilled. Even if a contract is made dependent on the occurrence of an uncertain future event and the event has yet to happen, the contract is nevertheless in existence. In other words, neither of the parties to this contract may unilaterally terminate the contract.[10] For instance, a father is obliged to gift a car to his son if the son passes his university entrance exams and is admitted to a law faculty. In this case, whether or not the son is successful in the university entrance exams and gains admission to a law faculty is a future uncertain event—*i.e.*, a suspensive condition. Even if the father's obligation to gift will only take effect if his son is successful in the university entrance exams, a contract to gift has been entered into between the parties, and neither party may unilaterally terminate it.

29.2.2 The Creditor's Expectant Right

Pursuant to TCO art. 171 par. 1, as long as the condition is pending, the debtor must refrain from any acts that prevent the performance of the obligation. With this provision, the legislature accepts that before the condition is fulfilled, the creditor has an expectant right.[11] If the debtor violates this expectant right,[12] then he is liable for the

[7]Tekinay et al. (1993), p. 333; Feyzioğlu (1977), pp. 352–353; Oğuzman and Öz (2016), p. 510.

[8]*Condition suspensive*, *Aufschiebende Bedingung*.

[9]Engel (1997), p. 846; Feyzioğlu (1977), p. 344; Oğuzman and Öz (2016), p. 505; Tercier et al. (2016), p. 284.

[10]Feyzioğlu (1977), pp. 348–349; Tekinay et al. (1993), p. 333; Oğuzman and Öz (2016), p. 516.

[11]Tekinay et al. (1993), pp. 333, 334; Eren (2015), p. 1173; Oğuzman and Öz (2016), p. 517.

[12]*Anwartschaftsrecht*.

damage of the creditor. For example, a professor working at the Sorbonne intends to be a visiting scholar at Istanbul University for a year if her application is accepted. The professor and a landlord in Istanbul make a lease agreement on the condition that the professor commences work at Istanbul University. In other words, this lease agreement is dependent upon a suspensive condition. The owner's obligation to make available the property and the professor's obligation to pay rent take effect when the professor's application is accepted. However, before the professor's application is accepted, the owner of the property sells the house to a third party. In this case, if the professor's application is accepted and she commences work at Istanbul University, then she may demand that the original owner pay compensation for damage resulting from the subsequent impossibility of performance (TCO art. 112, TCO art. 171 par. 1).[13]

Pursuant to TCO art. 171 par. 2, if a conditional right of a creditor is jeopardised, then the creditor is entitled to the same protections that he would have if the obligation was not conditional. For instance, in a contract of sale relating to immovable property that is dependent on a suspensive condition, if the seller attempts to transfer the immovable property to a third party, then the prospective buyer whose right is conditional may demand that the court impose an interim injunction on the seller in order to prevent the transfer of the property (TCPC art. 389 *ff*).[14]

In a conditional obligation, even if the creditor's right does not arise prior to the fulfilment of the condition, he may dispose of his expectant right. A conditional right may be transferred to a third party.[15] In addition, a creditor may demand that the debtor provide certain securities for his conditional claim.[16]

In an obligation dependent on a suspensive condition, the debtor is not entitled to perform the obligation before the suspensive condition is fulfilled. Despite this fact, if the debtor performs his obligation, then he may demand that the creditor perform restitution, provided that he is able to prove that he did not know that the obligation was dependent on a suspensive condition or that he believed that the condition had been fulfilled (TCO art. 78 par. 1).[17]

If the debtor performs the obligation knowing that the suspensive condition has not been fulfilled, then he may not demand that the creditor perform restitution (TCO art. 78 par. 1). Nevertheless, when it is understood that the suspensive condition will not be fulfilled,[18] the debtor may demand restitution of the performance (TCO art. 77 par. 2).[19]

[13]Oser and Schönenberger (1929), art. 152, N. 9; Oğuzman and Öz (2016), p. 517.

[14]Oser and Schönenberger (1929), art. 152, N. 7; Thévenoz and Werro (2012), art. 152, N. 20-25; Eren (2015), p. 1173; Tekinay et al. (1993), pp. 333–334; Oğuzman and Öz (2016), p. 518.

[15]Thévenoz and Werro (2012), art. 151, N. 41, art. 164, N. 63; Engel (1997), p. 856; Feyzioğlu (1977), p. 357; Nomer (2015), p. 430.

[16]Engel (1997), p. 856; Nomer (2015), p. 430; Reisoğlu (2014), p. 452.

[17]von Tuhr and Peter (1979), § 52, IV, 2, p. 479 *ff*; Thévenoz and Werro (2012), art. 152, N. 31; Oğuzman and Öz (2016), pp. 354, 518; Öz (1990), p. 85 fn. 39, 97–98.

[18]*Condictio ob causam futuram* or *condictio causa data causa non secuta*.

[19]Thévenoz and Werro (2012), art. 152, N. 32; Engel (1997), p. 856; von Tuhr and Peter (1979), § 52, V, pp. 487–488; Oğuzman and Öz (2016), pp. 361 and 518–519; Öz (1990), p. 98.

29.2.3 Suspensive Conditions in Dispositive Transactions

The general provisions of the Turkish Code of Obligations are essentially related to contracts that constitute obligations.[20] This is also true of conditional contracts. However, certain transactions that are dispositive may also be made dependent on suspensive conditions. For example, an assignment of a claim is a dispositive transaction with regard to the assignor[21] and may be made dependent on a suspensive condition. In addition, the transfer of the right of ownership of movable property may be dependent on a suspensive condition (TCC arts. 764–765). Further, a discharge agreement may also be made conditional.[22]

In cases where a dispositive transaction is dependent on a suspensive condition, the dispositive transaction does not take effect until the future uncertain event occurs. Therefore, the beneficiary's conditional right may readily be jeopardised. That is why the legislature aims to protect the beneficiary of a dispositive transaction by virtue of TCO art. 171 par. 3, according to which any dispositive transaction made before the fulfilment of the condition is void to the extent that the transaction impairs the effects of the suspensive condition. For instance, a chattel has been sold with a reserve of ownership[23] in accordance with TCC art. 764. In this case, even if the seller transfers possession of the sold item to the buyer, the latter may not become its owner unless he pays its price. That is to say, the transfer of ownership of the chattel is dependent on a suspensive condition, and the seller remains the owner of the chattel until the condition is fulfilled. The seller who has reserved the right of ownership may attempt to transfer ownership of the chattel to a third party. In such a case, if the buyer (prospective owner) pays the price of the sold item, then he may demand that the court determine the acquisition by the third party to be void. In this example, assume that the seller pledges the chattel to a third party (TCC art. 979 par. 1, TCC art. 939 par. 1). In this case, the buyer has the same rights and is entitled to assert the nullity of the pledge.[24]

29.2.4 Benefits Enjoyed in the Interim Period

In cases of obligations to give, even if the suspensive condition is not fulfilled, the object of the contract may be delivered to the creditor, and thus, he may obtain certain benefits arising from the subject matter of the contract. In such a case, if the suspensive condition is fulfilled, then the creditor has the right to retain the benefit obtained from it in the interim (TCO art. 172 par. 1). For example, a machine is sold

[20]*Acte générateur d'obligation, Verpflichtungsgeschäft.* See Chap. 7 fn. 5.

[21]*Acte de disposition, Verfügungsgeschäft.* See Chap. 14 fn. 5–6.

[22]Tekinay et al. (1993), p. 334; Oğuzman and Öz (2016), p. 519.

[23]*Reserve de propriété, Eigentumsvorbehalt.* Retention of ownership, reservation of title.

[24]Oğuzman and Öz (2016), pp. 519–520.

with ownership reserved to the seller (TCC art. 764) and is delivered to the buyer. The buyer rents this machine before the suspensive condition is fulfilled and obtains rental fees. After a period of time, the buyer pays the price of the sold machine—*i.e.*, the suspensive condition is fulfilled—at which time he becomes the owner of the machine. In this case, the buyer may retain the rental fees he received in the interim.

However, if the suspensive condition is not fulfilled, then the creditor is not entitled to retain the benefits enjoyed in the interim. Indeed, pursuant to TCO art. 172 par. 2, the creditor must return such benefits to the debtor. The restitution will be carried out in accordance with the provisions pertaining to unjust enrichment (TCO arts. 77–82).[25] It is apparent that the creditor must also return the subject matter of the contract, in the aforementioned example the machine, to the debtor.

29.3 Resolutive Conditions (Conditions Subsequent)[26]

According to TCO art. 173 par. 1, the termination of a contract may be made dependent on a future uncertain event, which is referred to as a resolutive condition. Where a contract is dependent on a resolutive condition, until the condition is fulfilled, the contract is effective as a non-conditional contract.[27] When the resolutive condition is fulfilled, the contract becomes ineffective (TCO art. 173 par. 2). In other words, so long as the resolutive condition is not fulfilled, the contract is effective, and thus, the creditor may demand the performance of the obligation arising from such a contract; similarly, the debtor must perform his obligation.

When the resolutive condition is fulfilled, the contract is automatically terminated. As a rule, unless the parties agree to the contrary or the nature of the circumstances requires it, this termination is not retroactive (TCO art. 173 par. 3). Indeed, in continuous contracts dependent on a resolutive condition, the parties generally do not agree that the termination of the contract will have a retroactive effect.[28] For instance, in a lease dependent on a resolutive condition, until the condition is fulfilled, the parties' obligations continue. However, with the fulfilment of the resolutive condition, their obligations are terminated. In such a case, the lessee must return the subject matter of the lease to the lessor. Nevertheless, the lessee is not entitled to demand restitution of the rent that has already been paid up to the time of the fulfilment of the condition.

---

[25]Oser and Schönenberger (1929), art. 153, N. 3, see and compare to Oğuzman and Öz (2016), p. 510 fn. 348.

[26]*Condition résolutoire*, *Auflösende Bedingung*.

[27]Engel (1997), p. 850; Feyzioğlu (1977), p. 369; Tekinay et al. (1993), p. 335; Oğuzman and Öz (2016), p. 525.

[28]Thévenoz and Werro (2012), art. 154, N. 14.

As a rule, in contracts performed by single acts of performance on each side ('instantaneous' contracts) and that are dependent on a resolutive condition, the termination of the contract has a retroactive effect.[29] That is why in such a case, if one of the parties performs his obligation, then the receiving party must restitute this performance upon the termination of the contract, in accordance with the provisions pertaining to unjust enrichment (TCO arts. 77–82). Moreover, the receiving party must not only make restitution but must also return or compensate for all benefits enjoyed as a result of the performance of the obligation.[30] It should be kept in mind that the parties may agree that the termination of the contract will not have a retroactive effect. In such a case, it is evident that any interim benefits may not be restituted.[31]

As to dispositive contracts[32] dependent on a resolutive condition, they also become effective at the time of their formation. However, when the resolutive condition is fulfilled, dispositive contracts are terminated. For example, an assignment of a claim is made dependent on a resolutive condition. In such a case, the assignment of the claim will become ineffective when the resolutive condition is fulfilled. Thus, the assignor will again become the owner of the previously assigned claim.[33]

Pursuant to TCO art. 292 par. 1, in contracts to gift, the donor may reserve the reversion of the subject matter of the contract should the donee die before the donor. In such a case, as soon as the contract is concluded, it becomes effective and the donor must transfer ownership of the subject matter of the contract to the donee. For movable property, the donor must transfer its possession (TCC art. 763 par. 1)[34]; for immovable property, the donor must request entry of the ownership on behalf of the donee in the land register (TCC art. 705 par. 1). With these transactions, the donee becomes the owner of the respective property. However, if the donee dies before the donor, then the resolutive condition is fulfilled and the ownership of the donee is terminated. In these cases, the legal nature of the donor's right is contentious. In the author's opinion, according to TCO art. 292 par. 1, the donor does not automatically become the owner of the subject matter of the donation. He may only demand that the donee's heirs transfer its ownership to him. Indeed, the second paragraph of TCO art. 292 supports this point of view, so that in the case of gifts of immovable property or of rights *in rem*, the right of reversion may be noted in the land register.[35]

---

[29]Thévenoz and Werro (2012), art. 154, N. 15; Oğuzman and Öz (2016), p. 527; Eren (2015), p. 1178.

[30]Oğuzman and Öz (2016), p. 527.

[31]Oğuzman and Öz (2016), pp. 527–528; Eren (2015), p. 1178.

[32]*Acte de disposition*, *Verfügungsgeschäft*. See Chap. 14 fn. 5–6.

[33]Becker (1941), art. 154, N. 6; von Tuhr and Escher (1974), § 86, IV, p. 276; Oğuzman and Öz (2016), p. 528; Reisoğlu (2014), p. 455; Tercier et al. (2016), p. 287.

[34]See Chap. 14 fn. 11.

[35]Steinauer (2007), p. 273, fn. 6; Tandoğan (1990), pp. 372–373; Oğuzman and Öz (2016), p. 529; Oğuzman et al. (2016), p. 214, fn. 666. See on the contrary, Eren (2015), pp. 1177–1178.

29.4 Common Provisions

29.4.1 Fulfilment of the Condition

In certain cases, the condition may consist of an act to be performed by only one of the parties. For instance, according to TCO art. 249, in the case of goods sold on trial or subject to inspection, it is at the discretion of the buyer whether or not to accept the goods. If the condition depends on a certain act of one of the contracting parties that does not have to be fulfilled personally, then this condition may be fulfilled by his heirs upon his death (TCO art. 174). It should be noted that the death of the counter-party is irrelevant.

29.4.2 Prevention Against Good Faith

If one of the parties precludes the fulfilment of the condition by acting contrary to the principles of good faith, then the condition is deemed to be fulfilled (TCO art. 175 par. 1). For example, a company undertakes to enter into a contract with another company on the condition that the latter wins a tender. However, the former precludes the fulfilment of the condition by rigging the bid. In this case, according to the aforementioned article, the condition is deemed to be fulfilled, and the party who has rigged the bid must enter into the contract as if the other party had won the tender.

Where one of the parties ensures the fulfilment of the condition by acting contrary to the principles of good faith, the condition is deemed not to be fulfilled (TCO art. 175 par. 2). For instance, an organiser of a marathon undertakes to give a prize to the athlete who wins the marathon. An athlete completes the race in first place, thereby winning the prize. However, it is later discovered that he had used prohibited substances and violated anti-doping rules. In such a case, the condition is deemed not to be fulfilled, and the athlete must return the prize.[36]

29.4.3 Prohibited Conditions

If a condition is stipulated in order to encourage an unlawful or immoral act or omission, then the legal transaction dependent on this condition is void (TCO art. 176). Therefore, if a contract is made dependent on the condition that one of the parties commits a crime or undertakes an immoral act, then this contract is void.[37]

---

[36]Tekinay et al. (1993), pp. 337–338; Feyzioğlu (1977), pp. 363–366, 368; Oğuzman and Öz (2016), p. 523.

[37]Eren (2015), p. 1168; Oğuzman and Öz (2016), p. 513; Reisoğlu (2014), p. 452.

Furthermore, conditions that are contrary to a provision protecting personal rights give rise to the same invalidity. For instance, if one of the parties undertakes to change his religion, not to marry, to adopt a child or not to acquire ownership of any property, then the obligations dependent on these conditions are void.[38]

Where a condition is initially impossible to perform, the following rules are applied: (1) if an impossible condition is suspensive, then the entirety of the legal transaction is void,[39] and (2) if an impossible condition is resolutive, then the transaction is valid as if it were not conditional.[40]

Where some of the provisions of the contract are invalid, as a rule, the other provisions of the contract remain valid (TCO art. 27 par. 2 sent. 1). Nonetheless, under TCO art. 27 par. 2 sent. 2, if it is obvious that the parties would not have concluded the contract without the invalid provisions, then the entire contract will be void.[41]

References

Aybay A (2011) Borçlar hukuku dersleri genel bölüm. Filiz, İstanbul

Becker H (1941) Kommentar zum Schweizerischen Zivilgesetzbuch, Volume VI, Obligationenrecht, 1. Abteilung: Allgemeine Bestimmungen, Art. 1-183. Stämpfli, Bern

Berger B (2012) Allgemeines Schuldrecht. Stämpfli, Bern

Engel P (1997) Traité des obligations en droit Suisse. Stämpfli, Bern

Eren F (2015) Borçlar hukuku genel hükümler. Yetkin, Ankara

Feyzioğlu FN (1977) Borçlar hukuku genel hükümler, vol 2. Fakülteler, İstanbul

Gauch P, Schluep WR, Emmenegger S (2008) Schweizerisches Obligationenrecht, Allgemeiner Teil, vol 2. Schulthess, Zürich

Helvacı İ (2014) Eski medenî kanunumuzla karşılaştırmalı olarak Türk medenî kanunu'na göre mirasın reddi, (mk. m. 605 - mk. m. 618). Filiz, İstanbul

Honsell H, Vogt NP, Wiegand W (eds) (2003) Basler Kommentar zum Schweizerischen Privatrecht, Obligationenrecht 1: Art. 1-529 OR. Helbing Lichtenhahn, Basel

Kılıçoğlu AM (2013) Borçlar hukuku genel hükümler. Turhan, İstanbul

Nomer HN (2015) Borçlar hukuku genel hükümler. Beta, İstanbul

Oğuzman K, Öz T (2016) Borçlar hukuku genel hükümler, vol 2. Vedat, İstanbul

Oğuzman K, Seliçi Ö, Oktay-Özdemir S (2016) Eşya hukuku. Filiz, İstanbul

Oser H, Schönenberger W (1929) Kommentar zum Schweizerischen Zivilgesetzbuch, Volume V: Das Obligationenrecht, Erster Halbband: Art. 1-183. Schulthess, Zürich

Öz T (1990) Sebepsiz zenginleşme. Kazancı, İstanbul

Özsunay E (1983) Borçlar hukuku I. Filiz, İstanbul

Pulaşlı H (1989) Şarta bağlı işlemler ve hukuki sonuçları. Dayınlarlı, Ankara

Reisoğlu S (2014) Türk borçlar hukuku genel hükümler. Beta, İstanbul

Schwenzer I (2009) Schweizerisches Obligationenrecht, Allgemeiner Teil. Schulthess, Bern

Sirmen AL (1992) Türk özel hukukunda şart. Banka ve ticaret hukuku araştırma enstitüsü, Ankara

[38]Oğuzman and Öz (2016), p. 513.

[39]von Tuhr and Escher (1974), § 84, IV, p. 259.

[40]Oğuzman and Öz (2016), p. 514.

[41]For further explanations see Sect. 5.3.2.

Steinauer PH (2007) Les droits réels, vol 1. Stämpfli, Bern

Tandoğan H (1990) Özel borç ilişkileri, vol I/1. Evrim, İstanbul

Tekinay SS, Akman S, Burcuoğlu H, Altop A (1993) Tekinay borçlar hukuku genel hükümler. Filiz, İstanbul

Tercier P (2004) Le droit des obligations. Schulthess, Zurich

Tercier P, Pichonnaz P, Develioğlu HM (2016) Borçlar hukuku genel hükümler. On iki levha, İstanbul

Thévenoz L, Werro F (éd) (2012) Commentaire romand code des obligations 1: art. 1-529 CO. Helbing Lichtenhahn, Bâle

von Tuhr A, Escher A (1974) Allgemeiner Teil des Schweizerischen Obligationenrecht, vol 2. Schulthess, Zürich

von Tuhr A, Peter H (1979) Allgemeiner Teil des Schweizerischen Obligationenrecht, vol 1. Schulthess, Zürich

Chapter 30
Earnest Money and Forfeit Money

30.1 Earnest Money[1]

An amount of money paid by a party when entering into a contract is not deemed to be forfeit money; on the contrary, it is deemed to be earnest money (TCO art. 177 par. 1).[2] That is to say, the money paid serves as proof that the contract is concluded. For instance, in a car sale contract, the buyer pays €10,000. If the parties' intention is not sufficiently determined in the contract, then this amount is deemed to be earnest money and is deemed to prove that the contract is concluded.

According to TCO art. 177 par. 2, unless otherwise provided by agreement or local custom, the creditor must deduct the earnest money from his claim. In the example mentioned above, if the price of the car is €50,000, then the seller must deduct €10,000 from the price and can then demand the remaining €40,000 from the buyer, provided that there is no agreement or local custom to the contrary.

[1]Aybay (2011), pp. 179–180; Becker (1941), art. 158; Berger (2012), pp. 645–649; Engel (1997), pp. 860–861; Eren (2015), pp. 1191–1193; Feyzioğlu (1977), pp. 374–382; Gauch et al. (2008), pp. 320–323; Honsell et al. (2003), Vorbemerkungen zu Art. 158-163, art. 158; Kılıçoğlu (2013), pp. 771–775; Nomer (2015), pp. 432–433; Oser and Schönenberger (1929), Vorbemerkungen zum dritten Abschnitt, art. 158; Oğuzman and Öz (2016), pp. 550–554; Özsunay (1983), pp. 161–162; Reisoğlu (2014), pp. 456–457; Schwenzer (2009), p. 494; Tekinay et al. (1993), pp. 338–341; Thévenoz and Werro (2012), Introduction aux articles 158-163 CO, art. 158, and von Tuhr and Escher (1974), pp. 287–289.

[2]*Arrhes, Haftgeld.*

İ. Helvacı, *Turkish Contract Law*, DOI 10.1007/978-3-319-60061-1_30

30.2 Forfeit Money[3]

In cases of forfeit money, either party may withdraw from the contract. If the party who paid the forfeit money withdraws from the contract, then he must relinquish the amount paid. If the party who received the forfeit money withdraws from the contract, then he must return twice the amount of the money he received (TCO art. 178).

The right to withdraw from the contract by asserting that forfeit money has been paid must be exercised before a principal obligation is performed.[4] For instance, in a lease contract relating to a dwelling house concluded for a period of 1 year, the lessee pays forfeit money of €3000. Subsequently, the lessee pays the rent that first becomes due, and the lessor transfers possession of the property to the lessee. In such a case, the lessee may no longer withdraw from the contract by asserting that he has paid forfeit money.

As to the question whether the creditor must deduct the forfeit money from the principal claim, TCO art. 177 par. 2 is applied by analogy.[5] Therefore, the creditor must deduct the forfeit money from his principal claim. In the aforementioned example, if the monthly rent is €5000, then the lessor must deduct the forfeit money of €3000 from the first rental payment.

It should be noted that forfeit money is not a penalty. That is why it may not be reduced by a judge on account of being excessive.[6]

Even if a party to a contract has paid forfeit money, he may withdraw from the contract according to the provision relating to the debtor's default in bilateral contracts (TCO art. 125).[7] In such a case, TCO art. 178 cannot be applied. Thus, if the withdrawing party is the party who paid the forfeit money, then he may demand repayment of the forfeiture.[8] Similarly, if the withdrawing party is the party who received the forfeit money, then he need only return the sum he received as forfeiture.

---

[3] *Dédit, Reugeld.*

[4] Thévenoz and Werro (2012), art. 158, N. 7; Oğuzman and Öz (2016), p. 553; Nomer (2015), p. 433.

[5] Oğuzman and Öz (2016), p. 553; Nomer (2015), p. 433.

[6] Thévenoz and Werro (2012), art. 158, N. 8; Feyzioğlu (1977), p. 381; Eren (2015), p. 1193; Oğuzman and Öz (2016), p. 553, See on the contrary Tekinay et al. (1993), p. 341.

[7] See Sect. 23.4.2.2.

[8] Oğuzman and Öz (2016), p. 553.

References

Aybay A (2011) Borçlar hukuku dersleri genel bölüm. Filiz, İstanbul

Becker H (1941) Kommentar zum Schweizerischen Zivilgesetzbuch, Volume VI, Obligationenrecht, 1. Abteilung: Allgemeine Bestimmungen, Art. 1-183. Stämpfli, Bern

Berger B (2012) Allgemeines Schuldrecht. Stämpfli, Bern

Engel P (1997) Traité des obligations en droit Suisse. Stämpfli, Bern

Eren F (2015) Borçlar hukuku genel hükümler. Yetkin, Ankara

Feyzioğlu FN (1977) Borçlar hukuku genel hükümler, vol 2. Fakülteler, İstanbul

Gauch P, Schluep WR, Emmenegger S (2008) Schweizerisches Obligationenrecht, Allgemeiner Teil, vol 2. Schulthess, Zürich

Honsell H, Vogt NP, Wiegand W (eds) (2003) Basler Kommentar zum Schweizerischen Privatrecht, Obligationenrecht 1: Art. 1-529 OR. Helbing Lichtenhahn, Basel

Kılıçoğlu AM (2013) Borçlar hukuku genel hükümler. Turhan, İstanbul

Nomer HN (2015) Borçlar hukuku genel hükümler. Beta, İstanbul

Oğuzman K, Öz T (2016) Borçlar hukuku genel hükümler, vol 2. Vedat, İstanbul

Oser H, Schönenberger W (1929) Kommentar zum Schweizerischen Zivilgesetzbuch, Volume V: Das Obligationenrecht, Erster Halbband: Art. 1-183. Schulthess, Zürich

Özsunay E (1983) Borçlar hukuku I. Filiz, İstanbul

Reisoğlu S (2014) Türk borçlar hukuku genel hükümler. Beta, İstanbul

Schwenzer I (2009) Schweizerisches Obligationenrecht, Allgemeiner Teil. Schulthess, Bern

Tekinay SS, Akman S, Burcuoğlu H, Altop A (1993) Tekinay borçlar hukuku genel hükümler. Filiz, İstanbul

Thévenoz L, Werro F (éd) (2012) Commentaire romand code des obligations 1: art. 1-529 CO. Helbing Lichtenhahn, Bâle

von Tuhr A, Escher A (1974) Allgemeiner Teil des Schweizerischen Obligationenrecht, vol 2. Schulthess, Zürich

Chapter 31
Contractual Penalty

31.1 General[1]

As a general rule, if a debtor does not perform his obligation at all or as required and he is at fault, then the creditor is entitled to demand that the debtor pay compensation for his damage.[2] Consequently, the creditor must prove the requirements for the debtor's liability for non- or improper performance of the obligation, in particular the existence and the quantum of his damage.[3]

In certain cases, proving the quantum of damage may be quite difficult. If a creditor does not want to assume this burden of proof, then he may instead benefit from a contractual penalty. Indeed, in a contract with a penalty clause or a contract relating to a penalty, the debtor generally undertakes to pay a fixed amount of money in the case of non- or improper performance of the obligations.[4] In practice, it is very common to come across such contracts or clauses. A contractual penalty may also deter the debtor from failing to perform the obligation and may encourage him to perform.[5]

---

[1]Aybay (2011), pp. 181–183; Becker (1941), art. 160-163; Berger (2012), pp. 636–644; Engel (1997), pp. 862–867; Eren (2015), pp. 1181–1190; Feyzioğlu (1977), pp. 388–408; Gauch et al. (2008), pp. 308–320; Honsell et al. (2003), art. 160-163; Kılıçoğlu (2013), pp. 775–790; Nomer (2015), pp. 433–443; Oser and Schönenberger (1929), Vorbemerkungen zu art. 160-163, art. 160-163; Oğuzman and Öz (2016), pp. 529–549; Özsunay (1983), pp. 163–167; Reisoğlu (2014), pp. 457–462; Schwenzer (2009), pp. 490–493; Tekinay et al. (1993), pp. 341–360; Tercier (2004), pp. 246–249; Tercier et al. (2016), pp. 427–434; Thévenoz and Werro (2012), art. 160-163, and von Tuhr and Escher (1974), pp. 277–287.

[2]For further explanations, see Tunçomağ (1963), Uçar (1993), Kocaağa (2003), Erdem (2006).

[3]See Sect. 22.2.3.3.

[4]von Tuhr and Escher (1974), § 87, I, p. 277; Oğuzman and Öz (2016), p. 533; Tercier et al. (2016), p. 427.

[5]Thévenoz and Werro (2012), art. 160, N. 2; Tekinay et al. (1993), p. 342; Oğuzman and Öz (2016), p. 530.

İ. Helvacı, *Turkish Contract Law*, DOI 10.1007/978-3-319-60061-1_31

As a rule, any obligation may be secured by a penalty, such as an obligation to give, to do or not to do (to refrain from doing something). However, according to certain decisions of the Turkish Court of Cassation, pecuniary obligations may not be secured by a penalty due to the fact that the creditor is entitled to demand default interest.[6] It is reasonable to accept that the parties may also determine a penalty in the case of pecuniary obligations.[7] However, in this case, the creditor is not entitled to demand default interest unless the parties agree to the contrary.[8]

In certain cases, it is not possible to determine a penalty for non- or improper performance of an obligation. For example, pursuant to TCO art. 346, the parties are not entitled to agree on a penalty for late payment of rental fees.

A penalty is generally agreed for contractual obligations. Nevertheless, obligations resulting from tort, unjust enrichment or the law itself may also be secured by a penalty.[9]

31.2 Legal Nature and Form

31.2.1 General

The obligation to pay a penalty is an obligation subject to a suspensive condition. The suspensive condition in this case is the non- or the improper performance of the obligation.[10]

An obligation to pay a penalty may be determined by the parties as a clause of a contract or as a separate contract.[11]

31.2.2 Form Requirements

If the contract, which gives rise to the obligation being secured by a penalty, requires a specific form, then this requirement also applies to the penalty clause or penalty contract.[12] For example, a sale contract relating to immovable property

---

[6]Oğuzman and Öz (2016), p. 532 fn. 394.

[7]Tekinay et al. (1993), pp. 343–344; Oğuzman and Öz (2016), p. 532.

[8]Oğuzman and Öz (2016), p. 532.

[9]Becker (1941), art. 160, N. 3; Oğuzman and Öz (2016), p. 531; Tekinay et al. (1993), p. 343; Eren (2015), p. 1182; Reisoğlu (2014), p. 458.

[10]Tercier (2004), p. 246; Tercier et al. (2016), p. 428; Oğuzman and Öz (2016), p. 531; Nomer (2015), p. 434; Berger (2012), p. 636.

[11]Thévenoz and Werro (2012), art. 160, N. 7; Reisoğlu (2014), p. 457; Tercier et al. (2016), p. 430; Oğuzman and Öz (2016), p. 531; Berger (2012), p. 637.

[12]Thévenoz and Werro (2012), art. 160, N. 7; Tercier (2004), p. 248; Tercier et al. (2016), pp. 430–431; Nomer (2015), p. 434.

must be concluded before a land registry officer (TCO art. 237 par. 1, LRA art. 26).[13] Therefore, if the parties intend to secure an obligation that arises from this contract, then they must comply with the form requirement of the sale contract. That is to say, they must insert the penalty clause in the contract that requires the official form. If the parties determine the penalty in a separate contract, then this contract must also be concluded before a land registry officer.

31.2.3 Ancillary Nature of Penalties

A penalty clause or a penalty contract provides the creditor with an ancillary right; thus, if the principal obligation to be performed is void, then the penalty will also be void. Pursuant to TCO art. 182 par. 2 sent. 1, penalties aiming to secure an invalid obligation, such as an illegal or immoral obligation, are void. The reason for the invalidity of the main contract is irrelevant.[14] For example, if the main contract is void due to simulation,[15] lack of form,[16] etc., then the penalty will also be void.

Moreover, an obligation, secured by a penalty, that is valid on the formation of the contract may become impossible to perform. If performance of the obligation becomes impossible on account of circumstances for which the debtor is not responsible, the creditor is not entitled to demand payment of the penalty. This is because the obligation to pay a penalty will also have become invalid (TCO art. 182 par. 2 sent. 1).

It should be noted that even if a penalty is invalid, or becomes impossible to perform on account of circumstances for which the debtor is not responsible, the invalidity or the impossibility of the penalty does not affect the validity of the obligation secured by the penalty (TCO art. 182 par. 2 sent. 2).

Furthermore, the contract that is subject to the penalty may be valid at the outset, but the creditor may withdraw (*ex tunc*)[17] from the contract or rescind it due to mistake, fraud or duress. In these cases, the penalty also becomes void.[18]

If the obligation secured by a penalty becomes time-barred, then the debtor may plead the fact that the obligation is time-barred and refuse to pay the penalty.[19]

---

[13]See Sect. 3.2.3.

[14]Eren (2015), pp. 1182–1183; Oğuzman and Öz (2016), p. 535.

[15]See Sect. 8.2.2.

[16]See Sect. 3.5.

[17]Termination of the contract takes effect retroactively (*résolution, Rücktritt*).

[18]Oğuzman and Öz (2016), pp. 536, 537; Nomer (2015), p. 437.

[19]Oğuzman and Öz (2016), p. 537.

31.3 Types of Contractual Penalties

31.3.1 General

In practice, parties generally agree on a fixed amount of money as a penalty.[20] Nevertheless, any act (prestation) such as an obligation to give or to do may be determined by the parties as a penalty.[21] Moreover, an obligation not to do may be determined as a penalty, provided that it has monetary value.[22]

According to TCO art. 181 par. 1, the parties may agree that in the event of the creditor withdrawing from the contract, the performed part of the obligation is forfeited to the creditor. Consequently, in a penalty clause or contract, the parties may agree that in cases of non-performance or of improper performance, the debtor who breaches the contract will lose certain rights or powers. For example, in a work contract, the parties agree that if the contractor does not perform the obligation by the due date, then he will lose a portion of his consideration. However, the provisions regarding sale with payment by instalments are not affected (TCO art. 181 par. 2).

31.3.2 Penalty in Lieu of Performance

According to TCO art. 179 par. 1, where a penalty is agreed for non-performance or improper performance of an obligation, unless otherwise inferred from the contract,[23] the creditor may demand either the performance of the obligation or the payment of the penalty. In such a case, as a rule, the creditor is not entitled to demand both the performance of the obligation and the payment of the penalty. For instance, in a car sale contract, the parties agree that the seller will transfer ownership of the car to the buyer, and if the seller fails to do so, then the buyer may demand a penalty of €20,000 in lieu of performance. In this case, if the seller does not transfer ownership of the car, then the buyer may demand specific performance[24] or payment of the penalty. If the obligation of the seller becomes impossible where he is responsible, then the creditor may demand only the payment of the penalty.[25]

---

[20]Engel (1997), p. 862.

[21]Thévenoz and Werro (2012), art. 160, N. 5; Reisoğlu (2014), p. 457; Oğuzman and Öz (2016), p. 534.

[22]Oğuzman and Öz (2016), p. 534, compare to Thévenoz and Werro (2012), art. 160, N. 5.

[23]Since the TCO art. 179 par. 1 is not mandatory, the parties may agree that the creditor has the right to demand performance of both. Engel (1997), p. 865; Feyzioğlu (1977), p. 393; Eren (2015), p. 1185; Oğuzman and Öz (2016), p. 539.

[24]See Sect. 22.1.2.

[25]Oğuzman and Öz (2016), p. 538; Nomer (2015), p. 437.

In cases where either performance of the obligation or payment of the penalty may be demanded, once the creditor demands payment of the penalty, he may not change his decision and is not entitled to demand performance of the obligation at a later time.[26]

Where the obligation is secured by a pledge or mortgage and the creditor demands payment of the penalty, these collaterals secure the penalty in lieu of performance.[27] However, a surety cannot be held liable for such a penalty (TCO art. 589 par. 4).

31.3.3 Penalty in Addition to Performance

Where a penalty is agreed for non-compliance with regard to the determined time or place of performance, the creditor may claim payment of the penalty in addition to the performance of the obligation, unless he clearly waives this right or accepts performance of the obligation without any reservation (TCO art. 179 par. 2).

This type of penalty is very common in practice, especially in the case of default by a debtor. It should be noted that this rule is not mandatory. Therefore, the parties may agree that in cases where the obligation is not performed at the set time or place, the creditor may demand either payment of the penalty or performance of the obligation.[28]

In cases where both performance of the obligation and payment of the penalty may be demanded, if the creditor accepts performance of the obligation without any reservation, then he loses the right to demand the penalty.[29] If he wants to preclude this consequence, then he must demand payment of the penalty before performance or, at the latest, at the time of performance. If he does not so, he must declare that he reserves the right relating to the demand for payment of the penalty during the period of performance.[30]

31.3.4 Withdrawal or Termination by Payment of Penalty[31]

In accordance with TCO art. 179 par. 3, the parties may agree that the debtor is entitled to withdraw from or terminate the contract by paying the determined

---

[26]Thévenoz and Werro (2012), art. 160, N. 11; Engel (1997), p. 864; Tercier (2004), p. 247; Eren (2015), p. 1184.

[27]Oğuzman and Öz (2016), p. 539; Nomer (2015), p. 441.

[28]Feyzioğlu (1977), p. 394; Oğuzman and Öz (2016), p. 540; Reisoğlu (2014), p. 459.

[29]Becker (1941), art. 160, N. 30; Tercier (2004), p. 247; Eren (2015), p. 1185.

[30]Oğuzman and Öz (2016), p. 541; Tekinay et al. (1993), p. 351; Eren (2015), pp. 1185–1186, compare to von Tuhr and Escher § 87, III, 1, b, p. 282.

[31]For further explanations Tutar (2016).

penalty. According to the Turkish Code of Obligations, as a rule, a party to a contract is not entitled to unilaterally withdraw from or terminate the contract. The legislature provides for an exception to this rule. Indeed, in some circumstances, a debtor has the right to pay a penalty instead of remaining bound by a contract.

In fact, in cases regulated by TCO art. 179 par. 3, there is no penalty for non- or improper performance of the obligation. On the contrary, the debtor voluntarily pays a penalty in order to be able to withdraw from or terminate the contract. Pursuant to TCO art. 179 par. 3, where a debtor claims that the parties agreed on a penalty for withdrawal or termination, then he must prove it.

31.4 The Role of the Debtor's Fault

In principle, in order for a creditor to demand payment of a penalty, the debtor must be at fault (TCO art. 182 par. 2).[32] However, as a general rule, even if the creditor must prove non-performance or improper performance of the obligation, he does not have to prove that the debtor is at fault. On the contrary, the debtor must prove that he is not at fault (TCO art. 112).[33]

Any type of fault on the part of the debtor is sufficient for his liability to pay a penalty—*e.g.*, gross fault (intention or gross negligence—*culpa lata*) or slight fault (slight negligence—*culpa levis*).[34] However, the parties may agree that the debtor will pay a penalty even if there is no fault on his part.[35]

In cases where the debtor is liable for non- or improper performance of the obligation in the absence of fault, the debtor need not be at fault to be liable to pay a penalty. For example, TCO art. 116 relating to the debtor's liability for assistants does not require the debtor's fault.[36]

In relation to a penalty determined as a result of a debtor's default in a pecuniary obligation, his fault is irrelevant.

31.5 The Role of the Creditor's Damage

For the payment of a penalty, the creditor's damage is irrelevant—*i.e.*, the penalty must be paid even if the creditor has not incurred any damage (TCO art. 180 par. 1). However, in certain cases, the creditor may have incurred damage exceeding the

---

[32]See on the contrary Eren (2015), pp. 1186–1187.

[33]See Sect. 22.2.3.2.1.

[34]Oğuzman and Öz (2016), p. 544.

[35]Oğuzman and Öz (2016), p. 545, compare to Eren (2015), p. 1187.

[36]See Sect. 22.5.

amount of the penalty. If the creditor demands compensation for his damage in excess of the penalty, then he must prove that the debtor is at fault (TCO art. 180 par. 2).

In the event that the debtor is either legally or contractually liable in the absence of fault, it is apparent that the creditor is not required to prove that the debtor is at fault in order to seek compensation for damage in excess of the penalty.[37]

In cases where the creditor withdraws from (*ex tunc*)[38] or terminates the contract (*ex nunc*)[39] by paying a penalty (TCO art. 179 par. 3), even if the creditor has incurred damage exceeding the amount of the penalty, he is not entitled to demand compensation for damage in excess of the penalty.[40]

31.6 Reduction of the Penalty[41]

As a general rule, the parties are free to determine the amount of the penalty (TCO art. 182 par. 1). However, a judge may reduce excessive penalties *ex officio* (TCO art. 182 par. 3). The judge may determine whether a penalty is excessive or not at his discretion. In the process of determination, the judge must take into account the parties' financial position and the debtor's conduct, especially the degree of fault. Nevertheless, the judge must not diminish the deterrent effect of the penalty.[42]

It should be kept in mind that the judge may not change the nature of the penalty.[43] For instance, if the parties agreed on an amount of money as a penalty, even if the amount is excessive, the judge cannot order that the debtor perform an obligation instead of paying the pecuniary penalty. Moreover, the judge is not entitled to quash the penalty completely on account of its excessive nature. The judge may only reduce the penalty.[44]

According to T.Com.C art. 22, merchants are not entitled to demand that the judge reduce the amount of a penalty, asserting that it is excessive. In order to apply this rule, the debtor must have the status of merchant, and the penalty must be determined in respect of a commercial obligation. Despite the said article, if the agreement relating to the penalty is immoral or contrary to the provisions protecting the personal rights of the debtor, then the debtor may demand that the judge reduce the amount of the penalty. According to the Turkish Court of Cassation, the judge

[37]Oğuzman and Öz (2016), p. 546.

[38]Termination of the contract takes effect retroactively (*résolution, Rücktritt*).

[39]Termination of the contract takes effect prospectively (*résiliation, Kündigung*).

[40]Tekinay et al. (1993), p. 359; Oğuzman and Öz (2016), pp. 546–547; Reisoğlu (2014), p. 460.

[41]For further explanations see Gülseven (2016).

[42]Feyzioğlu (1977), p. 402; Tekinay et al. (1993), p. 356; Oğuzman and Öz (2016), p. 547; Reisoğlu (2014), p. 462, fn. 22.

[43]Compare to Thévenoz and Werro (2012), art. 163, N. 9.

[44]Eren (2015), p. 1190; Oğuzman and Öz (2016), p. 547.

may decide on a reduction of, or even the invalidity of, a penalty in the event that the payment of the penalty would cause the debtor to become destitute.[45]

References

Aybay A (2011) Borçlar hukuku dersleri genel bölüm. Filiz, İstanbul
Becker H (1941) Kommentar zum Schweizerischen Zivilgesetzbuch, Volume VI, Obligationenrecht, 1. Abteilung: Allgemeine Bestimmungen, Art. 1-183. Stämpfli, Bern
Berger B (2012) Allgemeines Schuldrecht. Stämpfli, Bern
Engel P (1997) Traité des obligations en droit Suisse. Stämpfli, Bern
Erdem M (2006) La clause pénale: étude comparative de droit suisse et de droit Turc. Ankara
Eren F (2015) Borçlar hukuku genel hükümler. Yetkin, Ankara
Feyzioğlu FN (1977) Borçlar hukuku genel hükümler, vol 2. Fakülteler, İstanbul
Gauch P, Schluep WR, Emmenegger S (2008) Schweizerisches Obligationenrecht, Allgemeiner Teil, vol 2. Schulthess, Zürich
Gülseven H (2016) Cezai şartın indirilmesi. Seçkin, Ankara
Honsell H, Vogt NP, Wiegand W (eds) (2003) Basler Kommentar zum Schweizerischen Privatrecht, Obligationenrecht 1: Art. 1-529 OR. Helbing Lichtenhahn, Basel
Kılıçoğlu AM (2013) Borçlar hukuku genel hükümler. Turhan, İstanbul
Kocaağa K (2003) Türk özel hukukunda cezai şart (bk.m.158-161). Yetkin, Ankara
Nomer HN (2015) Borçlar hukuku genel hükümler. Beta, İstanbul
Oğuzman K, Öz T (2016) Borçlar hukuku genel hükümler, vol 2. Vedat, İstanbul
Oser H, Schönenberger W (1929) Kommentar zum Schweizerischen Zivilgesetzbuch, Volume V: Das Obligationenrecht, Erster Halbband: Art. 1-183. Schulthess, Zürich
Özsunay E (1983) Borçlar hukuku, vol 1. Filiz, İstanbul
Reisoğlu S (2014) Türk borçlar hukuku genel hükümler. Beta, İstanbul
Schwenzer I (2009) Schweizerisches Obligationenrecht, Allgemeiner Teil. Schulthess, Bern
Tekinay SS, Akman S, Burcuoğlu H, Altop A (1993) Tekinay borçlar hukuku genel hükümler. Filiz, İstanbul
Tercier P (2004) Le droit des obligations. Schulthess, Zurich
Tercier P, Pichonnaz P, Develioğlu HM (2016) Borçlar hukuku genel hükümler. On iki levha, İstanbul
Thévenoz L, Werro F (éd) (2012) Commentaire romand code des obligations 1: art. 1-529 CO. Helbing Lichtenhahn, Bâle
Tunçomağ K (1963) Türk hukukunda cezai şart. İstanbul üniversitesi, İstanbul
Tutar E (2016) Dönme cezası. Turhan, Ankara
Uçar S (1993) Hukukta cezai şart ve uygulanması. Alfa, İstanbul
von Tuhr A, Escher A (1974) Allgemeiner Teil des Schweizerischen Obligationenrecht, vol 2. Schulthess, Zürich

[45]Tekinay et al. (1993), p. 357; Eren (2015), pp. 1189–1190, compare to Oğuzman and Öz (2016), p. 549; Tercier et al. (2016), p. 432.

Part V
Assignment of Claims, Assumption of Debts, Transfer of Contracts and Joining a Party to an Existing Contract

Chapter 32
Assignment of Claims

32.1 General[1]

A claim arising from a contract or some other source of obligation, such as a tort or unjust enrichment, may be transferred to third parties.[2] A claim may be transferred by an agreement, by a court order or by law. In this section, assignment of claims[3] effected by agreement and those effected by a court decision or operation of law are analysed respectively.

32.2 Assignment of Claims by Agreement[4]

32.2.1 Conditions

In order for a claim to be assigned, the following conditions must be met[5]: (1) there must be an assignable claim, and (2) there must be an assignment contract between

[1]Aybay (2011), pp. 184–192; Becker (1941), Vorbemerkungen zu art. 164-174, art. 164-174; Berger (2012), pp. 741–779; Engel (1997), pp. 871–893; Eren (2015), pp. 1224–1243; Feyzioğlu (1977), pp. 613–665; Gauch et al. (2008), pp. 243–271; Honsell et al. (2003), Vorbemerkungen zu art. 164-174, art. 164-174; Kılıçoğlu (2013), pp. 790–809; Nomer (2015), pp. 447–454; Oser and Schönenberger (1929), Vorbemerkungen zur Abtretung von Forderungen (art. 164-174), art. 164-174; Oğuzman and Öz (2016), pp. 555–596; Özsunay (1983), pp. 183–193; Reisoğlu (2014), pp. 464–475; Schwenzer (2009), pp. 563–581; Tekinay et al. (1993), pp. 240–268; Tercier (2004), pp. 301–311; Tercier et al. (2016), pp. 515–531; Thévenoz and Werro (2012), art. 164-174, and von Tuhr and Escher (1974), pp. 329–373.

[2]For further explanations, see Kocaman (1989), Dayınlarlı (2008), Günergök (2014).

[3]*Cession des créances, Abtretung von Forderungen.*

[4]*Cession volontaire, Freiwillige Abtretung.*

[5]Becker (1941), art. 164, N. 4.

İ. Helvacı, *Turkish Contract Law*, DOI 10.1007/978-3-319-60061-1_32

the assignor and the assignee. It is not necessary for the debtor to give consent to the assignment.

It must be kept in mind that, in certain cases, claims that are expected to arise in the future—*i.e.*, prospective claims—may also be assigned.

32.2.1.1 Assignability of the Claim

A creditor may assign his claim to a third party unless the assignment is forbidden by law, by virtue of the agreement or by the nature of the legal transaction (TCO art. 183 par. 1). For instance, pursuant to TCO art. 322 par. 2, in lease contracts relating to dwelling houses or business premises, the lessee may not assign his right of use without the written consent of the lessor. Another example is that in agreements for lifelong support, the rights of the grantee cannot be assigned (TCO art. 619 par. 1).

As mentioned above, the parties to a contract may prohibit the assignment of the claim by agreement (*pactum de non cedendo*).[6] For example, in a lease contract, the rental fee is assignable, but the parties may agree to the contrary. Furthermore, in certain cases, the claim may not be assignable due to the nature of the legal transaction.[7] Indeed, in certain cases, there may be a strong relationship between the claim and the personal characteristics of the creditor. In other words, the assignment of such a claim will affect the content of the claim. For instance, as a divorced spouse who has the right to alimony (spousal maintenance) cannot assign his claim for alimony, neither may a member of an association assign his claims arising from that membership.

In the aforementioned cases, the creditor is not entitled to assign his claim. If he attempts to do so, the assignment is void, and the debtor may simply refuse the third party's demand by pleading that the claim is not assignable.[8] However, in cases where the assignment of a claim is forbidden due to an agreement, the creditor may nevertheless attempt to assign his claim. In such a case, the legislature protects a third party, provided that he acted in good faith. Indeed, pursuant to TCO art. 183 par. 2, if a third party acquires a claim in reliance on a written acknowledgement of debt that does not mention that the claim is unassignable, then the debtor is not entitled to object to the assignment on the ground that it was prohibited by an agreement.

[6]Tercier (2004), p. 304; Thévenoz and Werro (2012), art. 164, N. 32–35; Eren (2015), p. 1236; Tercier et al. (2016), p. 521; Engel (1997), p. 872.

[7]Eren (2015), p. 1237; Tercier et al. (2016), p. 522; Engel (1997), p. 872; Tercier (2004), p. 305; Thévenoz and Werro (2012), art. 164, N. 36.

[8]Tekinay et al. (1993), p. 247; Eren (2015), p. 1237; Oğuzman and Öz (2016), pp. 571–574; Tercier et al. (2016), p. 522.

32.2.1.2 The Assignment Contract

The second condition for the assignment of a claim is the requirement for an assignment contract. This contract must be concluded between the assignor and the assignee.[9] As mentioned above, the consent of the debtor is not required.

The assignment contract must be made in written form (TCO art. 184 par. 1). It must state the identities of the assignor and the assignee, the assigned claim and the parties' intention relating to the assignment. By analogy to TCO art. 14 par. 1, the assignor's signature is sufficient. The assignee's declaration of will (intention)[10] for the contract may be implied.

A divisible claim, such as a pecuniary claim, may be wholly or partially assigned.[11] Where a divisible claim is partially assigned, it is evident that the unassigned part of the claim remains in the assets of the assignor (principal creditor).

It should be noted that a promise to make an assignment does not require any particular form (TCO art. 184 par. 2). Such an agreement does not transfer the claim to the assignee, but, on the contrary, it obliges the assignor to transfer the claim to the assignee.[12]

An assignment contract is a dispositive legal transaction[13] with regard to the assignor.[14] Thus, with the conclusion of the contract, the claim that is the subject matter of the contract is assigned to the assignee. For this reason, the assignor must have the capacity to act and the power of disposition.[15] Although the assignor has the capacity to act, if he does not have the power of disposition, then the assignment contract will be void. For instance, if a claim has already been assigned to a third party, then any subsequent assignment by the assignor relating to this claim will be void.[16] This is on the basis that if a creditor has already assigned the claim, then he is no longer entitled to the claim and, thus, loses the power of disposition in respect of the claim.

The cause (*causa*) of an assignment may be *causa solvendi*, *causa donandi* or *causa credendi*.[17] For instance, creditor C has already promised to assign his claim to assignee A. When creditor C assigns his claim to assignee A in order to perform his obligation to assign, then the cause of the assignment is a *causa solvendi*. However, if a creditor wishes to assign his claim with the aim of making a gift,

---

[9]Becker (1941), art. 164, N. 5; Tercier (2004), p. 305; Tekinay et al. (1993), p. 240; Tercier et al. (2016), p. 522.

[10]*Déclaration de volonté*, *Willenserklärung*.

[11]Thévenoz and Werro (2012), art. 164, N. 20; Oğuzman and Öz (2016), p. 566.

[12]Oğuzman and Öz (2016), pp. 562–563; Reisoğlu (2014), p. 466; Nomer (2015), p. 449.

[13]*Acte de disposition*, *Verfügungsgeschäft*. See Chap. 14 fn. 5–6.

[14]Conversely, such a contract is an acquisitive transaction with regard to the assignee.

[15]*Pouvoir de disposer*, *Verfügungsmacht*.

[16]Tercier (2004), p. 306.

[17]Oğuzman and Öz (2016), p. 560.

then the cause of the assignment is a *causa donandi*. Where the creditor assigns a claim with the aim of acquiring a counter-claim, then the cause of the assignment is a *causa credendi*. For instance, in a sale contract, if a buyer entering into a contract assigns his claim with the aim of becoming entitled to a counter-claim, then the cause of the assignment is a *causa credendi*.

Certain scholars argue that an assignment of a claim is a causal legal transaction.[18] According to these scholars, if the cause (legal ground) of the assignment is invalid, then the assignment is invalid as well. For instance, assume that there is an invalid lease agreement between the lessor and the lessee. The lessee, in order to pay prospective rental fees, assigns to the lessor a pecuniary claim arising from another contract that is concluded with a third party. In this case, as the legal ground of the assignment is invalid, the assignment is invalid as well. However, certain scholars are of the opinion that the assignment of a claim is an independent (abstract) legal transaction and so even if the legal ground of the assignment is invalid, the assignment may be valid, but the transfer of the claim will constitute a case of unjust enrichment in the assets of the assignee.[19] The practical consequence of this view is that the assignee must assign the claim back to the assignor. If he fails to do so, then the assignor may bring an action in order to reclaim the assigned claim.

An assignment contract is void if the assigned claim does not exist.[20] However, even if the claim does not exist, a promise of assignment relating to such a claim may be valid. This is because such an agreement does not transfer the claim to the assignee but, on the contrary, obliges the assignor to transfer the claim to the assignee. In such a case, it is obvious that the promising party who is obliged to transfer the non-existent claim cannot perform his obligation and will therefore be liable for non-performance.[21]

A simulated written acknowledgement of debt is void (TCO art. 19 par. 1).[22] Thus, such legal transactions do not give rise to a valid claim. However, even if the written acknowledgement of debt is simulated, the alleged creditor may attempt to assign his pseudo-claim to a third party. In such a case, if the third party relies on this written acknowledgement of debt, then the debtor cannot plead that the transaction is simulated, and he must pay the amount mentioned in the deed (TCO art. 19 par. 2).

As indicated above, in certain cases, claims that are expected to arise in the future—*i.e.*, prospective claims—may also be assigned.[23] For example, in a lease

[18]Eren (2015), p. 1231; Tekinay et al. (1993), pp. 241–242.

[19]von Tuhr and Escher (1974), § 93, II, p. 333; Oğuzman and Öz (2016), p. 560; Reisoğlu (2014), p. 465; Becker (1941), art. 164, N. 1. For further explanations see Honsell et al. (2003), art. 164, N. 23–25.

[20]Nomer (2015), p. 449; Oğuzman and Öz (2016), p. 569.

[21]Oğuzman and Öz (2016), p. 563.

[22]See Sect. 8.2.2.

[23]Nomer (2015), p. 449; Oğuzman and Öz (2016), pp. 566–567; Eren (2015), pp. 1234–1235.

contract, a lessor may assign the prospective rental fees to a third party. In such a case, the assignor actually assigns an expectant right. Therefore, if the prospective rental fees are not payable due to premature termination of the lease, then the assignment contract relating to this expectant right will be void.

A claim that may arise from any contract subject to a suspensive condition (condition precedent)[24] is also able to be assigned.[25] However, if the suspensive condition does not occur, then this assignment contract will also be void.

Similarly, a claim that may arise from any contract subject to a resolutive condition (condition subsequent)[26] is also able to be assigned.[27] However, if the resolutive condition occurs, then this assignment contract will also be void.

32.2.2 Consequences

32.2.2.1 Transfer of the Claim

With the formation of an assignment contract, the claim that is the subject matter of the contract is transferred to the assignee.[28] The assignor is no longer entitled to the claim. Thus, the assignor may not accept performance of the obligation and is not entitled to discharge the debtor. Indeed, upon assignment, these rights belong to the assignee.[29]

If the debtor does not perform the obligation, then the assignee may bring an action for specific performance. In addition, if the conditions for an action for compensation for damage are met, the assignee may initiate proceedings. Nevertheless, the assignee is not entitled to withdraw from the contract or terminate it. This is due to the fact that the right of withdrawal or termination requires the withdrawing person to be a party to the contract.[30]

32.2.2.2 Transfer of Ancillary Rights

The assignment of a claim also includes the assignment of all privileges and ancillary rights, except those that are inseparable from the person of the assignor (TCO art. 189 par. 1). Privileges that are separable from the person of the assignor include certain rights that are bound to the claim, and they grant certain specific

[24]See Sect. 29.2.

[25]Thévenoz and Werro (2012), art. 164, N. 19.

[26]See Sect. 29.3.

[27]Thévenoz and Werro (2012), art. 164, N. 19.

[28]Tekinay et al. (1993), p. 250; Thévenoz and Werro (2012), art. 164, N. 61; Tercier (2004), p. 307.

[29]Tercier et al. (2016), p. 524; Oğuzman and Öz (2016), pp. 574–575; Eren (2015), p. 1238.

[30]Oğuzman and Öz (2016), p. 577.

priorities to a creditor in the event of a debtor's bankruptcy (TCBE art. 206). As mentioned above, these privileges are transferred to the assignee.[31]

In relation to privileges that are inseparable from the person of the assignor and, thus, are not transferrable to the assignee, circumstances that preclude the commencement of the limitation period may be given as an example. Pursuant to TCO art. 153 par. 1 subcl. 3, between spouses, the limitation period does not commence, or is suspended if it has already started, during the course of the marriage.[32] If one of the spouses assigns his claim to a third party, then the limitation period commences or continues from the date of assignment.[33]

As to ancillary rights, ancillary securities such as sureties, pledges and mortgages may be given as examples. It should be noted that in order for an assignee to benefit from a mortgage, entry in the land register is not necessary (TCC art. 891).[34] Moreover, in order for an assignee to benefit from a pledge, the transfer of possession of the chattel to the new creditor is not necessary[35] (*cf.* TCC art. 939 par. 1). If an assigned claim has already given rise to a lien[36] in favour of the creditor (TCC art. 950 par. 1), then this right is also transferred to the assignee with the assignment of the claim.[37]

According to TCO art. 189 par. 2, interest in arrears is also presumed to be assigned with the assignment of the principal claim. It should be kept in mind that interest that has not accrued will also belong to the assets of the assignee. TCO art. 189 par. 2 is not mandatory. Thus, the parties may agree that interest in arrears will not be transferred to the assignee.[38]

32.2.2.3 The Obligations of the Assignor

The assignor must deliver to the assignee the proof of debt, such as any bill, and other available documents evidencing the claim and must provide the assignee with the necessary information in order for the assignee to assert the claim (TCO art. 190). In particular, the assignor must deliver the deed from which the claim arises, such as the sale or lease contract. However, if the deed furnishes the assignor with certain other rights, then he does not have to deliver the document itself to the

---

[31]Feyzioğlu (1977), p. 641; Tekinay et al. (1993), p. 241; Oğuzman and Öz (2016), p. 575.

[32]See Sect. 26.4.

[33]Tekinay et al. (1993), p. 251; Oğuzman and Öz (2016), pp. 577–578.

[34]For further explanations, see Helvacı (2008).

[35]Thévenoz and Werro (2012), art. 170 fn. 30, *cf.* Feyzioğlu (1977), p. 651; Tekinay et al. (1993), p. 260.

[36]For further explanations see Çetiner (2010).

[37]Eren (2015), p. 1240; Oğuzman and Öz (2016), p. 576; Oğuzman et al. (2016), p. 1049, compare to Thévenoz and Werro (2012), art. 170, N. 9.

[38]Oğuzman and Öz (2016), p. 576; Nomer (2015), p. 450.

assignee; he may elect to only provide the assignee with a copy of the document.[39] For example, in a lease contract, if the lessor assigns only certain rental fee claims, then he will need the original lease in order to demand any unassigned claims.

Furthermore, the assignor must provide all documents to the assignee relating to the securities associated with the assigned claims, such as any surety bond, pledge or mortgage contract.[40]

32.2.3 *The Position of the Debtor*[41]

32.2.3.1 Performance in Good Faith

With the formation of an assignment contract, the claim that is the subject matter of the contract transfers to the assignee. The debtor may no longer perform the obligation in favour of the assignor. If the debtor attempts to perform his obligation for the benefit of the assignor, this does not result in the discharge of his obligation.

However, if the debtor does not know of the existence of the assignment, then he may attempt to perform the obligation for the assignor. In such a case, although the performance of the obligation for the assignor is not possible, TCO art. 186 protects the debtor acting in good faith. That is to say, if the debtor is not notified of the assignment by the assignor or the assignee and the debtor performs his obligation for the benefit of the former creditor, he is released from the obligation.[42]

In addition, according to the said article, in cases where a claim is assigned multiple times, if the debtor is not notified of the assignments and performs his obligation in good faith to one of the previous creditors instead of the latest, then he is discharged from the obligation. For instance, a creditor assigns his claim to a third party, and this third party reassigns the claim to another. If the debtor was not made aware of these assignments, then he may perform the obligation in good faith for the benefit of the original creditor. Furthermore, if the debtor was aware of the first assignment, but not the second one, then he may perform the obligation in good faith for the first assignee.[43]

32.2.3.2 Refusal of Performance and Deposit

If ownership of the claim is disputed, then the debtor may refuse to perform the obligation, and he may be discharged by depositing or delivering the subject matter

---

[39] Feyzioğlu (1977), p. 651; Tekinay et al. (1993), p. 259; Oğuzman and Öz (2016), p. 578.

[40] Thévenoz and Werro (2012), art. 170, N. 11; Oğuzman and Öz (2016), p. 578; Feyzioğlu (1977), p. 651; Tekinay et al. (1993), p. 260.

[41] For further explanations see Günergök (2014).

[42] Tercier (2004), p. 308.

[43] Thévenoz and Werro (2012), art. 167, N. 21; Oğuzman and Öz (2016), pp. 582–583; Nomer (2015), p. 452; Reisoğlu (2014), p. 470.

of the claim at a place determined by a judge (TCO art. 187 par. 1). For determination of the place of delivery or deposit, the debtor must apply to the court at the place of performance of the obligation. It should be noted that it is irrelevant whether the dispute has been brought before a court or not.[44]

Where the debtor is aware of the fact that ownership of the claim is disputed, it is not at his discretion to elect the person to whom the performance is directed. On the contrary, if he performs the obligation in favour of the erroneous creditor, then he must bear the consequences of this action (TCO art. 187 par. 2). That is to say, the debtor must perform the obligation in favour of the real creditor again, and then he may demand that the erroneous creditor return the performed obligation in accordance with the provisions relating to unjust enrichment.[45]

In cases where the dispute is brought before a court, the parties to the dispute may demand that the debtor deposit the subject matter of the claim, provided that the dispute is pending in court and the obligation is due (TCO art 187 par. 3).

32.2.3.3 Defences of the Debtor

The assignment of a claim may not exacerbate the position of the debtor. TCO art. 188 is written with this principle in mind. According to this article, the debtor may raise against the assignee the defences that he had against the assignor at the time he was notified of the assignment. Therefore, the debtor may assert[46] (1) that no claim has arisen due to the fact that the obligational relationship that allegedly gave rise to the claim is invalid or (2) that the claim has been terminated by performance, discharge or set-off. Moreover, if the claim is time-barred, the debtor is entitled to raise this defence. In addition, if the conditions of the *exceptio non adimpleti contractus* are met,[47] the debtor may also raise this defence.[48]

In the event of a debtor having a counter-claim that was not yet due at the time he became aware of the assignment, he may set off the counter-claim on the condition that it becomes due before or at the same time as the assigned claim (TCO art. 188 par. 2). For instance, A is obliged to pay €10,000 to B, and this claim will fall due on 22 September 2016. In addition, B is obliged to pay €20,000 to A, which will fall due on 25 December 2016. Assume that, on 3 April 2016, A assigns his claim to assignee C and B is notified of the assignment on 6 April 2016. In this case, when C demands that B pay €20,000 on 25 December 2016, B may set off his counter-claim against A with his obligation to C.

---

[44] Becker (1941), art. 168, N. 7; Engel (1997), p. 884; Thévenoz and Werro (2012), art. 168, N. 4; Feyzioğlu (1977), p. 656; Oğuzman and Öz (2016), pp. 583–584.

[45] Öz (1990), pp. 57–58.

[46] Tekinay et al. (1993), p. 252 *ff*; Oğuzman and Öz (2016), p. 586; Eren (2015), p. 1241

[47] See Sect. 18.4.2.2.

[48] Thévenoz and Werro (2012), art. 169, N. 11; Feyzioğlu (1977), p. 658; Oğuzman and Öz (2016), p. 587; Eren (2015), p. 1241.

32.2.4 *Warranty of the Assignor*[49]

32.2.4.1 In Assignments Without Consideration

Where a claim is transferred without consideration to an assignee, the assignor cannot be liable for the non-existence of the claim and the insolvency of the debtor (TCO art. 191 par. 2). In other words, the assignor does not give any warranty. Thus, if the debtor does not perform the obligation for the assignee, the latter is not entitled to demand that the assignor pay compensation for damage. The reason for this provision is that if a person obtains a claim gratuitously, he must bear the consequences of the possibility of the non-existence of the claim or the insolvency of the debtor. If the legislature had made an assignor liable in the case of gratuitous assignments, then this would result in placing the assignor in an inequitable position.

32.2.4.2 In Assignments by Law

The provision indicated above also applies to assignments carried out by virtue of law. That is to say, if a claim is transferred by law, the former creditor warrants neither the existence of the claim nor the solvency of the debtor (TCO art. 191 par. 2).

32.2.4.3 In Assignments for Consideration

In the case of an assignment for consideration, the assignor warrants the existence of the claim and the solvency of the debtor at the time of the assignment (TCO art. 191 par. 1). In the following cases, the assignment of claim is deemed to be for consideration. For instance, when D is obliged to pay €10,000 to C and the latter assigns this claim to A for €5000, the claim is deemed to be for consideration. Furthermore, instead of paying this sum of money, A may undertake an obligation to give or to do or not to do.

The liability of an assignor arises by virtue of the law. Consequently, even if a non-existent claim is assigned, and the assignment is thereby invalid, the assignor is liable. If the assignee knows of the non-existence of the claim, the assignor is not liable.[50]

The liability of an assignor does not require fault on his part. Thus, even if an assignor is entitled to presume that a claim exists and that the debtor is solvent, he may nevertheless be liable.[51]

---

[49]For further explanations see Engin (2002).

[50]Oğuzman and Öz (2016), p. 591.

[51]Oğuzman and Öz (2016), p. 593.

32.2.4.4 The Extent of the Liability

An assignee may demand the following from a liable assignor: (1) the return of the consideration paid together with interest; (2) the costs arising from the assignment; (3) the costs associated with recovery, and any unsuccessful attempts at recovery, of the claim; and (4) other damage, except where the assignor is able to prove that he is not at fault (TCO art. 193). For example, C asserts that D is obliged to pay him €10,000, and subsequently C assigns this claim for €6000 to A. However, D does not perform the obligation, and A must bring an action. The court dismisses the case due to the non-existence of the assigned claim. A incurs €1000 in procedural costs. In this case, even if assignor C is not at fault, he must nevertheless reimburse the consideration of €6000 plus interest and the procedural costs of €1000. If C is at fault, he must pay compensation for the damage suffered by the assignee, being €4000, which is the difference between the claim and the consideration.

If a creditor assigns a claim with the aim of performing an obligation without fixing the amount for which the claim should be credited, the extent of the assignor's warranty is determined according to TCO art. 192. For example, C asserts that D is obliged to pay him €5000. Furthermore, C is obliged to pay €10,000 to A, and so C assigns his claim against D to A with the aim of performing his obligation. In this case, there are three possibilities: (1) if assignee A cannot obtain performance due to non-existence of the claim or the insolvency of the debtor, then the whole obligation of assignor C will stand; (2) if assignee A obtains partial performance, for example a payment of €3000 from D, then this amount will be credited, and thus the balance of €2000 will stand; and (3) if assignee A could have recovered €5000 had he proceeded with all due diligence, then this amount will be credited.

32.3 Assignment by Court Order or by Operation of Law

The transfer of a claim may be by operation of law. For instance, when a creditor dies, his transferrable claims pass to his heirs automatically. Indeed, according to TCC art. 599 par. 1, the heirs acquire the inheritance as a whole on the death of the deceased by operation of law. Another example is regulated by TCO art. 127, according to which the fulfilment of an obligation by a third party satisfies a creditor but the obligation is not extinguished, and the claim therefore passes by operation of law to the performing third party.[52]

The transfer of a claim may also occur by court order. For example, a creditor promises to assign his claim to a third party. If the creditor does not transfer the claim to the third party, the latter may bring an action and demand that the creditor transfer the claim to him. If the court accepts this demand, the claim that is the

[52]See Sect. 24.2.

subject matter of the court order transfers to the claimant when the court order becomes final (TCO art. 185).

In the above-mentioned cases, the transfer is effective against third parties without requiring any form or the consent of the former creditor (TCO art. 185). As mentioned above, if a claim is transferred by law, the assignor warrants neither the existence of the claim nor the solvency of the debtor (TCO art. 191 par. 2). If a claim is transferred by a court order and this transfer is for consideration, TCO art. 191 par. 1 may be applied by analogy.[53]

32.4 Special Provisions

According to TCO art. 194, special provisions governing the assignment of certain rights are reserved. Indeed, the assignment of claims arising out of negotiable instruments, such as a bill of exchange, a promissory note or a cheque, is governed by certain special provisions of the Turkish Commercial Code. That is why it is necessary to comply with those special provisions in the assignment of these claims. For instance, pursuant to T.Com.C art. 681, any bill of exchange may be transferred by the endorsement and delivery of possession of it, even if it is not expressly made out to order.[54] However, it should be kept in mind that where the drawer has included the words ‘not to order’ or a clause that has the same meaning in the instrument, then the bill may be transferred only subject to the formal requirements relating to the assignment of a claim (T.Com.C art. 681 par. 2).

Moreover, the right of ownership and other rights *in rem* may not qualify as claims, and the transfer of these rights is governed by special provisions. For instance, a contract for the transfer of ownership of land must be made by a duly authenticated instrument (TCC art. 706 par. 1). Furthermore, as a rule, entry in the land register is required for the acquisition of ownership of land (TCC art. 705 par. 1). As to chattels, the ownership or other rights *in rem*, as a rule, do not require a contract in written form but do require the transfer of possession to the acquirer (TCC art. 763 par. 1).[55]

---

[53]Tekinay et al. (1993), p. 266; Eren (2015), p. 1227; Oğuzman and Öz (2016), p. 596.

[54]See Sect. 25.4.2, fn. 43.

[55]The transfer of possession is of a factual nature. The material transfer of possession must be complemented by the parties’ agreement (referred to as a real agreement) concerning the transfer of ownership or the constitution of rights in *rem*. The real agreement is a bilateral legal act and does not require any specific form. It may be formed by the parties’ express or implied declarations of will (intention).

References

Aybay A (2011) Borçlar hukuku dersleri genel bölüm. Filiz, İstanbul
Becker H (1941) Kommentar zum Schweizerischen Zivilgesetzbuch, Volume VI, Obligationenrecht, 1. Abteilung: Allgemeine Bestimmungen, Art. 1-183. Stämpfli, Bern
Berger B (2012) Allgemeines Schuldrecht. Stämpfli, Bern
Çetiner B (2010) Hapis hakkı. Filiz, İstanbul
Dayınlarlı K (2008) Borçlar kanununa göre alacağın temliki. Banka ve ticaret hukuku araştırma enstitüsü, Ankara
Engel P (1997) Traité des obligations en droit Suisse. Stämpfli, Bern
Engin Bİ (2002) Alacağı temlik edenin garanti sorumluluğu. Seçkin, Ankara
Eren F (2015) Borçlar hukuku genel hükümler. Yetkin, Ankara
Feyzioğlu FN (1977) Borçlar hukuku genel hükümler, vol 2. Fakülteler, İstanbul
Gauch P, Schluep WR, Emmenegger S (2008) Schweizerisches Obligationenrecht, Allgemeiner Teil, vol 2. Schulthess, Zürich
Günergök Ö (2014) Alacağın devrinde borçlunun hukuki durumu. Vedat, İstanbul
Helvacı İ (2008) Eski medenî kanunumuzla karşılaştırmalı olarak Türk medenî kanunu'na göre sözleşmeden doğan ipotek hakkı. On iki levha, İstanbul
Honsell H, Vogt NP, Wiegand W (eds) (2003) Basler Kommentar zum Schweizerischen Privatrecht, Obligationenrecht 1: Art. 1-529 OR. Helbing Lichtenhahn, Basel
Kılıçoğlu AM (2013) Borçlar hukuku genel hükümler. Turhan, İstanbul
Kocaman AB (1989) Alacağın temlikinin benzer üçlü ilişkiler karşısındaki teorik sınırı sorunu. Banka ve ticaret hukuku araştırma enstitüsü, Ankara
Nomer HN (2015) Borçlar hukuku genel hükümler. Beta, İstanbul
Oğuzman K, Öz T (2016) Borçlar hukuku genel hükümler, vol 2. Vedat, İstanbul
Oğuzman K, Seliçi Ö, Oktay-Özdemir S (2016) Eşya hukuku. Filiz, İstanbul
Oser H, Schönenberger W (1929) Kommentar zum Schweizerischen Zivilgesetzbuch, Volume V: Das Obligationenrecht, Erster Halbband: Art. 1-183. Schulthess, Zürich
Öz MT (1990) Öğreti ve uygulamada sebepsiz zenginleşme. Kazancı, İstanbul
Özsunay E (1983) Borçlar hukuku, vol I. Filiz, İstanbul
Reisoğlu S (2014) Türk borçlar hukuku genel hükümler. Beta, İstanbul
Schwenzer I (2009) Schweizerisches Obligationenrecht, Allgemeiner Teil. Schulthess, Bern
Tekinay SS, Akman S, Burcuoğlu H, Altop A (1993) Tekinay borçlar hukuku genel hükümler. Filiz, İstanbul
Tercier P (2004) Le droit des obligations. Schulthess, Zurich
Tercier P, Pichonnaz P, Develioğlu HM (2016) Borçlar hukuku genel hükümler. On iki levha, İstanbul
Thévenoz L, Werro F (éd) (2012) Commentaire romand code des obligations 1: art. 1-529 CO. Helbing Lichtenhahn, Bâle
von Tuhr A, Escher A (1974) Allgemeiner Teil des Schweizerischen Obligationenrecht, vol 2. Schulthess, Zürich

Chapter 33
Assumption of Obligations

33.1 Promise to Discharge from a Debt[1]

33.1.1 *General*[2]

According to TCO art. 195, a third party with respect to an obligational relationship may promise the debtor to discharge him from the debt. As a result of this agreement, the promising third party is obliged to discharge the debtor from the debt. For instance, debtor D is obliged to pay €10,000 to creditor C. A third party enters into a contract with debtor D and undertakes to discharge him from this debt.

The agreement between the debtor and the third party does not require a specific form. However, if the promising party is obliged to discharge the debtor without consideration, this agreement must be in writing. This is because such an agreement constitutes a promise of a gift (TCO art. 288 par. 1).[3]

[1] Aybay (2011), pp. 192–195; Becker (1941), Vorbemerkungen zu art. 175-183 (Schuldübernahme), art. 175-181, 183; Berger (2012), pp. 812–825; Engel (1997), pp. 894–909; Eren (2015), pp. 1243–1255; Feyzioğlu (1977), pp. 666–701; Gauch et al. (2008), pp. 272–287; Honsell et al. (2003), art. 175-181, 183; Kılıçoğlu (2013), pp. 810–829; Nomer (2015), pp. 420, 454–457; Oser and Schönenberger (1929), Vorbemerkungen zur Schuldübernahme (art. 175-183), art. 175-181, 183; Oğuzman and Öz (2016), pp. 597–627; Özsunay (1983), pp. 194–207; Reisoğlu (2014), pp. 476–484; Schwenzer (2009), pp. 581–591; Tekinay et al. (1993), pp. 268–284; Tercier (2004), pp. 316–322; Tercier et al. (2016), pp. 543–553; Thévenoz and Werro (2012), art. 175-181, 183, and von Tuhr and Escher (1974), pp. 380–403. For further explanations, see Kahraman (2013), Paket (2014), Kılıç (2014).

[2] *Reprise de dette interne, interne Schuldübernahme.*

[3] von Tuhr and Escher (1974), § 99, I, 2, p. 383; Engel (1997), p. 895; Oğuzman and Öz (2016), p. 599; Tekinay et al. (1993), p. 270; Eren (2015), p. 1245; Reisoğlu (2014), p. 477.

İ. Helvacı, *Turkish Contract Law*, DOI 10.1007/978-3-319-60061-1_33

33.1.2 Legal Nature and the Promisor's Performance

The agreement between the debtor and the promising third party is an obligatory transaction with regard to the promising party.[4] It does not transfer the debtor's debt to the promising party. If the promising party intends to perform his obligation to discharge the debtor, then he must perform the debtor's obligation or make an agreement for assumption of debt with the creditor in order to assume the debtor's obligation.

In cases where a promising party attempts to perform a debtor's obligation, the creditor must accept performance, provided that the promising party's fulfilment is possible (TCO art. 83)[5] and appropriate to the obligation.[6] Otherwise, the creditor is entitled to refuse the promising party's performance.[7] However, if fulfilment by the promising party is possible and appropriate to the obligation and the creditor refuses or rejects performance without any just cause, then he falls into default.[8] It should be kept in mind that if the debtor's personal skills are of importance to the creditor, then he is not required to accept performance by the promising party.[9]

If the promising party intends to assume the debtor's obligation, then he must enter into a contract with the creditor. However, the creditor does not have to enter into a contract with the promising party for the assumption of the obligation.

Furthermore, the promising party may persuade the creditor to discharge the debtor.[10] If the creditor and the debtor make a discharge agreement, then the debtor's obligation is extinguished (TCO art. 132). Moreover, the promising party may fulfil his obligation by novation.[11] In this case, the debtor's obligation is extinguished, and a new obligation arises between the creditor and the promising party (TCO art. 133).

Where the promising party does not perform his obligation to discharge the debtor, the latter may bring an action in relation to the claim. At this point, it is worth recalling that the promise to discharge an obligation may be made with or without consideration. If the agreement is concluded for consideration—*i.e.*, if the debtor undertakes a certain obligation for his discharge—then the debtor is not entitled to compel the promising party to carry out his obligation to discharge unless he fulfils that obligation (TCO art. 195 par. 2). However, this rule is not mandatory. Thus, the parties may determine the order of performance.[12]

---

[4]*Acte générateur d'obligation, Verpflichtungsgeschäft*. Chapter 7, fn. 5.

[5]See Sect. 16.2.

[6]Tercier et al. (2016), p. 547.

[7]Oğuzman and Öz (2016), p. 600; Thévenoz and Werro (2012), art. 175, N. 4.

[8]See Chap. 20.

[9]Tercier (2004), p. 318. See Sect. 16.1.

[10]Thévenoz and Werro (2012), art. 175, N. 4; Oğuzman and Öz (2016), p. 601; Tekinay et al. (1993), p. 270.

[11]Engel (1997), p. 896; Thévenoz and Werro (2012), art. 175, N. 4; Feyzioğlu (1977), p. 671; Tekinay et al. (1993), p. 270; Oğuzman and Öz (2016), p. 601.

[12]Eren (2015), pp. 1246–1247; Oğuzman and Öz (2016), p. 602.

The legislature aimed to protect the debtor by the enactment of TCO art. 195 par. 3, according to which if the promising party does not discharge the debtor from his obligation, the debtor may demand that the promising party provide security, such as a surety, a mortgage, a pledge, etc.

33.2 Agreement for Assumption of Debt

33.2.1 Formation of the Agreement

An agreement for assumption of debt[13] is formed by the creditor's and the assuming party's mutual and consistent declarations of will (intention).[14] It does not require any specific form.

The offer may be made by the assuming party or by the creditor. In the ordinary course of life, an agreement for assumption of debt may be made in order to perform a promise to discharge. That is why the legislature accepts that notification to a creditor of a promise to discharge by an assuming party, or with the authorisation of the latter, by the original debtor, is deemed to be an offer (TCO art. 196 par. 2).

Acceptance by the creditor may be express or implied (TCO art. 196 par. 3 sent. 1). Acceptance by the creditor is presumed if he accepts the assuming party's fulfilment without any reservation or if he consents to any other act by the assuming party acting in the capacity of the debtor (TCO art. 196 par. 3 sent. 2).

An offer for an agreement for assumption of debt may be accepted by a creditor at any time (TCO art. 197 par. 1 sent. 1). However, it should be kept in mind that for the conclusion of any such contract: (1) where an offer without a time limit is made to a person present, the offer lapses unless the offeree accepts it forthwith (TCO art. 4 par. 1), and (2) where an offer without a time limit is made to a person who is absent, the offer is binding for a reasonable time (TCO art. 5 par. 1).

The assuming party or the original debtor may set a period of time for the acceptance of the offer (TCO art. 197 par. 1 sent. 2). In such a case, if the creditor remains silent until the fixed period expires, then the offer is deemed to be refused (TCO art. 197 par. 1 sent. 3). If a new promise to discharge has been agreed upon and if, before the first promising party's offer is accepted, an offer is made to the creditor regarding this new promise, then the first promising party is released from his offer (TCO art. 197 par. 2). However, it should be kept in mind that in the formation of any other contract, it is possible that one or more offers may be made at the same time to the offeree, and he is free to accept any of them.[15]

---

[13] *Reprise de dette externe*, *externe Schuldübernahme*.

[14] *Déclaration de volonté*, *Willenserklärung*.

[15] Oğuzman and Öz (2016), pp. 607–608.

33.2.2 Legal Nature

As indicated above, a debtor may be released from his debt by an agreement between the assuming party and the creditor. On the formation of such an agreement, the assuming party becomes the new debtor (TCO art. 196 par. 1).

An agreement for assumption of debt is generally carried out with the aim of fulfilling a promise to discharge. However, a person may assume the debtor's obligation without such a prior obligation.[16] In the case of an agreement for assumption of debt, the debtor is substituted. In other words, a new debtor replaces the original debtor, who is thereby released from the debt. As a result, such an agreement qualifies as a dispositive legal transaction[17] with regard to the creditor. Thus, the parties must have the capacity to act, and the creditor must have the power of disposition.[18,19]

An agreement for assumption of debt is an independent (abstract) legal transaction. Thus, even if the legal ground—*e.g.*, the promise to discharge—is invalid, the agreement is nonetheless valid. However, the original debtor's discharge will create a case of unjust enrichment in his favour.[20]

As an agreement for assumption of debt is a dispositive legal transaction with regard to the creditor, if the assumed debt does not exist at the time of formation of the contract, then it is void.[21] This is because the object of the contract is impossible to perform at the time the contract is formed (TCO art. 27 par. 1).

33.2.3 Effects of Substitution of Debtor

As mentioned above, the principal consequence of an agreement for assumption of debt is that the debtor is released from the debt and the new debtor is obliged to perform the original debtor's obligation. The creditor may no longer demand performance by the original debtor. Even if the new debtor does not perform the obligation, the position of the creditor with respect to the original debtor is unaffected.[22]

[16] Thévenoz and Werro (2012), art. 176, N. 5; Gauch et al. (2008), p. 275; Oğuzman and Öz (2016), p. 604; Tekinay et al. (1993), p. 273.

[17] *Acte de disposition, Verfügungsgeschäft*. See Chap. 14, fn. 5. It should be kept in mind that an agreement for assumption of debt is an obligatory legal transaction with regard to the assuming party. Becker (1941), Art. 176, N. 2; Feyzioğlu (1977), pp. 685–686; Oğuzman and Öz (2016), p. 604; Eren (2015), p. 1248.

[18] *Pouvoir de disposer, Verfügungsmacht.*

[19] von Tuhr and Escher (1974), § 99, II, p. 388; Feyzioğlu (1977), pp. 685–686; Oğuzman and Öz (2016), p. 604; Eren (2015), p. 1248.

[20] Oğuzman and Öz (2016), p. 604.

[21] Eren (2015), p. 1251; Oğuzman and Öz (2016), p. 608.

[22] Oğuzman and Öz (2016), p. 610; Reisoğlu (2014), p. 478; Eren (2015), p. 1250.

As the new debtor assumes only the debt of the original debtor, the obligational relationship between the original debtor and the creditor stands; that is, the new debtor does not become a party to the obligational relationship. For instance, in a car sale contract, the buyer is obliged to pay €10,000. If a new debtor assumes this debt, the obligation of the seller relating to the transfer of ownership of the car remains in favour of the buyer. In other words, the buyer's rights relating to ownership of the car are not affected.

In addition to these consequences, the new debtor is in the same position as the original debtor with regard to the time and the place of performance, etc.

33.2.3.1 Ancillary Rights and Debts

As a rule, an assumption of debt does not affect the creditor's rights. In addition, the substitution of the debtor does not affect the ancillary rights of the creditor, unless they are inseparably connected to the person of the original debtor (TCO art. 198 par. 1). Thus, the creditor may demand that the new debtor pay interest[23] and penalties. If there is a maturity clause in the agreement between the creditor and the original debtor, then the creditor may exercise his rights under this clause.[24] Furthermore, if the original debtor has provided certain securities such as a mortgage or a pledge, the creditor may continue to benefit from these securities.[25]

The creditor may not set off his claim against the new debtor with the debt he owes to the original debtor.[26] Furthermore, if there are grounds that are inseparably connected to the person of the original debtor that preclude the limitation period from commencing or continuing,[27] then the limitation period commences or continues when the agreement for assumption of debt is concluded. For instance, if a husband is obliged to pay €10,000 to his wife, then the limitation period does not commence so long as they remain married (TCO art. 153 par. 1 subcl. 3) However, if a new debtor assumes the husband's debt, the limitation period commences.[28]

Pledges given by third parties and sureties extinguish when the debt is assumed by a new debtor, unless the pledgor and surety consent to the assumption of debt in

---

[23]It should be noted that it is contentious as to whether or not the interest or penalties accrued before the agreement for assumption of debt are transferred to the new debtor. Unless the contrary is understood from the agreement for assumption of debt, these claims transfer to the new debtor. Thévenoz and Werro (2012), art. 178, N. 3; Tercier (2004), p. 319; Engel (1997), p. 900; von Tuhr and Escher (1974), § 99, V, 1, p. 392; Becker (1941), art. 178, N. 2; Oğuzman and Öz (2016), pp. 610 611; Tercier et al. (2016), p. 548; Nomer (2015), p. 456, *cf.* Tekinay et al. (1993), p. 277.

[24]Oğuzman and Öz (2016), p. 610.

[25]Oser and Schönenberger (1929), art. 178, N. 9; von Tuhr and Escher (1974), § 99, V, p. 393; Engel (1997), p. 900; Eren (2015), p. 1250; Reisoğlu (2014), p. 479.

[26]Feyzioğlu (1977), pp. 686–687; Tekinay et al. (1993), p. 278; Oğuzman and Öz (2016), p. 611; Reisoğlu (2014), p. 480; Eren (2015), p. 1252.

[27]See Sect. 26.4.

[28]Feyzioğlu (1977), p. 687; Oğuzman and Öz (2016), p. 611.

written form (TCO art. 198 par. 2). In fact, for third parties who pledge or provide surety, the personal, moral and financial position of the original debtor are of importance. If the legislature had not enacted this provision, the securing third parties would have been faced with providing pledges or sureties to a person who is unknown to them.[29]

It should be kept in mind that if the securing third parties do not consent to the assumption of debt, this does not preclude the validity of the agreement. The only consequence of the absence of consent is the extinguishment of their securities. As noted above, the consent of securing third parties requires a written form. The consent is invalid if they do not comply with this requirement.[30]

33.2.3.2 Defences

The right to raise defences in relation to an assumed debt transfers to the new debtor (TCO art. 199 par. 1). For instance, the obligational relationship that gave rise to the debt may be invalid. In this case, the new debtor is entitled to assert that the assumed debt was never in existence. Moreover, the assumed debt may be extinguished, for example, due to performance, set-off or a discharge agreement. Thus, the new debtor may raise these defences against the creditor.[31]

If the assumed debt is already time-barred, then the new debtor may raise this defence against the creditor. Furthermore, if the original debtor has the defence of *exceptio non adimpleti contractus* against the creditor,[32] it is evident that the new debtor may also raise this defence.[33] Moreover, if the debt becomes time-barred after the assumption of debt, then the new debtor may raise this defence against the creditor.

Unless the contrary is inferred from the agreement for assumption of debt, the new debtor is not entitled to raise the defences that the original debtor personally had against the creditor (TCO art. 199 par. 2). Consequently, the new debtor may not set off his debt to the creditor with any claim that the original debtor may have against the creditor.[34]

Certain rights are dependent upon being a party to a contract. That is why if the contract constituting the original debtor's obligation is voidable, due to mistake, fraud or duress,[35] the new debtor may not rescind the contract. Moreover, the new

[29]von Tuhr and Escher (1974), § 99, V, 2, p. 393; Oğuzman and Öz (2016), pp. 611–612; Tekinay et al. (1993), p. 277; Eren (2015), p. 1251.

[30]Oğuzman and Öz (2016), p. 612; Eren (2015), p. 1251; Nomer (2015), p. 456.

[31]von Tuhr and Escher (1974), § 99, IV, 1, p. 390; Tekinay et al. (1993), p. 278; Oğuzman and Öz (2016), p. 614.

[32]See Sect. 18.4.2.2.

[33]Tekinay et al. (1993), p. 278; Feyzioğlu (1977), p. 686; Oğuzman and Öz (2016), p. 612.

[34]von Tuhr and Escher (1974), § 99, IV, 2, p. 391; Oğuzman and Öz (2016), p. 615.

[35]See Chap. 11.

debtor is not entitled to withdraw from the contract, which gives rise to the original debtor's obligation, due to the default of the counter-party. This is because these rights still remain with the original debtor. If the original debtor exercises these rights—*i.e.*, if he rescinds the contract (*ab initio*) or withdraws from it (*ex tunc*)[36]—then the obligations arising from the contract that have been rescinded or withdrawn are extinguished retroactively. As a result, in these cases, the new debtor's obligations are also extinguished.[37]

The new debtor is not entitled to raise against the creditor defences that arise from the promise to discharge (TCO art. 199 par. 3). As noted above, the agreement for assumption of debt is independent of the promise to discharge. Thus, the new debtor may not refrain from performing the debt by, for instance, raising the invalidity or the non-existence of the promise to discharge.[38]

33.2.4 When an Assumption Agreement Becomes Invalid

If an agreement for assumption of debt becomes invalid, the original debt and all ancillary liabilities stand, subject to the rights of third parties acting in good faith (TCO art. 200 par. 1). An assumption agreement becomes invalid especially when a party to the agreement rescinds it because his declaration of will (intention)[39] is affected by material mistake, fraud and duress. As mentioned above, with the formation of an agreement for assumption of debt, the original debt does not extinguish, and a new debt does not arise. The only consequence of the agreement for assumption of debt is that the debtor is substituted.

If an agreement for assumption of debt becomes invalid, as indicated in TCO art. 200 par. 1, the obligation continues to rest with the original debtor. As a result, securities, including any pledges, mortgages or sureties, continue. However, if the securing third parties do not consent to the assumption of debt in written form, then these securities are extinguished (TCO art. 198 par. 2). TCO art. 200 par. 1 aims to protect securing third parties acting in good faith. In fact, if the securing third parties are not aware of the invalidity of the agreement for assumption of debt and they do not consent to the assumption of debt, the extinguishment of their securities is unaffected by the assumption agreement becoming invalid. In addition, the creditor may demand that the assuming party pay compensation for damage resulting from the loss of securities obtained previously or for any other reason, unless the assuming party proves that he is not at fault[40] for the agreement for

[36]Termination of the contract takes effect retroactively (*résolution, Rücktritt*).

[37]Oğuzman and Öz (2016), pp. 615–616.

[38]Tercier et al. (2016), p. 549; Oğuzman and Öz (2016), p. 616; Eren (2015), p. 1252; Reisoğlu (2014), p. 549.

[39]*Déclaration de volonté, Willenserklärung.*

[40]See Sect. 22.2.3.2.2.

assumption of debt becoming invalid and for the consequential damage suffered by the creditor (TCO art. 200 par. 2).[41]

In fact, with the assumption of the debt, the creditor may lose the benefit of the third parties' securities or incur certain damage due to his belief in the validity of the agreement for assumption of debt. For instance, the creditor, relying on the agreement for assumption of debt, may have discharged the securing third parties from liability. In such a case, the assuming party is liable to compensate the creditor for damage unless he proves that he is not at fault for the agreement for assumption of debt becoming invalid and for the creditor incurring damage.[42] For example, if the assuming party induces the creditor to accept the agreement for assumption of debt by fraud or duress (TCO art. 39 par. 1), then, when the creditor rescinds the agreement on account of the fraud or duress, the assuming party cannot be released from paying compensation for the creditor's damage.

33.3 Cumulative Assumption of Debt[43]

According to TCO art. 201, a cumulative assumption of debt is an agreement concluded between a new debtor and the creditor. As a result of this agreement, the new debtor becomes liable jointly and severally along with the existing debtor. In comparison to the usual form of debt assumption, in the cumulative assumption of debt, the original debtor will not be released from his debt. On the contrary, he remains as a debtor. The remaining party and the new debtor become jointly and severally liable (TCO art. 201 par. 2).

It should be noted that the consent of the debtor is not necessary for an agreement relating to a cumulative assumption of debt to be valid. Furthermore, the new debtor's liability is not ancillary to the original debtor's debt.

An agreement relating to a cumulative assumption of debt does not require a specific form. However, TCO art. 603 should be considered. According to this article, certain provisions concerning suretyship apply to other personal guarantees provided by natural persons. Therefore, the provisions pertaining to form, the capacity to act as surety and the consent of the surety's spouse apply to cumulative assumptions of debt that are carried out for the purpose of providing a security. Consequently, in such a case, a cumulative assumption of debt must be in writing, and the amount of the new debtor's liability and the date of the agreement must be handwritten by the new debtor (TCO art. 583). If the new debtor is married, subject to certain exceptions, he must also have the written consent of his spouse, at the

[41]Feyzioğlu (1977), p. 688; Tekinay et al. (1993), p. 279; Oğuzman and Öz (2016), pp. 618–619; Reisoğlu (2014), p. 480.

[42]Eren (2015), p. 1252; Tekinay et al. (1993), p. 279; Oğuzman and Öz (2016), p. 619.

[43]For further explanations see Portakal (2016).

latest by the time the cumulative agreement for assumption of debt is formed (TCO art. 584).

In cases where the cumulative assumption of debt is carried out with the aim of securing the debt, if the new debtor performs the entire debt, then he may have complete recourse to the original debtor. However, if the original debtor performs the entire debt, he may not have recourse to the new debtor.[44]

33.4 Assignment of an Estate or a Business

33.4.1 General[45]

An owner of an estate[46] or of a business may assign the estate or the business with all its assets and liabilities to a third party. In such a case, the debts of the estate or the business transfer to the assignee. As mentioned above, the parties to an agreement for assumption of debt are the creditor and the new debtor. However, in cases where an estate or business is assigned, the parties are the assignor and the assignee. The debts of the estate or the business are transferred to the assignee upon conclusion of the assignment agreement and by the assignee's notification to the creditors or the assignee's publication of the assignment. As has been seen, the creditors' consent is not necessary for the transfer of the debts of an estate or a business.[47]

33.4.2 Conditions

In order for the debts of an estate or a business to be transferred, the following conditions must be met: (1) there must be an assignment agreement concerning the transfer of the estate or the business with all its assets and liabilities between the assignor and the assignee, and (2) the assignee must notify the creditors or publish a notice that he has acquired the estate or the business with all its assets and liabilities (TCO art. 202 par. 1).

[44]Oğuzman and Öz (2016), p. 621.

[45]For further explanations see Acemoğlu (1971), Arıcı (2008).

[46]*Patrimoine*, *Vermögen*. Patrimoine: " … *is the totality of an individual's economic assets and liabilities, for example those rights and duties which are capable of valuation in money terms.*" (See Dahl 2001, p. 243); more concisely the *patrimoine* is a collection of assets and liabilities attached to a person; Estate: "*The collective assets and liabilities of a person viewed as an entity capable of owing or being entitled to money, of being solvent or insolvent.*" (Simpson and Weiner 1989, p. 408). For further explanations see Ayiter (1968).

[47]Engel (1997), p. 905; Oğuzman and Öz (2016), p. 623.

The parties may specify the debts to be transferred in the assignment agreement relating to the transfer of the estate or the business. However, even if they do not specify the debts to be transferred, the agreement is nevertheless valid.[48]

In order for the debts to be transferred, the assignee must notify the creditors of the assignment or publish a notice that he has acquired the estate or the business. The notification of the assignment to the creditors does not require a specific form. As to publication, the legislature requires that an announcement of the assignment must be published in a nationwide newspaper. However, in the case of the assignment of commercial businesses, the announcement must be published in the Trade Registry Gazette (TCO art. 202 par. 1).

33.4.3 Consequences

When the notification or the publication of the assignment reaches the addressees, the assignee, along with the original debtor, becomes liable for the debts of the assigned estate or business. The liability of the original debtor continues for 2 years. This period of time for debts that are due commences on the date of notification or publication. As to debts that are not due at the time of notification or publication, the period of time commences on the date they become due (TCO art. 202 par. 2). As long as the assignee does not give or publish the notification, the two-year period does not commence (TCO art. 202 par. 4). In other respects, the assumption of debts by way of assignment of an estate or of a business has the same effect as the assumption of a single debt (TCO art. 202 par. 3).

It should be noted that since the original debtor's liabilities stand for 2 years, the third party's securities provided for the original debtor also continue for 2 years. At the end of this period of time, these securities are released. If the creditors do not want to lose the benefit of these securities, then they must persuade the securing third parties to give their written consent to the assumption of the debt before the period of time lapses (compare to TCO art. 198 par. 2).

33.5 Merger and Acquisition of Businesses[49]

Two businesses may be merged by mutually taking over the assets and liabilities of the other. In addition, a business may join another business. In these cases, the creditors of both businesses, having the same rights arising from the assignment of an estate, may demand their claims from the new business (TCO art. 203 par. 1). That is to say, the debts of the merged businesses are transferred to the new

[48]Oğuzman and Öz (2016), p. 624.

[49]Esin and Lokmanhekim (2003).

business. It should be noted that the liability of the original debtor does not continue.

The same principle applies to the debts of businesses owned by a single individual that are subsequently converted into a general partnership[50] or a limited partnership[51] (TCO art. 203 par. 2).

33.6 Special Provisions

33.6.1 General

Special provisions relating to an assumption of debt in the case of partition of an inheritance and in the case of transfer of encumbered real estate are reserved (TCO art. 204).

33.6.2 Partition of an Inheritance

Subject to certain legal exceptions, the debts of the deceased pass *ipso iure* to the heirs, and they become personally liable for the debts of the deceased (TCC art. 599 par. 2). If there are several heirs, then they are jointly and severally liable[52] for the debts of the deceased. As long as the heirs do not distribute the estate, their joint and several liabilities continue. However, the heirs may distribute the estate, and, in the partition proceedings, they may determine that the debts of the deceased will be entirely assumed by one of them. Moreover, they may decide which part of the debt is to be paid by which heir. In such cases, if the creditor explicitly or implicitly accepts the assumption or the partition of the debt, the joint and several liability of the heirs is extinguished. However, if the creditor does not consent to this partition, the joint and several liability of the heirs continues for a period of 5 years. This period of time commences for debts that are due at the date of partition. For debts that are not due at the time of partition, the period of time commences on the date they become due (TCC art. 681). If debts are not paid by the end of this period of time, then the heirs' joint and several liabilities are extinguished, and they become liable in proportion to their legal share of the inheritance.[53]

In the partition, if an heir receives movable or immovable property, which is a part of the inheritance, and which is pledged or mortgaged for the debt of the deceased, this heir assumes the debt secured by this property (TCC art. 655). In this

[50] Ansay and Schneider (2002), pp. 85–88.

[51] Ansay and Schneider (2002), p. 88.

[52] See Chap. 27.

[53] Dural and Öz (2015), p. 462.

case, for the assumption of the secured debt by the heir, the consent of the creditor is not necessary. In addition, if there are several heirs, their joint and several liabilities extinguish with this acquisition.

33.6.3 Transfer of Encumbered Real Estate

An owner of immovable property that is mortgaged in order to secure a debt may alienate his property to a third party. As a rule, the alienation of the mortgaged immovable property affects neither the liability of the mortgagor nor the personal liability of the debtor, unless agreed to the contrary (TCC art. 888 par. 1). Nevertheless, if a new owner attempts to assume the debt secured by the mortgaged real estate, the registrar of the land registry must notify the mortgagee that the new owner has attempted to assume the debt (TCC art. 890 par. 1). If the mortgagee does not consent to the new owner assuming the debt and the original debtor being discharged from the debt, then he must notify the debtor of this decision.

In cases where the mortgagee does not consent to the substitution of the debtor, he must give written notice to the original debtor within 1 year (TCC art. 888 par. 2) commencing from the date of notification by the registrar (TCC art. 890 par. 2). If the mortgagee does not notify the debtor of his decision within 1 year, then the new owner becomes the new debtor of the debt secured by the mortgage, and the original debtor is released (TCC art. 888 par. 2). As has been seen, the creditor's consent is not necessary for the new owner to assume the debt.[54]

References

Acemoğlu K (1971) Borçlar kanununun 179. maddesine göre malvarlığı veya ticari işletmenin devri. İstanbul
Ansay T, Schneider E (eds) (2002) Introduction to Turkish business law. Turan, Ankara
Arıcı MF (2008) Ticari işletmenin aktif ve pasifi ile devri. Vedat, İstanbul
Aybay A (2011) Borçlar hukuku dersleri genel bölüm. Filiz, İstanbul
Ayiter N (1968) Mamelek kavramı üzerine inceleme. Ankara
Becker H (1941) Kommentar zum Schweizerischen Zivilgesetzbuch, Volume VI, Obligationenrecht, 1. Abteilung: Allgemeine Bestimmungen, Art. 1-183. Stämpfli, Bern
Berger B (2012) Allgemeines Schuldrecht. Stämpfli, Bern
Dahl HS (2001) Dictionnaire Juridique Dahl. Paris
Dural M, Öz T (2015) Türk özel hukuku, miras hukuku, vol 4. Filiz, İstanbul
Engel P (1997) Traité des obligations en droit Suisse. Stämpfli, Bern
Eren F (2015) Borçlar hukuku genel hükümler. Yetkin, Ankara
Esin Gİ, Lokmanhekim ST (2003) Uygulamada birleşme ve devralmalar. Beta, İstanbul
Feyzioğlu FN (1977) Borçlar hukuku genel hükümler, vol 2. Fakülteler, İstanbul

[54]For further explanations Helvacı (2008), p. 326 *ff.*

Gauch P, Schluep WR, Emmenegger S (2008) Schweizerisches Obligationenrecht, Allgemeiner Teil, vol 2. Schulthess, Zürich

Helvacı İ (2008) Eski medenî kanunumuzla karşılaştırmalı olarak Türk medenî kanununa göre sözleşmeden doğan ipotek hakkı. On iki levha, İstanbul

Honsell H, Vogt NP, Wiegand W (eds) (2003) Basler Kommentar zum Schweizerischen Privatrecht, Obligationenrecht 1: Art. 1-529 OR. Helbing Lichtenhahn, Basel

Kahraman Z (2013) Karşılaştırmalı hukukta borcun dış üstlenilmesi (borcun nakli). Vedat, İstanbul

Kılıç M (2014) Türk hukukunda borcun üstlenilmesi. Yetkin, Ankara

Kılıçoğlu AM (2013) Borçlar hukuku genel hükümler. Turhan, İstanbul

Nomer HN (2015) Borçlar hukuku genel hükümler. Beta, İstanbul

Oğuzman K, Öz T (2016) Borçlar hukuku genel hükümler, vol 2. Vedat, İstanbul

Oser H, Schönenberger W (1929) Kommentar zum Schweizerischen Zivilgesetzbuch, Volume V: Das Obligationenrecht, Erster Halbband: Art. 1-183. Schulthess, Zürich

Özsunay E (1983) Borçlar hukuku, vol I. Filiz, İstanbul

Paket S (2014) Borcun dış üstlenilmesi. Yetkin, Ankara

Portakal SY (2016) Borca katılma. On iki levha, İstanbul

Reisoğlu S (2014) Türk borçlar hukuku genel hükümler. Beta, İstanbul

Schwenzer I (2009) Schweizerisches Obligationenrecht, Allgemeiner Teil. Schulthess, Bern

Simpson JA, Weiner ESC (1989) The Oxford English Dictionary, vol V. Clarendon, Oxford

Tekinay SS, Akman S, Burcuoğlu H, Altop A (1993) Tekinay borçlar hukuku genel hükümler. Filiz, İstanbul

Tercier P (2004) Le droit des obligations. Schulthess, Zurich

Tercier P, Pichonnaz P, Develioğlu HM (2016) Borçlar hukuku genel hükümler. On iki levha, İstanbul

Thévenoz L, Werro F (éd) (2012) Commentaire romand code des obligations 1: art. 1-529 CO. Helbing Lichtenhahn, Bâle

von Tuhr A, Escher A (1974) Allgemeiner Teil des Schweizerischen Obligationenrecht, vol 2. Schulthess, Zürich

Chapter 34
Transfer of Contracts and Joining a Party to an Existing Contract

34.1 Transfer of Contracts[1]

The transfer of a contract[2] is an agreement concluded between the transferor, the transferee and the remaining party to the contract. In such a case, all the claims and the debts of the transferor, and the legal position of being a party to the contract, are transferred to the transferee (TCO art. 205 par. 1).

The agreement relating to the transfer of a contract requires the same legal form as the contract to be transferred (TCO art. 205 par. 3). For instance, a sale contract relating to immovable property must be concluded before a land registry officer (TCO art. 237 par. 1, LRA art. 26). Therefore, if the contract to be transferred is a sale contract concerning immovable property, the transfer contract must also be concluded before a land registry officer. However, a sale contract relating to movable property, as a rule, does not require any legal form. Thus, even if the parties conclude this contract in a written form, the transfer contract does not require a specific form.[3]

A transfer contract may be concluded only between the transferor and the transferee. However, in order for this contract to be effective, the remaining party's consent is necessary (TCO art. 205 par. 2). This consent may be given before or after the formation of the transfer contract. It should be noted that there is no specific provision in the Turkish Code of Obligations relating to the form of this

[1]Aybay (2011), pp. 195–196; Becker (1941), Vorbemerkungen zu art. 164-174, pp. 765–767; Berger (2012), pp. 823–825; Eren (2015), pp. 1255–1256; Gauch et al. (2008), pp. 269–270; Kılıçoğlu (2013), pp. 829–834; Nomer (2015), pp. 445–447; Oğuzman and Öz (2016), pp. 627–635; Reisoğlu (2014), pp. 485–486; Schwenzer (2009), pp. 592–593; Tercier (2004), pp. 303, 311; Tercier et al. (2016), pp. 531–536, and Thévenoz and Werro (2012), art. 181.

[2]For further explanations, see Ayrancı (2003), Çayan (2016).

[3]Oğuzman and Öz (2016), p. 629.

İ. Helvacı, *Turkish Contract Law*, DOI 10.1007/978-3-319-60061-1_34

consent. Thus, it would be appropriate to infer that this consent does not require any specific form.[4] Moreover, this consent may be given explicitly or implicitly.

According to TCO art. 205 par. 4, subrogation cases resulting from law[5] and other specific provisions relating to the assignment of claims[6] and the assumption of debt[7] are reserved.

34.2 Joining a Party to an Existing Contract

In order to join a party to an existing contract, it is necessary that there be a new contract between the parties to the existing contract and the person wishing to be joined as a party to that contract.[8] As a result of this new contract, the joining party will have the same rights and obligations as the party to the original contract (TCO art. 206 par. 1). For instance, in a work contract, if the added party is joined alongside the contractor, then he will have the same rights and obligations as the contractor. Or if the added party is joined to the contract alongside the customer, then he will have the same rights and obligations as the customer.

In the absence of an agreement to the contrary, the added party becomes a joint and several creditor or debtor (TCO art. 206 par. 2). Therefore, the legal position of the new joint and several debtor will be governed by TCO arts. 162–168.[9] Similarly, the legal position of the new joint and several creditor will be governed by TCO art. 169.[10]

The form of the contract that enables the added party to be joined to an existing contract must be the same as the existing contract (TCO art. 206 par. 3).

References

Aybay A (2011) Borçlar hukuku dersleri genel bölüm. Filiz, İstanbul
Ayrancı H (2003) Sözleşmelerin yüklenilmesi (devri). Yetkin, Ankara
Becker H (1941) Kommentar zum Schweizerischen Zivilgesetzbuch, Volume VI, Obligationenrecht, 1. Abteilung: Allgemeine Bestimmungen, Art. 1-183. Stämpfli, Bern
Berger B (2012) Allgemeines Schuldrecht. Stämpfli, Bern
Çayan G (2016) Sözleşmenin devri. Adalet, Ankara
Eren F (2015) Borçlar hukuku genel hükümler. Yetkin, Ankara

[4]Nomer (2015), p. 446; Oğuzman and Öz (2016), p. 630.

[5]See Sect. 24.2.

[6]See Chap. 32.

[7]See Chap. 33.

[8]*Cf.* Tercier (2004), p. 303.

[9]See Chap. 27.

[10]See Chap. 28.

Gauch P, Schluep WR, Emmenegger S (2008) Schweizerisches Obligationenrecht, Allgemeiner Teil, vol 2. Schulthess, Zürich
Kılıçoğlu AM (2013) Borçlar hukuku genel hükümler. Turhan, İstanbul
Nomer HN (2015) Borçlar hukuku genel hükümler. Beta, İstanbul
Oğuzman K, Öz T (2016) Borçlar hukuku genel hükümler, vol 2. Vedat, İstanbul
Reisoğlu S (2014) Türk borçlar hukuku genel hükümler. Beta, İstanbul
Schwenzer I (2009) Schweizerisches Obligationenrecht, Allgemeiner Teil. Schulthess, Bern
Tercier P (2004) Le droit des obligations. Schulthess, Zurich
Tercier P, Pichonnaz P, Develioğlu HM (2016) Borçlar hukuku genel hükümler. On iki levha, İstanbul
Thévenoz L, Werro F (éd) (2012) Commentaire romand code des obligations 1: art. 1-529 CO. Helbing Lichtenhahn, Bâle

Article Index

İ. Helvacı, *Turkish Contract Law*, DOI 10.1007/978-3-319-60061-1

Subject Index

İ. Helvacı, *Turkish Contract Law*, DOI 10.1007/978-3-319-60061-1

MIX
Papier aus verantwortungsvollen Quellen
Paper from responsible sources
FSC® C105338

If you have any concerns about our products,
you can contact us on
ProductSafety@springernature.com

In case Publisher is established outside the EU,
the EU authorized representative is:
Springer Nature Customer Service Center GmbH
Europaplatz 3, 69115 Heidelberg, Germany

Printed by Libri Plureos GmbH
in Hamburg, Germany